Contents

Acknowledgements x

Introduction 1

PART I   EXPRESSION IN SPEECH

Chapter 1   Natural Speech 11
1.1   The production and perception of speech 12
1.2   The basic model 17
1.3   Developing a model to include expressive content 21
1.4   Evaluating lines of research 22
1.5   The perception of a waveform's expressive content 24
1.6   The test-bed for modelling expression 25

Chapter 2   Speech Synthesis 28
2.1   Modern synthesis techniques 28
2.2   Limitations of the synthesizer type 34

Chapter 3   Expression in Natural Speech 37
3.1   What lies *behind* expressive speech? 38
3.2   How does expression get into speech? 39
3.3   Neutral speech 40
3.4   Degrees of expression 41
3.5   The dynamic nature of expression 44
3.6   The 'acoustic correlates' paradigm for investigating expression 47
3.7   Some acoustic correlates 53
3.8   Hearing thresholds: the difference limen concept 56
3.9   Data collection 57
3.10   Listener reaction to expressive utterances 61

Chapter 4   Expression in Synthetic Speech 65
4.1   Synthesizing different modes of expression 65
4.2   What is needed for expressive synthetic speech? 69
4.3   Evaluating the results 71
4.4   Expression is systematic, but non-linear 73
4.5   Integrity of speakers and their expression 75

4.6	Optimizing synthesis techniques for rendering expression	78
4.7	Modelling naturalness and expressive content	82

Chapter 5 The Perception of Expression   86
5.1 The objective of speaker expression   87
5.2 Current limits to characterizing the acoustic triggers of
     listener reaction   88
5.3 Characterizing listener reaction to expressive signals   89
5.4 The listener's ability to differentiate signals   90
5.5 Non-linearity in the acoustic/perceptual relationship   91

PART II TRANSFERRING NATURAL EXPRESSION TO SYNTHESIS

Chapter 6 The State of the Art   97
6.1   The general approach   97
6.2   The representation of emotion in the minds of
      speakers and listeners   100
6.3   Defining emotion in general   102
6.4   Defining emotion in terms of acoustic correlates   105
6.5   Variability among acoustic correlates   107
6.6   The non-uniqueness of acoustic correlates   110
6.7   Reducing the number of variables   111
6.8   The range of emotive effects   113
6.9   The state of the art in synthesizing prosody   115
6.10 The theoretical basis   119
6.11 The state of the art in synthesizing expressiveness   121

Chapter 7 Emotion in Speech Synthesis   124
7.1 Type of synthesizer   125
7.2 Using prosody as the basis for synthesizing expression   129
7.3 Assessment and evaluation of synthesis results   132
7.4 Synthesis of emotions in speech: general problems   136
7.5 Linking parameters of emotion with acoustic parameters   140

Chapter 8 Recent Developments in Synthesis Models   150
8.1 The current state of thinking   150
8.2 Subtlety of expression   152
8.3 The expression space: metrics   153
8.4 Natural synthesis: feedback in the dialogue environment   154
8.5 Contemporary changes of approach to speech   158
8.6 Providing the synthesizer with listener feedback   160
8.7 Some production-for-perception considerations with
     expressive speech   164

Expression in Speech: Analysis and Synthesis

Expression in Speech: Analysis and Synthesis

Mark Tatham
and
Katherine Morton

OXFORD
UNIVERSITY PRESS

OXFORD
UNIVERSITY PRESS

Great Clarendon Street, Oxford OX2 6DP

Oxford University Press is a department of the University of Oxford.
It furthers the University's objective of excellence in research, scholarship,
and education by publishing worldwide in

Oxford New York

Auckland Bangkok Buenos Aires Cape Town Chennai
Dar es Salaam Delhi Hong Kong Istanbul Karachi Kolkata
Kuala Lumpur Madrid Melbourne Mexico City Mumbai Nairobi
São Paulo Shanghai Taipei Tokyo Toronto

Oxford is a registered trade mark of Oxford University Press
in the UK and in certain other countries

Published in the United States
by Oxford University Press Inc., New York

© Mark Tatham and Katherine Morton 2004

The moral rights of the authors have been asserted

Database right Oxford University Press (maker)

First published 2004

All rights reserved. No part of this publication may be reproduced,
stored in a retrieval system, or transmitted, in any form or by any means,
without the prior permission in writing of Oxford University Press,
or as expressly permitted by law, or under terms agreed with the appropriate
reprographics rights organization. Enquiries concerning reproduction
outside the scope of the above should be sent to the Rights Department,
Oxford University Press, at the address above

You must not circulate this book in any other binding or cover
and you must impose this same condition on any acquirer

A catalogue record for this title is available from British Library

Library of Congress Cataloging in Publication Data

(Data available)

ISBN 0199250677

10 9 8 7 6 5 4 3 2 1

Typeset by Newgen Imaging Systems (P) Ltd., Chennai, India
Printed in Great Britain
on acid-free paper by
Biddles Ltd., www.Biddles.co.uk

Contents vii

PART III EXPRESSION AND EMOTION: THE RESEARCH

Chapter 9	The Biology and Psychology Perspectives	167
9.1	Finding expressive content in speech	167
9.2	Is there a basis for modelling human expression?	168
9.3	Emotion: what is it?	169
9.4	The source of emotive content	172
9.5	Production of emotion: biological accounts	173
9.6	Production of emotion: cognitive accounts, with little or no biological substrate	177
9.7	Production of emotion: linking the biological and cognitive approaches	183
9.8	The function of emotion	187
9.9	Parameterization of emotion	189
9.10	Secondary emotions	189
9.11	Language terms and the use of words in characterizing emotion	191
9.12	The problems of labelling and classification	195
9.13	Concluding remarks	196

Chapter 10	The Linguistics, Phonology, and Phonetics Perspective	198
10.1	The nature of emotion	198
10.2	Databases for investigating expressiveness in the speech waveform	210
10.3	Speakers	216
10.4	Listeners	226

Chapter 11	The Speech Technology Perspective	236
11.1	Synthesis feasibility studies	236
11.2	Testing models of expression	250
11.3	Automatic speech recognition: the other side of the coin	259

Chapter 12	The Influence of Emotion Studies	264
12.1	How research into emotion can usefully influence work in speech	264
12.2	Emotion and speech synthesis	265
12.3	Prelude to an underlying model of emotion: the inadequacies of the speech model	267
12.4	An integrated physical/cognitive language model	269
12.5	Introducing a possible transferable model	273

12.6	Building a model for emotive synthesis: the goals	277
12.7	The evidence supporting biological and cognitive models suitable for speech work	280
12.8	Concluding and summarizing remarks	284

PART IV   DEVELOPMENT OF AN INTEGRATED MODEL OF EXPRESSION

Chapter 13	The Beginnings of a Generalized Model of Expression	289
13.1	Defining expressive speech	290
13.2	The simple composite soundwave model	294
13.3	Short-term and long-term expressiveness	296
Chapter 14	All Speech is Expression-Based	300
14.1	Neutral expression	302
14.2	Listener message sampling	303
14.3	The expression envelope	307
14.4	Defining neutral speech	310
14.5	Parametric representations	313
14.6	Data collection	320
Chapter 15	Expressive Synthesis: The Longer Term	327
15.1	What does the synthesizer need to do?	327
15.2	Phonology in the high-level system	331
15.3	Defining expression and transferring results from psychology	341
15.4	The supervisor model applied to expression	346
15.5	Is it critical how the goal of good synthesis is achieved?	347
15.6	Implications of utterance planning and supervision	349
15.7	Are synthesis systems up to the job?	349
Chapter 16	A Model of Speech Production Based on Expression and Prosody	355
16.1	The prosodic framework	355
16.2	Planning and rendering	357
16.3	Phonetics as a dynamic reasoning device	360
16.4	Phonological and Cognitive Phonetic processes	362
16.5	The speech production model's architecture	364
16.6	Prosodic and expressive detail	374
16.7	Evaluating competing demands for expressive content: a task for the CPA	380
16.8	Spectral and articulatory detail	383

16.9	Planning and rendering utterances within prosodic wrappers	384
16.10	Speaking a specific utterance with expression	386
16.11	The proposed model of speech production	387
Conclusion		389
References		393
Bibliography		411
Author index		413
Subject index		417

Acknowledgements

We should like to acknowledge the following for providing a supportive academic environment during our research periods in the United States: Professor Pat Keating and members of the Phonetics Laboratory at UCLA, and Professor John Ohala and members of the Phonology Laboratory at UC Berkeley. In addition, thanks are due to the University Library at the University of Cambridge.

We owe special thanks to Professor Peter Ladefoged for his long-standing generosity and encouragement, and to Jenny Ladefoged for her valued support.

Introduction

When people speak to each other they are able to communicate subtle nuances of expression. Everybody does this, no matter how young or old, or which language they are speaking: the existence of expression as an integral part of how speech is spoken is universal. This does not mean that every language or speaker expresses everything in exactly the same way: they do not.

The expression people bring into their conversation often says something about their feelings regarding the person they are talking to, or perhaps something about how they feel regarding what they are saying, or even how they feel in general today. This expression is incorporated in what a person says without changing the words being used or the way these are arranged into sentences. Different expressions are conveyed by changes in the acoustic signal—using different 'tones of voice'—rather than by altering lexical choice (which words are being used) or sentential syntax (how those words are arranged in the utterance). Of course this does not mean that people *never* alter the words they are using deliberately to convey expression: the point is that you can inform your listener directly about how you feel with words, or you can convey expression by a change in tone of voice. Tone of voice has expressive force, and is a very powerful means of telling people things the words themselves sometimes do not convey very well: what our attitude is and how we feel.

A consequence of the universality of tone of voice is that we never speak without it. We can imagine a kind of 'neutral' speech completely devoid of expression, but in practice it is safe to say this never actually occurs. Many researchers feel that a description of what neutral speech *would* be like is a good starting point for talking about different types of expression; but we shall see that this is likely to be an abstraction rather than anything which can actually be measured in an acoustics laboratory or deduced from people's perception. In real conversation anything we might call 'neutral speech' is speech with minimal or ambiguous expressive content, but it is not speech with *no* expressive content. In fact such speech would be extremely difficult to characterize precisely because it *does* contain expression but only in a minimally detectable way.

Listeners respond remarkably consistently to differing tones of voice. This means that, however subtle some of the effects are, they are part of our communicative system. If speakers regularly produce recognizable expressive tones of voice it follows that, at least at first, we should be able to detect in the speech signal differences which correlate well with listeners' feelings about expression. This is a very simple concept, but one which still largely defeats us. Tone of voice is apparently consistent for both speaker and listener, yet it remains quite elusive when we try to say something about what it is and how it works. It is part of the way in which we externalize our internal world using language.

Adding expressiveness to speech

It is usual to think of the speech signal—the acoustic manifestation of an utterance—as being the result of a complex chain of events which begins with some 'idea' or 'piece of information' the speaker wants to communicate. Most schools of linguistics feel that language is essentially a kind of encoding system which enables speakers' intentions to be turned into speech signals for 'transmission' to a receiving audience. Some of the encoding processes will be sequential, others will take place in parallel; and one of our concerns will be to decide at what stage expressive content comes into play.

Some of the properties of expressive tone of voice may be phonological in origin, associated with the planning of speech, before it is phonetically rendered or turned into an acoustic signal. Others may be phonetic in origin or associated with the control of how the phonological plan is rendered phonetically. How and where expression gets into the speech signal is very important, because this can determine how much control a speaker has over the expression. Extreme examples might be when a strong feeling of anger can make a speaker's voice tremble in an involuntary way, or when a speaker subtly injects a tone of irony or reproach into their speech.

The basic model we shall be suggesting consists of a planning stage followed by a rendering stage. These two stages correspond roughly to the levels of phonology and phonetics in linguistics. An important refinement of this basic approach is that the rendering stage is closely monitored and kept accurate as rendering unfolds, a process known as 'supervision'. Rendering is a relatively new term in speech production theory, corresponding to the earlier and simpler term 'realization'. We shall be developing this general concept and the concept of supervision as we proceed, but will leave more complete definitions till later.

A computationally oriented approach

Because we intend suggesting an *explicit* model of expression in speech we have chosen to make that model computational—that is, capable of being computed. This simply means that our descriptions are of algorithmic processes which have a beginning and an ending, and clearly defined linking stages. The purpose of developing a computational model is that it will run on a computer. Since it is based on experimental observation, the model is descriptive of how human beings speak with expression, but at the same time the model is formulated to be predictive. In particular, it predicts an acoustic speech signal incorporating expression, and we have chosen to set up the model in the test environment of *speech synthesis*. That is, we describe expression in speech in terms of how a soundwave might be created synthetically to simulate the speech of a human being.

There are problems with using a speech synthesizer to test models of human speech production and perception. One of the main difficulties is that the speech production and perception constraints at all levels have to be programmed in detail. In one sense this is a serious problem, because it means we have to know a considerable amount about how human speech production works and the constraints which operate on it. Perhaps surprisingly, the existence of this problem is precisely why computational modelling is so important and so revealing: gaps in our knowledge, inadequate basic assumptions, and shortcomings in our descriptions are clearly brought out, forcing careful consideration of every detail.

If our model of human speech production is descriptively and computationally adequate from the point of view of characterizing what we observe in the human being's behaviour, it follows that its implementation as a synthesis device (either for testing or for more general application) will take us as close as possible to a simulation of the human processes. This does not mean, however, that the model tries to be indistinguishable from what a human being actually does. On the contrary, this is what we do *not* want. A model which *is* what is being modelled is not a model at all, and therefore not able to fulfil the purpose of models: to cast light on the nature of the object being modelled. Such a model would have the same black-box characteristics as the object itself.

Speech synthesis

Because the computational model being used to create synthetic speech is based on our understanding of human speech production, the simulation incorporates the human properties which have been addressed. For example, in characterizing human speech it is appropriate to distinguish between a phonological planning stage and a phonetic rendering stage. This distinction gets transferred to the simulation: phonological planning is treated as something we call 'high-level synthesis', concerned with simulating cognitive processes in speech production, whereas phonetic rendering is treated for the most part as 'low-level synthesis'. Low-level processes are more about the physical production of the soundwave using descriptive models of the acoustic structure of speech.

The idea of high-level and low-level synthesis will be developed as we proceed with describing synthesizing expression in speech. But we might notice here that there is important and revealing interplay between the two levels. For example, if we are satisfied that we have a good model of how stops coarticulate with the vowels which immediately follow them in syllables, we are in a good position to model the high-level plan which will enable the coarticulatory model to produce a good soundwave. Coarticulation theory models how the results of interacting segments are revealed in the linear stream of speech; a good model will predict the kind of input needed for this to happen. That is, how we model coarticulation interacts with how we model the parts of the higher-level plan which are eventually to be involved in the coarticulatory process. We use coarticulation as an example, but it is worth remembering that segments need a theory of how they coarticulate only if the overall model assumes that there *are* segments. The same principle applies to a model of expression: we need to establish a suitable construct about what we *mean* by expression—something we shall consider when we discuss in detail a possible model of prosodically based speech production which incorporates expression.

A computational model of expressive content in speech

Since part of the research community's purpose in modelling the expressive content of speech is to generate synthetic speech both for practical purposes and for the purpose of testing the model of human behaviour, we consider that a computational model is not only desirable but essential. The model should have coherence and integrity by reason of the fact that it *is* computational, and should easily be able to be incorporated into high-level aspects of speech synthesizers. But we need to ask some questions:

- Is a computational model appropriate for dealing with the phenomenon of expression in speech?
- Does the concept of expression lend itself to being computationally defined?
- Can the acoustic correlates of expression be determined and stated in a way which feeds into the computational nature of the model?

If we feel that computational modelling of expression in general and the expressive content of the acoustic signal in particular is both appropriate and possible, the next step is to attempt to determine physiological, cognitive (including social), and language-based contributions to the overall production of the speech signal.

An integrated theory of speech production and perception

An integrated theory of speech production/perception is rarely broached in the literature, even in connection with simple segmental rendering. But it is even more rare to find discussion of a full theory of prosodics (including expression) which integrates production and perception. Under these circumstances it would be reckless to attempt more than to collate observations and try to begin the process of building a theoretical framework for modelling expressive content in speech. Bearing in mind that here there can be no last word claims, and that the best we can achieve is a statement coherent enough to be demolished, we shall discuss the preliminaries to a speech production model (Chapter 16) which integrates both speaker and listener perspectives on the one hand and segmental and prosodic perspectives on the other.

Let us repeat that this is no more than a useful working model which attempts to make sense of observations about human speech production and perception. Pending data to the contrary, there is the weakest of hypotheses that human beings actually work this way. We stress again, though, that the model is not and cannot claim to *be* the human being: it is just a device of the scientist. Separate models of production and perception fail to account for apparent interdependence between the two modalities; we propose that an integrated model takes the theory forward in the sense that it pulls in the observations the other models neglect.

Our account of modelling expression

Part I is a general treatment of expression in speech. We examine how researchers have been investigating natural speech and transferring their findings to speech synthesis. We include a section on how expression is perceived by listeners, in particular discussing the non-linearity of the relationship between the acoustic signal and perception. We conclude that perception is an act of assignment rather than a process of discovery. Part II moves on to the detail of how researchers have transferred ideas about natural expression to the domain of speech synthesis, and includes a discussion of recent developments of the technology. Our characterization of synthesis involves a formal separation of high and low levels, corresponding to cognitive and primarily physical processes in human speech production.

Part III is devoted to an appraisal of the background research. Several disciplines are involved and how they come together is critical if we are to have a comprehensive understanding of expression. We begin with the biological and psychological perspectives, and move on to linguistics, phonology, and phonetics. We then examine what these approaches mean for speech synthesis and how they might point to a way forward. We examine how models of expression might be evaluated in the light of synthesis requirements.

Our concluding section, Part IV, begins by outlining the beginnings of a general model of expression, with a view to proceeding to a fully integrated model based on the findings covered in Part III. We look at a way of formalizing the data structures involved, and discuss why this is crucial to an explicit model. We evaluate expressive synthesis in terms of longer-term developments which make prosody and expression central to the model. The final chapter moves to proposals for a model of speech production anchored in prosody and expression—an almost complete reversal of the traditional approach in speech theory. Expression, exemplified in emotion, becomes central to the discussion and envelops the model. Speech is characterized as a carefully planned and supervised process operating within the dominating requirements of expression.

Part I

Expression in Speech

Chapter 1

Natural Speech

Conversation between people is far more than a simple exchange of information communicated by the words we choose and the syntax which puts them into a particular order. Each word has what might be called its *intrinsic meaning*, or intrinsic semantic content—the kind of meaning found in an ordinary dictionary. But dictionary meaning changes, sometimes in subtle ways, when combined with other words in a sentence. And the meaning of a sentence is more than a simple sum of the meanings of the individual words it contains. Words and their intrinsic meanings interact within the sentence to produce an overall *sentence meaning*. Linguists often think of the sentence as the basic stretch of language within which we arrange words to communicate our meaning. But this is usually a little too idealistic: most people in conversation depart from the ideal, and false starts and broken sentences are very common. However interesting this 'real' language is to us, it makes sense to relate it to the concept of the ideal sentence if only to have some yardstick against which to relate what people actually say.

The ideal sentence is regarded as abstract for this reason: it does not occur in speech. Sentences—arrangements of words within the sentence *domain*—represent what we could call general cases of regularly ordered stretches of words that are said to underlie the actual utterances which occur. It is not common for mainstream linguistics to dwell too much on actual utterances. Linguistics is a fairly rigorous approach to characterizing language. We speak of the area of study of linguistics as being 'normalized' language—it is devoid of variability. But, as we shall see, some of the ways in which the phonology and phonetics of an utterance are manipulated to communicate expression do not fall easily within the normal descriptions of linguistics, since utterances are spoken language. In modelling expression, we will be dealing with actual speech as well as abstract representations.

1.1 The production and perception of speech

Much work has been devoted over the past twenty to thirty years to developing models of human speech production and perception. Usually the two modalities have been considered separately, though a number of researchers have pointed out that there are insights to be had from an integrated approach, some of which we consider in Chapter 15.

The position for integration can be justified by simply noting that, separately, neither speech production nor perception models are ideal. It seems clear that a good start to modelling both production and perception is to allow for an anchor point whereby each has an abstract representation which is ideal and which is not error-prone. So we could say that a speaker's intention is to produce a speech signal from some underlying ideal representation, and that a listener's intention is to assign to that speech signal a corresponding ideal representation. The errors creep in during the processes which take the ideal representation and convert it to a speech signal; they also arise during the hearing and perceptual processes. The perceptual side of our model does not focus on the 'recovery' of a representation *from* the signal, but on the assignment of a representation *to* the signal. For us, the final perceived representation originates in the listener's mind, not in the acoustic signal.

We could say that, ideally, communication between speaker and listener would result in a perfect or near-perfect copy in the listener's mind of the speaker's original intended representation. Ideal communication does not occur, however, because of imperfections in the system resulting in *passive* distortion of the final representation. We call this distortion passive because there seems no evidence, all things being equal, that the distortions have been deliberately introduced. Of course, there is scope for a speaker deliberately to mislead a listener by using an acoustic waveform which they know will be misinterpreted because it is 'out of context' or ambiguous in some way. And this kind of occurrence—the deliberate manipulation of the ideal communication chain to play on error—is the key to understanding the remarkable degree of collaboration which actually goes on between speaker and listener.

If speakers know enough about the sources of error in this chain and if they know what errors are likely to be produced they can deliberately set up either the data being processed (the representation) or the communicative environment (the context, linguistic or other) to cause a predictable error. But this knowledge can be used the other way round. If a speaker knows what sort of error can occur and when it can occur, they can compensate for the effect to make sure it does not occur. This is an oversimplification, but the point being made is that we are never entirely passive players in an act of communication when it comes to succumbing to defects in the system—we can do something about them, and we do.

1.1.1 Integrating production and perception

We need to consider whether there are comparable benefits when modelling prosodics, the vehicle for much of expression in speech. A gain would be apparent if such an approach could throw light on otherwise unexplained observations. At the segmental level the gains are fairly obvious:

- We get greater insight into why speakers vary their utterance precision (more precision is used when the speaker judges greater perceptual ambiguity).
- We can often explain how a listener is able to repair a defective utterance successfully (the speaker's plan is being shadowed in a predictive way), and so on.

It is worth investigating whether the evidence when dealing with non-prosodic elements that production and perception are not independent carries through to prosody. And then, from 'plain' prosody it is a short step to deducing that expressive content in speech works similarly.

Starting with production, we may want to consider how useful the production-for-perception approach is. In modelling the production of segments, elements, or gestures it seems useful to use this approach because it does look as though, as we have discussed, a speaker varies their production precision in correlation with their predicted estimate of the listener's difficulties. The term for the listener's workload is 'perceptual loading'—that is, the loading imposed on the perceptual process.

So, for example, a teacher using an unexpected technical term might well render it with increased precision of articulation. Increased precision is achieved by motor control adjusted to lessen coarticulatory effects. But coarticulation is directly dependent on the rate of delivery of an utterance: the faster the delivery, the greater the likelihood that coarticulatory processes will be enhanced. Rate of delivery, however, is an aspect of prosody, and an observation of tempo changes when a speaker shows sensitivity to a listener's perception loading is evidence of speaker–listener collaboration beyond the segmental level. Consider also that the speaker might introduce a slight pause before and after the difficult word—broadcast newsreaders often do this—thus disrupting the smooth flow of the utterance's rhythm. This is also collaboration in the area of prosody. Finally, the speaker might introduce greater amplitude on the difficult term's stressed syllable and/or locally increase the duration of the syllable or its nuclear vowel—areas at the interface between prosody and segments or gestures.

Already we are listing effects which are basically prosodic in nature and which arise from speaker–listener collaboration: they are not hard to find. The model at the prosodic level begins with the same observation we made earlier about segments: the predicted acoustic signal (or its underlying articulation) is altered in some way to influence the way it is perceived. Another way of saying this is to notice that speech production theory will predict that a phonologically planned utterance will, all things being equal, produce a particular acoustic signal which falls within the limits imposed by the mechanics, aerodynamics, and any other constraints which affect its production. But under increased perceptual loading on the part of the listener, the speaker distorts what is expected, and an acoustic signal outside normal predictions is produced.

The mechanism we have suggested in the past (Tatham 1995) for making such adjustments to utterance-rendering involves direct cognitive supervision and control over what is going on. The production scenario is modified by cognitively organized short-term adjustments of articulatory precision and concomitant prosodic effects. The result is a reduction of any spurious degradation of an otherwise ideal acoustic signal. Mechanical and aerodynamic effects which contribute to coarticulatory phenomena are reduced to a level which significantly reduces listener perception loading and consequently potential error. In a more contemporary approach, we have suggested that the actual physical mechanism for this is analogous to, if not the same as, Fowler's early tuning mechanism which has access to the coordinative structures highlighted in *Action Theory* (Fowler 1980) in such a way as to make direct short-term adjustments to the equations of constraint which govern or characterize articulator dynamics. For the supervisory model to be plausible, there needs to be a suitable mechanism available to carry out the proposed supervisory action.

1.1.2 *Production-for-perception and prosodics*

The production-for-perception model (Chapter 8) claims that a speaker has an ongoing perceptual model running in the background during the production process, which can be 'consulted' on demand. The purpose of the perceptual model is to trial specific production-rendering processes to test the perceptual robustness of their output in the current environmental context. This context could be linguistic, but it could also be social or acoustic. So before the production system produces an *actual* articulation or soundwave an internal perceptual pass is run on the *projected* soundwave to see if it will enable perception to work adequately in a particular context. If the result of the trial is positive, the phonetic rendering process is triggered; if negative, an iterative process of improvement in robustness is set running until the desired level of perceptual accuracy is obtained. The plan is then rendered, and an appropriate acoustic signal is generated. There are several possible refinements to this model. For example, the iterative process of progressive 'improvement' might span several utterances, but in principle what characterizes this model is continuous sensitivity to perceptual needs.

At a prosodic/expressive level, we can imagine a speaker wishing to convey anger during an argument. An internal trial of the projected acoustic signal makes the speaker feel that they are not going to communicate this anger with sufficient force. They deliberately proceed to accentuate the anger content of the acoustic signal. This case is extremely interesting to us because it presupposes that the speaker 'knows' what constitutes the anger-perceptual trigger in the acoustic signal and has independent cognitive control over its prominence.

In both segmental and expressive domains the hypothesis is that without some kind of supervised reinforcement there is scope for ambiguity or, in the case of expression, understatement. We are saying that the speaker has the ability to institute a process of 'refinement' by intervening cognitively in the normal state of affairs, and that this is consequent on an internal trialling of the projected perceptual results without the intervention. Production strategies evaluated and continuously modified can be characterized as probability-based. What seems to count is the probability of perceptual error, a violation of the speaker's goal to be perceived.

One argument against this optimization procedure is that speech is usually not optimal as far as we can tell; a speaker can usually do better when it comes to articulatory precision. It might be, however, that the result of the iterative process is not the optimal articulation but the most precise articulation *necessary to achieve the perceptual goal.* Hence we find that precision is continuously variable, sometimes high, sometimes low, and usually in between, but almost always achieving the goal.

Speakers, we are claiming, are able to make these adjustments to their articulatory precision because they continuously run a predictive model of the perceptual outcome of how they are about to articulate their utterances. It is not necessary for the speaker to postulate an internal soundwave for running through a predictive perceptual model: simply predicting the values of parameters with a high contrastive role would be enough. So, for example, if in some dialogue in French it becomes critical to distinguish between the two words *bon* /bõ/ and *beau* /bo/, where the phonological feature [±nasal] and the articulatory parameter of nasality bear most of the contrast, then the speaker makes pretty certain that good, clear nasality is achieved in one word and suppressed in the other. Enough contrast in the nasality parameter will be achieved to make sure the listener has no difficulties, especially with words like this pair, where the semantic and syntactic distances between them are comparatively small—*bon* and *beau* are both adjectives with fairly similar meanings.[1]

This internally generated evaluative feedback is not the only feedback the speaker receives, but it does come in advance of actually producing an utterance. We are also sure that there are stabilizing feedback mechanisms at work during an utterance, though we cannot say precisely how they interact with the abstract predictive feedback we have been describing, except to assist in tightening up on precision of articulation. The speaker also gets feedback from the listener's reactions to what is being said. This feedback may take a number of forms, from a puzzled look through to a verbal query or request for repetition, and invariably comes after the utterance has been produced. Notice that the speaker's own internally generated feedback results in an immediately optimized soundwave (all additional constraints being equal), but that reaction to externally generated feedback (observed from the listener, for example) gives rise to a delayed response by the speaker.

1.2 The basic model

There are several approaches to modelling speech production and perception within linguistics, each of which emphasizes purposes and achievements; a list of these might include cognitive

---

[1] Phonetic transcriptions in this book follow the principles of the International Phonetic Association (1999).

phonetics, task dynamics, articulatory phonology, optimality theory, and metrical phonology. These concern various ways of characterizing aspects of speech; but one property they share is that they deal mostly with non-expressive utterances. Our question is how we approach adding a characterization of expression in speech to what we already have in terms of the way researchers, of whatever school, already offer.

Ideally, the model would incorporate procedures which have access to the results of the cognitive processing involved in expression, and which know how these results might be implemented to produce expressive speech. Similarly, for completeness it should also compute both the physical and cognitive processing necessary for generating an acoustic signal—the physical manifestation of emotion (as a well-worked example of expression)—and the physical manifestation of cognitive assessment and evaluation of the appropriate cognitively determined prosodic structures of the acoustic signal.

All this leaves aside the question as to where the information leading to producing an appropriately expressive acoustic signal might reside. In the *model*, any information needed for feeding into the various processes which contribute to building expressive speech can be found in tables or in any appropriate form virtually anywhere in the model: without knowledge of principles deriving from understanding the human production of speech, information and processes get placed at suitable points in the model for producing the required output in an efficient way. Where information and sets of processes reside in the *human being*, on the other hand, is very much an open question when it comes to understanding exactly how a human produces expressive speech. One advantage of the proposed approach is that some of the questions facing researchers modelling human processes can be couched in computational terms, thus aiding a more explicit statement of hypotheses which might usefully lead to productive investigation.

It is important to reiterate that a model of an event or processes is a way of *accounting* for that event, but this does not mean that the model completely describes the event or that it *is* the event itself. Indeed, by definition, a model must *not* be exhaustive, and certainly not the event itself: this would completely defeat the object of building models. To possess a perfect model which throws up no questions—that is, to possess the object of investigation itself—is a useless position in science. If the model and the object being modelled converge to the point of being indistinguishable, no purpose will be served: the investigator is back where they started. A ridiculous parallel in our quest to synthesize human speech with expressive content would be to employ a human being to do the synthesizing, thus guaranteeing a perfect acoustic signal which would take us no closer to *understanding* what we had produced. Thus the computer system *is not* the human system—they may converge in terms of what they output, but the computer system generates the output in a transparent way which is not matched by the opaqueness of the human processes.

We begin with a very simple working definition of expression: expression is information about feelings and attitudes conveyed by speech, in addition to the denotation and connotation of the words and phrases themselves.

1.2.1 Preliminary assumptions

Taking general expressive content in spoken language first, we can enumerate certain basic assumptions:

- The speaker and listener share a similar linguistic code.
- Linguistic descriptions of 'normative' speech are adequate.
- Acoustic correlates of linguistic descriptions are discoverable.
- Acoustic correlates are measurable.
- Expression involves an interrelationship between prosodics and pragmatics.

Similarly, there are assumptions in the exemplar case of *emotional content*:

- The emotion effect is physiologically based—certainly in the case of the small set most clearly defined in the literature, i.e. the basic emotions: fear, anger, contentment, and sadness; other emotions are less clearly defined, and usually regarded as less basic—for example, irritation, woe or joy;
- Fear, anger, contentment, and sadness can be clearly associated with biological systems.

One reason why these four are most often mentioned in the literature—especially when it comes to synthesizing expressive content—is that they *are* well defined in terms of biological systems (see Chapter 9). Once these four can be simulated synthetically, perhaps differences between emotive content and style, and between style and expression, such as authoritative, pleasant, expansive, reflective, and thoughtful, can be attempted. In terms of the usefulness of a synthesis system it is these latter which prove more attractive. In the kinds of use to which dialogue systems, for example, are put, they will clearly be more needed than emotions like sadness.

In terms of basic physiological response we may make more detailed assumptions about the relationship between utterances (speaking) with expressive content and the speaker's physiological and cognitive capabilities

- There is a close link with the biological substrate.
- There is a physiological 'setting' for expression—expressing emotion is the expression of the physiological stance or the awareness of a physiological stance.
- The entire body participates in this physiological stance.
- The speech production mechanism is in a different basic setting from the 'norm' as described by phonetics, for each expressive state.
- There is a reflection or manifestation of the physiological setting in the correlating acoustic signal.
- Parameters and invariances can be teased from the acoustic signal which correlate with the underlying physiological setting.
- Physical setting can be modified by cognitive intervention.

There are other assumptions, of course. But these reflect a philosophy or generalized approach: the underlying acoustic detail in expressive speech is the way it is, in some instances, *because* of particular physiological settings. The obvious ones are anger—which can, if it is intense enough, produce a tightening of the vocal tract which involuntarily distorts the speech—or extreme contentment or ecstasy—which seems to have a similar kind of effect on the vocal tract, often altering formant values. Certainly such underlying physiological settings cause changes in speech which cannot be ascribed to cognitively sourced details of how speech is controlled.

1.3 Developing a model to include expressive content

In the psychology literature there are identifiable alternative models of emotion; this leads to discussions about their relative merits. The phonetics literature, however, seems to reflect that research has not yet reached this stage: there seem to be no competing models of how expressive content is represented in the acoustic signal.

The position taken in this book—that a productive way to characterize speech is in terms of a prosodically based architecture—is in line with certain schools of thinking in phonology and phonetics, and differs from a segmentally based architecture. This particular approach has the potential of making the characterization of expressive content more viable, simply because of its focus on the prosodics of speech—which seems to be the dominant carrier of expressive content. Later we develop this particular model from the point of view of a computational model of speech production rather than from the point of view of a general descriptive characterization of speech. The basic idea of putting the entire model (including segmental phenomena) into a prosodic framework is not new, and an early proposal to this effect is seen in Firth (1948; see also Hayes 1995). The gestural time-focused approach of Articulatory Phonology (Browman and Goldstein 1986) has some similar properties, although here the framework is not linguistic prosody but the apparent domain structure of motor control.

In theoretical terms, the prosodic framework proposes that speech production is usefully characterized as being cognitively dominated, whereas the Articulatory Phonology framework relegates a great deal of speech production to low-level processes and constraints. Articulatory phonologists have argued against overburdening phonology (or cognitive processes) with motor control detail, but their arguments have largely centred around segmental rather than prosodic aspects of speech. Articulatory Phonology appears to neglect prosody as a potential overall framework, whereas the approach we are advocating makes it the general envelope for the characterization. Our approach is explicitly designed to lay emphasis on underlying cognitive processes and de-focus the physical periphery. We retain the ideas of Task Dynamics (in Browman and Goldstein, after Fowler 1980 and others) and its self-regulating low-level structures, but direct attention toward cognition.

1.4 Evaluating lines of research

In any area of study, but especially in one which is comparatively new, we need some means of evaluating different researchers' methodologies and results. At this stage in the discussion it is worth considering some of the more basic questions:

- Is the purpose of the research fully explicit? We should perhaps be wary of statements like: 'The purpose is to determine the acoustic correlates of expressiveness'—without putting the notion of expressiveness into a proper theoretical context or perhaps not defining what a possible acoustic correlate might be.
- What assumptions about the data are being made? Assumptions about the data are perfectly legitimate provided they are explicit and expressed in terms preferably of testable hypotheses. So, it might be assumed that the acoustic signal does indeed encode expressiveness (even though this looks obvious). But the assumption should go on to propose how testing might be done in terms of a hypothesis: 'Anger is expressed by speaking louder and slower' could be a testable hypothesis, for example. But 'Let's see how anger is encoded' is much less secure an approach.
- Is the data used to derive an explicit model which is testable? The data is gathered in terms of hypotheses, and once processed, the data and the refuted or supported hypotheses can be used in the construction of a model which takes in more than the data measured—in other words, makes predictions which themselves are transparently able to be tested. Clearly an approach is more useful if it extends to the predictive stage.

- What are the explicit means of testing the proposed model—and is this done? Ideally the model based on the research should of itself suggest how it might be tested—formally, this means that it suggests the kind of data which might *refute* it. Good research will almost always proceed to this stage in the argument.
- Is the research directed toward a particular application—like the development of a synthesis system capable of expression? Some of the research in the literature has been conducted with a particular application in mind, but this is usually not the case. There is no particular reason why researchers *should* have applications in mind—though in the case of speech synthesis, a proposed application might itself usefully form the test-bed for the proposed model.
- How have researchers been transferring their ideas and findings about the acoustic correlates of expression to speech synthesis systems? What methods have proved useful and reliable? Since there are different types of low-level synthesizer and different approaches to high-level synthesis, it is not obvious how findings about speech production are transferable. We shall see, for example, that our approach to modelling expression requires it to be an overriding property of the model, dominating all phonological and phonetic processes. But clearly such a model would not transfer easily to a speech synthesis system which itself models expressive content as an afterthought, superimposed on an utterance predominantly generated as 'neutral'-sounding.
- Does the research have a spin-off not necessarily explicit in its report (such as additional application to automatic speech recognition, for example)? Most of the work in expressiveness in phonetics has been concerned with speech production and with the resultant acoustic signal. But in psychology, one focus of interest has been the perception of expression and the reaction of perceivers to expression. Since automatic speech recognition has potential as a test-bed for models of speech *perception*, it is an application which has clear connections with work in understanding expression in speech.

Some of the above might be just general questions, others might be used as explicit criteria for evaluating the accuracy or usefulness of a particular piece or line of research. It is obvious that most, if not all, synthesis applications would profit from being able to generate speech with expression. We may still be in the stage of development where some would argue that what we have is good enough for many applications—but then there were those who argued that colour film was a waste unless it was just used for spectacular entertainment productions or specialist research applications, or those who argued that wireless mobile phones were an unnecessary luxury which would not catch on. In the end, except for very special purposes where there is a reason *not* to have expression, all synthesis systems will have expressive capability and all will sound indistinguishable from human speech, whatever the state of the art now.

Similarly, developing models of speech production will not avoid this area of human communication which is so all-pervasive in our contact with one another. Our belief is that prosody (including expression) is in a sense the carrier medium of speech, and that a shift of focus in speech models and their underpinning theories is overdue. As we develop a model of expressive content in speech, it will become clear why we regard expression and general prosody as the 'wrapper' within which speakers formulate *all* utterances.

1.5 The perception of a waveform's expressive content

It is worth adding that speech synthesis is not the only area of technology which stands to gain by a greater understanding of expressiveness in speech. In dialogue systems, automatic speech recognition (ASR) needs to determine what it is the human user is saying.

ASR systems consist essentially of a set of procedures whose end product is the assignment of symbolic labels (like a phonetic or orthographic transcription) to a speech waveform. From a practical point of view, it is clear that ASR could benefit from an extension of its labelling processes to expressive content contained in the acoustic signal. This is work for the future, since not much progress has yet been made in recognizing the 'neutral' aspects of prosody, let alone its expressive properties. In general, ASR is less related to linguistics and psychology than speech synthesis, and owes much of its success to using signal-processing techniques based often on a statistical approach (hidden Markov or artificial neural network modelling) rather than on a linguistics or psychology approach.

An example incorporating expression modelling would be the use of an automatic speech recognizer to evaluate a model of the perception of expressive content in speech. The task of the recognizer would be to label stretches of utterances with appropriate expressive markers, analogously to the way recognizers currently provide phonological or orthographic markers. As a test-bed for perceptual research this approach would be invaluable, but there is little doubt that the current generation of speech recognition devices is based on strategies which would not be suitable for such a task. Current devices are not explicitly modelled on human perception—so the test might only trivially be of the ability of recognizers to do labelling, rather than of whether the model of expression perception is good.

1.6 The test-bed for modelling expression

Speech synthesis began with the segmental approach, based, in its early days, on the classical phonetics (CP) model. In CP, segmental and suprasegmental effects are described and classified separately, and very little is said about any interaction between the two types of phenomenon. The nature of segments is focused on the segment itself—and, later, on any changes these segments might undergo depending on variations in their occurrence in the context of other segments. Prosodic phenomena are described as affecting stretches of concatenated segments: rhythm and intonation are examples.

These days, some fifty years later, the focus is gradually shifting to one which integrates the two into a single phenomenon: dynamic speech. The most productive model here is one which characterizes speech in a hierarchical fashion, focusing on tiers of prosodics within the hierarchy. This hierarchy—as a complete network—constitutes the structure which derives an *utterance plan* which is to be rendered as an acoustic signal. The prosodic hierarchy is a descriptive framework which transparently characterizes, in an abstract way—no variability—what underlies the production of the acoustic signal. And wherever there is an explicit relationship between motor control and the acoustic signal, that too is covered in the plan.

The prosodic hierarchy underlying speech can be viewed as the interpretive framework necessary for speaking utterances. Within the hierarchy we recognize, for the purposes of clarity of the model, tiers or levels, and domains—well-defined stretches of utterance. When we focus later on detailed examples of expression models we shall further clarify these terms, bringing them together in an integrated model in Part IV.

The tiers or levels within the hierarchy involve domains focused ever more narrowly on the objects involved in speech processing; that is, they are represented with increasing granularity with newer, smaller objects being progressively brought into processing play as we descend through the hierarchy of tiers. The lowest level of the network has objects of extrinsic allophonic size (Tatham 1971), the highest of sentence size or greater (though these are prosodic, not syntactic domains). Elements within the network all contribute to the plan, rather than just the output layer: it is as though the derivational history of the output layer lives within it. It is important to remember that the layout of a model is initially aimed to make the thinking behind it and its workings clear and transparent. Later we may want to claim some special status for the layout of the model, for example that it reflects some independently verifiable cognitive or physical structure within the human being.

Our example of a suitable test-bed is based on a computational model (Tatham et al. 2000). Here the prosodic structure is modelled explicitly in high-level synthesis, though in a such a way as to simulate as closely as possible the dynamic human production process as a whole. The system has a dynamic prosodic structure which is at times algorithmic and at times declarative. So, for example, if a particular object or node in the output layer (say, a syllable boundary) is characterized by a particular node or juxtaposition of nodes in the declared data structure at this particular point in the hierarchy, then the process linking the node(s) and the derived syllable boundary is a dynamic process rather than a simple description designed to 'explain' the boundary occurrence. For an applicational speech synthesizer (rather than an illustrative or test-bed speech synthesizer) all such processes must be fully dynamic and algorithmic, with no gaps or omissions in the chain of processes linking and developing the declared data structures. It is one thing to 'explain' an acoustic signal; it is quite another to create that signal in a proper and principled way.

Chapter 2

Speech Synthesis

Speech synthesis is the creation of an acoustic signal which resembles human speech. One of the most productive approaches involves developing a strategy which parallels the way we view speech production in human beings, keeping separate how we model the cognitive and physical processes involved. Along with others we call the cognitive processes 'high-level' or phonological, to use the term from linguistics. The physical processes are called 'low-level' or phonetic. There are grey areas involving processes which are difficult to assign to either level, as well as a great deal of interaction between the two levels. But for transparency in our modelling it is useful to regard low- and high-level processes as relatively separate.

2.1 Modern synthesis techniques

Early attempts at speech synthesis do not form the basis of an adequate environment for our purposes. Although very high-quality speech was able to be produced by some systems there was much tweaking in evidence—often unprincipled and sometimes incompletely documented. Although one of the best, the Holmes system (Holmes et al. 1964; Holmes 1988), for example, so closely integrates the high- and low-level aspects of its approach to text-to-speech synthesis that is it difficult to know exactly what is happening. An example of this is the way nasal segments are handled by a rather awkward relationship between A1 and ALF (two parameters concerned with the amplitude of the first formant and the amplitude of 'low frequencies'), or the relatively broad band of frication achieved by 'combining' high formant filters. Details such as these make the precise control of the subtleties of expression in speech very difficult because they are at best simply design compromises for intelligible speech; they do not give full access to the variables needed for encoding expressive content.

For our purpose of trying to create synthetic speech with expression, it is important to have the working environment as transparent as possible, and this means at least a clear separation within the synthesis model of high- and low-level processes. This will ensure an unambiguous placing within the system of the correlating human cognitive and physical processes. Certainly a transparent synthesis environment for testing an assessment of expressive content in human speech is essential. Using a confused or opaque environment as part of the testing process would create a major problem in trying to determine whether any output errors were the result of the expression model or the test-bed itself.

We chose to mention the Holmes system, not because it was the best or the worst, but because it was the most accessible and customizable system of the period. But notwithstanding the early pioneer work in text-to-speech or rule-based synthesis systems, more recent systems developed since the 1980s are more detailed and versatile.

2.1.1 Traditional units for synthesis

Since our method of describing expression in speech rests on a clear identification of two stages in speech production in the human being, planning and rendering (see Chapter 16), our computational model must be testable on a synthesizer which itself makes just such a distinction. Above, we referred to high-level synthesis, and this is the part of the model which takes care of the planning stage. Low-level synthesis, on the other hand, is about rendering the plan. Any synthesizer which makes this distinction either explicitly or in an implied way qualifies for use in a system which incorporates explicit planning and rendering—in particular the planning and rendering of prosodic and expressive content.

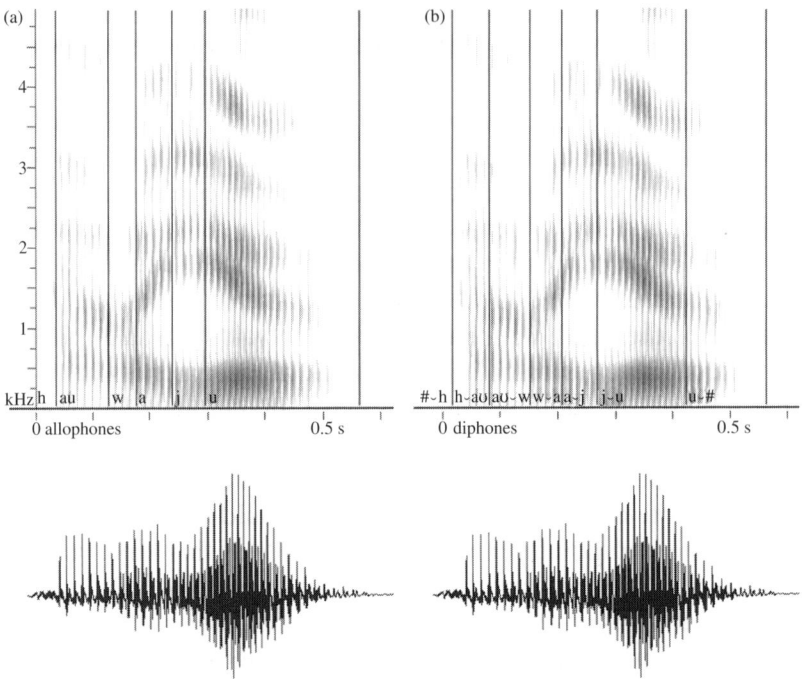

Fig. 2.1. Spectrograms of the utterance *How are you?* showing (a) allophone boundaries and (b) diphone boundaries. Notice the continuousness of the acoustic signal.

2.1.2 Units in modern systems

One or two modern synthesis systems have units of different sizes within the same system. Thus a system might contain a vocabulary of say 30,000 words in its inventory of units, but if called upon to speak a word not in the vocabulary could resort to piecing together the word from syllables found in among the words it does have. On the odd occasion when even the syllable cannot be found, such systems then retrieve allophones to reconstruct the necessary syllables (Tatham and Lewis 1999). Once again, the quality of the output is likely to degrade as the units get smaller and a larger number of critical transitions between them need to be computed.

Other modern systems increase the basic unit size, employing what are known as 'unit selection techniques' (Black and Campbell 1995). Such systems contain typically a large database of several hours of recorded human speech. Whenever the

Table 2.1. Example of unit selection. The longest appropriate units (shaded in the table) are selected from the database fragment, marked with a phonetic transcription, for insertion into the new target utterance. One unit, [ɜː], is not found in the database

Database fragment	Orthographic representation:
	'Unit selection is a sophisticated method of using variable length units in speech synthesis. We can now see how the method is attracting much attention.'
↓	Phonetic representation:
	[junɪt sɪlekʃn ɪz ə səfɪstɪkeɪtrd meθəd əv juzɪŋ veəriəbl leŋθ junɪts ɪn spitʃ sɪnθəsɪs. wi kə n aʊ si haʊ ðə meθəd ɪz ətræktɪŋ mʌtʃ ətenʃn]
New target utterance	'How it works is very interesting.'
	Concatenated rearranged units taken from the database fragment:
	[haʊ ɪt w ɜː k s ɪz v e ri ɪn t r e s tɪŋ]

synthesizer is called upon to synthesize an utterance it scans the database and selects the largest possible units available, including whole phrases. There are certain constraints on what can and cannot be used under certain circumstances, but in principle unit selection systems have the potential to produce very high-quality speech. Clearly, the longer the matching stretch of speech found in the database the more accurate will be the intersegmental modelling. We shall see later, though, that despite superior segmental rendering, unit selection systems have difficulties when it comes to utterance prosodics—the essential 'carrier' of expressive content.

Table 2.1 offers a simple example of how unit selection might work. The method of putting together a new utterance involves selecting from the database (here just a fragment) the longest sequence of units called for in the target utterance. In this particular example the longest sequence found was [tɪŋ], preserving the original transitions between the three segments. However, [ɜː] was not found in this particular fragment. It is easy to imagine that sometimes strings longer than the three-segment one here will be found; a much larger database increases the probability of finding any particular sequence.

2.2 Limitations of the synthesizer type

An interesting question is whether current methods of synthesizing speech—usually the lower-level system—are adequate for handling the parameters of expression. So, if we were considering the possibilities for synthesizing speech with emotive content using the Holmes or Klatt parametric synthesis systems we would be looking at whether the parameters offered, their range of variability, and the fineness of their control are adequate for the job. In addition the way the parameters interact with each other within the system is important—they might not be entirely independently controllable. But it is also the case that parameters interact within the listener, and this will be an important consideration when we come to modelling listener response to speech with expressive content. The kinds of interaction which might be important are the perceptual interaction between formant frequencies and fundamental frequency, the interaction between pitch and amplitude, and the relativity of the various parameters.

Ultimately it is clear that creating or evaluating synthesized expressive speech presupposes knowledge of just what it is in the acoustic signal which correlates with a particular expression, and how this translates into the variables available in the synthesis model under consideration. Even before we come to look at speech with expressive content, we can note that the human speech production/perception system seems to involve complex interaction of almost every level and every parameter: unravelling the contribution of each element in the system to the overall process is very difficult indeed, and it is by no means certain that the complexities of the basic system are understood by researchers even before we look at expression.

2.2.1 Unravelling the complexities

Under circumstances as complex as these, it is usual to use a traditional research paradigm to tackle the problem from each point of view separately. Thus building a good model of speech *without* expressive content would normally precede the addition of the complexity of modelling expression. However, this approach presupposes that the component parts are separable: they are for modelling purposes (because we can view them how it suits us), though things might not be so simple in the real world. Let us consider an example: phoneticians trained in experimental acoustic research are apt to think of the acoustic signal in terms of its spectral properties. For them, much of the insight of how the acoustic signal is an encoding of messages rests in the frequency domain, with the behaviour of formants, for example. The usefulness and appropriateness of this view is reinforced by our knowledge that the predominantly passive hearing system in the human being focuses on the spectral content of the acoustic signal as the result of performing a mechanical analysis of it in the cochlea (Daniloff et al. 1980).

The spectrograms we inspect in our labs are produced in a similar way to the spectral analysis performed by the hearing process. But the Fourier or LPC analysis of the acoustic signal used as the basis of spectrograms is nothing more than a mathematical transformation of the complex wave—there is no serious implication that the complex wave itself is *constructed* from the spectral analysis. The acoustic signal is a coherent entity: it does not incorporate the means of its own analysis—that is, it is not necessarily intrinsically biased in favour of the kind of spectral analysis that suits us. The lesser position is that it is, however, amenable to the kind of analysis we need for our research, and the kind of analysis our ears perform on it. It makes sense for the researcher to analyse speech in a way analogous to the way the ear analyses it. And it makes sense for the researcher to hypothesize that such an analysis is 'meaningful' to the perceptual system, since that is by and large what it has to work with. This principle was the basis of the thinking behind the selection of appropriate parameters in early parametric synthesis systems. The principle is distinct from the basic idea of the usefulness of parametric synthesis in general—bandwidth compression considerations were the driving force here (Lawrence 1953; Flanagan 1956).

2.2.2 *The adequacy of synthesis for testing models*

Using a synthesizer as a test-bed for a model of human speech presupposes either a completely transparent synthesis system which neither adds to nor subtracts from our model or a synthesis system in which the limitations and constraints are well understood. Constraints which are a property of the synthesizer being used can, if they are known, be allowed for or negated when considering the success of the synthesized expression model. For example, it may well be hypothesized that subtleties of fundamental frequency change in the course of a syllable-length portion of the utterance trigger the perception of a particular emotion. Here it is obvious that the synthesizer must not be constrained in such a way that fundamental frequency (f0) changes of such a short period of speech are not possible.

To use synthetic speech for model testing, we would need then to be sure that the system was up to the job. It would have to be capable of:

- producing a 'clean' and expressionless voice judged subjectively to be human, even if listeners are never likely to hear completely expressionless speech in real life;
- allowing the free manipulation of available parameters without generating any spurious artefacts based on interactions within the system;
- implementing a completely explicit computational model reflecting what we know of human speech production, with no obvious omissions or opaque patches to cover gaps in our knowledge—this is true of both the model and the synthesizer.

These criteria define our test-bed application. Under these circumstances, it does not matter whether our model of expressive human speech is one which presupposes a basic expressionless mode on which is overlaid expressive content, or whether expression is seen as a complex and unavoidable property of all human speech—the criteria for the basic synthesis test-bed engine define a system which can be used in both these scenarios. Another way of saying this is that the test-bed must not obviously favour one particular model's approach over another. The key consideration is complete transparency: it is essential to know the design motivation for every single process within the synthesis system and how each interacts with other processes, especially if some of them are motivated by practical considerations rather than by actual knowledge of the human system.

Chapter 3

Expression in Natural Speech

In addressing the differences between neutral and expressive speech, researchers have asked the question: How does speech which incorporates a particular expression, say an emotion or attitude, compare with neutral speech in which there is no obvious emotive content? Attention is not focused on how the acoustic signal got to be the way it is, nor on how such a signal makes the listener feel they detect this or that expressive content in the speech. In examining only the acoustic signal, a comparison between various modes of expression is usually made by reference to neutral speech. Almost all researchers have consistently made two assumptions:

- neutral speech does exist and is detectable, and
- it can be established as a base or 'canonical form' from which other styles of speech or tones of voice can be mapped.

The problem is to establish just what neutral speech *is*. Usually, experimenters take neutral speech to show no detectable expression of emotion or intention in its acoustic signal. Sometimes this is established formally by experiments involving listening panels, and on other occasions the speech has simply been judged by the researcher themselves to be neutral. A further technique is to define a particular style or environment as neutral and take a sample database from that environment. An example here might be to assert 'newsreader style' to be in general neutral, and to take samples of speech from newscasts containing no obvious additional expression content (but see Tams and Tatham 1995).

3.1 What lies *behind* expressive speech?

In talking about particular styles of speaking or the expressive content of someone's speech, we presuppose that there is an underlying abstract idea of expression. The question to ask for the moment is: What is expression? rather than: How is it rendered? Experiments based on the acoustics of speech collect data about the expressive characteristics of the waveform itself—the product of *rendering* expression. Clearly, it would help to know just what it is that has been rendered, say by setting up a simple model of speech production which isolates the rendering process from the processes which have built the utterance plan. The plan is a statement of *what is to be rendered*. In a more traditional but *static* model of speech production, we would refer here to the separation of phonetic and phonological processes respectively.

The question of what expression actually might be at the planning or pre-planning levels, and its answer, fall outside the domain of core linguistics, including phonology and phonetics. But if we are to describe characteristics of the speech wave which trigger particular feelings in listeners and which either have been planned by speakers or derive from some other, less obvious cognitive or physical source within the speaker, we need definitions of these underlying phenomena. This is especially true if we want somehow to distinguish between neutral and expressive *plans* and neutral and expressive *renderings*.

What is needed is a characterization of expression at an abstract level which correlates with the differences observed between the plan and its rendering. It may well be that one reason why researchers have had so much difficulty in finding the acoustic correlates of expression is that there is no firm underlying concept with which to correlate the acoustic signal. Much or perhaps all of the existing research begins by identifying various modes of expression (for example, different emotions experienced by the speaker) at an abstract level, then continues by analysing stretches of waveform which have prompted a listener to identify them. But what most of this research in the speech literature does *not* do is explicitly characterize these abstract modes of expression: they are just enumerated. Thus a speaker can be 'happy', 'determined', 'forthright', etc., and as a result they produce waveforms which somehow enable a listener to know this. But what *is* 'happy', and how has this happiness made the waveform special?

3.2 How does expression get into speech?

We suggest that expression is a manner of speaking, a way of externalizing feelings, attitudes, and moods—conveying information about our emotional state. We use the term 'expressive speech' to mean speech which gives us information, other than the plain message, about the speaker, and triggers a response in the listener. The reason we understand this idea is because all speech is spoken with expression: it is just that the expression varies. We are usually able to comment on the expression we hear in speech, and can recognize without much difficulty a speaker's feelings or intentions. Sometimes there are ambiguities and we might be confused as to a speaker's exact feelings, but often expression can be very clear. For example, anger or happiness in someone's voice are usually not difficult to detect, but subtly conveyed suspicion or irony may be more difficult or even misread by the listener.

Emotion is seen as a type of expression. Some researchers feel that there are a few relatively unambiguous 'basic' emotions—like the anger and happiness just mentioned—with the more subtle ones 'overlaid' on top of these or consisting of blends of these. Others see emotion as a cline. Yet others point to the fact that often strong feelings literally distort the physical vocal tract, leaving an unambiguous physical 'trademark' or imprint. Anger, for example, often involves a physical tension which can be felt throughout the body and certainly has an effect on the tenseness of the speech organs, which in turn creates a distinct acoustic effect. Happiness might involve a less total physical change, often just a smile which is 'talked through'. Listeners report that the physical change can be perceived—for example you can 'hear' a smile on a telephone voice. Note that these informal terms are readily used and understood by non-experts. Part of our task is to make such terms explicit. The tension of anger and the smile of happiness are distinct from the connotation and denotation of words and phrases in speech communication but nevertheless colour any speech that occurs simultaneously with the emotion. However, not all expression in the speech signal results from such linguistically independent physical effects. Sometimes there is expression which the speaker deliberately adds to speech and which can only be conveyed through speech. We shall examine these different types of expression in detail later.

3.3 Neutral speech

It can be claimed that it is not possible to speak without expression—even so-called 'deadpan' speech has expression, suggesting for example that no particular expression is intended. Deadpan speech may be considered a special case of expression—one end of a scale of expressiveness, perhaps—and is often referred to in the literature as 'neutral speech'. But the concept is used as a kind of baseline to begin a characterization of expression. In this approach, expression is seen as a modification of baseline neutral speech, or some kind of overlay imposed on this baseline. Perhaps we might think of neutrality as some kind of *carrier* which gets modulated to reveal other expressions. This might be a useful way of modelling the relationship between the different expressions, since in such a model they would be characterized as modulating the carrier differently.

Such ideas, though, look like a contradiction. On the one hand we are saying that neutral speech never occurs or is very rare, yet on the other we are saying that it can be used as a baseline from which to measure expressiveness. This concept is useful, and is not a contradiction if we consider the relationship between expressions in terms of a very simple hierarchy:

abstract underlying expression   neutral
$$\downarrow$$
surface expression   anger—fear—contentment—sadness

We use this very simple descriptive model of underlying expression and surface expression to enable us to picture the idea that in an abstract way any one utterance can be thought of as basically having neutral expression enhanced during the course of speaking into actual expressive content in the acoustic signal. The neutral speech is abstract because it never occurs on the surface.

3.4 Degrees of expression

This is a useful model because it enables us to introduce the idea of *scales* of expressiveness. Imagine, for example, that some otherwise neutral sentence is actually spoken with anger: John is angry that his bicycle has been stolen, and this is very apparent when he simply says: *Someone stole my bicycle*. But there can be degrees of such expression. We can tell from this simple utterance not just that John is angry, but how much he is angry—from very angry indeed to hardly angry at all. Any one of these emotions can assume different degrees. But what we think of as neutral expression might also be thought of as nothing more than anger, or happiness, or any other expression, quite simply so weakly expressed as to be imperceptible to the listener.

There is a point in saying that 'no expression' is simply 'zero anger' etc., which becomes clear as we push the capability of our model yet further. We shall want to say later that there is always potential for any expression in speech but that on occasion any one or more potential expressions are set to zero. This gives us the chance to think of *varying* expression while a person is talking as being a change in the balance of the values assigned to the range of possible expressions. We could say that there are *two* variables: one is the particular emotion, for example, and there is its value—how much there is of it.

How we are to express degrees of expression will depend very much on the model we choose to help account for phenomena such as emotional or attitudinal signals in speech, which in turn will depend on how emotion and attitude themselves are characterized. For example, if we believe that there are just a few basic emotions and that these combine to form what we might call secondary emotions, then we could imagine that it is not just which of the half dozen or so basic expressions that are combined, but *how much* of those which are combined. But if we take another approach to characterizing emotion and believe that different emotions can be thought of as zones along an emotional *vector*, then how we characterize degree has to be handled differently. The vector might be a cline of emotions shading into one another, with extremes at either end. In the vector approach, degree would simply be a reflection of intensity in a particular zone, or in other words the size of the zone itself. We can illustrate these two approaches.

3.4.1 The basic/secondary model of emotion

There are researchers who have developed the idea that most emotions can be characterized in terms of combined contributions from some small number of basic emotions—these secondary emotions are also called 'mixtures' or 'blends' (Lazarus 1991; Ekman 1992; Plutchik 1994; Oatley and Johnson-Laird 1998). Table 3.1 illustrates this.

In this example we identify four basic emotions, b1–b4 and four secondary emotions, s1–s4. The matrix defines the secondary emotions in terms of the percentage they 'owe' to each of the basic emotions. Thus secondary emotion s3 owes 10% to b1, 75% to b2, 5% to b3, and 20% to b4. This is a kind of abstract recipe for arriving at a secondary emotion. The recipe itself does not specify *degree* of emotion simply because this would be a specific instantiation of the emotion type, rather than its general definition. It is important to distinguish between the general

Table 3.1. How secondary emotions can be characterized in terms of contributions from basic emotions

	Secondary emotion s1 (%)	Secondary emotion s2 (%)	Secondary emotion s3 (%)	Secondary emotion s4 (%)
Basic emotion b1	50	25	10	0
Basic emotion b2	50	25	75	30
Basic emotion b3	0	0	5	60
Basic emotion b4	0	50	20	10

Expression in Natural Speech

definition which this type of matrix illustrates and a specific occurrence of the emotion. When it does occur, we can specify its definition and the *degree* to which it occurs like this:

- On any one occasion emotion s3 owes 10% to b1, 75% to b2, 5% to b3, and 20% to b4, and on this particular occasion has occurred with (say) 45% of its potential intensity.

3.4.2 The vector model of emotion

The vector model, on the other hand, places emotions in zones along a vector. Figure 3.1 illustrates this. The upper vector here represents the potential for n emotion 'zones' along the 'emotion vector'. Because the model is of *potential* emotions, each is represented with equal size (and therefore equal, but unspecified, intensity). In the lower vector we see an actual occurrence or instantiation of emotion. The speaker is experiencing emotion 3, with a slight mix of emotion 5; the remaining potential emotions appear vestigially simply to mark their positions on the vector, but they do not figure in the current emotional experience. The relative sizes of the zones along the vector depict the intensity of the specified emotion.

One of the aspects of our understanding of expression in speech which is difficult to get to grips with is just how we change the degree of expression and the different types of expression even within the course of a sentence. Perhaps even more intriguing, is the question of how listeners are able to track these

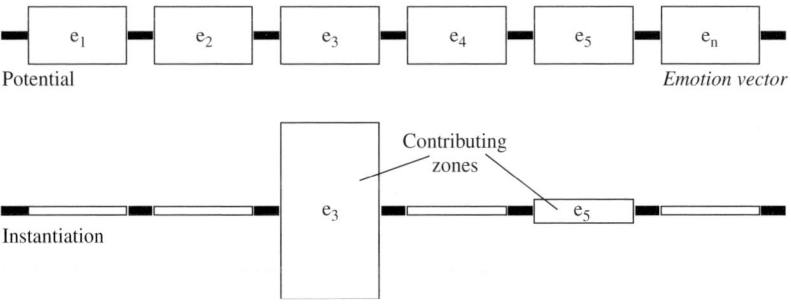

Fig. 3.1. Emotions modelled as 'zones' along a vector.

changes so accurately and skilfully. An apparent instantiation of 'neutral' emotion would be a close to zero value for all emotions.

3.5 The dynamic nature of expression

The idea that expression unfolds or changes as speech proceeds introduces a dynamic perspective into its description, and this is a relatively new concept in describing emotion or attitude in speech research. Up till now most effort has been concentrated on static descriptions which characterize, say, the acoustic characteristics of sadness or suspicion, etc., as though whole utterances or indeed longer stretches of speech have some kind of constant expressive content. But although this is in theory possible—just as in theory it may be possible to speak without communicating any expression at all—in fact it is rare enough to be discounted as a reasonable occurrence in real-world communication between people. People always communicate expression and attitude, and they always do so in a dynamic and adaptive way. Listeners can always comment on a speaker's attitude and can usually track how attitude unfolds during conversation.

Just as we can begin with an abstract starting point for describing expression itself—the neutral, special case of *no* or '*zeroed*' expression—so we can begin the characterization of how expression unfolds dynamically in speech with an abstract starting point in which expression is static or constant, not changing in the course of an utterance. The use of abstract reference points in modelling complex dynamic phenomena is not new—several approaches to psychology and linguistics rely heavily on this concept. Abstract reference points are introduced to provide a firm foundation on which to build our complex dynamic models of expression in speech.

As an example, we might think of a speaker reporting that they have just realized a misunderstanding which had led them to be unhappy. Figure 3.2 shows a graph of the change from unhappiness to happiness. This is not a graph of intonation but a graph of continuous change, as the sentence unfolds, between happiness (represented by the top line) and unhappiness (represented by the bottom line).

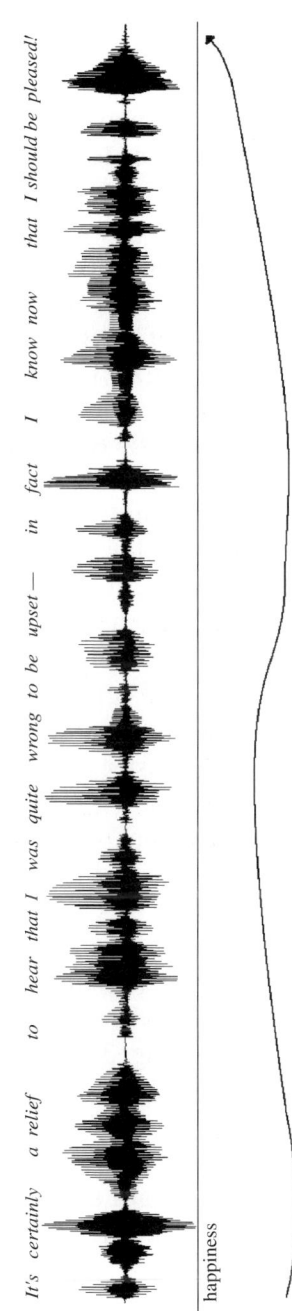

Fig. 3.2. The continuousness of movement from unhappiness to happiness as an utterance unfolds.

As the speaker is actually talking there is a change taking place in the way they feel, giving rise to a perceived change in their feelings. This graph handles only one emotion at a time: it takes no account of possible interplay of mixed feelings, and would have to be much more complex to do so. It is good enough for the moment, though, because we are trying to enumerate some of the properties of expression which we shall need to model quite carefully if we are to describe where expressive content in speech comes from and what acoustic form it takes. Here we are using a graph analogous to a musical score, except that we are not representing the discrete notes of a melody, rather the *continuousness* of changing expression. The range of the graph could be taken to be from 0% to 100% on a scale of the speaker's potential happiness with anything in their environment. What this kind of graph does well is capture subtle changes in a mood or attitude as time unfolds; the graph can also be directly related to the words being spoken by means of textual labelling. In addition, a waveform of the actual speech could form another track of the score. In a more complex model we could even indicate just how quickly an individual can experience emotion changes—there must be constraints on how fast we can alter our feelings—by putting limits on the steepness of the slope of the graph.

There are clearly several different ways we could represent expression and how it changes with time. But once we have assembled exactly what we need to capture in our model of expression we shall have a clearer idea of the best or optimum way of doing this so that we can bring out exactly what features of expression, its feeling in the speaker, and its perception in the listener that we need. Graphs like Fig. 3.2 report what might have happened, but they make few claims about why the events occurred or what constraints there are on their occurrence. As we move on we shall see that we need to refocus our attention, away from simply describing events toward trying to understand why the events are as they are. In our specific case, the events are particular characteristics of the acoustic signal; the objective is to characterize expression in such a way that we can begin to understand why the acoustic signal is like this.

3.6 The 'acoustic correlates' paradigm for investigating expression

Most research into expression in speech has been about discovering the acoustic correlates of various modes of expression. Thus the acoustic characteristics for example of 'anger' have been compared with those for 'sadness' or 'happiness', and so on. In this section we examine some general principles which have been used in research in the area of modelling expression in the acoustics of speech, and consider some which may not have been applied. We draw attention to one or two examples of work which investigates the possibility of setting up reliable acoustic correlates for various types of expression, usually the expression of particular well-defined emotions.

Establishing what represents this or that expression in speech is clearly desirable; but given the perhaps rather extreme subjective nature of expression in general it is doubly important to have a firm scientific framework within which to work. Unfortunately, it is not always clear what framework has been adopted.

There are three general areas of motivation for researching within the 'acoustic correlates' paradigm

- to discover how speaker emotions and attitudes are acoustically encoded;
- to establish how to synthesize expression;
- to model the cues listeners have for arriving at distinct expression percepts.

Thus the acoustic correlates research paradigm is not uniquely motivated. Its methodology and architecture cater for investigating how a physical object with a great deal of variability (the acoustic signal) relates to or correlates with an invariant cognitive object (the speaker's phonological description, or plan), how we can identify the acoustic properties of speech which need to be synthesized to incorporate the naturalness associated with expression, and how the variable acoustic signal correlates with listeners' perceptions of expressive content.

We can say that within the speaker/listener there is a subconscious mental object of which the language user (that is, both speaker and listener) can be made aware. By its nature this object does not vary. For the moment we are unifying the speaker's plan—an abstract or mental characterization of what is to be uttered—and the listener's decoded percept—an abstract representation of the listener's view of what the speaker intended to say—that is, their *plan*.

On any one occasion this mental object or plan correlates with a single physical object—the acoustic signal. But on many occasions the same mental object correlates with a large number of physical objects (in fact, in principle as many objects as there are occasions—i.e. each one is different). Put more simply: although a speaker's plan usually gets only a single acoustic encoding (unless the speaker repeats themselves) we know that the acoustic signal will vary on different repetitions of the same plan; and although some variations are predictable there is no obvious way of predicting *all* the possible variations.

That is, for the speaker there is a one-to-many mapping of the invariant utterance plan onto the actual acoustic, and for the listener there is a many-to-one mapping of the acoustic onto the invariant percept. We speak of correlation between speaker plan and the speech waveform, and correlation between the speech waveform and the listener percept of the plan—and it is this correlation which the acoustic correlates experimental paradigm seeks to explain. One of the tasks will be to discover which variations are predictable and which are not. Both types of variation need to be properly modelled. Figure 3.3 shows three instantiations of the invariant underlying plan *How are you?*, each spoken with no conscious intention on the part of the speaker to introduce any variation.

3.6.1 *Modelling variability: the one-to-many problem*

The range of varying acoustic signals has certain properties which we find when an utterance plan is rendered or encoded as a speech signal:

- all the variations correlate with a single particular underlying mental object—the plan;

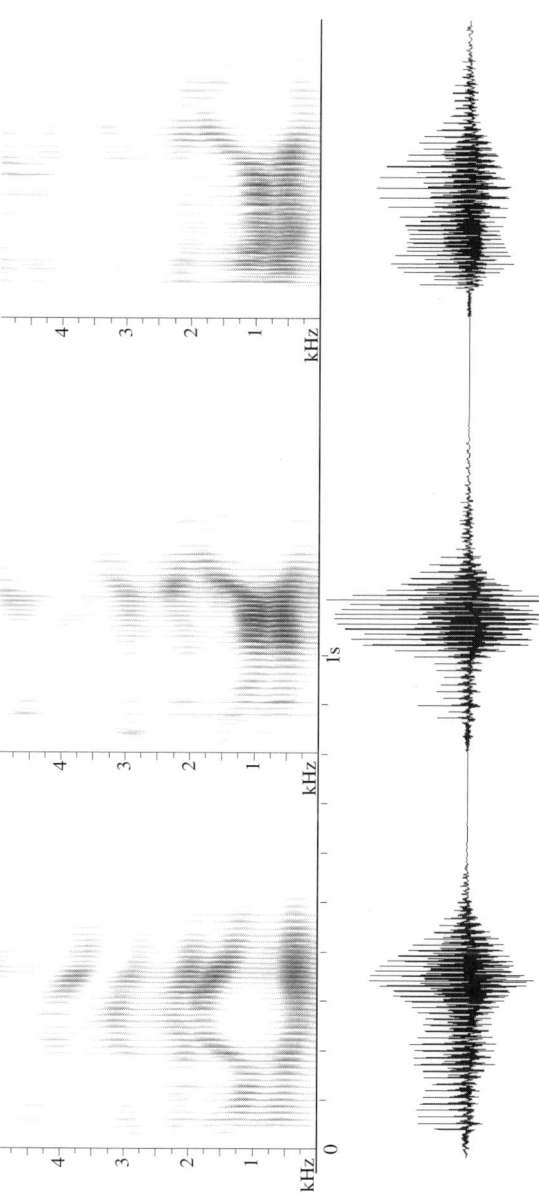

Fig. 3.3. Three waveforms of the utterance *How are you?*, showing variations between actual instantiations of the same underlying plan.

- the surface objects themselves are 'contained'—that is they have a describable structure of pattern themselves, independently of the underlying mental object—but nevertheless explained by it in terms of the fact that they occurred at all. The surface pattern is also explained by external constraints—for example, the limits within which the tongue can move.

The diagram below exemplifies the general case model. There is a single underlying object which derives a set of surface objects. The derivational process (the arrow connecting the objects) is constrained in a number of different ways—we show two, but there will be more. It is this constraint *pressure* which ensures the variety of surface objects which constitute instantiations of the underlying abstract invariant object.

single underlying object

{constraint set 1}→   ⇓   ←{constraint set 2}

{surface objects}

Typically, in the area of phonetics many of these constraints will be of a physical nature (e.g. coarticulatory phenomena). The variability among the set of surface objects is usually not entirely random. Although there are some random elements, much of the variability is patterned and can therefore be explained in principle. That is, for any one set of surface objects (the variable acoustic signals),

- membership of the set is explained by their correlation with a single underlying object;
- the range of variability is explained by the degrees of freedom of the surface object itself; and
- the actual occurrence of any one object within the set is explained by the constraints imposed on the conversion or transformation of the underlying object to the surface object.

3.6.2 Recovering from variability

The acoustic correlates experimental paradigm seeks to determine, for each underlying object, the correlating set of surface objects such that a unique relationship is set up between the two levels. In this sense, a plausible surface object or acoustic signal can be generated from the underlying plan, and in principle the underlying plan is 'recoverable' from the acoustic signals, say, by a listener. We are expressing the bi-directionality of the approach rather simplistically here; it is certainly the case that actual perceptual recovery of the plan is an extremely complex process, and involves many factors outlined in Part IV.

In the model of expression in speech which we are building throughout this book, we would say that there is a contained range of acoustic effects which point, when any one of them occurs, to an underlying correlate which is usually unique.

- If we detect acoustic effect A, we have determined that the speaker intended to communicate (or unconsciously 'felt') a particular emotion E. In this sense $E \rightarrow A$, and by extension A is, in fact, $\{A\}$—the set of all A associated with the underlying emotion E. For the speaker or perceiver, *which* A in the set is unimportant—but the listener may well detect a problem if it is the *wrong* A (even if for decoding purposes it does not matter which). So in a model designed to enable simulation there must be a proper means of going beyond describing that it could be any one of a set of A, and must, in fact be a particular A in $\{A\}$. In addition E', the listener's derived percept must be correctly recoverable from $\{A\}$. That is:

$$E \rightarrow \{A_1, A_2, A_3, \ldots A_n\} \rightarrow E'$$

What does this mean in plain language? Let us say that a speaker is going to use, consciously or unconsciously, a particular expression in their speech, for example 'happy'. The expression will be described as part of the utterance plan, whether the expression itself is ultimately derived cognitively or physically. The plan is invariant; that is, it is a once-only characterization of what is to be spoken. However, because of various constraints imposed during the phonetic rendering process, many potential variations on the plan can emerge. Some of these will be predictable, but others will not. But because, in the absence of deliberate repetition, a speaker generally utters the plan only once, there will be only one actual acoustic waveform for this plan. In an experimental situation we can elicit repeated renderings of the plan. This is a rather artificial situation, but almost all experimental paradigms create some degree of artificiality. However, the repeated renderings do give us some idea of the range of variability creeping into the rendering process, and indeed eventually enable us to spot patterns within the variability itself. Listeners must be able to derive a percept of the speaker's expression from the acoustic signal—but we shall discuss later whether this is achieved only from the signal or whether the decoding process is much more complex.

So, from a single utterance plan there are potentially a whole set of different renderings, each a variation of the abstract intention. In real life we rarely get to hear more than one of these renderings, but for the researcher the interest often lies in the potential variability itself. Aside from random variability, the actual patterning is important not just because it tells us something about the source of the variability and the limitations on the rendering process, but because listeners are sensitive to some types of variability and not to others. We discuss later this sensitivity and how we model the rendering process to focus on it.

Problems begin to arise if two underlying objects correlate with *overlapping* sets of surface objects:

- For the speaker/listener the problem is potential ambiguity.
- For the researcher the problem is the possibility of attributing one particular surface object to the 'wrong' underlying object.

These are, of course, the same problem, except that the listener has just one chance, whereas the experimenter would typically collect a large database of examples precisely to survey the range of variability. Listeners have to fall back on 'experience' or a database within their memories—a database which could not have been collected under the controlled conditions of the experimenter.

3.6.3 The basis of the acoustic correlates paradigm

Attempts to determine the acoustic correlates of expression are all based on the idea that, independently of the words being used in an utterance—that is, independently of its meaning—aspects of the acoustic signal itself convey expression for the speaker. The basic idea is that there are discoverable acoustic correlates for expression which are contained in the speech waveform.

This is a reasonable claim. In its simplest form, a listener is primed to detect expressive content depending on how this content is encoded in the acoustic signal; that is, a listener has a model of the acoustic correlates of expression. If you change the acoustic signal, you change the listener's reaction, and a different expressive content is detected. In short, this approach claims that a listener can tell a speaker's feelings or attitude simply from the acoustic signal: change the signal to change the expression. If this is true, it should be simple to discover what it is in the acoustic signal that carries the encoding. It should also be simple to re-synthesize the effect by changing the corresponding features of a synthetically generated speech waveform.

Indeed, there have been numerous experiments carried out to discover the acoustic correlates of expression on this basis. Later we shall discover that the approach does not work, and that there is much more to the way the acoustic signal is used to convey expression than a simple encoding of this or that type of expression depending on the speaker's feelings. We shall discover that it is often hard to isolate any one feature of the acoustics which has contributed in any unique way to the listener's perception of how the speaker feels or what their attitude is. But for the moment it makes sense to examine the paradigm further, since it is so common, and see what researchers have been able to resolve.

3.7 Some acoustic correlates

Researchers have not yet produced a formal definition of the highly abstract cover terms like 'emotion', or abstract terms like 'anger' or 'happiness'. So for this reason, while we are still surveying the field of expression in speech and trying to determine the scope of the subject areas, we shall confine ourselves to some examples of expressive content in speech. For example, listeners can hear an utterance and report: *The speaker is angry*, or *The speaker is happy.* We can then examine the waveform for consistent differences which reliably trigger these observations. On the one hand this is useful to us at this stage because speakers and listeners 'know' what these terms mean, and so we need not present a formal definition; on the other hand, however, the very fact that what such terms mean is in some sense 'known' leads many researchers to proceed without proper definitions—thus making comparison between different studies difficult, at the very least. The formal problem is one of first defining an object (the emotion) and then giving it an unambiguous label.

Bearing all this in mind, we begin our investigation of the acoustic correlates of expression, although some (like syllable rate) are phenomena computed from the signal rather than direct measurements taken from the signal. We proceed, knowing of potential pitfalls in the classification system, and realizing that what follows amounts to nothing more scientific than a cursory outline of what might be possible in more strict formal terms. The data presented in Table 3.2 is after Stibbard (2001), who presents a comprehensive review of the literature on acoustic correlates of emotion. The table shows six emotions (we avoid the question here of the relationship between basic and secondary emotions) and eight 'acoustic' parameters—that is, variables which can be derived from measuring the acoustic signal. The table shows how variables depart from some 'norm' for any given emotion:

- Anger tends to produce increased mean f0 (indicated by the plus sign in the cell where the anger row and the mean f0 column intersect).
- Sadness tends to have decreased (the minus sign) overall amplitude and reduced syllabic rate.
- Increased 'breathiness' is a property of speech with surprise expressive content.
- Surprise generates 'sudden excursions' in f0 variation
- and so on.

Without defining these six different emotions for the moment, we can set up a parametric classifier which can either be thought of as distinguishing them by their properties or as specifying how to achieve them. Stibbard based his table on the results of a

Table 3.2. Correlations between various emotions and properties of the acoustic signal (after Stibbard 2001)

	Mean f0	f0 range	f0 variation	Overall amplitude	High frequency amplitude	Stressed syllable durations	Syllabic rate	'Breathiness'
Anger	+	+	irregular	+	0	+	−	0
Hatred	−	+		+	0	+	0	+
Sadness	−	−		−	0	0	−	0
Fear	+	+	+	+	+	0	0	0
Happiness	+	+	smooth changes	+	0	0	0	+
Surprise	0/+	+	sudden excursions	higher on stressed syllables	0	0	0	+

consensus of many researchers or a majority agreement after they had examined the 'acoustic properties' of these emotions. We shall offer a review of some of the work in Chapter 10, but for the moment we shall use generally agreed findings as illustrative of the kind of properties discovered in the acoustic signal.

Most researchers relate the properties of the acoustic signal to those found for normal or neutral speech—that is, speech which does not appear to display any expressive content. We have argued above that such neutral speech does not exist in other than some abstract form—but this is not the view of the majority of researchers.

Mean f0 is the mean of all f0 measurements taken for the utterance; f0 range is the range from the largest to the smallest measured f0; f0 variation is an assessment of the regularity of changes of f0 (descriptive terms like 'irregular', 'smooth', 'sudden', 'slow' are often found to describe this regularity or lack of it); overall amplitude is the range of amplitude—found by taking the largest value during the utterance (the smallest value is zero); high-frequency amplitude is the average amplitude of 'high frequencies' in the signal; stressed syllable duration is the average duration of syllables bearing linguistic stress, or sometimes emotional stress; syllable rate is a measure of the number of syllables occurring each second on average in the utterance; an articulatory gesture is an articulatory movement for pronouncing a particular target—'extreme' is a vague term found in the literature which may relate to the degree of precision of the articulation; 'breathiness' refers to the degree of air flow leakage accompanying vocal cord vibration—high-pitched voices generally have more leakage than low-pitched voices, but deliberate leakage is often used for stylistic effect.

Many of the terms found in the literature relating to naming the parameters used for characterizing the expressive acoustic properties of an utterance seem rather imprecise; perhaps even more vague is the way they are used and the values they are given. Very often it is a case of a kind of impressionistic value assigned to a parameter; the best descriptions are the result of thresholding at a precise level, though perhaps describing a relative term. It is almost always the case that the values assigned, numerical or impressionistic, are relative to the neutral case defined by the researcher.

3.8 Hearing thresholds: the difference limen concept

As early as the 1930s (see a review in 't Hart et al. 1990: 26–37) researchers in psychoacoustics were keen to discover what they called 'difference limens' or 'difference thresholds'. These are definitions of what have also been called 'just noticeable differences'. The idea is to discover the fineness or 'resolution' of human hearing and perception for certain phenomena in acoustics. Consider as an example the fundamental frequency of the human voice. It would not be difficult these days to devise an experiment which asked listeners to report when they heard a *change* in a sample of f0; this could be done using fine control of the f0 of a synthesized vowel sound. The f0 would actually slide continuously, but most listeners would confine their judgements to imposing a stepping function on the continuum, indicating the fineness of their ability to perceive the change: it may well be that they can perceive a change only when the sliding tone has moved at least 2 or 3 Hz, for example (Flanagan 1957). The stepping value (in this case 2 or 3 Hz) is the difference limen for the perception of vowel fundamental frequency. Flanagan noted that the limen increases as f0 itself increases, so it is also the case that this suggested 2–3 Hz is a function of where we are on the f0 frequency range: 1 or 2 Hz may be the just noticeable difference at 100 Hz, but at 200 Hz the difference limen is a little greater; it is a non-linear function, perhaps logarithmic. There is no reason to suppose in advance that the just noticeable difference is itself a constant for any of the acoustic features we may choose to look at as candidate parameters for characterizing expression.

The reason for the query is that a particular difference limen may have been determined within a context inappropriate to our current needs, and therefore be 'wrong' for our purposes. For example, it would be ridiculous to observe a consistent acoustic 'cue' for a particular effect if it could be shown that human beings were insensitive to that effect. This does not mean that the effect should be left unaccounted for; it simply means that it is a correlate which has scientific interest, but that it cannot be the only correlate to trigger the perception of any particular expressive content.

There is also at least the possibility that, *in combination*, features of the acoustic signal may produce, in the technical sense, a 'subliminal' perceptual effect, even if it can be shown that to any one of these features there is limited sensitivity. What we mean by this is that listeners may unconsciously associate a particular combination of features with a particular expression. This is a difficult point, and is perhaps not one which has been shown to play a role in the perception of expression, but it is not something which can be completely ruled out, given the current state of our knowledge in this area. Researchers tend to identify this or that feature as correlating with this or that expression as though the choice between expressions were easy and clear. Results this simple are associated with experiments which correlate gross acoustic features with well-focused emotions like anger or happiness. At some point we do have to account for much more subtle perceptual effects which, we are suggesting, rely more on how acoustic features *interplay* with one another.

3.9 Data collection

Supposing we were considering an emotional mode of expression: anger. In a typical investigatory paradigm a subject-talker would be asked to speak some test phrases or sentences 'with anger'. Various techniques have been developed for gathering the data: these include

- using professional actors who it might be claimed know how to speak with particular emotions on demand;
- making large conversational databases in the hope that particular modes of expression will be included;
- tricking a subject into uttering phrases in particular expressive modes, etc.

There are various pros and cons associated with all data-gathering techniques which we shall be discussing later (Chapter 10), but for the moment let us assume we have a means of obtaining the required data samples.

These would be recorded and replayed to listeners in a perceptual test designed to confirm that indeed the phrases had been spoken with anger: that is, that they had been spoken in such a way that listeners readily perceive that the speaker is angry. Having confirmed that there is something in the acoustic signal prompting this perception, a detailed analysis is performed in an attempt to isolate characteristics of the signal which vary from 'neutral' speech or from some other emotional mode of expression used in the rendering process (for example, listener confirmation that this time the same sentences or phrases had been spoken in such a way as to convey happiness, or perhaps a lesser form of anger, irritation).

Since expression in speech is generally regarded as a prosodic or slow-moving effect, candidate parameters for the detailed acoustic analysis are changing fundamental frequency (not instantaneous f0), amplitude settings over relatively long stretches (not local, syllable-based amplitude readings), and long-term changes to timing which may disrupt the normal, expected rhythm of utterances.

It is clear that without some firmly focused description of the abstract expression—the intended speech with anger, for example, or the perception of the speaker's intention—such experiments trying to establish correlation between underlying expression and variables in an acoustic signal are going to be difficult to conduct in any reliable and repeatable way. So, to compare two examples of anger, for example, we would have to have a clear definition of anger (one of the examples must not be irritation, for instance) and a clear listener judgement that both examples trigger perception of anger (once again, not irritation or some variant).

3.9.1 Obtaining samples of speech

These simple approaches, however, either assume that there really *is* a speaking style with no expressive content at all or are prepared to compromise and find a minimally expressive style which gets labelled 'neutral'. More sophisticated approaches to obtaining samples of neutral speech are possible: inverse filtering and parametric estimation.

1. Inverse filtering. Here the method, analogous to the inverse filtering of a microphone signal to derive the source glottal waveform, is to filter out from a signal with obvious expressive content the factors responsible for that content, thus leaving behind the plain non-expressive signal. Like glottal waveform recovery, however, the technique presupposes that the characteristics of the filter are more or less known—and of course it is precisely these characteristics which we are trying to discover.

The paradox can be largely overcome by careful experimental design, and this is sufficient to produce a useful, though not quite complete, answer. For example, an experiment may be set up in which there is iterative interaction with the experimenter to change the signal progressively until it becomes relatively expression-free. At this point there would be some indication of the parameters of the expressive content and their values; these would be revealed by noting precisely what was having to be removed to achieve what the experimenter or a panel of listeners judges to be expression free speech.

This would not be a pointless experiment to perform. Almost all researchers up to now have worked in a slightly more informal but analogous paradigm which we may call the 'subtraction' methodology. In this technique a sample of expressive speech is examined to see what 'extra' elements it contains—these extra elements are revealed by comparison with neutral speech, such that we have

$$\text{expressive element} = \text{expressive waveform} - \text{neutral waveform}$$

and this paradigm makes the explicit assumption therefore that

$$\text{expressive waveform} = \text{neutral waveform} + \text{expressive element}$$

A slightly more complex version of this paradigm would assume that the expressive waveform is an interaction between the neutral waveform and the expressive element

$$\text{expressive waveform} = \text{neutral waveform} \times \text{expressive element}$$

This formulation implies that the neutral waveform is transformed rather than augmented by the expressive element, and the complication is that the nature of the interaction would need to be understood before the expressive element could be revealed—precisely the inverse filtering paradox we just came across.

2. Parametric estimation. Identifying and removing parts of a waveform is not a simple matter. Perhaps the most useful and certainly the commonest way is to establish normative values for a set of parameters which are found to vary with expressive speech. That is, the approach begins with a characterization of neutral speech, highlighting those areas or parameters which are thought to lend themselves to modification by the speaker for adding expressive content—while everything else remains unchanged. There are, however, some interactions between parameters, and everything else does not always remain unchanged—these interactions are often unintended, and are analogous to coarticulation.

The technique involves a systematic comparison for each parameter between samples of neutral speech and samples of expressive speech. The comparison reveals the differences in a systematic way, enabling not just comparison between neutral speech and each type of expressive speech individually, but

Expression in Natural Speech 61

potentially even comparison between different types of expression. The experimental paradigm is fraught with problems and misleading artefacts, but it is very common. For example, many researchers report systematic differences between the overall range of fundamental frequency of utterances for a speaker during periods of different expressive content; here, the range of f0 would be a salient parameter. Another often-quoted parameter which varies systematically for different modes of expression is tempo or utterance delivery rate.

3.10 Listener reaction to expressive utterances

Researchers who aim to characterize neutral speech as one expressive type among many have the basic problem of providing an adequate set of examples of neutral acoustic signals. The problem is actually easier when it comes to any expressive type *other* than neutral, underlining the claim made by ourselves and others that neutral speech is not easy to define from actual examples obtained from speakers. All the usual problems arise: should examples be collected from speakers unaware they are being recorded and who are therefore behaving relatively naturally? Should speakers be asked to switch on a particular expressive mode for the purposes of delivering a relatively clean set of data? Should actors be used to provide the data? And so on. What is special about obtaining neutral speech data is that neutral speech may actually not exist. Certainly, if a simplistic definition of neutral speech along the lines of 'speech devoid of any expressive content' is used then it is almost certainly the case that it can occur only very rarely indeed. But if it did, how would we recognize it? Presumably by listener reaction.

Acoustically, there are differences between speech identified by listeners as emotive and 'with speech expression'. Sometimes there is difficulty in identifying a particular mode of expression, but the prior question: 'Is there any expressive content?' can usually be answered clearly. One of the problems is that listener response appears to be context-sensitive. A calm voice can trigger a response which an agitated listener would welcome, whereas a bored-sounding synthetic voice would most likely have a quite different effect, depending on the listener and also the semantics of the utterance.

We can isolate one very important contextual factor among many which we can use to illustrate perceptual sensitivity to context: listener response appears to depend on the listener's prior emotion. Listeners can be thought of as objects within their own psychological environments. They are not detached from their own environments: they respond *within* them and are constrained *by* them. The context of psychological environment is so fundamental to perception that we cannot make sense of the perception of expressive content in speech without modelling how it develops within the environmental context. This idea is quite central to how we view the perception of emotive content in speech.

There is scope here for confusion. Linguists often refer to rules which are 'context-sensitive'. These rules usually characterize changes to linguistic units which are dependent on their immediate linguistic context. For example, in phonology we might want to note that in most accents of English unstressed vocalic syllable nuclei tend to be reduced in 'quality', so that the vowel in the initial syllable of the noun *concern* is [ə] rather than [ɒ]— [kən'sɜːn]. In English phonetics we might note that initial voiceless plosives are usually associated with a short period of devoicing associated with a following vowel or voiced sound (sometimes called 'aspiration' or 'voice onset time')—*cat* [kʰæt], *pleasure* [ˈpʰlɛʒə]. However, our meaning here is different. We are referring to the way in which listeners—perceiving the utterance—are within their own varying psychological environments. Their perceptual behaviour is sensitive to *their own* contexts— and what they are perceiving is sensitive to *its own* linguistic context. The linguistic stimulus—the utterance together with its expressive content—varies dependent on its own context quite independently of the listener. But the listener's perception of the stimulus depends not only on the stimulus but on the perceptual context within which it is perceived.

Expression in Natural Speech

Let us try to formalize this. Listener reaction is a function of the incoming signal *and* the psychological environment or state of the listener at the time:

$$\delta(\sigma_m, x_j) \to \sigma_x, \text{ but}$$
$$\delta(\sigma_n, x_j) \to \sigma_y$$

There is a rule δ such that the listener, in a certain psychological state σ_m and scanning a particular stimulus x_j, changes to a new psychological state σ_x; but if the listener is in a different psychological state σ_n and receives the same stimulus x_j, the change is to the new psychological state σ_y.

The listener is modelled here as a finite automaton capable of existing in a predefined set of psychological states and switching between these depending on an incoming stimulus; but the change depends not only on this incoming stimulus, but also on the existing or prior state of the listener. The format of the rule allows for different state changes while receiving the same stimulus, with the change being dependent on the existing emotional state, and the 'external' dialogue (social) context which may change.

The model helps explain how listener reaction to the *same* stimulus can be different on different occasions. There are two possible dimensions to this: if we think of the two different reaction states as σ_x and σ_y, then σ_y might be a variant of σ_x, or it might be a completely different emotion. It's here that we need to be quite clear about naming and classifying emotions: is there a basic set and variants on the members of this set, or is there a set in which each emotion is categorized as different? It is obvious that this point needs explicit and careful clarification. For the moment we just note the need for distinguishing between these approaches.

In our model of varying listener response to a set of incoming stimuli, the 'expression' we are continually referring to as able to be characterized as an acoustic trigger is the x in the above equation. Clearly, listener response, even with the two variables we are describing (not one) in operation, is not random and can be very simply characterized by the above equation.

The allied question, which we shall delay examining also, arises here: to what extent is the speaker able to predict listener response to the expressive content? Usually, if the speaker is aware at all of including expressive content in their speech, the speaker accepts the listener response, but occasionally the speaker is surprised by listener reaction to their expressive content: this may be an occasion where the predictive model of listener response held by the speaker fails.

Chapter 4

Expression in Synthetic Speech

Although in principle modern synthesis is able to provide a perceived intelligibility level which matches that of human speech, and is therefore able to provide speech which is often (especially for relatively short utterances) indistinguishable from 'unemotional' human speech, there is a considerable shortfall in rendering the kind of naturalness which derives from the inclusion of expression. There are many situations in which intelligibility is simply not enough to make the speech usable. An example is the issuing of warnings, with the need to convey authority and urgency. Another is the need in sophisticated interactive systems, involving both a synthesizer and an automatic speech recognizer, for the synthesizer to be able to respond to the expression in the voice of the human user in the same way that human beings engaged in a conversation do. There is little doubt that market penetration of commercial synthesis systems is being held back by such limitations. But before we tackle fully interactive systems, there is work to be done on understanding just how expressive content is coded in the speech waveform such that a listener can usually readily identify the speaker's tone of voice—their expression.

4.1 Synthesizing different modes of expression

To satisfy the need for synthetic speech which is natural-sounding to the point of faithfully reproducing tone of voice we need explicit characterizations of the acoustic encoding involved. Research has so far involved attempts to synthesize the so-called 'basic emotions' of anger, fear, contentment, sadness, and a few others. These are a subset of the emotions which a listener can identify, and emotions are a subset of expression in general. There is a terminological problem here, but as far as possible we shall keep to using the word 'expression' as the most general term capturing all forms of expressive content in human speech. Later, when dealing with the work of contemporary researchers, we shall move much more toward 'emotion' as expressed in speech, simply because this is the type of expression most commonly worked on.

There is no clear agreement in the literature on how to define emotion (see Chapter 9) nor exactly which of the emotions are basic, nor even why some should be regarded as more 'basic' than others. For the moment this will not bother us. Terms like 'anger' or 'happiness' have been clear enough to researchers to enable them to proceed with attempts to analyse and then resynthesize the correlating acoustic signals. However, discussion of a proper model of expression in speech will need formal definitions.

In discussing the state of the art in synthesizing expressive speech we begin by focusing on the quality of the synthetic output. This is usually measured in terms of the success of the acoustic signal in triggering listeners' perception of the intended expressive content of the synthesized speech. So researchers will often be looking to evaluate their results in terms of listener response.

4.1.1 Testing the accuracy of synthesis for expression

Two questions can be asked with a view to discovering not only how accurate the synthesized waveform is but also whether the results can be generalized to a wider characterization of expression.

1. How accurately have researchers succeeded in synthesizing expression in speech from the point of view of the ability of the output waveform either to trigger the correct perception in listeners or to enable direct comparison with natural speech? One test of the accuracy of synthesizing expressive content in speech is whether listeners report that they detect the intended expression. Among several different types of test, they could be asked to identify the expression without being prompted, or they could be asked to choose from a set list (a 'forced choice' paradigm). Some would argue that the results here would capture any *subjective* effects inherent in the perception of expression, and this of course is part of what we are aiming to characterize: how do listeners actually go about detecting and then identifying expressive content in speech? Perception is a non-linear process dependent on the nature of the stimulus and the nature of the perceptual processing itself. Subjective testing and evaluation of synthesized expression makes it difficult to separate these two variables.

A different kind of test would be whether the acoustic signal reflects the properties determined to be associated with the intended expression. No listeners would be involved in such an evaluation, except in determining the expressive content of the original human speech. Thus, example waveforms of human speech judged to incorporate the relevant tone of voice would be compared with example waveforms of synthesized speech, with a difference metric used to evaluate the accuracy of the synthetic version: the less the difference the more accurate the rendering.

In other words, as with other areas of focus in speech synthesis research, there are subjective and objective methods of evaluating the synthetic signal. The basis for choice between the two approaches, and variants on both, is not at all obvious. However, researchers should adopt a principled and explicit evaluation of their results so that comparison between different experiments and different approaches to the problem is transparent.

2. How have researchers approached the use of synthetic speech to test the accuracy of a model of how expression is conveyed in human speech? Here the primary question is not: How accurate is the result?—the acoustic signal—but: How accurate is the model it's based on? If we can be sure that we are generating synthetic speech which is accurate and has met evaluation criteria like those just discussed, we can move the focus away from the signal itself and begin considering whether the basis for our synthesis is a useful or even accurate computational model of how expression is encoded by human beings.

We need evaluation metrics to judge:

- whether a synthesis system is capable of synthesizing expressive content;
- how easy it is to incorporate expressive content;
- the success of attempting to match a naturally generated human waveform;
- success at convincing listeners they are hearing expressive human speech rather than synthetic speech;
- the usefulness of the synthesis for testing a model of human speech production with expressive content;
- the usefulness of the synthesis for testing a model of how expressive content is perceived.

The usual criteria for setting up the model have to be met. In our view, and certainly in the case of the model we are proposing in this book, it must:

- accurately reflect as much as possible of the necessary coherent data collected by researchers on the subject of expression in speech;
- be designed to look 'back' to its source in research on human speech production, casting light on the human processes and how they are constrained;
- look 'forward' to what is necessary for making the synthesis system work, identifying and explicitly dealing with any artefacts or constraints inherent in contemporary synthesis.

Testing its accuracy is critical in developing the computational model itself—if processes are introduced to patch the system to make it work we must be clear what these are and what their intention is: they should be considered no more than hypotheses to fill gaps in our knowledge while we await further experiments or insights. The knowledge in which we have confidence and which we have encapsulated in the model must be clearly identified to avoid any confusion with processes or knowledge introduced to make up for any shortfall in our knowledge.

One of the severe demands of a computational model is that it should 'run' from beginning to end, prompting the identification of areas of vagueness or uncertainty in our understanding. It is the algorithmic nature of computational models and the way they unforgivingly highlight incompleteness, errors, and omissions *and* test basic assumptions that makes them so valuable in approaching the understanding of human behaviour.

4.2 What is needed for expressive synthetic speech?

The development of a model suitable for creating synthetic speech which triggers in the listener the same feelings of expression as original human speech presupposes a number of conditions.

> Condition 1: There must be an explicit definition of just what expression *is*, and how different modes of expression are accommodated within the overall definition.

As a specific example, understanding *emotions* and how they are experienced by a person—as well as how they are detected and felt by another person—falls within the scope of the disciplines of psychology or bio-psychology. These areas of study are charged with defining and modelling how human beings generate and perceive emotion, attitude, and similar phenomena. The term used most often and the phenomenon most studied is 'emotion'. But what if the definitions in psychology, clarifying the nature and origins of emotion, for example, cannot be made to work with the definition of expression in linguistics, clarifying how it is coded in speech?

What we have to avoid perhaps is going too far back in the chain (from origin to acoustic signal and its perception) without examining how the various disciplines involved treat the various stages of generating, expressing, and perceiving emotions and attitudes. It is not necessary to know in linguistics, for example, how emotions arise—just as in linguistics it is not necessary either to know how a thought arises; linguistics is concerned with how thoughts are encoded, not with where they come from or even what they are. Following this lead, we might just want to be concerned with how emotion and attitude, etc., are encoded as expression, not where they come from. It will turn out, though, that it *is* important to have a feeling for what they are because it is important to know at the very least whether they are cognitive or physical in origin: in the sense that it may be significant to our model whether its input is from a cognitive or physical source. The reason for this is that a physical source (like facial muscular tension during anger) will involuntarily distort the acoustic signal because of its physical effect on the mechanism producing the signal, but a cognitive source also involves neural signals to the speech musculature to produce a signal which might be described as an intended modification of the signal.

> Condition 2: The supporting model of expression at the higher psychological level would ideally be parametric and have a close correlation with a manipulable parameter set at the phonological (planning) and phonetic (rendering) stages of speech production.

For reasons internal to linguistics, in particular phonology and phonetics, and also internal to acoustics, the most useful model to us is probably one based in a parametric approach. It would be helpful if the underlying model from psychology were also parametric. Psychologists do not always take the parametric approach (see Chapter 9), and when this is the case we shall need to reconcile any parametric modelling of our own in phonetics with what they offer.

> Condition 3: Criteria for evaluating the resulting acoustic waveform should probably be established in advance.

There are two possibilities when it comes to establishing the basis for evaluating any synthetic speech, but especially expressive speech:

- Does the output match a human generated waveform with similar expression? [the fully objective evaluation], or
- Is the signal objectively accurate or not, does it trigger the right judgements in a human listener? [the controlled subjective evaluation].

Evaluation plays an important role when it comes to designing a speech synthesis application. It is in principle important that our computational model designed for resynthesis applications should incorporate the means of its own evaluation. We discuss this in some detail in the section on model evaluation (Chapter 7; also below, 4.4). The synthesizer itself must be able to respond to control signals on a repeatable basis—that is, must always react identically to any repeated sequence of control data. The synthesizer must either be guaranteed to introduce no artefacts which could be construed as part of the data, or must itself be so well described that any artefacts can be systematically quantified and their effects offset in evaluating the output. This last approach is fine if the evaluation is objective; but if it is subjective it is probably not possible to be explicit about the effects of errors (however well the errors themselves are described) on the listeners in the evaluation task. The only way around this would be to conduct prior experiments to try to determine the effects of the artefacts and hope that their interaction with the desired signal is either inconsequential or entirely describable, but this is too elaborate and fraught with potential for error.

- Is it sufficient to create a waveform which measures up to scrutiny as a genuine human speech waveform (evaluated objectively, for example, by measuring selected features), or is it necessary to go further and produce the waveform from as accurate as possible a computational model of human speech production?

Early attempts at speech synthesis were often satisfied if the speech sounded good or intelligible. But as devices improved, intelligibility became less of an issue and attention was refocused on the method of producing the waveform. An example with a parametric system would be whether the choice of parameters could be justified in terms of what is known about human speech production. Most types of speech synthesizer aim to recreate fairly accurately the acoustic model of speech production (Fant 1960), though few go further and attempt a simulation of the neurophysiology involved.

4.3 Evaluating the results

In Chapter 7 we discuss the need for evaluation of speech production and perception models as well as speech synthesis. Here we are concerned in a preliminary way with what criteria might be used to evaluate the waveform output of a synthesiser. There are two main criteria.

1. Is the synthesized speech a good match with a human version of the same utterance? Such an objective evaluation would need clearly defined parameters, and features of the acoustic signal would need to be selected as reliable indicators of goodness. Clearly, the acoustic features cannot be selected at random; some may show wide variability, yet be good indicators of success; others may vary very slightly and yet throw the whole system. To ask the synthesizer to match exactly a human produced waveform is also extremely difficult. How would we know whether the human waveform was truly representative? In a trivial sense it is guaranteed to be right because it was produced by a human being, but it could still be at the extreme of acceptability. What is to say that the synthesizer is not also right even if it is at the other extreme of the same variability?

One thing it seems that humans latch onto when they assess speech (real or synthetic) is its 'integrity'. Integrity of speech is its *internal consistency*, and a good way of discovering this is to ask the questions:

- Was the entire utterance clearly spoken by the same person on a single occasion? or
- Was it various pieces of utterance spoken by the same person but glued together? or
- Was it sections of utterances spoken by people that sound a bit like the same person, but are clearly not? etc.

What we need is an objective measure of integrity. Sometimes, for example, it is possible to see discontinuities in the synthetic waveform (or its derivative spectrogram) which can be detected by the listener—and perhaps there are other similar features which could be looked for.

2. Does the synthesized speech trigger a listener to declare that it is a good match with a human version of the same utterance? Integrity is a key here also:

- Is the entire utterance spoken by a single person on a single occasion?

or, in other words,

- Is the utterance internally coherent?

The design of subjective tests for the quality of synthetic speech is extremely difficult. There is a good discussion of the major pitfalls of both subjective and objective assessment of the intelligibility and quality of synthetic speech in Childers (2000: 473–7).

Criterion 1 above (the synthetic speech matches a human version of the same utterance) maintains a fully objective approach to evaluation and judgements of quality—but rests on two assumptions:

- We know what to measure.
- We know what range of values indicates a good synthesizer.

Unfortunately there is certainty about neither of these points. In the end most researchers declare the importance of objective measurements, but concede that the best synthesizer is the one which sounds the most human-like under a wide variety of conditions (not just on a single utterance). What we are saying is that what matters is whether the synthesizer can produce an acoustic signal which triggers the right response in the listener: one of being satisfied that the signal has been produced by a human being and has the right level of integrity. It is going to be a bonus if an experienced researcher in the acoustics of speech also declares the signal to have been produced by a human being (although it was in fact produced by a synthesizer) and therefore confirms that it exhibits no awkward or unexplained discontinuities or other anomalies visible on analysis of the synthesized waveform.

4.4 Expression is systematic, but non-linear

That a speaker regularly produces *particular* expression and that a listener can identify which expression is being used means that the use of expression in speech is systematic and not random. Perhaps part of the expressive content is not within the cognitive control of the speaker—as when they 'choke' with sadness uncontrollably—but the effect is still systematic. These systematic effects sometimes have physical origins and sometimes cognitive origins: sometimes perhaps both (see Chapter 9).

Adding expressive content to synthetic speech necessarily presupposes, therefore, an understanding of the range of feelings in a speaker which are to be expressed, and how these correlate with particular properties of the acoustic signal. But in addition we also need an understanding of how listeners detect and react to the acoustic signal. We know from our experience of speech perception in general that the relationship between the physical signal—the acoustic waveform—and the perception or identification of the signal and its elements is by no means straightforward. We speak of the entire chain of events as being *non-linear*. We can represent this chain diagrammatically:

Speaker   Signal   Acoustic   Signal   Identification of the 'intended'
expression/ → production → signal   → detection → expression/emotion
emotion

The relationship indicated by the arrows in this progression is non-linear and might also be context-sensitive. For example, a particular acoustic signal identified as coming from a speaker experiencing a particular emotion on one occasion may well convey something else on some other occasion and in some other context. It seems to be the case that the non-linearity of expressive content in speech is responsible for much of the difficulty we have in building successful models of exactly what is happening. If what we are saying about the non-linearity and context sensitivity of expression is true, it is probably the case that to neglect either when adding emotion to synthetic speech will result in listener detection of unnaturalness. Listeners *expect* non-linearity and context-sensitivity, and will react uneasily to failure to implement an adequate model of either.

Here we face head-on an important point in model building in a science dealing with human beings, their behaviours and reactions. We model phenomena, and we do so to give coherence to observations, and in so doing to tease out some explanation as to what is going on. But we are trying to do more. Not only do we want a model of the expressive content in speech which explains

Expression in Synthetic Speech

detail of the observed acoustic signal, but we also want to use that model as the basis for creating synthetic speech which will convince a listener that what they hear is real human speech. The model is not therefore just investigative in orientation—it is also contextualized to listener reaction. Put another way, the model needs to incorporate as much as possible of what we know of the acoustic signal and how it came about, and in addition as much as possible of what we know of how expression is perceived in speech.

In our specific example, the expectation of contextual non-linearity on the part of the listener is critical; and although it is not necessary to dwell on this in the investigative model, it *is* necessary to make it central to the listener-oriented model. The reason for this is that ambiguity in the model only becomes important when we consider how a listener disambiguates. We discuss such considerations in more detail when accounting for listener-centred speech production (Chapter 8) and the perception of expression in general (Chapter 5). Considerations of this kind are also central to deciding whether speech should be synthesized to produce an accurate acoustic signal or whether it is more important to produce accurate listener reaction: the two are not necessarily the same thing.

4.5 Integrity of speakers and their expression

In the design of a speech synthesis system—at both high and low levels—a major concern is integrity. Integrity is the internal coherence of an utterance which defines it as coming from a single speaker. Integrity of the utterance is readily detectable by listeners, particularly if it fails. For example, one of the major problems with concatenated waveform synthesis is maintaining integrity of speaker. Even when the concatenated units come from a single database recorded by a single speaker, integrity can fail. But there are many reasons why a synthesized utterance may fall short of this requirement, causing a listener to react to the synthesis process rather than its message.

Work by Cooke (Cooke and Ellis 2001) has been examining the possibility of modelling the auditory organization of speech, including for example how listeners can separate two voices which are mixed together in perceptual experiments, or hear 'through' apparently serious intermittent masking (following Bregman, e.g. 1990). The mixed voices effect can best be illustrated, perhaps, using a completely different aspect of language, syntax, and lexical selection. It is not difficult, for example, to unravel the interweaving strands of two separate sentences in the following 'composite' sentence:

> *She gathered John worked out bundles of beautiful regularly flowers in the gym.*

We could easily develop a model of coherence and integrity within sentences based on syntax or the probability of one lexical item following another, for example.

Listening to an acoustic signal is much more difficult to model and understand, but some progress is being made. There is no doubt that the speech of one person has an internal integrity which a listener can appreciate, and even 'track through' sections of speech from a different speaker—this has to be a similar property of synthetic speech to achieve complete naturalness. This internal cohesion involves consistent properties for adjacent units like segments and syllables, and involves tracking contours or trends in the flow in a satisfactory way. The syntax of a sentence flows in a predictable grammatical way, and similarly its acoustic signal flows without unexpected discontinuities.

Listeners are sensitive to a speaker's adherence to an established *profile* of identifiable and consistent parameters, and their ability to track these profile 'contours' as an utterance unfolds could form part of a basis for measuring or evaluating what the speaker is doing. Producing and perceptually tracking contours through the signal is so strong an effect in speech that deliberately violating a predicted contour can be used for stylistic effect—and even to convey feelings.

Take an obvious parameter of the acoustic signal which can easily be used to illustrate this point: fundamental frequency or f0, which is used to render a speaker's planned intonation. The way f0 changes during the course of an utterance is largely predictable: that is there are rules for how f0 should behave. Uttered sentences

Expression in Synthetic Speech

which are plain statements of simple fact usually show a progressively falling f0 from some key word in the sentence (Fig. 4.1). However, suppose we break the f0 contour for this sentence by 'resetting' the downward contour upwards immediately before the word *girl*, and then resuming the fall (Fig. 4.2a). Immediately the listener feels that the speaker is trying to express something unexpected about the meaning of this sentence. Alternatively resetting the downward contour to continue to the end with a slight rise beginning immediately before *held* (Fig. 4.2b) might make the listener feel that the speaker is asking if they know exactly what is meant, or that there is some covert subtext to the statement.

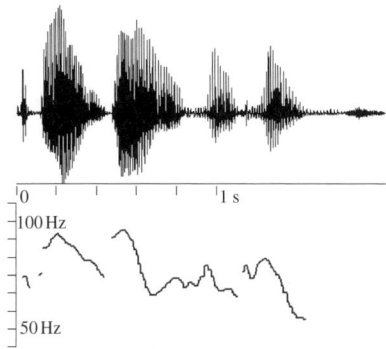

Fig. 4.1. Waveform and fundamental frequency contour during the utterance *The boy and girl held hands*, spoken with no strong expression.

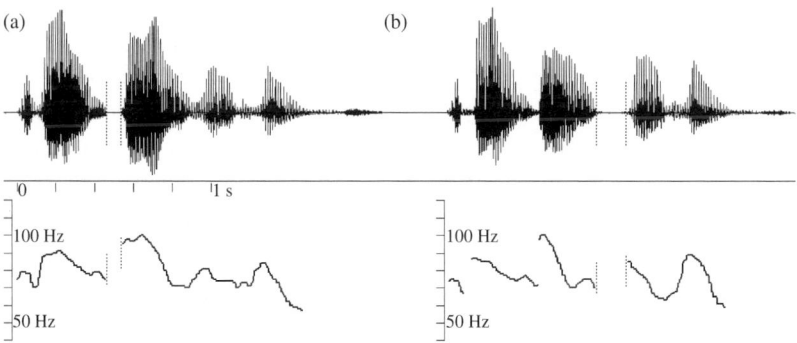

Fig. 4.2. f0 contours of the utterance *The boy and girl held hands*; (a) the f0 contour is reset immediately before the word *girl*; (b) the contour is reset immediately before the word *held*.

For the listener, the close following of expected contours can be a measure of the internal coherence of an utterance. The very fact that breaking the expectation adjusts listener reaction means that coherence has been broken—and that the expectation must have been strong. That a speaker can change the expectation means that the speaker knows how to use contours to convey the coherence of meaning of an utterance, and that they know that the listener knows this too.

But we have not only coherence of the semantics and pragmatics of an utterance, but also pervasive characteristics of a speech waveform which define the *integrity of the speaker*—they convey that the speech comes from a single speaker. These are in addition to the characteristics which define the coherence of meaning and its closely related property, expressive content. These facts must figure in our model of expression in speech, whether we are simply trying to characterize how speech is produced and perceived, or whether in addition we are trying to synthesize a waveform to produce the most natural-sounding artificial speech.

4.6 Optimizing synthesis techniques for rendering expression

It is one thing to have collected data about expression in speech; it is another to have this data organized as the basis for a coherent model expressly developed for an application, like improving synthetic speech. For applications, we would expect the nature of the model to have been in part determined by the way it is going to be used. As an example, consider improvements to a concatenated waveform low-level synthesizer. Because the frequencies and amplitudes of individual formants are not controllable in such a synthesizer, there would be no point in including measurements of these in assessing the acoustic correlates of expression—even if they subsequently turn out to be significant. The discovery that they are important would, however, prompt changing the choice of low-level synthesizer to one which can control these features independently—a parametric synthesizer of the Klatt type, for example. But not all features are equally important, and under certain circumstances it might be that in the real world of speech synthesis applications the amplitudes and frequencies of formants may be weighted as only minimally significant compared with other emotion-bearing acoustic features which *are* manipulable in a concatenated waveform synthesizer. If this were the judgement, there would be a discussion as to whether 'losing' two features would outweigh the general gains associated with this synthesis method.

There is no doubt that the introduction of successful concatenated waveform synthesis of the diphone-based type (Moulines and Charpentier 1990) or the word/syllable-based type (Lewis and Tatham 1991) or the large unit selection database type (Black and Campbell 1995) represent a very significant step forward in achieving high-quality speech synthesis.

The reason is clear: the units in concatenative wave synthesis are intrinsically superior acoustic models of stretches of speech than we had earlier in the allophone-based parametric systems. The improvement has two dimensions:

- Because the model involves a non-parametric representation, an improved result is guaranteed, compared with a parametric representation which may fall short of capturing all the relevant properties of the acoustic signal, particularly spectral detail varying in time—especially true of allophone-based systems.
- Lengths of pre-recorded speech (even if they have to be manipulated to adjust timing and fundamental frequency) are inherently superior at capturing time dependent features of the signal like the transitions between segments described by coarticulation theory (Hardcastle and Hewlett 1999).[1]

---

[1] The problem with early parametric systems was the informal basis of the choice of parameters. In theory the parameters were chosen according to their perceptual relevance, but at the time these early systems were developed there had been no significant work done to justify fully the use of the particular parameter sets chosen from the point of view either of production or of perception. It is true that after the fact some arguments were mounted that some systems with as few as a dozen parameters could produce an acoustic signal 'indistinguishable' from human speech (Holmes 1988), but it wasn't until the multi-parametric system of Klatt, which had sufficient parameters to enable proper experimentation, that we were able to research easily the choice of parameters.

But there is a problem with concatenated waveform speech: it is fine at modelling the acoustics of the segmental properties of speech (for example, modelling the acoustic differences between *cat* and *cap* or *top* and *tip*), but poor at modelling the prosodic properties of speech. In fact, normally speech prosody modelling is avoided. Some synthesis systems explicitly store their acoustic models with prosodic features (other than micro-intonation) deliberately normalized—all fundamental frequency movement is removed when preparing the database of acoustic models of syllables (Tatham and Lewis 1992).

With the possible exception, in theory at any rate, of unit selection techniques which might be able to include usable prosodic content in their units (though this would multiply exponentially the number of acoustic models needed to be stored in the database), waveform concatenation models have to move all prosodic modelling to the 'higher level' of the system and compute every detail. For practical purposes this may be fine, but it places prosodic modelling in danger of being computationally top-heavy.

The problem is to avoid the kind of modelling which can easily incorporate everything and account for nothing in human processes. An extreme of this occurs in automatic speech recognition, where a perfectly good statistical model may successfully label whole stretches of utterances, yet say nothing at all about how human beings achieve similar symbolic labelling in their perception of speech. Automatic speech recognition models are not usually designed to simulate human perception because not enough is known about the processes involved, so in that sense they do *not* fail, though they are unhelpful if simulating human perception is what we want to do! Similarly, a computationally intensive model of prosodics is going to suffer the same fate—there is no guarantee that without carefully formulated constraints it tells us anything at all about speech production. Success is, however, more likely with synthesis than recognition, simply because we happen to know more about the nature of the production of prosodics (though only so far in rather static descriptive models).

4.6.1 Synthesizer type and quality trade-offs

There is a trade-off between quality and synthesizer type which would, at one time, have presented us with a difficult decision. Early formant synthesizers like Lawrence's serial formant system or Holmes's parallel formant system were able to produce excellent speech quality provided that what was required of them respected one or two important constraints. Most of the early systems had always had in mind the need to keep computer memory and transmission bandwidth requirements within strict limits—narrow bandwidths (low bit rates) and memory saving were the original purpose behind the design of such systems. Consequently there was a cost in terms of speech quality: intelligibility was eventually very high indeed, but the ability to meet the requirements of synthesizing *particular* voices or *particular* expression characteristics was poor. This inevitably led to a level of naturalness which falls short of what we are currently looking for in speech synthesis. Modern versions of formant synthesizers, however, have no need to continue to conform to constraints imposed by memory costs or the needs for reduced transmission bandwidths, and are able, with the introduction of many more variable parameters than was earlier the case, to meet some of the heaviest demands of models of expression in speech.

The story is unfortunately very different with waveform concatenation systems. With these systems, the building-block stretches of real recorded speech used to create the synthesizer's output waveform are taken from a stored database. Techniques vary depending of the size of the building block, anything from allophones or diphones, through syllables or words, to variable length units, depending on the sophistication of unit selection techniques used for choosing appropriate chunks of speech. All, however, rely on a stored database of recordings of human speech, varying from recordings of spoken isolated units, to units spoken in frames and then excised, through to passages of continuous read or spontaneous speech. With waveform concatenation systems it is possible successfully to vary such acoustic parameters as overall intensity, fundamental frequency, and overall rate of utterance, and there are various well tried techniques for doing this (Moulines and Charpentier 1990). Local variations in utterance rate (say, on a syllable-by-syllable basis for accommodating rate changes during a word or phrase) are more difficult, but still possible.

Some of the acoustic properties which vary with expressive content are, however, not normally manipulable in waveform concatenation systems: these include the various parameters of formants (centre frequency, bandwidth, amplitude) and the subtlety of formant transitions over brief periods of time. One possible answer to this problem is to set up alternative databases that the system might draw upon when necessary. Thus a database of neutrally spoken recordings might be augmented with one where the original speaker was clearly angry or happy. What defeats such systems is the sheer size of the database needed. This is not a storage problem, but a problem of actually making the original recordings and accessing them quickly once they are stored within the system. However, this kind of solution would clearly have a use in limited domain systems which are specifically designed to operate with small vocabularies in an application having restricted semantic content—for example spoken stock exchange quotations or weather forecasts. There are two dimensions in which the domain may be limited: the semantic and lexical domain (confining what is to be spoken to a particular subject area), and the expressive domain (confining any expressive requirements to a narrow range such as 'normal' and 'with increased authority'—a constraint which might serve well in a telephone information system, for example).

4.7 Modelling naturalness and expressive content

A prerequisite to determining what is meant by naturalness and expressive content for synthesizing natural-sounding speech is a clear idea of what speech synthesis is actually about. Do we want to generate a waveform which is indistinguishable from a speech waveform produced by a human being when the two signals are compared in the laboratory? Or is it about generating a waveform which a human listener judges unambiguously to be a speech signal produced by a human being? We favour the second definition. For us, speech synthesis is mostly about creating a perceptual illusion, and it is for this reason that we place such emphasis on how speech is perceived. The model in this case is about speech production-for-perception: we view speech production as having a goal which is not just a simple waveform, but a waveform which will trigger the intended listener reaction.

In the early days of speech synthesis there was no doubt that the dominant idea was to create waveforms matching those made by a human being. But the use of listeners to judge the effectiveness of synthesis brings in unknown subjective factors; and unless these are properly modelled the resultant evaluation has little value. The finding that listeners judged the speech to be intelligible in the early days was too often interpreted as an evaluation of the 'accuracy' of the waveform. In one sense it *is* accurate—it has triggered the correct percepts in the listener—but in the other sense—that the waveform is similar to a human waveform—there is no guarantee of accuracy unless the effects of listener perception processes can be removed from the evaluation. Few researchers attempted such a normalization of their perceptually based evaluation results.

4.7.1   *Research questions*

The strategy for synthesis is to discover the acoustic correlates of the expression of an emotion, attitude, or style, and program the synthesizer to make its otherwise expressionless speech reflect the emotion and convey a suitable style.

The kinds of question researchers have been asking are:

- How does speech which expresses a particular emotion/attitude compare with neutral speech in which there is no obvious emotive content?

Our comment here is that neutral speech is itself a style.

- What is the difference between neutral speech and expressive speech?

Acoustically, there are differences between speech identified by listeners as neutral and as having expression. What researchers have been calling neutral speech (that is, speech with no perceptible emotive overlay) does not appear, of course, to trigger the same strength of response within the listener. But strong response is not a necessary characteristic of emotive speech. A calm voice can trigger a response which an agitated listener might welcome, whereas a bored-sounding synthetic voice (which can be guaranteed to have no expression) would most likely have a quite different effect, depending on the listener. The difference between 'calm' and 'plain message voice' (one betraying no emotion) as produced synthetically is very difficult to specify and model acoustically.

- How do the acoustic correlates of one emotion differ from those of another emotion?

4.7.2 Research strategies

We have looked in a preliminary way at several lines of research. In some of the more promising ones researchers have come up with useful ideas about:

- defining speaker emotions and attitudes;
- expressiveness or tone of voice—the acoustic correlate of speaker emotion;
- style of delivery;
- the acoustic correlates of style.

What is recognized here is a long-term effect—style—and a shorter-term expressive mode primarily based on emotion or attitude. We feel that this division needs to be carefully refined in the model of expressiveness. We shall see that this is particularly important when we come to consider that for a given style there are the same expressive modes available as for another style. The interplay between long-term and short-term expressive content needs careful examination.

The basic research and the applications work over the past few years have proceeded from different basic assumptions, and for that reason the results probably cannot yet be integrated into a single well-defined approach to a general characterization of expressive content in speech. We will explore whether a more coherent model could be put forward, and suggest possible ways of integrating these differing approaches.

Based on this initial survey of where we are now in terms of understanding expression in speech and resynthesizing it, we now turn to asking such questions as:

- What tools have researchers developed and made available?
- What methods of dissemination of results have been used and where are the results to be found? Are there schools of thought, trends, agreements, disagreements, etc.?
- Can we identify the more promising strands of research in terms of their basic scientific assumptions, their general and applicational models, their evaluation and external verification of claims?
- How have researchers been transferring their ideas and findings about the acoustic correlates of expression to speech synthesis systems? What methods have proved useful and reliable?
- What successes have there been, and how were these evaluated? Do the evaluations themselves point to developments for future research?
- Have the actual types of synthesizer used imposed constraints on researchers' approaches to synthesizing emotion? More generally: has the design of synthesizers constrained the way in which emotion (or its acoustic correlations) have been modelled?

Researchers have been searching for a productive strategy for understanding expression in speech and synthesizing it. However, the work turns out to be a little disparate, and there is as yet no real consensus about approach. *Outside* the field of synthesis a number of models have been proposed to describe and account for emotive expression. However, these models do not appear to specify enough details for use in speech research. In particular, exploiting symbolic representations of expressive content in speech has not been fully addressed.

Chapter 5

The Perception of Expression

The speech waveform, to reiterate, codes the speaker's emotive or attitudinal state in some way, but at the same time it triggers a listener's emotional response. The listener response can be either recognition of the speaker's emotion or a listener's own emotion generated as a response to what the speaker says. But whether or not the listener is aware of these, they are not the same thing:

$$E_{speaker} \to A \to \begin{Bmatrix} E'_{speaker} \\ E_{listener} \end{Bmatrix}$$

where E is the speaker's emotion, A is the acoustic signal, $E'_{speaker}$ is a listener percept of the speaker's emotion, and $E_{listener}$ is an emotion triggered in the listener.

This presents us with an experimental dilemma. If we are examining the acoustic signal within the acoustic correlates paradigm, we need to be sure that the speaker's intention was to produce this or that expressive content before we start to examine the signal for traces of the expressive content. The standard method would be to do listening tests on the data to get listeners' agreement as to what they are listening to. There is no serious reason to doubt the method, so long as we are sure that listeners' judgements do indeed reflect accurately the speaker's intent. The usual way to be sure of this is to use a panel of listeners rather than a single individual (and certainly not the experimenter). It also helps to have the speaker's view on what they were trying to do. An agreement threshold would need to be established for the panel (a simple one would be: so many per cent agreement, for example) before proceeding with acoustic analysis.

5.1 The objective of speaker expression

As a result of the observation above, clarification is needed particularly before any experiment as to whether the focus is on $E'_{speaker}$ or on $E_{listener}$. That is, a systematic three-way distinction must be made between a speaker's intent to convey their feelings, a speaker's desire to create a specific reaction in the listener, and a reaction in the listener which was not intended by the speaker. For example

- *I could tell he was upset by the way he told me the news*. A listener is reporting here that they have detected and labelled the speaker's own reaction to the news they are reporting.
- *He upset me by the way he told me the news*. Here the listener is not reporting the speaker's feelings but the feelings the speaker's expressive content generated (perhaps even 'requested' deliberately) in the listener.
- *I couldn't tell how he felt, but I think he didn't realize that the way he told me the news upset me*. Here the listener's unrequested emotive reaction may even mask out recognizing the original speaker's emotion.

The way we model how expression communicates emotion, among other things, needs to be able to handle these two things separately. We can see that a speaker can communicate their own feelings, and separately have an influence on the listener's feelings—and the speaker's and listener's emotions could be different.

- *The sadness in his voice was catching: I couldn't help but share his feelings*. Here the listener is reporting detection and labelling of an emotion, and experiencing themselves a similar emotion.
- *I could tell he was sad at the news he gave me—but I was amazed he was suffering*. A speaker conveys news that has saddened them. The listener is aware by the speaker's tone of voice that they are sad, but this sadness triggers a feeling of surprise in the listener.

There is clearly a whole range of combinations possible for the interaction between speaker and listener feelings, generating subtleties which so far defy explicit modelling. We need to adopt a modelling strategy which can handle this interplay, characterize the subtleties, and at the same time remain simple, replicable, and testable.

5.2 Current limits to characterizing the acoustic triggers of listener reaction

In characterizing how the acoustic correlates of one emotion differ from those of another, we have to deal with considerable non-linearity in the system. Researchers have reported the gross acoustic characteristics of the expression of various major emotions and attitudes, but one problem which has not been addressed sufficiently is the mismatch between the 'distances' between the acoustic cues and the perceived emotions. Table 3.2 above incorporates most of the findings up till now, and thus illustrates just how far we are from any complete characterization. But what is important is that classifications of this type illustrate how far we are from establishing any distance metric between acoustic cues or between the emotions they reflect in the speaker or trigger in the listener. When we come to develop a more comprehensive model in Part IV, we shall see that most people are able to respond meaningfully to suggestions about the 'distance' between emotions. Questions like:

- Do you feel sadness to be closer to anger or to happiness?
- Would you say that irritation and anger go together better than irritation and joy?
- Can you place the following along a linear scale: happiness, sadness, anger, irritation, fear, authority, gentleness, ecstasy, fury, etc.? Or would you prefer to place them along several different scales?

Listeners may be able to answer these questions—some easily, some with difficulty, some with remarks like: 'But they shade into one another'. But all in all, people have a good idea of the differences and relationships between different feelings. These ideas are not, of course, formal—though they can often be *formalized.* By contrast, corresponding acoustic measurements, of course, are formal and can be explicitly related.

What happens when we try to match the two is that 'closeness' of expressions according to people's judgements does not correspond exactly with closeness of acoustic measurement. Two expressions might be felt to be fairly distant in terms of feelings (anger and happiness, for example) but not share that distance on any reasonable acoustic scale; in their extreme forms both may introduce a tremor into the voice, which can appear in the acoustic waveform. Ideally our characterizations of the two should resemble each other in terms of factors like distance metrics, if only to make the relationship between expression and its correlating acoustic signal as transparent as possible. The apparent non-linearity between speakers' and listeners' feelings about expression and the acoustic signal itself becomes serious when it comes to setting up a system for synthesizing expression.

5.3 Characterizing listener reaction to expressive signals

Attempts have been made over the past few years to synthesize speech expressing some of the emotions described as 'basic'. However this is not normally the type of voice output interactive systems are seeking to provide—these systems would not normally be expected to exhibit anger or happiness. More likely requirements include attitudinal expression such as authority and calmness. Perceptual tests generally give mixed results—certainly nothing as reliable as comparable tests done on human speech, indicating the poverty of the underlying model.

There is some doubt as to the classification of even these basic emotions from the listener's perspective, let alone expression of a more natural, frequent, and subtle type; this problem will be discussed more fully in Part III. The point here is that although it seems difficult enough to work out the acoustic correlates of major expressiveness which can be easily recognized and agreed among listeners, it is very much more difficult to continue to consider *subtle* expression. Yet it may well be that, for practical purposes in speech synthesis, it is just this particular kind of expressiveness which would be more frequently needed than the extreme types. This is a real research dilemma. It would seem obvious that the most fully described models of the acoustic correlates of expression will be those relating to extreme or basic emotions, yet it is equally obvious that speech in an automated interactive enquiry system, for example, needs this type of expression much less than it needs less intense expressiveness to increase its naturalness and credibility.

This is really an extension of the discussion on research strategies. The subtleties of expression which can be reliably produced and perceived seem numerous and very finely differentiated, and for this reason seem to defy description for the moment. There is a case for divorcing the research strategy, just for this particular purpose, from the characterizations of underlying speaker emotion or attitude, and deflecting it to consider just the interactions between an acoustic signal (*any* acoustic signal) and listener emotive reaction. Understanding the relationship between a speaker's emotion and the listener's perception of that emotion conveyed by the expressive content of the intervening acoustic signal may be too great a research task for us to consider for the moment.

5.4 The listener's ability to differentiate signals

Looking at the idea of a distance metric, the characterization is usually in terms of position along a vector: so, for example, irritation is often closer to anger than happiness is to anger. Even 'closer' would be detectable differences like 'quite irritated' and 'rather more irritated, but not particularly angry', and so on. We discussed the idea of zones along a vector in Chapter 3 above; there we were concerned with characterizing the speaker's underlying emotions, but the idea can be carried over to a method of describing speaker's reactions to expressive content.

However, this closeness of emotions on some perceptual or cognitive scale does not necessarily translate well to an acoustic scale. To say that conceptually 'quite irritated' is less forceful

The Perception of Expression

than 'very irritated', and that these fall closely together on a descriptive vector, is to say something about characterizing emotions in some cognitive space. 'Quite happy' and 'very happy' might be thought of similarly in this cognitive space, but probably not along the same vector; the perceptual space in the vector model might be populated with several such vectors. It is not necessarily the case that such a perceptual characterization transfers directly or even well to the acoustic space—although it is usually assumed, often without overt discussion, that this is the case. Usually, as we have seen, the acoustic space is described in terms of a number of features or parameters; there is no suggestion that these parameters correspond to the vectors of this particular perceptual space model.

The claim is that degree of expressiveness in the signal may not correlate with strength of *detected* expressiveness. Another way of saying this is that more of a particular acoustic feature does not necessarily prompt listener feelings of a more intense expression—increasing the range of f0 in the signal, for example, does not necessarily prompt a listener to assign a greater level of anger to the speaker's emotion. There are exceptions—hence the use of the word 'necessarily'. Listener detection of boredom on the part of the speaker might be triggered by a relatively narrow fundamental frequency range in the speaker's utterance; greater interest, however, is signalled by a wider f0 range. Notice the use of relative terms—'narrow', 'wider'—here on the grounds that the listener is not detecting f0 range in terms of actual frequency. *He increased his fundamental frequency range by 25 Hz, so I knew he was becoming interested* is not a possibility! But *His speech became more lively, so I knew he was becoming interested* is definitely a possibility, where *lively* correlates quite well with a wider frequency range for f0.

5.5 Non-linearity in the acoustic/perceptual relationship

The standard strategy for synthesis seems simple and logical: discover the acoustic correlates of the expression of an emotion, attitude, or style and they can be programmed into the synthesizer to make otherwise expressionless speech reflect the emotion and convey a suitable style. The problem is that the simplicity and obviousness of the strategy conceals enormous difficulty in its implementation.

One flaw in the argument, and the downfall of the simple correlates paradigm, is the expectation that the acoustic correlates are actually there to be found; and furthermore that they can be inserted into a characterization which closely reflects the speaker's utterance plan. Yes, logically there must be correlates of speaker emotion, etc., if listeners can accurately report the emotion, and logically those correlates are capable of the same discrimination between emotions as the listener's discriminative ability because they are the triggers for those cognitive discriminations in the listener. But it is not necessarily true that the correlation is transparent.

We can put this another way: if listeners report detecting expressive changes in the audio, and if they discriminate these changes into categories which correspond by and large to the speaker's report of their feelings, then there is a clear correlation between all three stages: speaker, signal, listener. The speaker must have signalled a given emotion in a given expression and the listener must have detected the given expression to be able to provide a label for the emotion which closely matches the speaker's own labelling of their own emotion. But despite the obviousness of the claim and despite the simplicity of its formulation, the paradigm is fraught with difficulty.

Let us leave expression for the moment and take an easier example, derived from the production and perception of plain individual segments in English. In some accents of English, word-final plosives are not released although plosive articulator contact is established. Thus in the four words *bit, bid, Bic, big* (*Bic* is the brand name of a ballpoint pen) there is often no plosive release to help the listener disambiguate these words. They are easily disambiguated, however, by listening to the vowel. The final consonants' 'place of constriction' parameter is implied by the characteristics of the vowel's off-glide—a simple coarticulatory phenomenon. In our four-word example this supports the place parameter distinction for the consonants. The voice/voiceless distinction is similarly not conveyed by the consonant, but by the length of the vowel—the 'missing' voiceless consonants being preceded by proportionally shorter vowels than the missing voiced consonants. In this segment-oriented model of speech production, which includes segment deletion and coarticulation between segments, we have an example of transferred distinguishing features—the cues for disambiguation are not where they might be expected from a simple consideration of the underlying phonology or the utterance plan, but on some adjacent segment.

In the above examples, listener disambiguation of the words is reported in terms of segments other than those for which the listener provides labels: *It ended in a 'd'* is a common answer to the question: *How did you know the word was 'bid'?* The listener is labelling acoustically non-realized segments—with the basis of the labelling coming from elsewhere. When queried, the listener responds as though the cues had been provided by the non-realized segments, and usually seems 'unaware' that the cues have come from elsewhere.

Now, extending this segment-based example, disambiguation between expressions might not take place just where it might be expected or indeed where it is reported. This is one of the main reasons why we have to be careful of the acoustic correlates approach: the parameters of the underlying abstract states of expression might not correspond in any obvious transparent one-to-one or linear relationship with the parameters of the rendered speech. Consider the processes involved:

- A speaker develops a plan for an utterance, a plan of how it is to be spoken.
- The speaker takes the plan and turns it into an acoustic signal.

Thus

$$underlying\_planned\_utterance \times rendering \rightarrow derived\_acoustic\_signal$$

> where the term 'rendering' covers all the phonetic processes involved in generating the acoustic signal

The simplistic formulation of the equation conceals the possibility that the underlying representation and the acoustic signal may not 'correspond', that is, that the process of rendering may be non-linear. Thus

$$underlying\_plan_{segment\_A} \times rendering \rightarrow derived\_acoustic\_signal_{segment\_B}$$

is not uncommon in segment rendering, and there could be a similar situation with prosodic rendering. The corresponding equation relating the acoustic signal to the listener's label would be

$$derived\_acoustic\ signal_{segment\_B} \times perception \rightarrow label_{segment\_A}$$

Here we see that the perceptual process results in a labelling 'segment A' despite the fact that what the listener heard was an acoustic signal related to segment B. The overall result has been a labelling of segment A (the 'correct' segment) despite the fact that segment A did not exist as a distinct or 'discoverable' entity in the acoustic signal. This model is still too simplistic, because we could say that in the speaker's rendering process some feature of segment A was transferred to segment B and then recovered. Whilst more complex, this model is still non-linear.

The argument transfers from the segmental representation to the prosodic representation which is largely responsible for expressive content in speech. A particular prosodic acoustic effect may not necessarily relate directly or in a one-to-one fashion with the actual emotion being rendered. Its subsequent perception may 'transfer' the labelling back to the original speaker intention, but meanwhile the acoustic signal does not give the researcher a linear acoustic characterization of the speaker's intention.

Part II

Transferring Natural Expression to Synthesis

Chapter 6

The State of the Art

Over the past two or three decades there have been many studies of the acoustic correlates of expression in speech and some attempts to recreate expressive speech using speech synthesis. Most of this work has centred on a particular type of expression—emotion—and for this reason that is what this chapter will concentrate on.

6.1 The general approach

Researchers often refer to a speaker's 'emotional state', and are concerned to discover what it is in the speaker's acoustic signal which enables a listener to detect and identify this emotional state. A great deal of research effort has been directed toward investigating emotional states by psychologists and biologists (see Chapter 9), but although we can now identify some of their main acoustic correlates there is still no entirely satisfactory model of the entire chain from speaker to listener.

Researchers use the term 'perceptible correlates of emotional state' to refer to the relationship between the experience of an emotion in the speaker and the listener's reaction to the detection of that emotion (Murray and Arnott 1993). The apparent weakness in current models concerns the way these two relate. One reason for the difficulty is that the relationship is clearly non-linear. For example, one thing we lack is a good assessment of the relative perceptual status of acoustic correlates. There may be acoustic correlates which a listener cannot even hear because the signal may not reach some auditory discrimination threshold—not a question of perception, but a question of relatively passive hearing. A usable acoustic correlate must meet certain minimum criteria. For example, it must be:

- audible;
- perceivable;
- valuable (able to be used).

But the situation is actually more complex that this, because the status of an acoustic effect varies. Not only does the production vary; the same signal will be audible or perceivable on some occasions but not on others.

We can easily appreciate that the underlying emotions vary—they vary in *definition* (may be perceived as shading into one another) and in *intensity* (may be stronger or weaker)—and that therefore the correlating acoustic signal will also vary. An emotion which produces a clear, unambiguous correlate on one occasion may produce a less clear signal on another. Many observations of this kind can be made, making it difficult to produce a clear statement of how this or that emotion correlates with this or that acoustic effect.

Murray and Arnott, in their survey of the literature on the acoustic correlates of emotion, suggest three 'voice parameters' that a speaker's emotion affects:

- Voice quality

    It is not entirely clear what this means. The term is ambiguous: it could refer to the spectral content of the overall signal, as seen for example in a spectrogram, or it could refer to specific properties of the voice *source* signal. Most researchers use the term to mean properties of the source, citing Laver's classification (1980) of various types of voice source. However, it is also the case that the overall spectral content of the signal can depend on emotion—as, for example, when a speaker is very tense and their normal relationship between formant frequencies is affected because the usual shape of their vocal tract has been distorted. If, for example, a tense speaker raised their larynx the probable effect would be an overall raising of the frequency of F1 (formant 1)—meaning that the 'new' relationship between F1 and the other formant frequencies would provide a cue for the tensing and hence for the presence of anger.

- Utterance timing

    Timing of utterances has been interpreted differently by different researchers. Here are the main candidate measures:

    overall utterance duration;
    average duration of syllables, usually stressed syllables;
    average duration of syllable vowel nuclei;
    rhythm—the timing of rhythmic units or feet.

    If timing is a cue for emotional content in the waveform it is always taken as a relative measure rather than an absolute one, as are the other parameters referred to by Murray and Arnott. So a particular emotion would correlate with a speeded up rhythm, for example, when compared with this speaker's normal rhythmic rate. This falls in line with the generally accepted paradigm of comparing expressive speech with neutral or non-expressive speech, also vaguely defined.

- Utterance pitch contour

    The pitch contour of an utterance refers to the way in which the fundamental frequency changes during the course of the utterance. Relating the sample contour to the speaker's 'neutral contour' reveals a difference which, it is assumed, cues the addition of expressive content to the signal.

It may be important when considering these voice parameters to distinguish between primary-level and secondary-level effects. With voice quality, for example, the primary effect would be vocal tract tensing brought on by a general tensing associated with strong feelings of anger, and a secondary, consequent effect would be a change to the formant distribution in the frequency domain. Thus a formant distribution different from what might normally be expected would signal to the listener that vocal tract tensing had occurred, which in turn would signal that the speaker is angry. It is not clear from published research whether unravelling cascading effects such as these would bring benefits to synthetic modelling. It is usually the case, though, that models of any behaviour do benefit from attempting to discover what lies behind surface effects.

The encoding process in human beings is not straightforward, since there are a variety of different ways in which someone's speech is affected: generalized physical distortions of the vocal tract or larynx, mechanical and aerodynamic inertial effects (coarticulation), muscular contractions under voluntary control, and those under reflex control—to name just the main ones. The way in which each of these effects works on the waveform is different. Ideas about manipulating parameters of the speech waveform synthetically are bound to be a little simplistic if they assume that all acoustic effects are somehow equal in controllability, or affect the waveform in similar ways.

The fundamental difficulty being highlighted here is that speech synthesizers are not good analogues of human beings in respect of how they actually produce the soundwave. Human beings produce or manipulate their speech waveforms by changing how the sound is produced, whereas almost all synthesizers operate by changing the soundwave itself. The link between the two is the soundwave, and although we do understand much of how the soundwave is actually created, we understand much less about how it is used to encode linguistic content, and even less about the encoding of expressive content.

6.2 The representation of emotion in the minds of speakers and listeners

A question which the theory of expressive content in speech must address is how the acoustics of emotion is represented in the minds of both speakers and listeners. Is the representation in terms of

- the acoustic signal itself, or
- the articulatory control which produces the acoustic signal?

Although a speaker may not be consciously aware of their acoustic or motor objectives, we can ask whether the speaker's goal is to produce a particular waveform or to produce a particular motor procedure, which will automatically bring about the right waveform. At the surface the result is the same, but underlying the surface effect is how the goal is represented in the speaker's mind.

The same question can be asked of listeners. Is their interpretation of what they hear associated directly with the acoustic signal—*Am I hearing the acoustic signal I associate with an angry speaker? If so, this speaker must be experiencing anger*—or directly with the underlying motor effects—*Am I hearing the acoustic signal I associate with the kind of articulatory effect produced by an angry speaker? If so, this speaker must be angry.*

This is analogous to the distinction between the early motor and analysis-by-synthesis theories of speech perception (see the discussions in Lieberman and Blumstein 1988). The motor theory claimed that speech perception used a model of speech articulation held by the listener, in which they reinterpret the acoustic signal in terms of speaker articulation. The analysis-by-synthesis model, on the other hand, dealt directly with the acoustic signal using the listener's model of speaker production of utterance waveforms. In the motor theory case, listener representation of speech was in terms of articulation or motor control, and in the analysis-by-synthesis theory case, listener representation of speech was in terms of the acoustics only. Phonologists faced the same question concerning mental representation when considering the feature set necessary in distinctive feature theory: should the features be predominantly articulatory, acoustic, or perceptual?

If it is true that the acoustic signals a speaker produces are not linear correlates of vocal tract shape or motor control, then it is necessary to include articulation somewhere in the representation. A weak reason for this is that a speaker could not predict a direct acoustic goal without an intermediate articulatory level, and a listener could not infer speaker intention directly from the soundwave. The reason is weak because non-linear relationships are predictable provided the non-linearity does not vary, though the relationship might be very complex.

But there is a much stronger reason. Speech waveforms appear to have a double underlying source, and the above explanation assumes just a single underlying source—motor control with a near-linear relationship to the planned utterance. However, we have suggested that supervision of motor control distorts any predicted linear relationship in a variable way (Tatham 1995), and this is enough to need speaker and listener alike to have some kind of representation of motor control in their minds. The complete underlying speaker intentions cannot, it seems, be directly deduced from the speaker's acoustic signal.

This discussion about representation has focused on speech perception theory where researchers were concerned with segmental representations rather than prosodic or expressive effects. But we can easily imagine extending the argument to emotional content. Because of the complexities of speech production supervision, it seems reasonable to model expressive speech production and perception goals to include articulatory or motor representations as well as acoustic representations.

6.3 Defining emotion in general

We discuss elsewhere (Chapters 9 and 10) the various definitions of emotion to be found in the research literature. Before considering attempts at resynthesizing emotion in speech, it will be helpful to introduce some of the definitions with a direct bearing on synthesis and speech production modelling.

Scherer (1981), for example, thinks of emotions as 'the organism's interface to the outside world'. This is not strictly a definition, but an attempt to define by example or statement of function—a legitimate exercise in view of the extreme complexity of the topic. For Scherer, emotion has *function*, though this is not necessarily entirely communicative. For example, when people experience emotion they are put in touch with the 'relevance and significance' of the external stimuli which brought about the emotion. Thus the emotion is a kind of mediator, or interpreter of the impact of a stimulus. In this capacity emotions serve to prime a person for appropriate action—fear may prompt flight, for example; or anger may prompt fighting back, either physically or verbally. But Scherer draws our attention also to the fact that experiencing emotion may be witnessed by a third party—another person can see emotion being experienced (somatic contortion, facial expression), or hear emotion (a cry, or the distortion of a verbal signal by the addition of expressive content).

The State of the Art

For Scherer an emotion is a state, or an event, arising from an evaluation of stimuli. The evaluation, which is not necessarily conscious, sets up the person for a reaction. At the same time an emotion communicates 'state and behavioural intentions' to third parties. Apart from this communicative function, overt expression of an emotion is not necessary. For this reason we might ask whether expression of an emotion is part of the emotion itself or whether it is a *side effect*, which when present happens to inform others. We have to be careful here to distinguish between *feeling* or experiencing an emotion (an internal event not requiring external expression) and *expressing* an emotion (the expression being consequent on the internal event). But Scherer goes further: not only is the emotion expressed, but it may be expressed *in order to* communicate state and behavioural intention. If this is so, the expression of emotion can be deliberately designed to communicate with others—it is not a side effect. Emotions are also expressed, of course, when it is known that there is no one available with whom to communicate—that is, when speaking to oneself.

Earlier, Izard (1977) had expressed concern that a definition of emotion should be as complete as possible, extending beyond cognitive factors to events or procedures in the 'brain and nervous system', and what are called the 'observable expressive patterns of emotion'. We might call this last part of the definition 'externalized emotion'. So, building on Izard, let us run through the chain of events:

1. Speakers feel an emotion—the feeling is cognitive and so involves an internal *representation*.
2. If they speak while experiencing the emotion (or perhaps even later recounting it—we need a term for this 're-run experience') they *express* the emotion.
3. Eventually there is an 'altered' acoustic signal—one which *reflects* the emotion.

We could say that an internal representation dominates a chain of events resulting eventually in an acoustic signal. In our view, a clear statement of what this internal representation involves is essential for the model. We do have to make provision also for the possibility of *delayed* communication of emotion, the 're-run experience'.

Frequently definitions of emotion arise from theories which seek to establish different types of emotion, or at least different levels of emotion. We refer elsewhere to ideas about so-called *basic* emotions. Some researchers invoke this notion to help simplify the task of accounting for the large number of reported emotions and shades of emotion which a human being can experience—assuming the number of words in the language is a reflection of how many emotions there are to define. Influential among the researchers using the idea of the existence of a small number of basic emotions we find Izard again and, more recently, Oatley and Johnson-Laird (1987), with early reference to the idea by Tomkins (1962), cited by Ortony and Turner (1990). These and some more recent researchers agree that there is this small number of emotions which in some way underlie the entire range able to be experienced by a person. But it should be pointed out that this view is not the only possibility. What they do *not* agree about is how these 'primitive' emotions combine. Neither do they agree as to whether they are attempting to characterize the concept of emotion or are accounting for the complexities of the subject.

As Ortony and Turner point out, it is important to establish whether the notion of basic emotions is based on sound evidence. This bears on the idea of the universality of emotion (see the discussion in Ohala 1984). It matters whether the basic emotions are biological or cognitive in origin, because if they stem from biological properties of the organism they are almost certainly universal, but if they stem from cognitive properties they *may* be universal, but not necessarily. The term 'hard-wired' is sometimes used when referring to biological origins (Murray and Arnott 1993); this is a term from computer science which implies that these particular emotions are part of the biological design specification of human beings—they are genetically endowed. Cognitive origins, however, are harder to pin down in terms of universality. Although it is the case that there are probably universal cognitive functions, for example as reflected in human logic and many aspects of human language (one of the basic premises of Transformational Generative Grammar), it is also the case that the cognitive functions can be learned and are shaped, perhaps as part of local culture. To cast light on this last possibility, experiments have been conducted to try to determine whether experiencing certain emotions and detecting them in other people varies between cultures. The results are not yet definitive, however. This is partly because there are in fact three possibilities for the origins of emotion:

- biological;
- cognitive;
- cognitive effects interpreting residuals of biological origins.

This last possibility, which combines both the biological and cognitive approaches, is in our opinion the approach most likely to yield explanations of what we observe in human emotional behaviour. Emotions which have direct biological origins may well be universal in terms of biological state, but they will not necessarily be universal in terms of the cognitive reaction or evaluation made by the person experiencing the biological state. This is quite distinct from the idea that a small set of basic emotions can be combined to form cognitive secondary emotions. The question is how these various basic and secondary emotions are represented in the mind of either those experiencing the emotions or those witnessing the experience.

6.4 Defining emotion in terms of acoustic correlates

It has been suggested that three voice parameters (Murray and Arnott 1993)—voice quality, utterance timing, and utterance pitch contour—are a good starting point for describing the acoustic correlates of emotion. Despite lack of an agreed definition of emotion itself, work has proceeded on identifying details of the acoustic parameters involved. There is, however, tacit agreement as to what emotion means in general, and this has led to some valuable research in identifying the relative contribution of these parameters to listener reports of speakers' emotional experiences.

Voice quality has attracted attention because there is a reasonable body of literature characterizing modes of voice in non-emotive speech. From this basis it has been possible to gain some idea of how emotive use of voice quality can be characterized, since some of the terms needed and the scope of the various possibilities for voice have been described (Laver 1980). Laver's discussion, however, does not propose an explicit model of the characteristics of voice quality, how the various types might be controlled, or how they might be represented in terms of motor control or as an underlying mental image.

Laver and Hanson (1981) identify five phonation modes which systematically differ from normal phonation: falsetto, whisper, creak, harshness, and breathiness. These labels suggest that these phonation modes are physically quite discrete. This is probably not so in the case of production, though they may well be assigned discrete labels in perception. With the exception of whisper, all these different phonation modes retain the possibility of fundamental frequency (f0) changes. But for each there is a different background against which any f0 changes occur. Placing the glottis into one of these modes may constrain f0 possibilities. Suppose, for example that one of these settings involves a general increase in tenseness; it may well be that f0 range is constrained to be narrower than usual, with f0 average increased. Several researchers report that voice quality is itself used to signal particular emotions—breathiness might go with fear, for example.

Work by one or two researchers has indicated that in whispered speech it is still possible to detect emotive content. This is especially interesting because this is the one setting (among these five) which does not have vocal cord vibration, and most studies of the acoustic correlates of emotion put various aspects of vocal cord vibration as a primary cue—average fundamental frequency, frequency range (the difference between the highest and lowest values during an utterance), and floor (the lowest value during an utterance) are all favourites. The other four phonation modes are characterized by some kind of interference with or departure from normal phonation: falsetto is a pitch-doubling effect associated with high tension, creak is an irregularity in periodicity, harshness has some tensing and periodicity irregularities, and breathiness involves vocal cord vibration along only part of the length of the vocal cords, with varying degrees of air leakage along the non-vibrating length. Accurate details of phonation types are hard to describe in non-technical language, but it is enough to say that certainly all five of these particular types make production and perception of fundamental frequency less than ideal—with whisper being the extreme case: no vocal cord vibration.

So, if whisper has no vocal cord vibration, and these other types have less than ideal vocal cord vibration, it must be the case that there are acoustic cues other than fundamental frequency which contribute to the detection of emotive content in the soundwave. This means that fundamental frequency is perhaps not the main or only parameter, and that listeners can and do shift around between parameters as and when necessary. There are parallels in the perception of segmental speech; for example, there are multiple cues for identifying particular syllable initial plosives (burst frequency, voice onset time, and formant 'bending' in the following vowel). It is hard to answer which of these is primary, if indeed that is the right question: we may not yet have an adequate perceptual model for dealing with multiple cues of this nature. In emotional speech, though, it is clear that there are a number of factors coming into play, and it is important to characterize the soundwave in terms of all candidate parameters, since we do not always know which are the important ones.

6.5 Variability among acoustic correlates

The acoustic correlates of emotion show wide variability both between speakers and within an individual speaker, and this is often linked with the difficulty of obtaining authentic natural emotional speech. We discuss this elsewhere under research issues (Chapter 10), but here we just highlight the problem of the trade-off between obtaining large quantities of possibly unreliable data if researchers record actors, and obtaining small quantities of reliable data either by recording spontaneous conversation or by attempting to provoke 'real' emotions in subjects. Because of the wide range of scores in the data it is good to have as much as possible so that an assessment of the variability can be made, particularly in respect of the potential overlap in scores between different emotions.

It may well be that we know so little about the acoustic correlates of emotion that authenticity is a minor problem for the moment. All data, no matter how obtained, should be checked by listening tests as to whether it reflects the speaker's and researcher's intentions—so there is a sense in which, if the data is judged by these tests to express the correct emotion, then it is adequate for the experiment. In our view, provided like is compared with like, it is perhaps premature to worry too much about the source of the data: speech from a person in whom anger is provoked may be different from speech from an actor who is acting angry, but for the moment the differences may be too subtle to worry about.

However, the variability does have to be dealt with and modelled in a reasonable way. A good starting point is to look at the way sources of variability are modelled in segmental speech and see if a corresponding model can be built for expressive content. If we treat emotion in speech in a phonemic vs. allophonic way we would say that there is a phonemic or underlying representation of an emotion which needs phonetic rendering. By comparison with the underlying representation—the plan—the phonetic rendering is in several ways unstable. This instability leads to a range of possible acoustic renderings—'allophones'. The perceptual system is able to take this relatively unstable rendering and, by a process of label assignment, 'reduce' it back to a phonemic representation analogous to the original plan. We might say that listener cognition neutralizes instability or we might say that cognition is 'intolerant' of instability—so much so that neither speakers nor listeners can say much about instability, and cannot say how it is produced or how they deal with it in the perceptual process. Prosodics and expressive content show the same paradox as segmental speech: speakers and listeners are aware of a stability which so far has not been found in the soundwave.

Just as most speakers of English will claim identity for the sound at the beginning of *tack* and the sound at the end of *cat*, so they will be unaware of the variability of expressive content in what they are hearing.

There is one major difference: speakers of English do not refer to 'degrees of /t/', though they might well refer to degrees of anger. It is hard to get a speaker to say that there is more of a /t/ at the beginning of *tack* than there is at the end of *cat*, but not hard for them to recognize and comment on how one person sounds more angry than another, or how one person's anger has subsided during the course of a conversation. With segmental aspects of speech we are referring to the difference between extrinsic and intrinsic allophones. Extrinsic allophones are the product of choice-cognitive planning decisions made at the phonological level—whereas intrinsic allophones are usually mechanical or aerodynamic artefacts produced notwithstanding a speaker's intentions. Apart from a genuine random element, mechanical or aerodynamic variability is usually called 'coarticulation'.

However, we see *degree* of expressive content as usually reflecting fairly accurately how the speaker is feeling. Depending on the source of the emotion, (cognitive or biological) degree is in some sense intended. Variability in the signal which cannot be ascribed to this kind of intention is analogous to involuntary coarticulatory effects. No one would argue against maintaining the distinction between variables introduced in phonology and those introduced in phonetics, and we feel that maintaining a comparable distinction between voluntary and involuntary effects in producing expressive content in speech is essential for the same reasons. The following diagram shows the parallel:

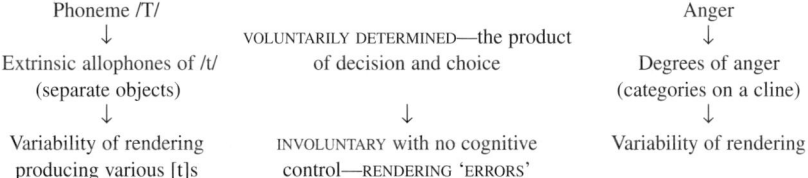

For example:

1. *I am angry.*
2. *My anger comes into the category 'very angry'.*
3. *I express this anger* (act of rendering).
4. *'Very angry'* in the signal shows variability.

Thus, just as what constitutes a particular allophone is not a fixed measurable quantity in a waveform, so what constitutes any one degree of anger is not fixed.

6.6 The non-uniqueness of acoustic correlates

It is well known that linguistic stress and expressive emphasis in English are rendered acoustically as an interplay between duration (timing differences), fundamental frequency, and intensity or amplitude. This was noted by Fry (1955; 1958):

- Duration relates either to the duration of the vowel nucleus in a stressed syllable or to the duration of the entire syllable—it is longer if the syllable is stressed or emphasized.
- Fundamental frequency relates to the average fundamental frequency of the vowel or syllable relative to those around it—depending on the direction of the intonation contour the f0 of the stressed syllable will be displaced higher or lower than the general curve.
- Intensity relates to the amplitude of the vowel or syllable relative to others around it—a stressed or emphasized syllable will show greater amplitude.

The values of these three parameters are relative to their context but also to their intrinsic values for the vowels or syllables in question. Thus, for example, the vowel [ɑ] has greater intrinsic intensity than the vowel [ɪ], so much so in fact that a stressed [ɪ] may have less intensity than an unstressed [ɑ] on some occasions. This complication of relative and intrinsic parameter values is of no consequence to speakers and listeners who are normally unaware of the problem.

The State of the Art

But what is interesting is that even when the relative measures have been accounted for there is no reliable predictive formula for the mix of these three parameters. Researchers have revealed that probably all expressive content in the soundwave involves more than one acoustic parameter and that the interplay between these parameters is itself a source of variability. It is true that often we are able to say that one parameter dominates, but this does not detract from the difficulty researchers have faced in modelling the non-uniqueness of parameters for expressing particular emotions.

If we take a collection of acoustic parameters and call them the correlates of expression in speech, and furthermore if we begin to identify how they mix and match to identify particular expressions, we discover that they are the same parameters used for general prosodic and many segmental features of speech. The parameters of our models of expressive content are the same as those for non-expressive content. This leads to difficulties among researchers in deciding whether expression is overlaid on non-expressive content or vice versa. The question asked: are the parameters used first to express the non-expressive content and then modified to add expression, or does the non-expressive content set the parameter values first, only to have them modified later by expressive content? For formal and other reasons, our model puts utterances into an expressive wrapper which has an *independent existence* dominating speech in general (see Chapter 16): the expressive content is determined first.

6.7 Reducing the number of variables

We have seen that the parameters of the soundwave are used to encode not only segmental but also general prosodic and expressive content. Recognizing this, and in an attempt to reduce the number of variables, researchers have tried to narrow down the problem by attempting to separate normal semantic content from emotive content. This is a different approach altogether from trying to separate influences on the acoustic signal, because it concentrates on very high-level or abstract features of the utterance.

On the grounds that at the acoustic level the residual encodings of meaning and expression are mixed, the idea is to remove meaning and leave just expression by removing semantic content at a high level.

However, since away from the purely abstract world semantic content cannot be entirely removed by a speaker, researchers have generally taken one of several different approaches to biasing the signal before measurement and attempt to isolate emotive content:

- Subject the waveform to a signal processing technique which will distort it in such a way as to make it impossible to recognize the words, and hence the meaning—while preserving prosodic effects. [Problem: this prejudges what is relevant and what is not and ignores possible interactive effects—e.g. does fundamental frequency contour *never* relate to semantic content?]
- Measure only known non-verbal parameters in the signal—the researcher simply ignores parameters, such as formant values, which convey meaning. [Problem: this prejudges again and cannot predict interaction—e.g. as before, do formant frequencies *never* signal expressive content?]
- Keep the semantic content constant while varying the emotive content—ask speakers to repeat the same sentence with different emotions. [Problem: speakers find the situation contrived, and there may also be an unexpected interaction between the 'fixed' meaning with the different emotive states requested—e.g. are we sure that a speaker can really not be influenced by the meaning of what is being spoken?]
- Give speakers meaningless material to speak—make up 'sentences' using numbers or letters of the alphabet. [Problem: the sentences or lists are not 'real' and speakers will find it difficult to apply expressive content to them—e.g. speakers may well be able to do this, but we cannot be sure they would use expressive content in the same way with material which does mean something.]

Each of these techniques might either remove semantic content or make it easy to normalize the data in such a way as to minimize the intermix between semantics and emotive content. But there are clear difficulties with all the techniques, making them less than perfect. In all cases the biggest problem is that we really do not understand the sources of interaction well enough to be certain that such techniques really do isolate what we are looking for.

The usual approach to understanding the emotive content of the waveform involves correlating a known emotion in the speaker with particular features of the signal. However, a smaller number of researchers have concentrated on assessing listener reaction to features of the waveform. Scherer (1974) was one of the first to attempt to correlate perceived emotions with acoustic variations. Scherer's work is also interesting because he is one of the first to parameterize both sides of the equation: certain mixes of various acoustic parameters stimulate listeners to perceive certain parameters or dimensions of emotion. Scherer comments that 'the attribution of emotional meaning from auditory stimuli is based on characteristic patterns of acoustic cues'—emotional meaning being indicated parametrically and the patterns of acoustic cues being an assessment of the relative weightings to be given to the acoustic parameters. He bases his conclusions on listeners' reactions to data produced electronically to provide only emotive cues, rather than a mix of semantic and emotive. This is really only half the experiment—it needs completing by manipulating human speech in the same way as the *significant* electronic tones were manipulated to assess whether listeners' reactions are similar. In other words: stage 1 discovers the relevant acoustic parameters (albeit artificially) and then uses this information to manipulate human speech. The human speech would have to be *resynthesized* rather than generated each time by a human being. The argument against this experiment is that there is little guarantee that what listeners *can* do with non-speech signals is the same as what they actually do with speech signals—a perennial problem with experiments based on manipulated or resynthesized speech.

6.8 The range of emotive effects

For the most part the correlation most frequently addressed is the one between the speaker's emotion and the soundwave produced.

Occasionally the investigation centres on the correlation between the soundwave and the perceived emotion. In general, researchers have assumed that there has to be a unique combination of acoustic parameters which relate unambiguously to the speaker's feelings. It is clear from numerous studies setting out the obvious acoustic parameters, however, that there is a great deal of ambiguity. The ambiguity in the research results appears to exceed the ambiguity experienced by listeners. This indicates perhaps one of two possibilities:

- The acoustic parameter set is wrong or incomplete.
- Listeners do not rely wholly on the acoustic signal to decide what expression they are hearing.

We suggest that it is the second of these which is causing difficulty in establishing a reliable correlation between emotion and the acoustic signal. The preferred solution currently, however, seems to be the first: researchers continue to try to refine their handling of correlates.

The parameters on the acoustic side of the correlation usually relate to prosody. That is, they are parameters which do not relate directly to segmental units. If the non-expressive features of prosody can be established and are taken as the 'norm', expressive effects are seen as modifications or extensions of this norm. The acoustic parameters—or those derived from the acoustic signal—generally thought to contribute are fundamental frequency range and contour, intensity, rhythm or rate of delivery, and voice quality. Of these, voice quality is the least well defined, and usually refers to features of the 'voicing' signal produced in the larynx, such as periodicity (or lack of it) and breathiness ('leakage'). Occasionally voice quality refers to properties generally associated with defining segmental units; for example, smiling and an angry tensing or raising of the larynx result in a departure from the expected or normal formant distribution for a particular speaker.

Murray and Arnott (1993) make a distinction between effects associated with emotion in general and effects correlating with specific emotions. Their findings are summarized in Table 6.1.

The State of the Art 115

Table 6.1. Summary of human vocal emotion effects (after Murray and Arnott 1993)

	Anger	Happiness	Sadness	Fear	Disgust
Speech rate	Slightly faster	Faster or slower	Slightly slower	Much faster	Very much slower
Pitch average	Very much higher	Much higher	Slightly lower	Very much higher	Very much lower
Pitch range	Much wider	Much wider	Slightly narrower	Much wider	Slightly wider
Intensity	Higher	Higher	Lower	Normal	Lower
Voice quality	Breathy, chest tone	Breathy, blaring	Resonant	Irregular voicing	Grumbled, chest tone
Pitch changes	Abrupt, on stressed syllables	Smooth, upward inflections	Downward inflections	Normal	Wide, downward terminal inflections
Articulation	Tense	Normal	Slurring	Precise	Normal

In brief, the answer to the question: How is this or that emotion expressed in speech? is a major key to our understanding of how the communication of emotion works. The correlation is between the speaker's experience and the detail of the soundwave itself: both need an appropriate characterization for incorporating in the correlation model. What an emotion actually is has to be described (Chapters 9 and 10). We feel that work which, say, assumes we know what anger or sadness or joy actually are, and then proceeds to talk of pitch changes, etc., is really addressing only half the problem. There is an important opportunity here for workers in more than one aspect of psychology, speech production theory, and speech acoustics to collaborate on a comprehensive model.

6.9 The state of the art in synthesizing prosody

Speech synthesis systems which are based on models of the segmental aspects of speech fail in one very important respect: they are poor models of any of the prosodic features of speech. Such systems include most of the parametric or formant systems (such as the Holmes or Klatt models which are based on allophone-sized units), and linear predictive coding (LPC) and concatenated waveform systems which rely on similar sized units, including diphones.

6.9.1 Unit sizes for synthesis

Early systems used acoustic models of small linguistic units, for example:

- An *extrinsic allophone* is the smallest unit of speech sound which a listener (constrained by their perceptual system) can recognize—a word like *cat* has three: /k æ t/—there are perhaps 150 or so of these in English, combining to form all possible words; this is a closed set, thus exhaustively enumerable.
- A *syllable* is the next largest identifiable unit, always consisting of a single vowel 'nucleus' which can be preceded by from zero to three consonants and followed by from zero to four consonants in English: + k æ t +. Perhaps around 8,000 syllables are used in English to form the set of words; this is a closed set, thus exhaustively enumerable.
- *Words* are used as units for acoustic modelling in some systems. These may be monosyllabic or contain several syllables in a variety of stressed/unstressed patterns; around 100,000 words might be a useful number, though fewer word models would be needed in a limited domain system. This is an open set, thus not exhaustively enumerable.

The above units are justified on the grounds of the roles they play in speech as linguistic units—that is, they are linguistically principled. Early forms of concatenated waveform synthesis, however, favoured another unit, the diphone, which has no justification in linguistics. There are one or two different definitions for the diphone, but it can be thought of as a unit beginning either halfway through an allophone or at a point of minimum change measured by, say, the frequency of a number of formants, through to a similar point within the following allophone. Thus a diphone 'encloses' or captures a characterization of the transition between adjacent allophones. This is useful because such transitions have proved difficult to describe adequately in terms of how segments 'blend' into or coarticulate with one another. English needs around 1,400 diphones for a good characterization of all combinatorial possibilities. Diphone models compare badly, though, with syllable models, since by definition the syllable is likely to include a larger number of coarticulatory transitions between segments.

6.9.2 Extended unit sizes

It is possible to base the synthesis system on a large, continuously recorded database. Usually this database is the source for a unit selection system in which, depending on the utterance required to be spoken, the system searches for the longest possible stretches of recording from which to build the utterance. The database itself may remain as the recorded waveform, which limits manipulation to timing and fundamental frequency, or it may be parametrically represented using the parameters appropriate to the low-level synthesizer being used; a parametric representation enables greater useful manipulation than a waveform based system, so long as appropriate parameters have been chosen (such as formant centre frequencies, bandwidths, and amplitudes).

Provided long enough stretches of speech are represented by using either a parametric or a concatenated waveform system, the segmental model can be very good indeed, and much of the concatenation problem created in early systems by the calculation of coarticulatory effects when segments are abutted are avoided in such systems. However, the usability of acoustic representation is essentially segment-based, and fails completely to capture any prosodic structure, except perhaps the relative stressing of strong and weak syllables. The problem arises because the sample waveform may well have been taken from a prosodic structure different from the one required by the new target utterance. In principle some of this problem could be overcome with huge databases and sophisticated unit selection techniques; but to capture everything the database would need to be very large indeed.

In fact, of course, very early systems, like the speaking clock or rail station announcements, were concatenated waveform systems with little or no signal processing. They relied on careful recording and a very limited grammar describing a small set of possibilities for combining the recordings in the database. In the very first speaking clocks the grammar was literally mechanical in nature, relying on sprocket wheels to switch between words and phrases. Some telephone-based announcements (like the directory information service) rely still on concatenation with little signal processing: the database contains two or three versions of each of the ten numbers, zero through to nine, with different intonation contours (say, one rising, one steady, and one falling) to compose a six- or seven-digit phone number, using the appropriate 'version' ('level', 'rising', 'falling' contours) of the digits. For example, the number 555 1234 might be composed of

$$\text{five}_{\text{level}} \text{ five}_{\text{level}} \text{ five}_{\text{rising}} \text{ one}_{\text{level}} \text{ two}_{\text{level}} \text{ three}_{\text{level}} \text{ four}_{\text{falling}}$$

These systems are not always very satisfactory, but detailed computation and processing of the appropriate intonation contours is avoided.

6.9.3 High-level and low-level prosody

One or two synthesis systems (Ogden et al. 2000; Tatham et al. 2000) have been based around a prosodically centred model. That is, in these systems the segmental properties of utterances are subordinate to their prosodic properties. There are some sound theoretical reasons for approaching a model of speech production in this way, and the consequent integration of the characterizations of abstract phonological prosodic contours and physical phonetic changes in the direction of fundamental frequency produces a more explicit and altogether more satisfactory result in terms of the naturalness of prosodic rendering. Systems of characterizing prosody or aspects of prosody, such as the intonation model proposed by Pierrehumbert (1980) and the ToBI system (Silverman et al. 1992) for characterizing intonation (both high-level phonological models), are bound to be less satisfactory because they have no really explicit way of integrating high- and low-level characterizations of prosodics with a corresponding segmental model.

6.10 The theoretical basis

Despite the fact that much has been written since the early 1960s on parametric synthesis describing the relative merits of the various low-level systems, not much has been written discussing the theoretical basis for early high-level systems. The early high-level, or 'synthesis-by-rule' systems (e.g. Holmes et al. 1964) used parametric synthesis at the lower level, but the fact that they are based on the theory of the time does not necessitate using parametric systems for their output: this is coincidence. If the first rule-based systems had used low-level concatenated waveform systems they would have had phoneme-sized units as their basis and single segment-sized units in their recorded inventories in just the same way as the parametric systems had.

At the time that attention turned to developing high-level (or 'text-to-speech') systems, the then current model of speech production focused on the 'phoneme-sized' unit or 'speech segment' of classical phonetics (Gimson 1962; Abercrombie 1967), and resolved the problem of explaining how such invariant units could be reconciled with the observed continuousness of the speech waveform by introducing Coarticulation Theory (Öhman 1966; MacNeilage and DeClerk 1969) in the middle 1960s. Treated historically, there can be little doubt that coarticulation theory was introduced to support the concatenated invariant unit idea—indeed, when introduced it was presented and discussed in just such terms. Later presentations and discussions were more sophisticated and were able to make much more reasonable claims about the interaction between speech sounds—see, for example, the idea of 'co-production' introduced by Fowler (1980), which, although also about coarticulation, was more realistic. The co-production model of coarticulation is much more about overlapping segments expressed parametrically than about the non-parametrically represented 'blended' segments of Coarticulation Theory.

The early systems of Holmes and, at Haskins Laboratories, Mattingly (1968) appear to have simply taken over the ideas in the extant theory of speech production and implemented them formally. As engineers, these key researchers had accepted the views of phoneticians, though these were intended as descriptive of human speech rather than as models for deriving simulations of the human speech production process: this came much later. There is a considerable difference between a descriptive system like classical phonetics, which aims to characterize a phonetician's impressions of the surface patterns of speech, and more recent algorithmic models, which aim to describe and formalize the processes *underlying* the surface classical phonetics attempted to describe. Early synthesis-by-rule systems used the surface descriptive model as though it were a speech production model—and for this reason it is not surprising that there are errors. Classical phonetic theory is much more like today's phonological theory in that it avoids mention of most sources of linguistically irrelevant sources of variability, which are nevertheless essential to characterizing the 'humanness', and therefore the naturalness, of speech. Omit these, and some of the humanness is lost.

In principle, then, high-level synthesis is a computational model of the linguists' phonology, even though in the early days there may have been no more than a dozen or so 'rules' in synthesis systems. There are a number of reasons for equating the synthesis model with phonology:

- The system was process-based, lending itself to a rule-based characterization—though other approaches were later tried (for example, there have been a number of artificial neural network systems developed which do not use rules, e.g. Cawley and Green 1991).
- It reflected knowledge the system must have to process input strings—that is, there was an implicit distinction between a permanent set of rules (the contemporary linguists' 'competence') and their use on occasion, dependent on a particular input ('performance').
- Although necessary in a particular language, the rules were not necessary as part of how human beings produce speech in general—that is, they were language-specific variables which modelled cognitive choice-based processes and not necessarily

universals. Any universality might be coincidental (for example, the phonological rule in most if not all languages that lengthens vowels in syllables having a voiced consonant as coda is cognitively universal by coincidence: the 'lengthening' is in fact either a by-product of phonetic rendering or perhaps an inappropriate modelling of final voiced consonant devoicing).
- The units and the rules combining them were invariant within a particular language—though the rules may have had either obligatory or optional status.
- At the high level the continuousness of the articulatory and acoustic signals of real speech was not reflected, as is the case in contemporary phonology: the only *time* variables are rather abstract—unit sequencing, or relative notions such as 'length'. This approach accurately reflects the cognitive status of this part of the overall model: planners of speech (speakers) and those who perceive it (listeners) are not concerned with low-level matters such as coarticulation and real time.

Finally, it is interesting to observe that, as high-level synthesis systems have developed, their use of phonology has been roughly in step with the phonological theory of the time. Pierrehumbert's ideas of a prosody which overlaid segmental phonology is a good example, as are the small number of contemporary systems which have shifted the focus to the prosodic domain (Tatham and Morton 2003).

6.11 The state of the art in synthesizing expressiveness

Over the past few years, as speech synthesis technology has matured in general so the research goals have shifted a little. In the early days researchers were concerned with simple intelligibility, and often the speech output was evaluated solely in terms of to what extent it was intelligible. As intelligibility became taken for granted, researchers turned to improving the naturalness of the speech being produced. It has now been realized that a major contributor to naturalness is expressiveness—the listener expects the speech to incorporate expressiveness, because arguably all *human* speech does so. To fail to include expressiveness virtually guarantees a lack of naturalness.

- It does seem that some synthetic speech which does not sound completely natural is, in fact, probably adequate as far as its segmental and 'neutral' suprasegmental properties are concerned. It does not sound completely natural because neutral suprasegmental properties are never found in natural speech. The synthesized speech, however good, lacks naturalness because it lacks expressiveness, and expressiveness is a *sine qua non* for naturalness.

The original goal, therefore, was simply to go on improving the naturalness of the speech. This was driven by scientific curiosity: how natural can the speech be made by including expressiveness, and how shall we do this? But latterly developments in speech technology are being driven by the demand for usable interactive systems communicating information to a lay public. Scientific curiosity has given way to the demands of practical engineering on some fronts.

There is one other original goal: the provision of a test-bed for the development of theories of speech production and perception remains as a research objective. More manipulable and reliable systems have improved the usefulness of synthesis as a model development tool, because its intrinsic accuracy is better. Researchers need to worry less whether a particular effect in the speech output is the result of a bug in the synthesizer or a bug in their model—they can be more confident today that it is their model which is failing, not the synthesizer.

However, we are beginning to realize that the division of the model into segmental and suprasegmental aspects might be unhelpful in the way it has been implemented. In almost all synthesis systems, suprasegmental rendering has taken second place to segmental rendering. Thinking is beginning to turn on this subject, and we are starting to see the emergence of models which focus primarily on the prosodic structure of an utterance and use this as a basis for synthesis. As yet this is confined to high-level systems: there are no low-level synthesis systems which do not concentrate on modelling the acoustics of the segment, seriously neglecting prosodic effects. In those overall systems where prosodics is becoming the focus, the shortcomings of the low-level system are being covered by heavier computational load at the high level. In the short term this will do, but it is at best makeshift in its approach.

6.11.1 *How do new lines of research differ?*

Current lines of research are a little different from what has gone before for the reasons outlined above, and especially because of technological improvements and the fact that engineering rather than scientific needs are beginning to have an influence on the research development.

However, there is just so much that can be done with the pure engineering approach, and, as researchers have found with automatic speech recognition, there are limits to what can be achieved in modelling a human system without taking more account of what the human is actually doing. In automatic speech recognition the purely statistical approach has provided us with systems which are excellent and very successful compared with early approaches based on poor models in linguistics; but times change, and the approach of phonetic and phonological theory has changed considerably since the earlier important decisions to focus on statistical approaches. The last ounces of error may eventually be eliminated from recognition systems by returning to models of human utterance perception. Similarly, though ideas about human speech production have never been completely eliminated from speech synthesis, there is now scope for improving the quality of synthetic speech by taking account of developments in the characterization of human speech production.

Chapter 7

Emotion in Speech Synthesis

As we have seen, many researchers in the fields of speech synthesis and expression studies feel that synthesis has reached the point where it is sufficiently stable and sufficiently natural to warrant moving forward to include expressive content. Some go further, feeling that the use of speech synthesis in information systems and the like will only become widespread when expressive content is there. Particularly in dialogue systems, listeners notice that something is not quite right, even when for short stretches of utterance or single words the signal produced is indistinguishable from human speech. In longer utterances or during a dialogue, listeners expect expressive content.

There is a need for a comprehensive account of the emotions underlying the acoustic signal, as well as an account of the signal itself. Only then will a correlation be discovered suitable for forming the basis of resynthesis. We would add to this the need for a full understanding of how the soundwave is processed by the listener. The perception of expressive content is one of our main concerns because of our observation that the relationship between the acoustic signal and the processes involved in assigning labels to it are non-linear. We would not feel confident in, say, rank ordering the parameters of a waveform according to expressive 'weighting' just on the basis of the fact that they are present when the speaker feels a particular emotion. The parameters of the acoustic signal relate to the experienced emotion roughly according to Murray's and Arnott's table (see Chapter 6), but we may not assume they related to a perceived emotion in the same way.

Considerations of perception are central to our own understanding of the goal of speech synthesis. There are two possibilities for this goal:

- the creation of a speech waveform indistinguishable from human speech when measured in a phonetics laboratory;
- the creation of a particular percept in the listener such that they confidently assign the appropriate labels or symbolic representations to the soundwave.

Our preferred aim is the second of these for two reasons. We believe that *human* speech production is perceiver-centred, and the acoustic signal itself is insufficient to predict how it will be perceived (the non-linearity condition). For these reasons our *synthesis* needs to be perceiver-oriented, and it therefore follows if we are right that we need to understand and model the entire chain of relationships from the emotion as experienced, through the soundwave, to the process of assigning appropriate emotional labels by the listener.

7.1 Type of synthesizer

The type of system used for synthesizing expression will introduce its own specific constraints on what can be achieved.

7.1.1 Formant synthesis

Formant synthesis is chosen for creating expressive speech either because it is comparatively easy to use and there are one or two systems readily available, or because it is highly manipulable. For example, Murray and Arnott (1995) attempted a few basic emotions using the DECTalk synthesizer, though the results as judged by listeners were uneven. At the time DECTalk was a combined high- and low-level synthesizer with possibly some internal interaction between the two levels; it is not entirely clear how Murray and Arnott corrected for this. The parameters of formant synthesis systems are normally completely under the researcher's control, and so it is easy to vary values on demand. Most researchers, however, have underused this feature because of self-imposed limitations on how the input utterances are marked up. In general the hand mark-up, and even a special case of semi-automatic mark-up, called by Murray and Arnott 'emotion-by-rule', sets the parameter values for whole utterances and makes no provision for *variable* emotion.

7.1.2 *Waveform concatenation synthesis*

Waveform concatenation systems include diphone-based and other systems using fixed units and unit selection systems using variable length sections of speech. Schröder (2000) and others tie diphone systems to waveform concatenation, but there is no reason why formant synthesis systems should not also be diphone-based, or indeed based on any size of utterance including stretches of variable duration as in large database unit selection systems. There are strict limitations on concatenation synthesis which are not found in formant systems. The general technique (discussed in Chapter 11) is to conjoin recordings of human speech (using the appropriate chosen units) and then process the result for fundamental frequency and timing. As yet, detail of the frequency *structure* of utterances cannot be altered by these techniques, so that only the acoustic correlates of expressions which use f0 and timing can be manipulated. This is a serious shortcoming to using waveform concatenation synthesis.

Although timing is not difficult to alter in waveform concatenation synthesis it is generally the case that timing and rhythm models are phonetically or phonologically based. That is, the units which form the basis of rhythm are primarily the syllable and also individual segments. Timing and rhythm adjustments therefore require a marked-up waveform where syllable and segment boundaries have been determined and properly aligned with the acoustic signal. With syllable- and allophone-based concatenation systems this is no more difficult than alignment of symbolic marking with natural speech, but it is more difficult with concatenated diphones. There is a paradox here: for some researchers diphones are preferred to allophones because their use avoids some of the difficulties associated with modelling coarticulation in allophone conjoining; but at the same time without such models the marking of a syllable or allophone boundary *within* a diphone is hard and has plenty of scope for error.

We should point out that in any case trying to align an abstract symbolic representation with a physical waveform is theoretically an impossible task, even if it is regarded as necessary for practical purposes. The timing within an utterance cannot be altered unless we can identify where the change is to take place, and *all* models purporting to enable us to do this are based on abstract aoristic symbolic representations.

Because of the constraints inherent in waveform processing of frequency domain components like formants, several researchers—for example Edgington (1997) and Rank and Pirker (1998)—have tried to assess whether it is possible to use just f0 and timing manipulation to introduce expressive content into speech. The results are largely inconclusive: there is some success, but the identification of expressive content is not reliable, probably because the relative contribution of f0 and frequency domain components is not fixed but varies between emotions—and indeed potentially *within* emotions. There is clearly also the possibility that in natural speech the relative contribution of the various parameters may be speaker-specific or vary within a single speaker on different occasions. Variables such as these introduce statistical processing difficulties in reducing the data obtained from such experiments because they widen the variability (and therefore increase uncertainty) considerably. Ideally the source of each variable should be isolated and independently dealt with.

To summarize: the major difficulty with all forms of concatenated waveform synthesis is the manipulation of voice quality (defined here as simply the spectral content of speech rather than various types of larynx signal). Efforts to determine how much can be done by manipulating time and f0 alone are inconclusive and unsatisfactory. It is reasonably clear that concatenated waveform synthesis comes second to formant synthesis when dealing with signal manipulation for expressive content.

7.1.3 Improvements to waveform concatenation systems

Waveform concatenation synthesis relies on the use of a database of pre-recorded natural speech. This is always the case with whatever units are employed: allophones, diphones, syllables, words, phrases, or variable unit selection periods. We can hypothesize that whatever expressive content was incorporated in the original data will come across in any resynthesized signal. It is for this reason that those speaking the database are often instructed to speak as 'neutrally' as possible in an attempt to avoid expressively biasing the system.

However, if this requirement to speak without expressive content is removed and the database is of sufficient size we can imagine that it will include a range of expressive content. This will depend of course on how the recording is made and how contrived the data is. It is a short step from the normal methods of unit selection—namely to search and retrieve the longest or most appropriate stretch of speech based on *segmental* content—to include also that the appropriate stretch is constrained to be one in the correct expressive domain. The technique has been tried by Marumoto and Campbell (2000). The probability of usefully satisfying the additional constraint as well as the segmental content requirement is pretty low unless the database is very large indeed. This is especially true if f0 and interacting spectral parameters of expressive content are both included in the set of constraints. However, we do not know exactly what the probability is, and more work needs to be done to determine whether searching large single databases for stretches of speech with particular expressive content is really feasible.

One or two researchers have introduced multiple databases into concatenative waveform systems (particularly unit selection systems) in an attempt to produce working systems which demonstrate expression in synthetic speech. For example Iida et al. (2000) report resynthesizing anger, joy, and sadness by having the same speaker record three separate unit selection databases. Around 75% success in identifying the particular emotions was reported, but it is not clear whether a greater success rate could have been achieved with the original recordings—that is, the control environment for the experiment is not explicit. Much more work needs to be done to determine just how much of the database speaker's *spectrally* defined expressive content is preserved when the database is used for resynthesis. In particular, any results need to be reviewed in the light of the scores for perceiving the expressive content in the original database before it is manipulated.

The success of multiple databases is limited by their size. There is probably a diminishing returns factor associated with unit selection systems, but nevertheless size is a real problem, particularly in terms of how rapidly the database can be searched to retrieve the appropriate units. However, in practical limited domain situations—where semantic and expressive content can be controlled—there may well be a use for such systems, as there is, of course, as a research tool (see Iida et al. 1998).

7.2 Using prosody as the basis for synthesizing expression

It is often claimed that prosody is the main vehicle for cueing emotion and other expressive content in speech. Schröder's (2000) survey of synthesis of emotive content cites several researchers who manipulate prosody, often by rule, as the basis for including expression in their output. However, there is often a confusion here: there is a difference between prosody—a highly abstract concept in linguistics—and the acoustic correlates of prosody. The problem is that the majority of linguistic models of prosody, e.g. the ToBI mark-up system (Silverman et al. 1992), are not really about the acoustic signal but are characterizations of speakers' and listeners' impressions using a symbolic representation. Any practical synthesis system which uses linguistic prosody has also to specify how it correlates with the acoustic output. And the problem here is that all synthesis systems fail to a certain extent to generate good prosody. In fact, away from work on expressive content, good prosody in synthetic speech is still regarded as the last frontier, which has still to be reached. The relatively poor intonation and rhythm achieved by even the best systems is still regarded as a barrier to general acceptance of synthetic speech in the human/computer interface.

Our understanding of the relationship between symbolic representations of prosody, which may fairly accurately reflect speakers' and listeners' feelings, and the correlating acoustic parameters is apparently quite limited. For this reason any approach to modelling expression using prosody as its basis must proceed with caution.

What we do know is that for the most part the acoustic parameters which convey general prosody are also used for expression, and that measurements of average f0, range of f0, rhythm, etc. can be compared for their roles both in prosody and in conveying expressive content. How prosody and expression interact at the parametric acoustic level is another matter, but results of studies are almost always couched in terms like: 'The f0 range is wider if the speaker is excited', meaning that whatever the 'normal' range of f0 within this speaker's prosody, it widens under certain emotive conditions. This leads some researchers to model expression as a global phenomenon, and to set global parameters for synthesizing expression. Most synthesis systems have default settings for parameters such as average f0, f0 range, etc. and it is a simple matter to reset these defaults using information based on the differences between normal prosody and prosody with 'added expression'.

In effect, this is an informal approach which compares well with our speech production model presented in Chapters 15 and 16, with its hierarchical arrangement of 'wrappers'. In that model we see prosody as wrapping utterance segmental content, and expression as wrapping prosody:

```
<expression>
  <prosody>
     <utterance₁/>
     <utterance₂/>
     <utteranceₙ/>
  </prosody>
</expression>
```

(The XML notation used here is explained later, in Chapter 16.)

This outline model has a sequence of utterances to be characterized within a prosodic framework, with the prosody in turn dominated by an expressive framework. Our model incorporates the concept of inheritance, so that setting or resetting expressive defaults would in turn be inherited through the network down to the utterance level. The appropriate parameters behave differently according to parameter settings which are passed down the hierarchy, and without any intervention expressive content would trickle through the system to appear in the utterance's acoustic signal.

Models which adopt the prosodic approach, or an approach working on the acoustic correlates of prosody, include 'rules' relating normal prosody with prosody altered by expression. As we point out, though, they usually take the form of global rules resetting defaults. However, it would also be possible, though more complicated, to introduce modifications to the detail of, say, intonation contours (Mozziconacci and Hermes 1999). Again the literature is confused: would this be the detail of abstract symbolically modelled intonation contours, or the detail of acoustically modelled f0 contours? Again, we have to make the distinction because of the non-linear relationship between the two. Changes to the detail contours of intonation or its f0 correlate might be considered to be local rather than global settings, and are candidates for intervention in default or reset global parameters. So, a possible arrangement might be:

```
<expression>
 <prosody>
  <global_settings>
    <local_settings>
      <utterance₁/>
    </local_settings>
    <local_settings>
      <utterance₂/>
    </local_settings>
    <local_settings>
      <utteranceₙ/>
    </local_settings>
  </global_settings>
 </prosody>
</expression>
```

Inheritance still has a trickledown effect through the hierarchy, and the model shows that local settings inherit the properties of global settings, but in addition make room for local changes to details of the utterance: global settings are reset locally.

There is also the problem of what we call 'drift settings'—settings which migrate between local and global. The mechanism for such detailed changes within the overall speech production framework does not seem to have been discussed in the expression literature.

7.3 Assessment and evaluation of synthesis results

In the early days of synthesis, assessment of the speech output was usually informal: there were no agreed techniques for evaluating output quality. In more recent times, however, many research projects have developed evaluation methods. These techniques have been usually set up without expressive content in mind, initially simply used to assess intelligibility. As intelligibility becomes less of an issue for developers of synthesis systems, more refined techniques are needed for assessing the effectiveness of the more difficult areas, such as prosody and expression. So far there are evaluation methods inherited from early trials of synthesizers, but we do not yet have an agreed evaluation paradigm nor agreed or well-defined standards for prosody and expression. Standards are necessary as benchmarks against which to measure the success rate of different systems.

It is not clear whether, in terms of techniques, the assessment of expression in synthetic speech should be any different from earlier assessments of 'accuracy'. Many researchers have carried over the techniques used for early intelligibility ratings. Evaluation can be either 'subjective'—involving the judgements of panels of listeners—or 'objective'—involving assessing the measured accuracy of the actual waveform produced.

Subjective assessment must take place within the constraints of a clear model of perception. There is no point in telling us what listeners think if we do not know *how* they arrive at judgements or assign labels. For example, if we believe that labels are somehow contained within the soundwave and are there to be extracted by listeners, our assessment would be of whether we have succeeded in encoding them in the signal. But if we believe that there are no labels in the signal but only rather poor cues for listeners to assign their own labels, our assessment would be of whether we had cued the assignment task satisfactorily. These are very different approaches and call for different interpretations of the results.

Objective assessment, on the other hand, presupposes an explicit and well-motivated model of the acoustics of expressive content in speech. The difficulties of evaluating subjective assessment are avoided, but on the other hand difficulties of knowing if the acoustic model is accurate are raised.

7.3.1 Subjective evaluation

Subjective evaluation involves assessment by listening panels. In the case of expressive speech the test often consists of setting up a number of sentences judged to be semantically 'neutral', and having the synthesizer speak them in a range of expressions—usually a range of emotions accepted as being relatively unambiguous in natural speech. The more basic emotions are the ones usually chosen: anger, sadness, contentment, etc. Subtle tones of voice are generally avoided in assessing the overall potential of a synthesizer to handle expressive speech. The reason for this is quite simple: their subtlety makes them candidates for ambiguity even in natural speech, and this obscures the contribution the design or workings of the synthesizer itself may be making to any confusion experienced by listening panels. With some exceptions, evaluation is usually of a synthesizer's performance with modes of expression whose acoustic signal has been modelled relatively clearly.

The tests themselves most commonly follow the 'forced choice perception' model, in which listeners hear an utterance and assign to it an expressive label by choosing from a fixed number provided by the experimenter. The list does not usually contain dummy labels, but is confined to the actual emotive types occurring in the test data. Listeners are therefore asked to discriminate between the categories on offer. A refined alternative to this technique is to supply listeners with no labels at all, but simply ask them to identify the expression type they hear without pre-empting novel choices—that is, labels of types not occurring in the data.

Interpreting the results of subjective tests is not easy because there are several objective and perceptual variables involved. For example, an emotion may well be detected by the majority of a listening panel as anger, but what is the degree of anger being expressed, and is it either slight enough to be confused with irritation, or even severe enough to be confused with irritation? The tests of themselves do not explain how confusions and perceptual errors arise, but above all they do not explain how *correct* answers arise. Was the correct expressive type detected because it was, on its own, exactly the way a human being would have performed? Or was it anger because it was not sadness—clearly identified in another utterance? Listening test design is a highly refined science within the field of experimental psychology, and fraught with difficulties. Most of the tests devised by researchers have been, for this reason, relatively informal, and seek to provide only a rough indication of how well the synthesizer has handled expressive content. They rarely seek to tease out the various factors contributing to correct identification or confusion.

The problems associated with evaluating expressive synthetic speech are not unexpected, given the fact that the acoustic models we have are still incomplete and the resultant synthetic speech is still comparatively crude. It is not uncommon for an excellent result to be obtained by accident, and we would often have to confess that we cannot explain why this or that result is particularly good or particularly bad, or even just surprising.

These are some of the questions subjective testing might answer:

- How natural is the speech? How human-sounding is it?
- Is the naturalness due to the fact that expression has been added? Is good synthetic speech without expression rated 'unnatural'? Can human speech ever be rated unnatural if it is emotively neutral?
- Can the intended type of expressive content be identified—with or without prompting?

- Has the expression come across with the intended degree of intensity? Is degree assessment by a listener as important as type assessment?
- Which types of expression are most likely to be confused with each other? Can we set up an 'expressive perceptual space' within which to establish coordinates and distances, plotting errors among 'correct' coordinates?
- Does confusion depend on type or degree of expression, or both, and in what mix?
- What is the interaction between semantic and expressive content? Is there any difference between the perception of human and synthetic speech in respect of this interaction?
- What happens when semantic and expressive content conflict, and are the results similar to those obtained for such conflicts in natural speech?

There are yet other questions. There is no doubt that we have only sketchy answers in general to most of these questions for synthesized expressive speech. Establishing an evaluation paradigm to determine answers for a particular model—or to compare models—is something which has yet to be achieved. Part of the reason for this is that parallel experiments with human speech are difficult to perform and evaluate.

7.3.2 Objective evaluation

Many researchers prefer a more 'objective' evaluation of their synthesis. Here the question asked would be whether the acoustic signal generated by the synthesizer could have been produced by a human being—on demand and in an appropriate situation, and not by accident.

In some ways objective evaluation is more attractive than listening tests for evaluating synthetic speech, though it too has its share of difficulties. If we are to say whether the signal could have been produced by a human being—and is therefore a 'good' signal—we have to have a clear model of what a human being would produce. No researcher would yet claim that our acoustic models of various emotions or expression types are completely accurate. But we do have a fairly good idea of the parameters involved, and some idea of how they interact to produce the perception of emotion, at least for the strong, unambiguous emotions.

The evaluation paradigm involves comparing natural speech with synthetic speech. Usually a rather more abstract approach is taken: we compare a *model* of expression in natural speech with the synthesis. And more explicitly, we compare the *predictions* of a model of natural speech with the results of the synthesis. If we make the assumption that, although by no means perfect yet, our models of expressive content are adequate to begin assessment, the next stage is to establish an explicit procedure for deriving a distance metric between what our model of natural speech predicts and what our synthesizer has produced. One reason for the common adoption of a parametric approach is that it establishes a checklist against which scored values for natural and synthetic speech can be compared. That is, the distances between scores can be arrived at for each individual parameter, if necessary by simple subtraction—to be extended to an overall distance arrived at by combining the weighted scores from all relevant parameters. How the scores are to be weighted for overall evaluation is a matter for discussion still, since there is no agreement.

7.4 Synthesis of emotions in speech: general problems

Most of the work so far on synthesizing emotion in speech has concentrated on the 'basic' emotions. The argument is that so little is understood about the details of expressive acoustic signals, and how to synthesize them, that it is better to stay with emotional states which are clear rather than subtle. This is not to say that the clear, perhaps exaggerated, states occur more frequently.

7.4.1 What to synthesize to illustrate a model of the acoustics of emotion

The argument against working with the clearer basic or primary emotions is that there is a danger of confusing category labels with objects within the category. As category labels they are rather like the phonemes of segmental speech as opposed to instances of objects *within* the category. If they are objects within the category rather than labels, there is a danger that they are not truly representative of the category, but selected on an unprincipled basis. The argument is perhaps overly subtle: the fact of the matter is that, properly, attempts to synthesize expressive speech are not waiting for complete models of the acoustics of expression—after all, synthesis is part of how we validate our models, however incomplete.

Nevertheless we have to bear in mind that there are two possible definitions for the primary—or indeed, any emotions:

- Primary emotions are category labels; or
- They are simply clear physical exemplar instances.

If the primary emotions are regarded as category labels akin to phonemes, we need a layered hierarchical model within which to categorize them, and there are no worries about their being 'typical'. If they are 'extremes' on a scale of clarity or precision, we need a flatter model. We need also to worry about how representative they are.

7.4.2 The minimum hierarchy

The approach to synthesis can be either speaker-oriented or listener-oriented, depending on whether the acoustic signal is judged in terms of how it matches typical human examples of the same emotions in terms of the response of listeners. If the aim is to model the whole emotion communication process the model will need to be multi-layered. Three layers is the minimum requirement:

- a plan layer, reflecting how a speaker plans their utterance and the plan itself;
- an acoustic layer, modelling the acoustics of expressive content;
- a percept layer, reflecting how a listener assigns appropriate labels to what they hear.

Layer linkage is by processes which convert between them. The acoustic layer is the one usually regarded as the key because it pivots between speaker and listener: it is the layer for handing over information. The plan gives rise to the acoustic signal, and it is also this signal, which gives rise to the percept (with or without active contributions from the perceiver). It is arguable that it is essential to deal with the expressive acoustic signal in terms both of where it has come from and of where it is going to.

7.4.3 Representation at the acoustic level

We have discussed the way most researchers adopt a parametric approach for representing emotion at the acoustic level. Because the research is still in its early stages, these parameters—f0 mean, f0 range, and overall utterance tempo are the most common ones—are usually treated as global. This means that their values are expressed as 'settings' over an appreciable length of utterance. The real problems begin when we try to model how these global settings can be subtly varied on a local intra-utterance basis. There has been no appreciable modelling of these effects. This becomes particularly important when we realize that precise linguistic correlations—like f0 contour reflecting phonological intonation—have significant local detail, and interact with sentence syntax.

As an example of how syntax alters the phonological and acoustic parameters of prosodics, we can see that contrastive emphasis on a single word, which may involve a quite sharp drop in the contour's shape (perceptually a 'high fall'), distorts significantly the running f0 contour. The use of the intonation contour to signal a switch from declarative to interrogative sentence type (perhaps overall falling vs. rising contour) must have some effect on the encoding of expressive content: is anxiety in a statement identical acoustically with anxiety in a question? Another example is the intonation contour and correlating f0 contour used with lists which varies significantly between languages: standard British English, for example, does this differently from American English or French.

Related to the representation of both global and local expressive content in utterances is the problem of modelling how emotions blend into one another during the course of an utterance or during a sequence of utterances. Obviously the models which only set the parameters for each utterance separately at its boundaries cannot handle changes *within* the utterance. Phoneticians aiming to tackle the question of how emotive speech reflects blending and shading of emotions are hampered by what seems to be a gap in the psychology literature. Not many researchers have addressed how emotions alter in a person as stimuli mix and blend—how a person's feeling of anger can modify as someone else explains to them that a misunderstanding has occurred. These changes are time-dependent and not always sudden, but when they are gradual they are not linear: people's feelings under these circumstances are likely to change relatively gradually, and not necessarily in a continuously even way.

One of the basic difficulties is improving our understanding of how speech production and perception actually works in general. This in turn will reflect our approach to synthesis and, for example, promote the drawing of a conceptually sharp distinction between high- and low-level synthesis.

There will have also to be a greater understanding of how synthesis itself actually works. A good example here is the success of unit selection techniques in concatenated waveform synthesis: neither the basic idea of concatenation nor the idea of selecting units from a database is conceptually accurate as a model of how human beings produce speech. In fact it is unlikely that these ideas *could* be incorporated in a speech production model or an expression model. They are engineering approaches reflecting good practice, and which result in good speech—but this does not guarantee that they, or other engineering approaches, make a good basis for understanding what human beings do. A system based on the parameters of speech production and perception which can transparently model the dependencies between production, soundwave, and perception is far more likely to be useful and help improve our understanding. This is not to decry engineering approaches *per se*—independently of our concern with expressive speech we want and need *good* synthesis, and academically based or 'scientifically accurate' systems are *not* delivering yet. But our understanding of emotive content in speech is so sparse at the moment that there may be a case to be made for not introducing too many additional problems by putting too much emphasis on little-understood engineering solutions.

7.5 Linking parameters of emotion with acoustic parameters

Some researchers in speech and synthesis have classified emotions in terms of a number of parameters, though it must be stressed that the labels and what is actually parameterized here do not entirely accord with similar ideas among the biologists and psychologists modelling emotion. The three most commonly used by recent speech researchers are 'arousal', 'valence', and 'control' (Schlosberg 1954). An alternative set of labels for the same parameters uses the terms 'activation', 'evaluation', and 'power'. These parameters are usually characterized as scalar—that is, as vectors along which values indicating degree of the dimension are found. The parameters can be defined (Schröder et al. 2000) as:

- *activation*—degree of readiness to act;
- *evaluation*—degree of liking and disliking;
- *power*—dominance/submission.

The idea is to categorize emotional 'states' (anger, sadness, etc.) in terms of values along these three scales. The parameters create a space within which emotional states can be located. Among writers who have used such a parametrically represented framework for categorizing emotions there is a basic assumption of linearity within the framework, although emotional categories may bunch along the vectors or in various spots within the space created, forming 'clumps' of unambiguous emotion. However, without knowing for certain that this is the case, a good working hypothesis is that the vectors should initially be treated as linear, rather than try to guess at preferred 'hot spots' along them. The main thing is that such a system allows for continuous representation and 'shading' of emotions.

Emotion in Speech Synthesis

At some stage in an overall model of the *communication* of emotion, a correlation might be established between the space used to describe emotion in the speaker and the corresponding perceptual framework in the listener. A spatial representation for both seems appropriate, but we should not assume that the degree of non-linearity within each space is similar, or that the correlation between the two is linear. It would, however, be useful if we could model the *experience* of emotion in the speaker and the *perception* of emotion by the listener using a common framework. Such a framework would be useful in evaluating synthesis systems using emotional parameters as a basis for generating expressive speech, because the evaluation could be based on comparing the two to compute a distance metric—potentially a measure of the success of the synthesis.

7.5.1 Category labels vs. parameters for driving the synthesis

An emotion experienced by a speaker can be characterized as a simple label or, some speech researchers believe, as a combination of three values, using as a first approximation the activation–evaluation–power framework just described. The parametric framework has the advantage of pointing to direct class relationships among emotions. So, for example, anger and excitement may both belong to the class of 'high activation' emotions. Using overall or 'cover' labels alone obscures this class relationship.[1]

This idea parallels the use in classical phonetics of phonetic symbols (the label approach) as well as place/manner classification charts (the parametric approach) or the distinctive feature approach of phonology. Place/manner classification and distinctive features enable greater generalization by dealing with classes of objects rather than isolated objects. For example, the labels /t/ and /d/ share little if anything as labels, but parametrically both belong to the classes [stop] and [alveolar] in English. This enables us to capture a generalization by writing a rule about alveolar stops rather than individual rules for each label category.

---

[1] There is need for caution here. The speech work is not exactly in line with the work by biologists and psychologists. Here we are confining the discussion to speech researchers. We discuss the approach of biologists and psychologists in Chapter 9.

Similarly, the acoustic correlates of emotion are modelled in a parametric way. Parameters, like f0 average and range, are commonly used in combination to characterize the acoustic correlate of this or that emotion. These acoustic parameters form the basis of models for manipulating synthetic speech to reflect expressive content. If the synthesis system is set up to have the same parameters as used in the characterization of the analysis, the values should transfer easily from analysis to synthesis. Almost all attempts to synthesize emotive content have followed this general procedure.

The next stage is to move the parametric representation 'back' from the acoustic analysis level to the level of emotional experience in the speaker. In other words, the labels become simple 'cover symbols' for the experiential space defined by the parametric representation. The synthesis strategy in such a system operates by establishing correlations between values on the emotional vectors and the set of acoustic parameters. Equivalence is between two parameter sets, rather than between a label and a single (acoustic) parameter set.

The power of such a model is dramatically greater than the label equivalent, since the combinatorial results of the equivalence rise exponentially and quickly become infinite. The focus of the model now shifts to highlighting the constraints which pull us back from the combinatorial explosion. In terms of the science involved in understanding emotion and its expression in speech, such constraints are formulated as hypotheses which cumulatively define the limits of expression. In terms of engineering an expressive synthesis system, many more subtleties become possible, ranging from discriminating between 'close' categories like anger and irritation, or sadness and distress, to having a clear picture of how to go about synthesizing degrees within a particular emotion: very vs. extremely angry, for example. Although not relevant to synthesis, the parametric approach to characterizing emotion also enables a better model of the sources of the various constraints involved—perhaps pointing the way to a greater understanding of the relationship between physical and cognitive sources (see Chapter 9).

7.5.2 The notion 'prosodic profile'

Schröder et al. (2000) refer to what they and a number of other researchers have called the 'prosodic profile' of an emotion. Based on the idea that emotions are expressed prosodically in speech, they are scored as to the relative contribution of various prosodic parameters. In effect the prosodic parameters define a space within which emotions can be located. The task of synthesizing emotional speech begins by establishing prosodic profiles from a large acoustic database. They aim to profile particularly what they call 'weak' emotions—that is, those beyond the simple strong emotions of anger, fear, sadness, and contentment or happiness and one or two others. Note, however, that among the biologists and psychologists (see Part III) even secondary emotions can be considered 'strong': for them 'secondary' does not mean 'weaker'. The profiles are established by analysing the database acoustically according to an aligned mark-up based on listeners' judgements as to what emotions are being expressed. So if a listening panel decides that a particular section of the database reveals the speaker to be, say, moderately pleased, the prosodic profile is assessed for the utterance(s) concerned. The collection of profiles is then used as the basis for synthesizing the emotions. The work differs in a couple of ways from parallel attempts by other researchers to establish the acoustic correlates of emotion:

- Weak emotions are being analysed.
- Time is included to assess how the profiles change as a speaker's emotions change.

The second point here is particularly important because much of the gain in naturalness achieved by synthesizing expressive content can be cancelled out by having the emotion remain constant over long periods. Our models of the acoustics of emotion must reflect the dynamics of emotion, as a speaker's tone of voice changes progressively with cascading utterances.

The first point—the profiling of what some speech researchers have called 'weak emotions'—is still, however, problematical. Profiles are very 'noisy'. Even for strong emotions they reflect enormous variability, much of the source of which we are as yet unable to determine. 'Noise' is a general technical term for unwanted signals or measurements which defocus the accuracy of a profile. There is a good chance that in the case of weak emotions the noise will be so great as to 'bury' the signal and make it impossible to discover the subtleties of the profile. There are effective techniques for minimizing noise, but they depend usually on a good model of the noise itself and its source—something we do not yet have for the acoustics of expression. There is no doubt, however, that there is progress to be made in profiling emotions in this way.

It is important to be clear that the term 'prosodic' is used here to refer to the correlating acoustic parameters of prosody, not to prosody itself. In linguistics, prosody is an abstract phonological concept which includes linguistic properties of an utterance such as stress and intonation. As such, prosody reflects cognitive rather than physical properties of an utterance, and it may be misleading to refer to prosody as an exponent of expression or emotion. It is more helpful to say that in terms of their acoustic correlates prosody and expression share the same physical parameters. It follows that they are differentiated by the mix of these parameters and their degree, relative to each other. A problem facing researchers is to work out how they are mixed or overlaid on one another.

The problem of using the term 'prosody' to refer to a linguistic abstraction *and* its acoustic exponents is aggravated by its inconsistent use in the literature, which often confuses the two. Thus traditionally phoneticians, as we have seen, will refer to a 'high fall' on a word or syllable as a cue for contrastive emphasis—for example: *It was his ↘ bike he crashed*. Terms like 'high fall' refer to a speaker's or listener's impressions of all or part of an intonation contour, and the contour itself is an impression reflected in a non-linear way by events in the acoustic signal. It is misleading to imply that (to continue our use of this particular term, though the same is true of others) that high fall means an unusual lowering of fundamental frequency, because of the non-linear relationship between the two. For example, how much the f0 needs to fall to give rise to the impression probably varies

Emotion in Speech Synthesis

depending on its current value and direction of change; it also depends on the amplitude of the signal, since a high fall is often associated with a local increase in amplitude.

There is an argument which says that so long as we remain with one single domain—either the abstract or physical domain—there is no problem. A traditional phonetician knows what a high fall is within their terms of reference, and an acoustic phonetician will also know what the term means. Our problem is that if we are to synthesize expression effectively we need to be able to relate impressionistic descriptions with physical values. So far there is no reliable or agreed basis for doing this. However, prosodic profiling as a means of classifying or discriminating emotions is a useful approach. The technique will remain productive so long as it continues to refer to the acoustic correlates rather than the abstract impressions of prosody.

7.5.3 Criteria for selecting acoustic parameters

On the assumption that emotions are expressed using speakers' acoustic signals, it is reasonable to set up acoustic prosodic profiles referred to in the previous section. From a purely descriptive point of view any non-linearity in the relationship is not too important, and descriptions are tolerant of a certain amount of noise. But any non-linearity or noise does become important if we are to derive general principles from these profiles in order to recreate expressive waveforms. The reason is that we are uncertain of exactly how the acoustic signal is interpreted by listeners, and need to be careful of obscuring detail which is important for naturalness in the synthesized signal. The adequacy of psychologists' or linguists' descriptive models is not generally measured in terms of whether they work for synthesis, and it is not guaranteed that what is good for one purpose is good for another. In science and engineering, models are built with a particular purpose in mind; this puts constraints on the final model which vary according to purpose. In our case the detail necessary for a perceptually convincing synthesis may not be necessary in the model describing a speaker's behaviour.

Three fundamental criteria play a role in selecting acoustic parameters; they must be measurable:

- in the acoustic signal;
- as controllable variables in the synthesis;
- relevant to both producing and perceiving acoustic expressive content.

Schröder et al. (2000) list a number of settings they consider relevant to manipulating emotional content in synthesis. They are categorized according to prosodic effects, though these are a mixture of abstract and physical features. Their 'prosody' allows for intonation (an abstract category), tempo (abstract and physical), intensity (physical), and voice quality (abstract and physical). These are the features of the prosodic profile which are used to characterize various emotional effects in the acoustic signal, as seen in Table 7.1.

Some features in the table need comment.

- 'Intonation' is an abstract term in phonology/prosodics which correlates fairly well with changes of fundamental frequency to set up intonation or f0 'contours'. The correlation is non-linear, and on occasion brings in other parameters such as intensity. Global settings are unhelpful when it comes to the dynamics of expressive content: expression is a continuously variable phenomenon needing effective local adjustment to mean and range of fundamental frequency.
- The local parameters suggested for details of intonation have been used by several researchers to model the acoustics of emotion,

Table 7.1. Some claimed correlations between prosodic parameters and synthesis parameters (after Schröder et al. 2000)

Prosodic parameter	Synthesis parameter
Intonation (global)	Overall fundamental frequency mean and range
Intonation (accent structure)	(a) No. of f0 maxima/minima per unit time
	(b) Duration, magnitude, and steepness of f0 rises and falls
Tempo	(a) Duration of pauses
	(b) Articulation tempo
Intensity	(a) Intensity mean and range
	(b) General dynamics: the difference between mean intensity for intensity maxima and overall mean intensity
Voice quality	Spectral slope

Emotion in Speech Synthesis 147

and correlations have been established—though once again there is a great deal of noise in the experimental data and probably non-linearity. Since all synthesizers have the means to change fundamental frequency locally there should be no difficulty in working with these parameters.

- 'Tempo' is often an abstract term in phonetics. Here it is used in a more physical way to quantify the rate of occurrence of pauses (and their durations), and the rate of occurrence of segments. Rates for segments can be deceptively simple, and it is very important to take into account the segmental structure of larger units like syllables and accent grouping. 'Rallentando' effects, for example, at the end of utterances (which may be just phrases) are phenomena which differentially affect segments depending on this higher-level structure. Even without considering the hierarchical structure of utterances, different types of segment behave in quite different ways when tempo is altered—for example, vowels alter their durations differently from consonants as rate of delivery increases or decreases.
- 'Intensity' is a vague term, but here we take it in the physical sense. There are important details of intensity, though, which could be overlooked. For example, local spectral changes of intensity are important in signalling, say, that the vocal tract is tense (perhaps because of anger or excitement): the first formant here can assume a generally higher centre-frequency value relative to the other formants, and can have a lower than expected intensity relative to the other formants. Changing a global intensity setting for formants could not satisfy this detail. Similar spectrally local intensity effects can occur with fricatives: angry voice, for example, can and does differentially increase the amplitude of the [s] fricative compared with other fricatives and other types of sound. This is the so-called 'hissing anger tone'.
- 'Voice quality' changes are taken here to mean changes to the voicing source, such as the degree of airflow leakage (breathy voice) referred to earlier. There are also detailed changes to the overall spectral content of the signal which are due not to source change but to mechanical changes in the vocal tract affecting its filtering characteristics. The term 'voice quality' is

used in the literature ambiguously to refer both to source effects and to overall spectral content.

These proposals are fairly comprehensive and usually work. The idea of prosodic profile proposed by several researchers fits well with the synthesizer parameters they list, and it is easy to see how they tie together the acoustic parameters of real speech with the manipulable parameters of synthesizers. It is early days to extend the overall model to take care of non-linearities in the correlations, and the general noise to be found in the acoustic measurements. By noise we do not mean acoustic noise, but statistical noise due to types of variability cascading within the measurements.

7.5.4 The role of voice quality

Scherer (1996) feels that one problem with many attempts to synthesize good emotive speech has been the lack of means to alter voice quality—where voice quality means the detail of the voicing source. This is particularly true of concatenative systems in which voice source is not a manipulable parameter except in respect of fundamental frequency. Many researchers have reported that voice quality plays a significant role in conveying expression in speech, and we would expect, along with Scherer, that systems in which the synthesized voice quality depends entirely on the original recordings would therefore be seriously constrained. Scherer claims that both intelligibility and acceptability are affected by this limitation. If 'intelligibility' refers to the ability to decode accurately the semantic content of an utterance we doubt this claim, but if it means the pragmatic content then the claim will be true for those expressive elements which depend on voice quality. Acceptability to a listener is often a matter of preference and context, but under certain conditions acceptability in general will fall below an ideal level.

Other researchers are divided: there are several for whom acceptable results can be obtained with concatenative systems (e.g. Edgington 1997; Montero et al. 1998) and several who obtained much poorer results (e.g. Heuft et al. 1996; Rank and Pirker 1998). This kind of work is particularly important in assessing whether expressive content can be synthesized with current technology because:

- It focuses on the limitations of particular synthesizer specifications and techniques.
- It highlights areas which need reappraising in terms of the basic theory of how expression is encoded in the speech waveform.

Chapter 8

Recent Developments in Synthesis Models

Momentum is gathering in the quest first to establish what the acoustic correlates of expressiveness in speech actually are, and secondly to bring these in a useful way to the problem of improving naturalness in speech synthesis.

8.1 The current state of thinking

The research paradigm itself is undergoing some useful consolidation, though differences do occur consistent with varying approaches to the subject and varying goals for individual researchers or research groups.

8.1.1 Features of the research paradigms

The main features of the research paradigms are stable for the moment, and make some assumptions along the following lines:

- The acoustic signal of a person's speech communicates something of their emotions or attitudes.
- Variables in the acoustic signal which do this are extra to that part of the signal which communicates (or triggers) the basic meaning of an utterance.
- A listener can detect and interpret these variables to decide on the speaker's expressive stance.
- This stance may be voluntary or involuntary, conscious or subconscious—that is, the speaker is not necessarily aware that they have somehow injected expressive content into their utterance or what that content is.

8.1.2 The research procedure

The research procedure is to have listeners assess utterances as to their expressive content using score-sheets which name possible expression labels (happy, angry, informative (a style or attitude), etc.). When the researcher has settled on a set of utterances which show the minimum of ambiguity, the acoustic signal is examined with a view to determining the acoustic correlates of the labels. This procedure is no different from the one adopted in the heyday of acoustic experiments in phonetics, when researchers were seeking the acoustic correlates of speech units or prosodic phenomena. In those experiments an utterance judged to include the segment in question was analysed acoustically to determine the acoustic properties of the segment.

If there is a criticism of this approach, it is that listeners' judgements about utterances can be flawed in the sense that it is probably the case that the acoustic signal serves only as a trigger for the listener perception—it does not supply the actual signal perceived. There are many ways of demonstrating the justification for emphasizing the active nature of perception; but if it is right that speech perception is an active process of assignment, not 'recognition', it does mean that a listener's judgements as to what they are hearing, as opposed to perceiving, may not be quite right. A listener will tend to identify the signal with the resultant percept, believing them to be one and the same thing, and may be quite unaware that the relationship is not necessarily one to one. Put another way, we can say that the listener, when confirming that an utterance contains a particular segment or other phenomenon, is in fact confirming not that the object is there, but that there is *something* present which triggers them to believe that the object is there. All this says is that the relationship between a physical object and the label assigned to it is not straightforward.

Knowledge of this pitfall in the experimental procedure, however, should make it possible to introduce checks to make sure it is avoided. So, a set of utterances is used as the experimental data—and, given the variability of human speech, the set would include many examples of each correlation candidate.

8.2 Subtlety of expression

One of the questions which arises from time to time concerns just how subtle expression is in speech. For example, psychologists and bio-psychologists may wish to know how many different emotions and degrees of emotion are actually possible; a speech researcher might wish to have some idea of just how fine is the listener's ability in perceiving different amounts of expression in the soundwave. So far, considerations as detailed as this are thought to be important in the long term, but for the moment there is one major question for speech:

- Can synthetic speech be produced which is more subtle than the 'basic' emotions? For example, is it possible to produce friendly, patient speech?

There may be scope for changing or modifying the approaches of the speech researchers. For example, we have seen that by and large researchers, understandably in such a new and challenging area, have been first analysing and then (for some), resynthesizing the 'basic' emotions in the initial stages of work on expressiveness in speech.

But we need to assess whether the current approaches, and indeed the current synthesis techniques, can be pushed beyond this primary level into areas of greater subtlety. For example, it is possible to create and distinguish unambiguously between friendly and unfriendly spoken with patience—these are tones of voice regularly adopted by teachers: the speech exhibits patience, but that patience is easily classifiable as either friendly or unfriendly. Our guess is that the acoustic signal here is very hard to analyse with a view to isolating the correlates of the two shades of expression. But *listeners* do not have this difficulty, and although the differences between these two modes of expression are subtle at the cognitive level, and we presume subtle also at the acoustic level, we confidently hypothesize that this subtlety does not significantly confuse a listener. It would be reasonable to assume, however, that the 'facilitating cues' in the acoustic signal do vary in ambiguity, and it is also reasonable to assume that the more subtle the expressive content the greater the ambiguity—though we are far from agreeing what subtlety means in terms of expression.

Researchers need to address more fully the listener's 'degree of confidence' in labelling a particular utterance as having been produced with this or that expression. Some researchers have produced confusion matrices in respect of listeners' responses during discrimination experiments, and these are based on a mismatch between a 'known' encoding of particular expression and the listener's perception of which expression is being encoded. In the model, this labelling involves invoking the listener's cognitive characterization and relating it to the acoustic characterization. Under conditions of subtlety or ambiguity we know that listeners can assess their own confidence in their labelling, but we would like to see development of the idea of an 'expression space' designed to provide a metric for indicating 'closeness' in expressions, either cognitive or acoustic. This idea is based on the fact that listeners are able to report how close a particular percept is to another.

8.3 The expression space: metrics

Referring to the idea of degrees of expression mentioned above, a hypothesis we might put forward is that a listener's degree of confidence reduces in correlation with closeness within the expression space; but we may well discover that this is a non-linear function. Consider, for example, that when two emotions e_1 and e_2 are very distant or quite distant, confidence may be equal; but at some point a threshold is passed and confidence begins to lessen as distance between e_1 and e_2 continues to decrease. The emotional distance would decrease linearly but the correlating expression of confidence would not therefore decrease linearly, and linearity might alter as critical distance thresholds are passed.

The metrics for characterizing emotion

- at source (either in the bio-psychological or the cognitive arenas),
- in the subsequent acoustic signal, and
- in the listener's perception

have been for the most part separately explored, with correlations being either rough or tentative. At the source level, characterization has been by label or symbolic representation (the speaker is 'angry', 'thoughtful', 'worried', 'happy', 'irritated', etc.), and within the confines of the source level it is not too difficult to place such symbols within a speaker's emotional space. Similarly, a parametric analysis of the acoustic signal can be used to create a space; and again at the perceptual level labels or symbolic representations can attempt to mirror the expressive space in the speaker. But what we really lack is an explicit mapping between these three spaces. Such a mapping would have to involve not just spatial 'position' but spatial 'weight'—weight being used to indicate relative 'significance' of points or zones within the spaces. There is little or no significant discussion in the literature yet of the complexity of such multi-dimensional representations (but see, for tentative approaches, Eskenazi's style space (1992), and Cowie et al.'s perceptual space experiments (2000), and the earlier work both researchers cite).

8.4 Natural synthesis: feedback in the dialogue environment

During a conversation between two individuals there is a continuous awareness of the needs and difficulties of the opposite speaker—this is the basic claim of production-for-perception theory (see Chapter 10). Listeners communicate to a speaker when they are unsure how to interpret what has been said, and there are a variety of extralinguistic ways of doing this. The result can be repetition of what has just been said, or an improved or enhanced (to the point of caricature) rendering of the feature in subsequent speech. So if a speaker intends to convey mild irritation and their listener doesn't pick up on this, the speaker will tend to increase the degree of expression of irritation until the listener signals, often covertly, that the point is being made adequately.

A terminology-based question arises here: does the speaker increase the degree of irritation or does the speaker move further along the vector towards anger? There may be an irritation–anger

Recent Developments in Synthesis Models   155

cline, but in addition to this, *intensity of application* of the cline is also important. For any one point on the cline there may be 'extent of application'—so consider the cline:

$\leftarrow$ delighted $\leftrightarrow$ pleased $\leftrightarrow$ don't care $\leftrightarrow$ irritated $\leftrightarrow$ angry $\rightarrow$

This is a flat cline, but at any point along it we can introduce degrees of application. So we might have: 0.4 pleased, or 1 angry, or 0.5 don't care—indicating the strength of the particular feeling. So, strongly expressing irritation does not mean expressing anger—and weakly expressing pleasure does not mean mildly saying you don't care.

This point is important. Many researchers have defined irritation and anger, for example, as degrees of basically the same emotion; happiness and ecstasy might be another example. With this model in mind, we can think of irritation as a kind of weak anger, or ecstasy as a kind of enhanced happiness. But we might find that a three-dimensional model is more appropriate: for any one categorical point on the cline (like delighted, pleased, don't care, irritated, and angry in the illustration above) we can imagine depth or intensity:

```
+      ↑           ↑             ↑              ↑            ↑
0   ← delighted ↔ pleased ↔ don't care ↔ irritated ↔ angry →
−      ↓           ↓             ↓              ↓            ↓
```

We can see from the diagram how each category along the cline can be increased or decreased in intensity. This approach makes sense if we feel that, for example, increased irritation is not the same as anger, or reduced pleasure is not the same as 'don't care'.

However, if listeners signal to speakers their success in interpreting a speaker's 'intentions' (explicit or tacit) with this degree of detail, the question is whether an adequate level of feedback signalling interpretive success can be supplied in the synthesizer–human conversation environment. If it can, then the synthesizer would no longer be working by feedback-deprived 'dead reckoning', but would immediately acquire a human ability so far not simulated in synthesizers: awareness of the perceptual success of what is being spoken—awareness via some means of feedback which in turn triggers an iterative process of increasing 'clarity' or optimization of what is being said. Optimization does not necessarily imply increased precision, simply an improved ability to do the job in hand.

We know of no synthesis system which regularly takes into account the degree to which the goal of communication—creating a particular percept in the listener—is successful (but see Chapter 15). Current synthesizers have one input—the utterance plan—but human speakers have an utterance plan *and* listener feedback. Absence of listener feedback causes an uncomfortable feeling sometimes in the speaker. In a dialogue environment, for example, the human being is talking to a computer which, with the currently available technology, is hardly likely to provide adequate feedback to minimize human unease about communicative success.

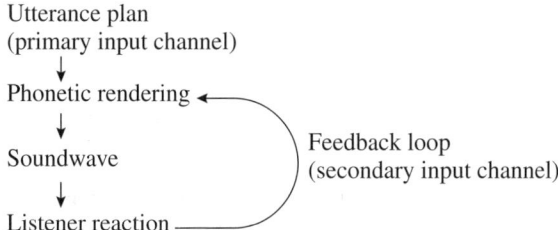

The theory of production-for-perception suggests an always-on iterative loop by which a speaker is constantly receiving feedback as to the success of the communicative events or speech being generated. The diagram illustrates this. This enables a speaker constantly to adjust certain communicative parameters (only one of which is the soundwave—others might be eye contact, hand gesture, etc.) to optimize the communicative goal: the creation of a particular percept in the mind of the listener.

In the production-for-perception literature the focus is on the basic 'linguistic' aspects of speech production and perception; but we are proposing here an extension to this idea into expression. In our cognitive phonetics paradigm, the rendering of the speech plan is under constant supervision (Tatham and Morton 2003). Part of the information available to the supervisory agent within the model is feedback which derives from listener reaction to what is being said. We have distinguished several levels of feedback: long-, mid-, and short-term and modelled these as global and local supervisory effects, but only tentatively extended the feedback model to include expressive content. But we can extend the model here by beginning to ask the question: What does the supervisor have at its disposal?

If we regard the supervisor's task as management of rendering, then, besides a copy of the utterance plan, this agent must also know the details of how rendering takes place to be able to predict the outcome of rendering the plan. But in addition to this, optimal supervision will depend on being able to predict how the rendered version of the plan—the acoustic signal—will succeed in its task of creating the appropriate perceptions, and for this purpose a predictive model of listener perception will be necessary. This perceptual model must be a generalization able to cope with the basic perceptual properties attributable to any listener, with ad hoc feedback giving the details of any particular listener properties. Listing these necessities, we get need to provide the speaker supervisor with at least:

- a copy of the utterance plan [static information source];
- a model of the rendering process [static information source];
- a general model of listener perception [static information source];
- feedback from the current listener about any problems, or general success or failure of the communicative goal of creating appropriate percepts in the listener [dynamic information stream];
- a means to interpret dynamic listener feedback stream [dynamic feedback interpreter];
- a means to act on interpreted feedback and appropriately modify production control—interfering with the rendering process [dynamic control ability].

We feel that a synthesis system with supervision would need to have access to these sources of information as well as to the control system for producing speech. Supervision is a method for optimizing speech production, whether in the human being or in a synthesis system (other words spring to mind: fine tuning, emphasizing, etc.). The process, whatever it is called, presupposes a basic specification for an utterance which is to undergo supervised rendering or revised rendering: this is the 'utterance plan'.

We suggest that to achieve movement forward in speech synthesis theory and practice, a means must be developed of making the synthesis system aware of faults in the delivery of expressive speech, leading to choosing and maintaining the best style for the situation. If we go down this route we are saying that the supervisor's domain extends beyond the sphere of just managing the rendering of the plan. The role of supervisor would be extended to one of *mediator* between listener and planner.

One major investigation for research in the future is whether the supervisory agent is capable, in the longer term, of changing the utterance plan itself. That is, does the supervisory domain extend to the high-level plan generator, or is the domain restricted to a lower-level managerial role? In linguistic terms this translates to whether processes or methods within phonetic rendering have access rights to phonological primes and processes. Our intuition is to answer yes to this question, in the belief that phonetic rendering is a far more active and complex set of methods over a more extensive domain than had previously been thought; that domain extends to utterance planning and to the supervision of expressive content. Investigating what it means for a human being to use expressive speech and to attempt to simulate this using synthetic speech in a true dialogue environment is beginning, for us, to prompt a fundamental re-evaluation of what might actually be involved. But this is for the future, and there are gaps to be filled in our current thinking before we proceed.

8.5 Contemporary changes of approach to speech

This section examines some new approaches and estimates their chances of success. A good example is the relatively new idea that speakers are subconsciously much more aware of their listeners' strategies for extracting meaning from the speech signal than had previously been thought. An important question here is whether we might be able to detect in the acoustic signal any subtleties of production which might reveal a strategy on the part of the speaker to pre-empt listener difficulties. In expressive speech studies research on the acoustic signal has strictly followed the acoustic correlates paradigm, in which features of the acoustic signal are assumed to have a largely linear relationship with an underlying expression or emotion, etc. in the speaker. But it is almost certainly the case that the acoustic correlates paradigm is flawed in detail. The relationship is clearly non-linear, in the sense that there is a systematic variability in the acoustic signal which relates to aspects of the 'expressive environment' which have not hitherto been investigated in depth. The acoustic correlates of expression vary no less than do the acoustic correlates of segmental and suprasegmental features.

With segmental features we have long recognized that the phonetic environment creates a systematic variability in the output—this is coarticulation, and the variability is characterized symbolically in the theory in terms of strings of intrinsic allophones. This variability is distinct from the underlying variability of *extrinsic* allophones, which derives from systematic contextual variation (assimilation) introduced by phonological processes. It is not difficult to show that segmental and suprasegmental features are varied, particularly in terms of the precision with which they are rendered, in a way dependent on the speaker's judgement of perceptual ambiguity. This idea was originally developed systematically in the models associated with the theory of cognitive phonetics (Tatham 1986a,b; Morton 1986). The same is true also of prosodic features. And it may be true also of expressive features.

Controlled and principled variability among acoustic expressive features—even when the underlying planned (consciously or subconsciously) expression has minimal variation—is to be expected, and might contribute toward the wide variability and sometimes contradiction found by researchers seeking a 'constant' set of acoustic features to relate to defined expressions or emotions. What is needed here is an analysis of the variability to see when it is systematic and, when it is, to explain it in terms of speaker sensitivity to perception. This work has yet to be done, but when it is it will mean that the variations in the acoustic correlates of this or that underlying expression will be mapped in such a way that they can be used to inject a further level of naturalness into synthetic speech. This line of research promises to improve synthetic speech considerably.

8.6 Providing the synthesizer with listener feedback

There is no major discussion in the published synthesis literature of production-for-perception or of feedback channels conveying listener reaction, though it is mentioned in connection with the high-level synthesis model (Tatham and Morton 1995). However it is clear that speakers do adjust their utterances to take account of two perceiver-oriented sources of information:

- a predictive model of what the perceiver will do (internal origin: the speaker's mind; timing: pre-acoustic signal);
- listener response via a feedback-sensitive mechanism for adjusting future speech in line with detected perceiver reaction to the current acoustic signal (external origin: the listener; timing: post-acoustic signal).

These channels of feedback—one internally generated and the other sourced externally—potentially have some effect on the speaker, either on the utterance plan or on the way it is rendered. It is therefore reasonable to suppose that a speech synthesis system would be deficient if it did not take account of such feedback. It is difficult to imagine a text-to-speech system modifying its utterance plan, since in most circumstances the text is a given, say in situations like reading email or some similar text out aloud. But in those situations where text is being generated on the fly, say as an interim stage in a dialogue system, or where concept-to-speech synthesis is in use, the text to be spoken could be modified according to listener perception or according to some internal model of perception. In any system, listener or internally sourced feedback could be made to adjust plan rendering.

An example of the kind of rule which might be brought into play would be something like: 'The listener is having difficulty with the technical words in this sequence of utterances, so these should be spoken with greater precision and at a slower rate than other parts of the utterance', or in pseudo-code:

```
var
listener_difficulty: range [1 - 9];
articulatory_precision: range [1 - 9];
current_word.technical_difficulty: range [1 - 9];
{
  begin
    while listener_difficulty > 7 and (if
    current_word.technical_difficulty > 4) do
    begin
      articulatory_precision = 8;
      next_word = current_word;
    end;
  end;
}
```

It is not difficult to imagine that the perceived listener difficulty could be analysed in terms of linguistic problems (phonological, syntactic, or semantic ambiguity, for example, including 'unknown lexical subset') or sociological/psychological problems ('Listener is not a native speaker, does not have the necessary background education, is not bright enough'), or even environmental ('too much ambient noise').

Some contemporary thinking about the production-for-perception concept includes the notion that there is collaboration between speaker and listener to produce the desired goal: perception. It is well known that a speaker can and does adjust their speech (usually in terms of precision of articulation, rate of delivery, and rhythmic distortion: Tatham and Morton 2002) to assist the listener's task. The degree of assistance varies—there is a principle at work: assist no more than is judged to be necessary, the judgement resting with the speaker. Thus, for example, under conditions of high ambient noise a speaker will tend to speak louder, more slowly, and with greater articulatory precision (a tendency to rein in the extremes of coarticulation). This phenomenon was discussed by Tatham (1971) and made central to the theory of cognitive phonetics (Tatham 1990).

On the assumption that something of the same phenomenon might be occurring with expressiveness in speech, we might hypothesize that a speaker is sensitive to a listener's strategies and, under certain circumstances, will acoustically encode expressiveness in different ways. The idea carries across to speech synthesis.

The first major problem here is the probability that we will not find an invariant acoustic correlate of a particular mode of expression or of a particular emotion. The descriptive label we have may be invariant, for example 'angry', but its acoustic rendering will depend not only on normal variability but also, perhaps, on how much the speaker feels the need to firm up their rendering for the listener, given the particular communicative environment (for example the rule in the fragment of pseudo-code above). Since no synthesis system at the present time goes beyond a very rudimentary attempt to model the perceptual effects of utterance rendering, it may well be the case that any attempt to incorporate perceptual feedback-driven adjustments will result in some improvements in naturalness. Refining such a model will not be easy—if only because of the difficulty of obtaining supporting data—but there is no doubt that synthesis models are defective in this area. The variability would be the same kind of variability as is introduced at the segmental level already, for example in coarticulatory contexts, except that it would extend also to variability of the prosodic structure of the utterance—and this is where expressiveness comes in to refine the rule given above.

Experiments to determine whether there is a production-for-perception factor in prosodics or in the expressiveness carried by the prosodics will have to sort out, as did the corresponding experiments at the segmental level, which types of variability are optional and which might be feedback-dependent. It will be necessary to design the experiments very carefully, and there are bound to be difficulties in gathering the data.

We discuss the arguments for and against different approaches to data gathering in Chapter 10, but we need not just enough data to make correlations between, say, an emotion of happiness felt by the speaker and the expressive content of the acoustic signal, but enough to analyse the variability of the acoustic signal in terms of these differing types. At the least significant level will be the involuntary variability due to 'jitter' in the system—the failure of human, mechanical, and other systems to replicates events precisely even when called for. And at the highest significant level will be those variations introduced because of the perceiver-sourced feedback we have introduced into the model.

But, as we saw earlier, there are two channels for listener influence on speech production. One derives from a generalized model the speaker already has of perception, and this one will still operate under the experimental conditions described, even if the removal of the listener takes away the other influence, direct feedback of an actual listener's performance.

There is, then, a major problem in data collection, perhaps unforeseen in early attempts to gather data to discover the acoustic correlates of expression (Murray and Arnott 1993). Even later researchers do not mention the problem, though all use their data as though it were representative of emotive speech, lessened only by problems of stylization and hypercorrection.

Our suggestion is to define the parameters of expressiveness and establish a vector for each of the parameters, along which will fall some score on any particular occasion. If the data is somehow of the 'citation' type, then parameter values will still fall on the vectors in question, though perhaps not in the same range as with more natural conversational speech. We would seek to establish the parameters and their values, or ranges of values, first. Then, looking at one or two different 'artificial' utterances—citation form, read speech, newsreader speech, etc.—establish points on these vectors. Although casual, natural speech doing exactly what we want it to is difficult to gather in large quantities, we can nevertheless enter scant data within the ranges defined by the vectors we have established from the earlier less natural data. This suggested approach goes some way to allowing for the pitfalls of using acted speech or citation forms.

8.7 Some production-for-perception considerations with expressive speech

To summarize the production-for-perception position: a speaker knows how they feel and knows how to convey their feelings; and the speaker also knows, or can model, how the listener will deal with reconstructing the impression of that feeling. The listener can correct any error the speaker may produce, in part because the listener is a speaker. Being a speaker means 'can model how speakers plan and render'; so listener and speaker are in this way collaborating in achieving a communicative goal—they collaborate by anticipating the other's processes. In this sense we can say that listeners are also taking account of speaker constraints, just as speakers are taking account of listener constraints. The communicative goal in this case is the conveying by speaker to listener of the speaker's feelings, as encoded by the expressive content on the acoustic signal. Following our earlier comments, it goes without saying that the speaker may be completely unaware that their feelings are being communicated.

A question here to ask of the psychology literature is: When a listener perceives a speaker's expression or emotion, does the listener themself feel that emotion? In other words, does the listener simply label the speech as having a particular expressive content, or does the listener share the expression or emotion? And would this depend on the semantic (or other) context?

We term this phenomenon 'expression induction'. Expression induction is about to what extent the speaker's feeling is induced in the listener. This is not really the kind of question we can address here; we bring it up simply to underline the complexity of the processes involved, and the variety of situational and other contexts in which expression can occur for both speaker and listener.

Part III

Expression and Emotion: The Research

Chapter 9

The Biology and Psychology Perspectives

In comparing human speech production with synthesis voice output, we can ask: what do speakers do that machines do not do? We can see that current speech synthesis systems lack several features that are basic to human communication:

- Sensitivity to the listener's perception. Speakers are aware of the effect of their utterances on a listener. Current voice output systems lack a means of feedback as to how the message is being interpreted.
- Appropriate emotive content. Much of daily speech is about our feelings and beliefs, conveying by tone of voice the views that cannot easily be transmitted by the plain message. Employing emotive content associated with the plain message can convey this information, and can trigger an attitude or feeling the synthesis system wishes to encourage the user to have.
- Precise use of language. Researchers still need to determine the extent to which the choice of words and syntactic constructions interact together with tone of voice in synthetic speech. For example, speakers can say *I am happy* with an intonation that normally triggers sadness. In this case the emotional tone detected may be interpreted as sardonic, or simply generate confusion if inappropriately used.

9.1 Finding expressive content in speech

Since the goal for synthesis is to build a simulation of expression that is accepted by the listener on an equivalent basis as human speech, we need to be clear about what it is that is being simulated. Do we aim to replicate human speech acoustic features, without looking at the expression source? Or might we look at what humans do that can result in emotive effects and model the source, for a clue as to what to look for in the waveform? We, along with some other researchers, pick the latter, and choose to look at what human speakers do to produce speech judged to have emotive content.

We can also increase our understanding of how language works. For example, by carefully selecting the words in a dialogue system and observing the interactions with the acoustic characteristics of the waveform, we may be able to synthesize a few 'basic' emotions and modify them with the appropriate choice of word. Thus it might be possible to synthesize an overall general emotion 'happy', but use words in the text to augment or diminish the effect of the basic synthesized happiness effect, such as *Well done!* to a learner, to provide encouragement with happiness emotive overtones, or *OK* to tone down a general effect of happy to create the impression of acceptance.

9.2 Is there a basis for modelling human expression?

In this book, we review work by researchers using synthesis to replicate a speech waveform judged to contain 'expressive content'. We also propose an alternative but quite generalized way of dealing with the emotion effects in speech. The approach requires modelling a biological base subserving variable cognitive intervention to produce emotive speech content.

Taking the view that understanding models of human expression production would enable researchers to find information in human speech as to what constitutes emotive content, we looked at some of the biological and cognitive models proposed to account for emotion. The obstacle, however, is clear: it is extremely difficult for researchers outside studies of biological and cognitive function to obtain a reasonable grounding in these fields. We addressed this difficulty by reading in a relatively narrow area, and were selective in what seems useful for our purposes only: emotive content in speech.

Biology and Psychology 169

We have looked at research we believe has produced models which are simple, coherent, internally consistent, and computationally adequate. We outline a computationally adequate model incorporating what we understand as expression and emotive content for speech synthesis. However, we do not see our suggested models dealing with emotive content and expressive content in speech as contributing to biological and cognitive research; the following sections present an overview *for speech*, and are not a critical commentary.

9.3 Emotion: what is it?

Emotion is a concept that has proved difficult to define, but one idea is fairly widespread: it can be seen as a topic that requires different levels of analysis (e.g. Tomkins 1962; Panksepp 1991; Lazarus 1991; Leventhal and Patrick-Miller 1993; Scherer 1993; Solomon 1993; Averill 1994; Clore 1994a; Ekman and Davidson 1994; Plutchik 1994; Harré and Parrott 1996; Strongman 1996; Oatley and Johnson-Laird 1998; Bechtel and Mundale 1999; Dalgleish and Power 1999; Ekman 1999; Gainotti 2000; Johnstone and Scherer 2000; LeDoux 2000; Deigh 2001; Ochsner and Barrett 2001). These different levels of analysis, correspondingly studied from different points of view, range from essentially biological reactions (e.g. Pribham 1980; Panksepp 1994; Rolls 1999; Adolphs and Damasio 2000; LeDoux 2000) through to interpretive conventions with little or no biological contribution (e.g. Zajonc 1980; Ortony et al. 1988; Izard 1993; Averill 1994; Lazarus 2001). At points between these two polarizations there are studies which include both biological and cognitive contributions to the experience of emotion, or which proceed from a biological base with cognitive interpretation (e.g. Borod 1993; Davidson 1993a; Frijda 1993; Mandler 1999; Adolphs and Damasio 2000; Clore and Ortony 2000; Lane et al. 2000; LeDoux and Phelps 2000; Johnstone et al. 2001).

Panksepp (1991: 60) at the beginning of the 'decade of the brain' (the 1990s) states the problem: 'the concept of emotion is notoriously hard to define in scientifically useful ways, and it is difficult to extract empirically useful and conceptually consistent guidelines from the vast array of existing perspectives.' And at the end of that decade, the difficulties continued in developing concisely stated models based on accepted principles which could give rise to testable model-derived hypotheses and to useful agreed methods for collecting reliable data. The problem of defining the term 'emotion' and the phenomenon it represents is reiterated at the beginning of the current decade: Ochsner and Barrett (2001: 39) state the problem as a question: 'Are emotions the product of complex cognitive appraisals, or are they the product of simple programs embedded in our genes and brains?'

The question is about defining emotion states as sourced by biological or cognitive processes, or as the result of non-conscious automatic processes interacting with intended and conscious processes. During this time, researchers in speech have become aware of expressive content as a major factor in judging synthetic speech as sounding more human-like, but our characterizing human expressive speech in terms of a set of measurable acoustic features has not been particularly successful. One major obstacle has been the difficulty in reading the appropriate research literature in physiology, cognition, and bio-psychology, since most of the speech researchers have a background in linguistics, psycholinguistics, phonetics, or software engineering.

The difficulty for non-specialists who feel the need for models from physiology and cognition studies, as well as from linguistics and studies in cultural modification of behaviour, is stated by Dalgleish and Power (1999: 779): 'Cognition–emotion relations are conceptualised at a number of levels of analysis: the neurobiological, the functional, the social and the cultural.' The need for detailed theoretical models of emotive human behaviour has been recognized for over a century, and researchers have directed their attention to various aspects of the study of emotion and expression. These proposals range from early work by Darwin (1872), James (1884), and Wundt (1902) to recent modelling such as Hebb (1946), Frijda (1986), Lazarus (1991), Johnson-Laird and Oatley (1992), Goldsmith (1993), Leventhal and Patrick-Miller (1993), Solomon (1993), Averill (1994), Strongman (1996),

Panksepp (1998), Ekman (1999), Lazarus (1999), Rolls (1999), Gainotti (2000), Johnstone and Scherer (2000), LeDoux (2000), and Ochsner and Barrett (2001).

The main difficulty seems to centre around a definition and classification of significant physiological and cognitive features which can precede model building and theory construction. Psychologists and biologists do not agree on a suitable classification of emotion; linguists and phoneticians have rarely looked at models of expression in natural language production suitable for their purposes. But a specification of expression and emotion is needed by speech researchers who are looking for the appearance of acoustic features in the waveform that obviously relate to expressive and emotive content. We need models that will provide sufficient detail so that expressive speech systems can be built that will automatically generate the appropriate waveform.

Since the waveform is the result of speech production, we reference here some texts which discuss the speech process. Simply stated, we produce speech by manipulating the aerodynamics of the moving vocal tract (Borden et al. 1994), thus producing an audible speech waveform (Ladefoged 1996). Patterns for movement of the articulators are well described in the articulatory phonetics literature. Most of these descriptions characterize non-expressive speech; expressive content in speech is often considered separately, and is thought of as either intended—that is, the speaker wants to produce a particular effect—or unintended. In this latter case, the speaker produces a waveform that is the result of physiological constraints on the vocal tract configuration. Within limits, these constraints can be manipulated under cognitive control.

For example, when speaking fast, the tongue cannot move throughout its whole range, and the intention to say the /t/ in *mists* is for some speakers of English barely or even not realized. There are many examples of varying degrees of precision in articulation under various conditions. One of these conditions is obvious to listeners—speech in an emotive mode: angry, frightened, or perplexed speakers produce a tone of voice which conveys information to the listener, instantly recognized from their speech characteristics.

A basic assumption in linguistics is that language output is a cognitive event, and therefore intended. Linguistics proper describes the resulting output, either written or spoken. The internal patterns of language units, the construction of language, and the relation among the major components of semantics, syntax, and phonology are described in formal and explicit terms (Chomsky 1965; Aitchison 1998; Jackendoff 2002). In spoken language, properties of the physical system produce characteristic effects which can be correlated with acoustic features in the waveform. The assumption we make is that emotion can modify acoustic features because emotion has effects on the physiological and cognitive properties of the speaker; we also assume the listener can recognize these acoustic features and make some inferences about the emotion state of the speaker.

9.4 The source of emotive content

Among specialist researchers in emotion, there are many different perspectives. Ideally, we would have an object, 'emotion', clearly defined, and then try to account for how it could be recognized and produced. In the case of emotion, although the concept has not been sufficiently defined for our purposes, we can look at how emotion might arise. We shall outline some of the ways this concept has been characterized. We regard emotion as a construct referring to a subjective experience about which the individual may be either aware or unaware. That is, although the expression of emotion can be observed, the experience of emotion is within the individual. Consequently, the research we find most useful can be broadly grouped according to three models of the source of emotion: physiological, cognitive, and a bio-psychological linkage. The latter consists of a basic biological setting, with cognitive interpretation or intervention; this research considers both physiological and cognitive activity as essential for emotion.

9.5 Production of emotion: biological accounts

We begin with an outline of biological sourcing of emotion states described from a perspective that lends itself to computational modelling.

Isolating and stating specific physiological descriptors associated with emotion has not been done on a large enough scale to detail fully all specific structures, their interrelation, and associated invariant predictable functions (LeDoux 1996). But a sufficiently good description of some neurological systems has been proposed; they are structurally dissimilar, and promote different functions that are central to a biological account of emotion states (e.g. MacLean 1990; Levenson 1992; Ekman and Davidson 1994; LeDoux 1996; Panksepp 1994; 1998).

One well-documented approach to the biological basis of emotion has been to disentangle the neural circuitry which appears to mediate emotion behaviour, and leave open the question as to how much cognitive intervention there might be at some stage in the reaction and subsequent observed response of the animal or human to changes in the environment. The outcome of this research is a proposal for a basis for a biological substrate (Panksepp 1998). Panksepp has noted that at the most basic physiological level, four different coherent neurological systems operate in situations identifiable as associated with the foundations of animal and human emotional response. These reaction states are labelled: 'fear, rage, seeking, and panic/distress'. These four emotion states have been reported by human subjects and also have been associated with animal response. The four groupings are described here, since we find this approach useful for our particular model of expression-based speech production incorporating emotion states. The following points paraphrase Panksepp:

- Neural circuits which energize the body to seek, claim, and defend territory are associated with anger. The organism is geared to be aggressive in seeking food, a mate, and territory. If unsuccessful, it will react with anger and/or frustration.

Behavioural changes in animals can be correlated with reports using 'anger' words by humans.
- A different set of circuitry will enable an animal to flee or to freeze under conditions of external threat if the animal cannot fight back. The reaction of fear is a protective device enabling a chance of survival by running away or not moving. These circuits are activated when anger is not appropriate. Words associated with fear and anxiety, 'nervous' or 'frightened', are used by speakers. What determines whether fear or anger will prevail appears not to be known. In fact, the activation could be characterized as a 'decision' taken by the organism. But it is difficult to predict what such a decision might be, since environmental conditions vary from event to event for the same organism, and different decisions appear to have been made within a given population in what might be seen as similar environments.
- Making a decision implies cognitive activity, since the choice of fear or anger response does not fit into the commonly agreed reflex response. (Note that a reflex response involves the spinal connection only, whereas an automatic response includes rapid reaction which involves brain centres: Toates 2001). However, to what extent a cognitive decision is involved, what parts of the brain may co-relate with this decision, and how the neural circuitry may be interlinked is not clear.
- A third set of reactions occurs if an animal or human is lonely or separated from its kind. Sorrow and sadness are associated with this activity, and are manifest by inactivity, whining noises, or slow purposeless activity. This behaviour is different from the unmoving posture if the organism is frightened. Reports by human subjects consist of 'sad' words.
- A fourth set of circuits is activated when there is no threat to the organism, or there appears to be no obvious loss of something important in the environment. In addition, caring for the young, or for a mate, lust and play, reported as 'happiness' or 'love' by humans, result from activity in this system.

Later work by Panksepp (2000) addresses the question of emotion states and possible cognitive activity.

9.5.1 Broader issues and the complexity of physiological systems

Rolls (1999) queries the term 'cognitive element'. In this researcher's view, activity is based on a complex system of learned responses and feedback from behaviour. For example, certain tastes can be assumed to be experienced, but with little or no cognitive intervention except for the acceptance or not of these tastes. The response of the animal can be to eat or not eat: it is not necessary to characterize the behaviour as a result of a decision process. The biological explanation adequately accounts for such behaviour. For a detailed description of a current way of modelling brain structure and function, see Rolls and Treves (1998).

Davidson (1993b: 143) describes cortical function in emotion behaviour; and later Davidson and Henriques (2000: 269) distinguish between 'the perception of emotional information' and 'the production of emotion'. They investigate whether the localization hypothesis provides a plausible framework for associating emotional state with regional brain activity.

Borod et al. (2000) report a componential approach to emotion processing involving posed and spontaneous expression, perception, and experience across facial, prosodic, and lexical channels. The componential biological approach may be compared with the cognitive approach across components (e.g. Frijda 2000; Johnstone and Scherer 2000). Borod (1993) also looks at common cerebral mechanisms for physical (facial) and prosodic expression.

Even when the physiological correlates can be modelled, it is not possible to say that cognitive activity can always be related to specific physiological activity. For example, many brain circuits may be involved in a single activity: MRI (magnetic resonance imaging) scans, along with other investigative procedures, do not necessarily reveal the neural origin of an action, but may show up a collection point for activity that originated elsewhere (George et al. 2000). Other physiological signs such as blood pressure readings and heart rate do not always positively correlate with reported or observed putative emotive events (Toates 2001). Cacioppo et al. (2000) discuss somatovisceral afference in emotion: a pattern of somatovisceral activity can be associated with more than one designated emotion, and different patterns of activity can be associated with the same designated emotion. Biunique mapping seems to be out of the question as yet in associating biological reactions and particular emotions, as described. See also Schumann (1999) and Sedikides (2001), who discuss the principle of mapping between biological reactions and emotions and evaluate the effectiveness of current techniques.

Other researchers have sought to postulate biological reaction as an underpinning for essentially cognitive characterizations of human activity (Treves and Samengo 2002). Adolphs and Damasio (2000: 195) propose that an emotion 'comprises a collective change in body and brain states in response to the evaluation of a particular event'. The state changes result in detectable changes in physiological function, and in the way the brain processes information. Gainotti (2000) focuses on subcortical structures that underlie both emotion and cognition, thus suggesting a model which relies on low-level activity for both cognition and emotion and links them through similar structures.

9.5.2 Cognitive activity which recognizes a biological substrate

If there is plausible evidence for the neural circuitry and its response to the change in the environment, are there also plausible cognitive models to account for the processing resulting in modification of these responses? Among the cognitive models proposed, we have selected those which would appear to be most useful to consider as a basis for computational modelling.

Some researchers agree that emotion is primarily cognitive in function, although they recognize that emotion states arise initially from biologically based activity: 'An emotion is one of a large set of differentiated biologically based complex conditions that are about something' (Clore and Ortony 2000: 24). Central to this particular cognitive approach, which recognizes the biological bases for detecting and physiologically reacting to a change in the environment, is separation of (a) the signal that might have emotional impact on the organism and (b) its significance to the individual. This approach, which distinguishes between the *stimulus* which may trigger a response and the *meaning* that stimulus might have, is not fundamental to all cognitive models.

Clore and Ortony (2000: 55) comment: 'The cognitive view maintains only that the trigger for emotional processes lies in the representation of the significance of a stimulus rather than in the stimulus itself.' In addition to the significance attached to the signal, there is also the possibility that the response itself, detected by the individual, might also have significance. If one function of emotion is to provide information, this might be relevant. For example, Niedenthal et al. (1999) discuss categorizing events by use of emotional response. This may be of especial interest to speech researchers when trying to determine what acoustic stimuli could function as a category probe: what acoustic features could be employed by listeners recruiting emotion responses to new situations.

Thus there are four components mentioned so far: the stimulus, the potential reaction, the possible significance of the stimulus, and the potential significance of the response itself. Paraphrasing Leventhal and Scherer (1987), perhaps the following statement sums it up for the purpose of speech researchers: 'emotions develop from simple reactions to more complex ones involving cognitive modification by means of experience and ability to access memory and perform cognitive processing.'

9.6 Production of emotion: cognitive accounts, with little or no biological substrate

Precise characterization of a totally cognitive, non-physiological, component of emotion is a minority view. Many researchers, however, do consider that emotion can be modelled as a separate subjective experience, and build cognitive models based on inferences about processing characteristics of emotion. These processes do not draw on descriptions of physical activity. In an earlier work Ortony et al. (1988: 14) state:

> there are four main kinds of evidence about the emotions: language, self reports, behaviour and physiology. The latter two kinds of evidence concern the consequences or concomitants of emotional states, but not

their origins, which we think are based upon the cognitive construal of events. For this reason we largely ignore behavioural and physiological evidence, focusing instead on language and self reports.

Thus it is useful for speech research to distinguish between cognitive models that address emotion associated with *cognitive* processes, and research that acknowledges an association with physiological *effect*. Additionally, cognitive processes may be interpretive or they may be modelled as themselves giving rise to the emotions.

9.6.1 Defining cognitive processing

Is it possible to determine what 'cognitive processing' is taken to mean? Recognition of sensory processing as having a cognitive element via perception of events implies some cognitive contribution to a potential emotion state (Ekman and Davidson 1994). On the other hand, as a result of external events in the environment, active cognition may play no part in the recognition of emotion but be the result of social conditioning (Frijda 2000). 'Cognitive' may, for some researchers, also refer simply to all that is not physiological processing.

The relation between cognition and emotion can be modelled in two quite separate ways; emotions and cognition can be considered separate functions, operating independently of each other (Zajonc 1980; 1989). Lazarus, on the other hand (1992), argues that cognitive processing is required before an emotion occurs. In this case, emotion is a function of the particular cognitive processing that takes place, however it may arise.

Clore et al. (1987) take a different approach: the task is to describe a relationship between the emotion, the situation that provided the stimulus, and how the individual construes these situations. They formulate a set of descriptive rules with a view to characterizing the emotions on the basis of different cognitive processes which could be hypothesized to underlie different emotions. The rules are couched as IF–THEN conditions, thus specifying the environment within which labelled emotions might occur. Intensity variables were seen to influence emotions in a patterned way. Speech researchers might find this approach quite useful, since a systems description is presented in computational terms, a familiar method.

If emotion cannot be defined easily and unambiguously, can the types of emotion be simply recognized and classified? Ekman (1992) points out the fundamental problem is that basic emotions have been described variously as separate, discrete, or differing in type of expression, manner, intensity, judgement as to importance to the individual (paraphrase of p. 170). Or basic emotions are considered discrete but differ in only one or two dimensions, or they differ in terms of positive/negative state. Ekman himself rejects the positive/negative distinction as a basis for classification and presents a list of features which could be used to characterize emotions (p. 175). The suggestion for a distinctive feature classification system is familiar to many speech researchers, and although the article was written in the early 1990s the outline presented may be helpful in understanding the classification approach.

9.6.2 Is cognition essential?

Most researchers (e.g. Ekman and Davidson 1994: 234) acknowledge that emotion can occur without the individual being aware of cognitive mediation. And many would agree that some cognitive processing is, in fact, required for most emotion. Not all conditions described as emotion, though, are uppermost in the awareness of the individual. In human activity, identification of emotion is usually on the basis of reporting. Although some notice may be taken of physiological changes such as increased heart rate, or behavioural changes such as becoming quiet or aggressive, the individual may be unaware of being in a state of emotion and hence unable to report directly: 'emotions are inferred constructs' (Lewis 1993: 223). Lewis goes on to point out that 'emotional states can occur without the organism's being able to perceive these states'. But the effect of being in a particular state may be observed by others, and may be detectable in the physiological settings of the individual.

Another approach is to regard emotions as the *result* of cognitive activity, not the activity itself: '*if* an individual conceptualises an emotion in a certain kind of way, *then* the potential for a particular type of emotion exists' (Ortony et al. 1988: 2; see also Lazarus 1992). Emotion is a result of cognition, in this view, but it is not clear whether the individual is always aware of cognitive processing.

Fundamental to these models is the hypothesis that the individual identifies discrete emotions in terms of the positive or negative value of the event to the individual (sometimes called 'valence'), and 'dimension', the degree of intensity of the effect.

The appraisal approach has been called 'subjective modelling', though probably it would be better to speak of modelling the subjectivity of appraisal itself: it is the object of the modelling which is subjective, not the models. Appraisal is about the state of the individual, variability of individuals, and both the variability of contexts in which events arise and the variability of the individual's ability to report consistently on their evaluation in terms of how events are thought to be good or bad, advantageous or disadvantageous to the self. Since appraisal depends on reports by subjects, one research task is to determine the reliability of reports by subjects, and to work out the repeatability of the research method. Schorr (2001) discusses some of the points to consider when doing experimental work in this area.

In appraisal theory, the identification of emotions is seen as a function of interpretation and evaluation of events by the individual. There are several points of view within the general approach; Lazarus (2001) suggests a two-stage appraisal process: The primary stage:

> This process has to do with whether or not what is happening is relevant to one's values, goal commitments, beliefs about self and world, and situational intentions, and if so, in what way. (p. 44)

The secondary stage:

> This process focuses on...environment relationship—the coping options, the social and intra-psychic constraints against acting them out, and expectations about the outcomes of that relationship. (p. 45)

The first stage evaluates the information; the second stage accesses ways of dealing with the results of the appraisal. This two-stage model could be of interest to speech researchers, since it provides a base from which choices can be made by the individual as the result of an initial processing in stage 1.

9.6.3 Modelling 'appraisal'

Scherer (2001: 370) defines the objective of appraisal theory: 'The major task of *appraisal theory* is to predict which profiles of appraisal under which circumstances produce such emotion episodes and which type of emotion is likely to occur.' He outlines the framework of appraisal modelling which begins with information from an incoming event. This is initially processed by an individual. The result is evaluated for its significance for that individual. It is the evaluation *process* which is termed 'appraisal'. The appraisal process is carried out by applying criteria which are concerned with the *needs* and *values* of the individual. The actual process can be conscious or non-conscious. Zajonc (1980) identified the possibility of non-conscious emotions and later proposed separating emotion states from cognitive activity. Johnstone et al. (2001) state that the criteria can be described in dimensional terms such as activation/intensity, valence/quality.

Judging whether an event is of benefit or is harmful to the individual before responding to the event is central to appraisal theory. Whether to ignore an event, be angry, attack, or flee, or any one of many responses, implies choice and decision. This type of activity can be regarded as cognitive-sourced, without mention of possible physiological correlates. It involves assessing and evaluating the change in the environment and making choices as to subsequent action.

Johnstone et al. (2001: 271) point out the need for 'solid theoretical underpinning for the assumption that different emotions are expressed through specific voice patterns'. They go on to outline a model which proposes that the results of appraisal produce physical changes which can be associated with changes in the speech waveform. Tatham and Morton (2003) also posit a relation between physical changes and varying speech waveforms (quite independently). We generalize further to say that the resultant physiological stance produces a corresponding vocal tract configuration which will constantly change throughout expression. These changes are hypothesized to be associated with acoustic features identifiable in the waveform. We extend this to say that expression can be both cognitively and biologically sourced for each waveform. We also agree that the lack of solid theoretical underpinning constrains research when interpreting experimental results.

Johnstone et al. (2001) further suggest that appraisal affects the physical *system:* they posit a set of conditions on the appraisal process, with varying values resulting in varying appraisals. To paraphrase p. 285: the effects on the production of a speech waveform will result from appraisal processes acting on the physiological mechanism—after having taken into account regulation of emotion responses constrained by interaction of the individual in the social/cultural context.

From a different point of view, Oatley and Johnson-Laird (1998) propose a theory whose objective is to integrate the biological approach with features of cognitive activity such as attention, readiness to act, memory access, problem-solving ability, and goal management. They suggest that emotions arise after evaluations of events are made, related to perceived goals. The purpose of emotion is to communicate, to provide information to others about ourselves, but also to give information to oneself, which can contribute to, for example, deciding on the best course of action in the perceived circumstances. Their Communicative Theory is a dynamic model which accounts for changing emotions via a process of secondary evaluation of events, allowing for a monitoring of changing events.

A feature of computational modelling is the capability to predict fully and explicitly. Wehrle and Scherer (2001) describe a computational approach involving appraisal—the aim is to suggest a more formal way of differentiating reported emotion. This implementation includes prediction of emotion as the outcome of the computational model. More success was reported in working with facial expression than in assignment of emotion word labels. However, this is a systematic rule-governed approach which might be very useful in the future. It may benefit from a formal parametric characterization of emotion which could perhaps then be linked with speech waveform parameters.

For a brief history of the appraisal approach and development of cognitive theories of emotion, see Lazarus (1999). For a discussion of the development of appraisal theory, see Scherer (1999). Since appraisal is seen as a major component of many cognitive models, speech researchers may find an understanding of the principles of appraisal and evaluation useful.

9.7 Production of emotion: linking the biological and cognitive approaches

The previous sections on biological and cognitive modelling have taken the line that the two areas approach the study of human activity from quite different perspectives. However, there are researchers who have discussed the possibility of closely linking the two—an approach which could strengthen the concept that appraisal processes directly influence the physiological correlates of an emotional state.

A demarcation between the areas of study, physical and cognitive, has been a research position considered by many as basic and reasonable in the study of the human being (Descartes 1649). The dualist approach, the recognition of two separate areas, has been variously and commonly labelled 'mind/brain distinction', 'mind/body separation', 'physiological/cognitive differences', and so forth—although functioning within one unit, the individual. Damasio (1994: 222), for example, states: 'Body and brain are usually conceptualised as separate, in structure and function.' *But externally*, 'body proper *and* brain participate in the interaction with the environment.'

Although the status of the two major points of view is different, and the models constitute hypotheses about human activity that can be built in two ways it is recognized that at some point it would be desirable to map from one model set to the other. And if the concept of dualism is useful in emotion studies, it is possible to ask some questions:

- How are the two levels of physiological reaction and cognitively derived reporting related within one individual?
- How does brain function influence mental processes and overt action?
- What does the phrase 'cognitive intervention' mean? How can it affect brain function?
- How might cognition interpret neurological activity in a meaningful way that is open to study?

Pecchinenda (2001) links the cognitive approach with the physiological models by discussing how appraisal affects both the internal state capable of creating a physiological change *and* movement of the individual in the environment. 'First, appraisal theory outlines the process that leads to specific emotional reactions.' 'Second, appraisal theory posits that physiological activity is determined by the personal meaning ascribed to the situation through the appraisal process' (p. 302). Thus physiological measurements of changes can be hypothesized to be related to a common source. However, as Pecchinenda points out (p. 307), since the neurological systems that mediate behaviour (physical and cognitive) are complex and interconnecting, some caution is perhaps indicted as to strong associations between the result of an appraisal process (a theoretical construct) and identifying what stimuli and what resulting physiological effect there might be (see also Gray 1994).

Another view is to consider that emotion is a cognitive event and exploits the basic neurological circuitry. Evidence for such a connection between cognition and brain is from LeDoux (1996: 289): 'Emotional reactions are typically accompanied by intense cortical arousal.'

He further discusses how emotion relates to the amygdala and its projections to many parts of the cortex (pp. 267–303). During the past thirty years a small brain structure, the hippocampus and the amygdala associated with it, has been studied as a possible structure that may be a way of relating cognitive processes to a neurobiological base (O'Keefe and Nadel 1978;

Wilshaw and Buckingham 1990; LeDoux 1996; Ochsner and Kosslyn 1999).

At the level of the brain-stem, there are systems which 'regulate arousal and alertness according to both internal states and environmental events' (Bloom 1988, quoted in Tucker et al. 2000). Tucker points out that the problem is to explain how the lower levels could 'coordinate with higher cortical systems to control behaviour adaptively' given the following conditions:

- if a vertical model is structurally adequate;
- if a dynamic model of function could describe how fixed-action lower circuits could respond to variations in activity of higher-level circuits;
- if major emotion control circuits can be shown to exist.

It has also been reported that the cerebral cortex plays an important part in certain types of emotion behaviour (e.g. Davidson 1993b). In functional terms this is saying that the cognitive properties (thinking, mental processing) can override the basic biological functions of detecting incoming information and processing it automatically. It is claimed (e.g. Panksepp 1998) that there is some evidence that this is one of the properties of the cortex: it is capable of inhibiting lower-order activity. The implication for a model of emotion is that a cognitive contribution can be either recognition of the physiological effect or suppression of it. In this case there may be a difference in the total body stance between suppression of emotion reaction and a lack of awareness, or a lack of reaction to an external event.

It is useful if the framework for a simple model can be outlined as:

biological_reaction ← cortical_reaction

This describes a connection between cognitive and physiological activity, and implies that cognition can instantiate a neurological effect in the cortex. As a result, if there are processes to the lower brain, activity in the lower brain can be inhibited. Thus the emotion felt and reported may be different under similar external conditions, because the internal conditions vary. The implication for speech research is that expected speech acoustic features can be suppressed, necessitating, for example, the inclusion of very explicit detail for precise dialogue system design, taking adequate account of the environment. However, a thorough going explanation of the relation between cognitive function and the associated underlying neural activity still eludes researchers (Rolls and Treves 1998; Treves and Samengo 2002).

9.7.1 *Collections of disparate brain processes?*

At a different level, even if it is possible to arrive at generally accepted physiologically and cognitively based models of emotion, and to relate cognitive constructs to different brain processes, a serious theoretical problem remains. LeDoux (2000: 129), among others, addresses the question: 'the terms "cognition" and "emotion" do not refer to real functions performed by the brain but instead to collections of disparate brain processes.' Examples are given of terms such as 'visual perception'—which can be described as a set of higher-level processes such as form, colour, and motion, which in turn can be modelled in terms of some underlying physiological and neurological processes across several sites of activity.

Thus emotion in LeDoux's terms can be described as 'made up of a variety of component functions (subjective experience, stimulus evaluation, physiological responses,... and so on)'. He points out the relation between cognition and emotion requires not only definition but a statement as to how the processes underlying these constructs can be related, since these constructs have a different status within the theory. If we really are dealing with 'collections of disparate brain processes', then terms like 'cognition' and 'emotion' are *abstract* labels on these processes. It may or may not be possible to proceed without referring both to the processes themselves and to their labels—in which case it would be necessary to group the processes in a principled way depending on their physical origins or their cognitive origins or both. Bechtel and Mundale (1999) discuss whether and to what extent it is possible to construct a scientifically plausible mapping which can directly relate the organization of brain systems with the organization of cognitive systems as both sets of systems are currently described.

The parallel problem in linguistics is whether or not it is scientifically possible to map phonological processes and objects onto phonetic processes and objects. We address this particular problem when discussing the development of a possible speech production model which might be able to assist in understanding how expressive content becomes embodied in the final acoustic waveform (see Chapter 16).

A major development during the past two or three decades has been the connectionist or artificial neural network (ANN) approaches (McClelland and Rumelhart 1986). The ANN paradigm rests on a formal system explicitly designed to be used in modelling the behaviour of neurons, but which can also be used very successfully to model some types of cognitive processing. Models developed from these two approaches can characterize the biological and the cognitive in similar ways. Direct linear mapping between biology and cognition is still not possible, but understanding their relationship is brought a step closer by relating them via a common mathematics. This is a potentially productive idea, but its application for this unifying purpose so far has been varied, and awaits clear proof of concept.

To paraphrase Schrödinger (1944): it may not be possible adequately to relate these constructs except in simple or directed ways for special purposes. It has been noted by many scientists that there is a problem in identifying physical and cognitive phenomena and mapping from one to the other. The two areas are not regarded as having equal status as objects of scientific enquiry. As Schrödinger says, the focus of the problem is that the mind cannot assess the world picture because 'it is itself that world picture' (p. 128).

9.8 The function of emotion

Clearly, emotion functions as a major integral part of our lives and has relevance to many aspects, such as our perception of current events, anticipated events, consequent decisions, relationships with others, our state of well being, and in general simply permeates how we live. Some major functions of emotion have been suggested:

- Emotions can direct attention to significant events in the environment (Ohman et al. 2001).
- Emotions are a way of relating to the environment, and of detecting change and responding appropriately—'a readiness to act' (Greenberg 1993: 501).
- Emotions arise as a result of determining that certain often novel events are important to the individual. Positive emotions are a result of concluding that the event is a good thing for the individual; negative emotions arise if the event is appraised as harmful. Thus emotion occurs after the event is detected and after an appraisal of whether the effect of the event will help or harm the individual (Frijda 1988).
- Emotions play a role in providing information about internal processing systems, integrating them so that 'both automatic and deliberative processes aim at common goals' (Leventhal 1984).
- Emotions enable the individual to adapt to changes in the environment. Each discrete emotion has a discrete function for adaptation, but there are individual differences in emotion activation (Izard 1992; Scherer 2000).
- Emotion functions as a way of categorizing events according to emotional response. Emotions can provide information both about the external environment and about our individual reactions to changes as they occur (Niedenthal et al. 1999).
- A possible function of emotion is to give information about the extent to which the information processed will be of consequence to the individual. If the incoming information is irrelevant to the individual, no action need be taken. If it is important, some action may be necessary, either internally or by effecting a change within the environment (Roseman and Smith 2001).

Although differing in detail, these characterizations of the function of emotion in human beings treat emotion as an alerting, classifying, identifying, or discriminating stratagem associated with environmental pressures on the individual.

9.9 Parameterization of emotion

Ideally, if all the processes involved in the characterization of emotion could be stated in parametric terms, they could be mapped onto speech characterizations. The reason for this is that speech has already, at two levels, been characterized this way: phonologists use distinctive features (Jakobson et al. 1952; Chomsky and Halle 1968), and classical phoneticians use articulatory features (Cruttenden 2001) to describe speech from an abstract, cognitive viewpoint; they also use acoustic parameters in discussing the acoustic characteristics of speech. The latter form the basis of all parametric synthesis systems. Some approaches to describing emotion have sought to create a set of features by which different emotions could be identified (e.g. Frijda 1986). Leventhal and Patrick-Miller (1993) have a useful discussion of dimensional vs. categorical classification of emotion (see Chapter 7 above, where we discuss the parameterization of expression, and how this can be linked to parameters in speech synthesis).

9.10 Secondary emotions

Emotions have been categorized as 'basic' or 'non-basic'. The non-basic emotions are classified variously as 'blends', 'combinations', 'mixed', or 'secondary'. To paraphrase Lazarus (1991: 59), emotion states may be ranked as dimensions 'on the basis of within-category strength' as, for example, when irritation as a mild anger is different in perceived intensity from rage.

The initial task for research is to identify differing types; researchers have compressed identification of emotion states into a grouping of six to eight basic emotions. But the difficulty is how to characterize what appears to be overlapping emotion categories such as reports of being simultaneously 'happy' and 'sad'.

Reports of subtle awareness of an internal state such as 'guilt' can be accounted for to some extent by assuming that this type of self-report is indeed an emotion state, and proposing that this type of state consists of 'emotion blends'. An example is the word 'smug' referring to a blend of 'happiness and anger', (Lazarus 1991: 195). A blend is secondary to the basic emotions from which it is composed. The concept 'blend' differs from another term, 'combinations' of emotions, (p. 229), which retain their core meaning. An example of a combination is 'bitterness' seen as identifiably both 'anger' and 'sadness'.

Plutchik (1993: 57) presents a graphical representation of eight primary emotions and the relation between them in terms of blends and intensity. The analogy with colour is made 'in the same sense that some colours are primary and others are mixed'. That is, 'hostility' can be considered a mix of 'anger' and 'disgust', themselves two of the primary emotion constructs. 'Guilt' is composed of 'joy' and 'fear', again two primary emotions. This method structures emotion states in such a way that it can show relationships between emotions based on eight primary, multiple secondary, and many degrees of intensity.

An account of the development and emergence of emotion states is posited by Oatley and Johnson-Laird (1998: 92), who suggest a dynamic mechanism: 'individuals can react to events by making more than one cognitive evaluation, and such evaluations can create distinct emotions in parallel or in rapid alternation.' The term 'mixture' is used to refer to the resulting emotion state. This model goes beyond description of categories, and suggests how emotion states might develop.

Another developmental model is proposed by Lewis et al. (1998), who suggest that 'derived' or 'secondary' emotions emerge from six primary emotions in the process of cognitive development. They are graded according to stages of development: 'those needing the least cognitive support emerge first, and those needing more emerge later' (p. 159). An outline model is presented (p. 160) which illustrates how 'self-conscious emotions' such as 'pride' and 'guilt' may be derived through interaction of basic emotions with developmental capacities associated with the idea of the self.

LeDoux (1996), among others, draws attention to a basic problem in defining and classifying emotion (p. 121). Some of the difficulty may lie in the choice of words used to refer to emotions 'rather than the emotions implied by the words'. We also wonder if the words used may not necessarily accurately reflect or precisely detail the concepts implied by the words. The varying usage of non-technical language creates problems for the researcher who does not have an intuition about the meanings of words referring to the identification of emotion constructs.

9.11 Language terms and use of words in characterizing emotion

Clore et al. (1987) collected a set of affective word terms relating to emotion. In this collection the words refer to 'internal mental states that are primarily focused on affect'. In their study, 'affect' is defined as meaning a basic feeling of 'goodness' or 'badness', which is then coloured by variants, such as degree, of this basic quality of feeling.

Thus, 'happiness' is described as a 'good feeling' with a special attribute that distinguishes it from 'joy', which is also a 'good' emotion. Both these terms are distinguished from 'depression', which induces a basic 'bad' feeling, but is itself differentiated from 'sadness', also a 'bad' feeling but with a different quality from 'depression'. In addition, what modifying effect do adjectives have? Is it possible to evoke the same feeling as 'depression' with the phrase 'malignant sadness' as used by Wolpert (1999), or does this phrase have a slightly different meaning and set of inferences from the word 'depression' and 'sadness' for both speaker and listener? A question here is:

- Do words refer to the emotion itself, or to a recognition of this emotion which can give rise to a general feeling of goodness or badness for the individual?

Another approach has been to identify and list words that refer to emotional *experience*. The sets of words collected are terms from ordinary non-technical language, listed with a view to reflecting a set of observations about the identification of emotion.

9.11.1 A reduction to 'basic' emotions

In early work Tomkins (1962) suggested eight emotions, based on deriving universals of modes of expression. Plutchik (1984) reported identification of a larger set of 140 words classified according to three reference terms claimed to reflect emotional states. However, in a later study (Plutchik 1994) this number was reduced to six 'basic emotions' labelled by six words (in English only) which could be used to describe the following emotions: 'fear, anger, joy, sadness, disgust and surprise'. Plutchik proposed a link between the reported feelings of his subjects in the experiments and these six basic terms. Others agree on six (Levenson 1992; Ekman and Friesen 1998). Izard (1992) suggested eight. Some researchers are uncommitted as to any actual number, but research more general reactions (Davidson 1993b; LeDoux 1996). Ekman's (1994) list, on the other hand—anger, fear, happiness, sadness, disgust, and surprise—is related to facial movements identified as expressing emotion.

But even within the paradigm centring on basic emotions from which others may be derived, there is some disagreement as to exactly how few concepts and their associated word labels are necessary to describe basic emotions. With numbers for basic emotions varying from four to six, the words 'fear, anger, joy, sadness', and 'disgust' are most commonly used to describe five basic emotions.

Johnson-Laird and Oatley (1992) examined the kind of words we have for emotions, and arrived at five for basic emotions—a similar list to Ekman's, minus 'surprise'—but later revised this number to four: happiness, anger, sadness, and fear (Oatley and Johnson-Laird 1998). Panksepp (1994; 1998) had suggested four basic emotions: 'fear', 'anger', 'joy/play', and 'sorrow'. These can be directly related to identifiable neurological activity. Secondary or derived emotion words have been suggested as describing 'variations' or 'blends' of basic emotions (Plutchik 1994). Although this idea has been discussed extensively in the literature, it leads to a relatively unconstrained computational explosion in the range of possibilities for emotion categories and associated words, particularly when each may, for some researchers, have different 'degrees'. Speech work must ultimately take account of the diversity of emotions and the use of language labels which characterize the emotion state. It would seem to be another case of the need for parameterization and mapping between two sets of objects: emotion and the labels available in the language of the speaker/listener.

Taking an approach which intends to parameterize emotion terms, Wierzbicka (1992) derived fifty semantic terms which can be applied across languages. A cluster of these terms can be associated with specific words and word categories; the words, and categories such as adverbs, are associated with the intention to express a range of emotions. Emotion words are classified in a feature matrix of word connotations associated with expressive content. This model is intended to be applicable in all languages, enabling cross-comparison of emotion terms in different languages. This goes some way toward providing a sounder linguistic base for labelling emotion-related events. As Wierzbicka points out, different languages are described differently in terms of syntax and habits of use.

9.11.2 Terminology: emotions and 'moods'

Another term is used to describe a particular class of emotion states—'moods'. These describe affective states which occur with minimal cognitive mediation (Clore 1994b; Frijda et al. 2000), and also characterize a condition which may be basically an emotion state, but the features of which prevail over a period of time and can result in an inability to adapt appropriately to the constant changes in the environment (Whybrow 1998). There seems to be agreement that an emotion state is transient, and occurs when a person is adapting to a short-term, even sudden, change in the environment. Moods, on the other hand, can filter some stimuli from the environment. For example, if the garage is hit by lightning, and your mood is generally buoyant, the ability to deal with the problem may be greater than if you feel depressed and hopeless. For examples see Lazarus (1991), Frijda (1993), and Whybrow (1998).

9.11.3 The general use of language labels

Whether emotion has primarily physiological or cognitive origins, on many occasions an emotional experience is expressed through *language*. Physically expressing emotion occupies a great deal of our speaking life, and is constrained by social and moral convention. If there are basic emotions which can be expressed with varying degrees of intensity, language seems to provide us with a set of quite subtle labels. For example, we can say *I feel sad*, or *distressed*, or *overwhelmed*, thereby expressing various degrees of what might technically be considered the same basic emotion, 'sadness', in contrast with another basic emotion, 'happiness', which also can be expressed in degrees, such as 'content', 'joyous', 'ecstatic'.

It is useful to remember that language can be thought of as a code. A word is a label on an object or event in the world. The speaker/listener interprets the word to refer to some emotion or quality. A speaker/listener can report an awareness of emotion in language terms, but the researcher also uses language to describe and label the result of experiments or observations, and as the basis for terminology in a *model* of emotion and emotive content of speech. Although researchers in emotion recognize the need to be careful in the use of the words, the labels may not mean the same in their lay and specialist uses. In the study of emotion, for example, researchers variously use the words 'feeling' and 'emotion' to refer to the same concept. Others connect the word 'emotion' with physical reactions, and 'feeling' with cognition. (For a history of developments in emotion studies, see Jenkins et al. 1998.) Referents vary and are not always agreed upon, and in any case just using a label does not mean the phenomenon itself has been identified. As Harré (1996: 344) points out: 'Psychologists have always had to struggle against a persistent illusion that in such studies as those of the emotions there is something there, the emotion, of which the emotion word is a mere representation.'

In speech research, word lists have been compiled relating words to emotion. But drawing the conclusion that because a word exists in the language to describe an emotion or feeling, therefore there exists such an emotion or feeling may be placing too much emphasis on the descriptive power of a list of words. Put simply, the existence in ordinary language of words relating to particular phenomena does not of itself mean that these phenomena exist in the scientific sense.

Biology and Psychology

Words in word lists should perhaps have the same status. The words belong to syntactic categories having different functions in the language—so a noun such as *anger* is different grammatically from an adjective *angered* or *angry*. If these words are to be labels for emotion, and if they function differently in the language, the class of words used may add differing interpretations of the meaning of the labelled emotions themselves.

Words such as *anger, fear, happiness, sadness* also have their opposite meanings. Basic emotions are appraised as good or bad. But we may ask: do the labels and the appraisals match up? Perhaps Appraisal Theory would find it useful to check the words as labels carefully (see Borod et al. 2000 on lists of good and bad emotions in an experimental setting). Just as a model is not the object being modelled, so the word-label is not the object it labels: it is in fact best regarded as a cognitively derived symbolic representation. The symbolic representation may or may not stand in a linear relationship with the object it represents; but it is as well to take the precaution of assuming that it does not. Quite clearly, emotion labels do not stand in a one-to-one relationship with characteristics of the acoustic signal—which is one reason why there is still so much apparent confusion in determining the acoustic correlates of emotion. Returning to the caution on using labels, these examples are for English only. An obvious question is: do the principles expressed work as well in other languages? The question remains to be answered.

9.12 The problems of labelling and classification

Researchers in the field of emotion are aware, of course, of the scope of the inherent problems. For example, Averill (1994) has drawn attention to difficulties of working in an area which is as yet not well defined, and has an unwieldy classification system. As researchers themselves have pointed out, they should pay careful attention to methods of investigation, evaluation, and interpretation of results. Classification systems useful for investigations within different disciplines such as biology, psychology, linguistics, and philosophy may not be suitable across disciplines, and it is necessary to be wary of moving across systems or approaches which may work well in some allied discipline. Labelling and classification is the basis of modelling, in a sense, but, like modelling, they are approached with particular aims and viewpoints in mind—these will almost certainly differ between disciplines, even if they *should* have similar aims. Researchers must be alert to problems in drawing conclusions that overgeneralize, that cannot be validated by independent external evidence, or that proceed from different points of view (Leventhal and Patrick-Miller 1993; Solomon 1993; Oatley and Johnson-Laird 1998). These principles are basic to all science, but researchers in emotion studies appear to be particularly sensitive to the implications of the many ways possible to carry out their work.

As a simple example, consider that it is commonly observed that similar external events elicit different emotions from different people, and different responses can be reported as emotion from the same person on different occasions. Clearly a consistent linear mapping from environment to emotion response is still not possible, limiting the predictive power of what theory we have.

9.13 Concluding remarks

To sum up three perspectives on the multi-component approach: paraphrasing Panksepp (2000: 137), many aspects of emotion arise from brain processes that occur in all animals, other aspects from interaction of these processes with environment and social experience, and others from our ability to use language effectively to conceptualize matters of importance.

From a slightly different point of view, Johnstone and Scherer (2000) outline three components that constitute emotion reaction:

- subjective experience,
- neurophysiological response patterns in the central and autonomic nervous systems,
- expression by face movements, voice, and other body gestures.

These three concepts constitute 'emotional reaction'.

LeDoux (1996: 40) on the other hand, also generalizes these components: 'However, in emotions, unlike in cognitions, the brain does not usually function independently of the body. Many if not most emotions involve bodily responses. But no such relation exists between cognition and actions.' We can think, understand, and produce language, mathematics, music, all without obvious bodily responses. Cognition does not necessarily produce obvious action, but emotion is generally seen as having physical correlates—although some researchers see a direct relation between cognition and emotion with no obvious associated physical action. Cognition here seems to be being modelled more abstractly, because actually thinking does involve brain activity. MRI scans show some areas of the brain changing whilst subjects report cognitive activity; increased glucose use has also been observed during 'abstract' cognitive activity. Perhaps it is worth reiterating yet again that in modelling human behaviour we should be wary of confusing the object with the *model* of the object.

We have found that working out modelling procedures and developing plausible models for dealing with expressive speech now requires some understanding of the human speech production and perception systems. Emotion can be seen as biologically based, cognitively–biologically based, or cognitively based (including social constraints and cultural demands), and at the same time seen to be cognitively influencing physiological function. For our purposes, the detail of how speech could be studied in both domains is necessary for understanding human speech production in general. Some kinds of expression are linguistically based, others seem to be emotion-based. Two important questions for speech researchers seem to be:

- How can two different types of expression (biologically based and cognitively based), seemingly needing different approaches to modelling, appear together in the speech waveform?
- In what way does the acoustic signal vary along some biological/cognitive and linguistically distinctive division in terms of elements like fundamental frequency change, intensity, timing—which are the acoustic features we work with?

Chapter 10

The Linguistics, Phonology, and Phonetics Perspective

This chapter covers the current research in the area of expression in human beings from the language perspective. We focus on the approach a theory of emotion could take, and look at current methods of investigation, in particular the use of databases of emotive speech.

10.1 The nature of emotion

The investigation focuses not just on how expressive content is apparent in the acoustic signal a speaker produces but also on listener reaction to the signal. Listeners are able to detect and label expressive content, and react to the signal, sometimes in a way which mirrors the speaker's emotion, sometimes in quite different ways. We consider the research which sets out to account for perception of expression via more than one input modality.

10.1.1 Whose task is the development of a theory of expression in speech?

Researchers in a number of different disciplines have an interest in the area.

- Biologists and bio-psychologists will be interested in physical and somatic aspects of emotion ranging from areas such as hormonal changes (Scarpa and Raine 2000) correlating with the experience of an emotion through to motor control (LeDoux 1996).

- Psychologists and those working in the general field of cognitive science have an interest in a characterization of emotion as a psychological phenomenon both in speakers and in listeners. For example,
    emotion in the speaker experienced prior to speaking, but reflected in the speech (choice of words or tone of voice);
    how speaker and listener attitudes might change during the course of a conversation;
    how the speaker is able to recognize different expressive content;
    or indeed whether there is expressive content at all.
  Does content arise wholly from the heard acoustic signal or does some of the labelling of what is perceived originate in the mind of the listener, forming part of a label 'assignment' rather than a label identification task?
- Linguists may be interested in correlations between the semantics of utterances and the way they are spoken, or in the way words are chosen to express thoughts when there is strong emotional influence. Like psychologists, linguists will be interested in whether there are any universal or innate basics to expression or emotion.
- Phoneticians want to investigate how emotion or expression in general alters the way utterances are delivered, either from an articulatory or motor control viewpoint or the resultant acoustic signal. They are interested in the correlations of expression which articulation and acoustics embody. Phoneticians working in the area of the perception of speech will have many of the same aims as psychologists, trying to model the way listeners are able to identify (detect and then label) spoken expressive content.

All the researchers from the above disciplines would be involved in developing the general theory. Our focus from a phonetics perspective is on the expressive content of the acoustic waveform of speech, and the associated articulations and their control, rather than on the origin of the emotion or attitude being expressed.

A general theory of expression will include the source and nature of a biological/psychological phenomenon; this is the emotion, mood, or attitude as experienced by a person. The theory also will account for how the phenomenon is expressed in the articulation and acoustic waveform of utterances spoken, whether this expression is deliberate or not, or whether the speaker is aware or not that their feelings are being communicated. In addition the general theory will characterize the reactions of a listener, both in terms of how the listener perceives the expressive content of the signal they hear and in terms of their own emotional or attitudinal reaction to what they hear.

10.1.2 Questions for a theory of emotion

Researchers have asked a number of questions which collectively help specify what a theory of emotion would look like and the areas it would address.

1. Emotion originating in the speaker

- What are emotions?
- How do they arise?
- How are they physically manifested?
- How are they cognitively manifested?
- How are they sensed and interpreted by the originator?

Emotions are usually defined in terms of the way they are manifested in the person experiencing them. Some researchers in biology relate emotional category labels to such things as hormonal balance and activation/inhibition of the nervous system. There is discussion as to how emotions arise to differentiate between externally and internally derived stimuli. Their *manifestation* can also be physical or cognitive, and they will affect the way in which the expressive content of an acoustic signal is produced. Finally the person who is experiencing the emotion often senses the experience and is able to interpret it, though not necessarily in the way a listener would.

2. Emotion affecting the environment

- How do emotions impinge on the environment (e.g. how they are reflected in a soundwave)?

- What is a suitable way of representing the expressive content of the acoustic signal?

The manifestation of emotion in the speaker is encoded in the speech signal. Sometimes this is an automatic effect and sometimes a voluntary effect—but it may be either physically or cognitively based. How the expressive content itself is to be modelled is an important question, particularly because it is almost certainly the case that the correlations with both speaker and listener reaction are non-linear. That is, there is probably no straightforward one-to-one correlation between speaker 'experience', acoustic 'rendering', and listener 'reaction'.

3. Emotion detected and interpreted by the listener

- How are the environmental changes detected by another person?
- How is what is detected measured by the other person?
- How are the measurements interpreted?
- How are the labels assigned?

The most important and interesting aspects of the perception of emotion from the soundwave are those relating to the non-linearity of perception, implying that the labels listeners use for what they perceive are not present in the soundwave but assigned by a reasoned interpretive process. This idea is further reinforced by the fact that the interpretation of expressive content in the acoustic signal is often, if not always, context-sensitive.

10.1.3 *What is emotion for speech researchers?*

Many speech researchers who are not psychologists have, often without discussion, adopted descriptive accounts of what emotion is. Since emotion is something 'experienced', they feel that its characterization falls properly within the domain of psychology, and accept what they understand of what psychologists have to say. We have compared this to linguistic theory, which can be thought of as being about how ideas in a speaker's mind get encoded as soundwaves, which in turn get decoded back into copy ideas in a listener's mind. Linguistics, though, usually has little to say about the nature and origin of the ideas themselves: this falls within the domains of psychology and perhaps philosophy.

Another cognitively based approach common in recent speech work is the social constructivist perspective (Averill 1980; Harré and Parrott 1996). In contrast with the cognitive perspective on appraisal, the social constructivists claim that the appraisal of an event—in our terms, its interpretation—rests not just on the event itself, its detection and its cognitive interpretation, but depends also on social constraints as to how it is to be appraised. Hence

$$\text{event} \rightarrow \text{appraisal} \rightarrow \text{label/emotional experience}$$
$$\uparrow$$
$$\text{social constraints}$$

Since many social constraints are culturally dependent, this particular model is able to explain why certain events trigger different emotional reactions in different cultures. Furthermore, social constructivists claim that how we actually display our emotions is also culturally constrained. Whether this idea can be extended to how expressive content is reflected in the speech soundwave is still a matter needing further investigation.

10.1.4 Measuring expressive content in speech: the 'neutral standard'

The problem of providing a benchmark for measuring expressive content in speech is not a trivial one, and elsewhere we discuss what neutral speech—speech without expressive content—might be (see Chapter 3), and how it might be used as a benchmark in studies of the acoustics of emotion. One or two researchers have tried synthesizing a standard neutral speech and transforming it under known conditions. This is almost certainly not what human beings do, but it does enable us as scientists to keep track of what might seem like endless variability in prosodic and expressive rendering of utterances (Stibbard 2001).

Just as at the segmental level we find that speakers and listeners report a constancy, so we find them reporting constancy of prosodics. We argue elsewhere (Tatham and Morton 2003) that what is being reported is not some objective view of the actual acoustic signal but an idealized abstraction. What we need for our benchmark is an uncoloured instantiation of this ideal. This is very easy to illustrate formally, and probably impossible to achieve in real life from a human speaker. But because it can be expressed formally we may be in a position to synthesize utterances—albeit false ones—without any expressive content. The irony is that the single most important contemporary difficulty with synthetic speech is its very lack of expressive content; but this does not mean automatically that what we have synthesized is 'neutral' speech. The reason for this is that the synthesis has been based on real speech which is never neutral.

But even if we could produce speech which is neutral—more realistically, speech which has expressive content but where this is set so low as to be unrecognizable—we would expect to find context-sensitivity (Cauldwell 2000) operating here too. In other words, what sounds relatively neutral in one context may not do so in another. If this is right, it seriously impedes any attempt to base any model of expressive content on some *measured* neutrality because it would mean that identifying the neutrality to measure would be a suspect process. The research paradigm which says 'Here is some neutral speech and we will now measure how this expressive speech is different from it' becomes difficult to sustain if we agree that neutral speech either could not exist or is context-sensitive when it does. However, if we could reconstruct somehow an abstract version of what neutral speech *might be*, the paradigm might continue to have some value.

Put another way, we might argue that it is possible in the theory of speech production to assert that there can be something we call 'normal' which is untouched by context because it is *defined before context arises*. But since there is always context, this normal is by definition abstract. This is exactly the same as phoneme theory at the segmental level. The procedure is highly abstract and quite artificial at both the segmental and suprasegmental levels because normally context comes *before* the objects we are trying to regard as normal. In the real world—not the one constructed by our science—segments exist only when enveloped or 'wrapped' by segmental context, and prosodic features similarly exist only within a suprasegmental context.

There are different ways of considering the concept of normality in speech.

- Any process of deriving abstract normal or neutral or context free segments from actual speech is a process involving reversal of the contextual process: reversing coarticulation will cause the extrinsic allophone (the *planned* allophone) to appear, then reversing the phonology will cause the underlying phoneme to appear. This is the technique used in Classical Phonetics to 'discover' the phonemes within a real utterance (see Laver 1994: esp. 41–2). The technique can easily be extended to a theory of accent, for example, in which you could have an underlying pronunciation for 'the language' with transformations to achieve pronunciations in various accents—but the underlying form would be the same for all accents, and indeed for all speakers.
- There can be many 'normals' *not* necessarily related to the abstract underlying representation. The normal form emerges from examination of a stretch of utterance which is likely to reflect normality. So: what is normal for any one speaker on any one occasion? Suppose we call yesterday's normality '4'—but we notice that wherever the speaker was using '4' yesterday today they are using '6'; perhaps they have a cold. At this point we have a choice of models:

   Either we say normal yesterday was '4' and normal today is '6', or

   we can say that there is an abstract normal which is '2' and which yesterday could be recovered from '4' by dividing by a contextual '2', but which will have to be recovered from '6' today by dividing by a contextual '3'.

The existence of '2' and '3' is the daily changed context constraining how the 'abstract 2' occurs. In this latter model 'abstract 2' would never occur—the closest would be 2×1, which is not the same as 2. That is, 'abstract 2' would always be 'realized' within a context, even if that context were '1', which does nothing except pull 'abstract 2' to 'instantiated 2'.

But whichever technique we use for arriving at some characterization of normal speech we cannot escape the fact that normal speech never occurs at the surface—there is always a transformation, even if the transformation is so slight as to apparently give a surface 'normal'. A good example from segmental phonetics would be the assertion that the pronunciation of [t] is different in the two utterances [ata] and [iti]—but that the pronunciation of [a] in [ata] and [aka] is *not* different, and is therefore a 'normal' pronunciation. This position is taken sometimes in Coarticulation Theory (Hardcastle and Hewlett 1999) on the grounds that some segments 'dominate' coarticulatory processes and themselves are minimally coarticulated. This is not the best model: it is better to say that *all* surface segments have been transformed, even by a factor of 1 (as above): this makes for complete consistency of description at the surface level—and a consistency in the way in which all surface objects are related in the model to their underlying objects. We would not say that 'the phoneme /t/ does not show up at the surface in these examples, but that the phoneme /a/ does'—in neither case does the phoneme show up: it cannot because it does not exist in this world.

10.1.5 Dimensional representation of emotion

There have been a number of proposals in the speech research literature over the past two or three decades to classify emotions according to their locations along a number of abstract dimensions (cf. Davitz 1964b). In these circumstances, three dimensions are proposed: arousal, pleasure, and power:

- arousal: the degree of emotional intensity;
- pleasure: how positive or negative the emotion is;
- power: how much control there is; does the feeling come from within the speaker or from the outside environment?

Arousal is also known as 'activation' or 'activity', pleasure as 'valence' or 'evaluation', and power as 'strength', 'control', or 'dominance'.

Sometimes adjectives applied to the person experiencing the emotion are used to define the dimensions, though strictly these are not definitions but statements of correlation. This moves the meaning of emotion from an object experienced to the feeling of

Table 10.1. The relationship between emotion 'objects' and their 'feeling'

Emotion 'object'	Effect on the person—'feeling' or 'experience'
Pleasure	happy/unhappy, pleased/annoyed
Arousal	agitated/calm, excited/apathetic
Power	powerful/powerless, dominant/submissive

the experience. Clearly these are not the same thing, if only because the feeling can be context-sensitive whereas the object itself is in some abstract sense independent of context. It may be helpful to make a clear distinction (Table 10.1).

Experiments attempting to place different emotions within this early three-dimensional space have not given entirely unambiguous results. The basic emotions which are strongly felt, like anger and sadness, score fairly unambiguously when rated by the person experiencing the emotion and when rated by someone perceiving how the experience is reflected in the emotive content of the acoustic signal. But, as is usually the case as we move away from these strong emotions, ambiguity creeps into the classification—that emotions can be differentiated as strong or weak is not agreed by cognitive psychologists.

In general, with 'sadness', power rates low as far as the speaker is concerned, and for sadness the features arousal and excitement usually rate low too. 'Anger' scores high on arousal, particularly extreme anger, whereas 'happiness' scores high on the pleasure dimension. We cannot summarize all the experimental findings here, but there has been some agreement about placing the various emotions within the space created by these three dimensions, though the results do not provide unambiguous discrimination between them.

There is an argument, emanating from more recent biopsychological studies, for taking a more formal approach to defining parameters for characterizing emotion. For example, the work of researchers such as Zajonc (1980), Leventhal (1987), Lazarus (1991), Plutchik (1994), LeDoux (1996), and Panksepp (1998) takes a general approach which can be characterized as more rigorous in terms of definitions and theoretical framework.

10.1.6 Push and pull effects

Scherer (1995) repeats an earlier suggestion (Scherer 1985) that it is useful to distinguish between 'push effects' and 'pull effects' in emotion determinants. Push effects involve physiological processes (the example given is 'muscle tone') which 'push vocalisations in a certain direction'. Pull effects involve external factors (the example is 'expectations of the listener') which 'pull the affect vocalisation toward a particular acoustic model'. The constructs of push and pull are linked to the self: push means pushed away from the self, and pull means pulled toward the self.

Scherer claims enhanced muscle tone when there is sympathetic arousal resulting in a push effect of higher f0. Pull effects derive from 'cultural conventions' which are able to 'influence the production of signs required in social situations by specifying a particular acoustic target pattern, as opposed to mental concepts or internal physiological processes which push out expression'.

He may be saying that there are intrinsic properties to acoustic expressive content deriving from two sources: 'mental concepts' and 'physiological processes'. These are the push effects. In addition there are social factors which pull expression toward a particular acoustic *profile* ('model' is perhaps the wrong word). We assume that he does not mean these to be mutually exclusive, but is suggesting that the final acoustic signal depends on influences from both directions. A number of questions would arise from such a claim:

- Are push and pull factors mutually exclusive? Is it a question of either one or the other? Scherer suggests antagonism between push and pull factors. Some physiological arousal might increase a speaker's f0 at the same time as there is a conscious attempt to pull it down (to 'show control')—producing a 'contradictory message'.
- If the two interact, is one logically or temporally prior to the other? For example, is there an initial push 'formulation' which is subsequently modified by socially determined pull? Or are push factors determined within the context of prior pull factors? The whole formulation of the model and subsequent

claims for its explanatory power will depend on which of these two is the case.
- If there is no logical or temporal priority, what is the 'mix' of coexisting push and pull factors. Does this vary with particular emotions, or with particular cognitive or social contexts? Can any one emotion be identified with this or that mix? For example, is the expression of 'anger' predominantly push-determined, or are there pull conventions which determine how it is expressed? But perhaps it is the case that the mix of push and pull varies depending on the contextual factors (cognitive or social context) of the moment.

It is not clear what is to be gained by a push/pull perspective. There is a parallel in speech production theory: the pushed targets of speech sounds are pulled by coarticulatory factors which are mechanically and aerodynamically context-dependent—sometimes push dominates and sometimes pull, even for a given sound; the entire process of coarticulation is temporally governed. In coarticulation theory push is logically prior to pull. A refinement of coarticulation theory—Cognitive Phonetics—however suggests that speakers can and do predict pull and adjust their push in a compensatory gesture. This kind of idea suggests that push and pull (if the speech production analogy is valid) have a relationship which is far from simple. Extending Scherer, we might hypothesize that a speaker can anticipate social pull and opt to minimize, maximize, or optimize its effect—a subtle speaker-controlled play on the acoustic signal. In the case of Cognitive Phonetic Theory the goal of such a push-pull control mechanism is the creation of certain perceived effects in the listener; perhaps speakers can and do also control the relationship between push and pull effects in the expressive content of their speech waveforms with the same goal of influencing listener behaviour.

Scherer (2000) emphasizes time, focusing on how 'constantly changing affective tuning' is based on 'continuous evaluative monitoring of the environment'. Presumably the evaluative monitoring is cognitive. In effect, then, he is proposing an ongoing amorphous emotional state—we would call it an abstract emotion—which is tuned—modulated—in accordance with the results of the organism's evaluation of its environment. An organism would thus, we suppose, always have some emotive state, and this is in direct agreement with our own position. We claim that emotion is not switched on or off, or switched between this or that qualitative property, but is an *evolving* 'object' possessing the important feature of a 'time constant' which constrains, for example, rate of change between emotional states. Along with Scherer, we believe that too much emphasis has been placed on category switching and category labels. What for us at any rate is important is the temporal progression of evolving emotion. This has presented some problems in our XML data structure declarative system, but we believe these have now been overcome (see Chapter 16).

There are parallel ways of looking at speech production, and these parallels are important for us in the way in which the recognition of emotion in an individual is later expressed in any acoustic signal produced by that person.

- One particular speech model focuses on categories of speech sounds, their linear juxtaposition and coarticulatory overlapping processes which 'convert' a string of discrete objects into the continuousness readily observed in the acoustic signal. In the Classical Phonetics model (Gimson 1967; Cruttenden 2001) these discrete objects are simply declared as 'abstract', though in Cognitive Phonetics (Tatham 1990) they are declared as objects with cognitive 'reality'. Perception is a process of deriving appropriate category labels for the acoustic signal.
- Another, more recent model (Browman and Goldstein 1986) focuses on the continuousness of the signal, denying or minimizing categorical relevance during the speech production process. Speech is characterized as multi-parameter gestures which 'flow' rather than 'sequence'. They do, of course, relate to cognitively based categories, but do not necessarily derive from them in a linear fashion.
- The third speech model integrates these views in a unified approach to speech production and perception, making a distinction between cognitive and physical processes, and

between static and dynamic modelling of planning and rendering (Tatham and Morton 2003). In this model perceptual labels are 'assigned' rather than 'derived'.

Scherer's (2000) model focusing on the dynamics of expressiveness is a recent important step forward in the conceptualization of emotion, and brings the continuous and changing nature of expression to the forefront. When we consider phonetic rendering of expression later, we shall see that static modelling of any kind of expression is becoming less tenable.

10.2 Databases for investigating expressiveness in the speech waveform

As with almost all research into the acoustics of speech, investigation of the acoustic correlates of expression needs a large representative database of material to work with. This does not mean, though, that it is not possible to work with small data sets, and indeed there are researchers who prefer this on the grounds that large data sets inevitably result in data reduction techniques which can normalize out important details, particularly of an individual speaker's way of talking.

When it comes to assembling data for studying expressive content, researchers are torn between a number of different methods, the main ones of which are:

1. Ask actors or non-actors to:
   speak spontaneously using particular modes of expression;
   repeat previously learned utterances using different modes of expression;
   read out utterances using different modes of expression.
2. Ask actors or non-actors to read out utterances which by reason of their content cause the reader to assume a particular mode of expression.
3. Induce an emotion in a speaker while talking with them.
4. Eavesdrop on conversations hoping that particular modes of expression will turn up.

Each of these techniques has its drawbacks. Whether actors or non-actors are used in approach 1 it can never be assumed that people know how to 'turn on' expressive content in their speech properly. Even if it is felt that they have got it right, there is no guarantee that what they are doing is exactly what happens when the expressive content is spontaneous. Similarly with approach 2—there is no guarantee that this is natural expression. Approach 3 has its merits, especially with strong emotions like anger and fear, though there are serious ethical questions which detract from any popularity for this approach. Approach 4 gives the most reliable results from the point of view of guaranteeing the expressive content to be genuine, but it is extremely difficult to ensure that exactly the right content arises during the conversation—or whether there will be enough examples of this or that expression to feel that what has been captured in the recording is truly representative.

The list of data sources above distinguishes between the kind of consciously intended expression—'on-demand' expressive content (1 and 2) and expressive content which is the result of emotions, etc. which are actually experienced by the speaker (3 and 4)—'on-experience' expressive content. The pre-research question which needs considering, even if it cannot be answered, is whether on-demand expressive content is the same as on experience expressive content in terms of the actual acoustic signal produced. The signals may be different even if listeners report the expression to be the same.

In the end, most researchers continue to resort to using actors or non-actors responding to requests to read out sets of utterances in a variety of different emotions and to repeat the sentences a given number of times. At least this way, it is argued, the data set is complete, and this completeness outweighs for most researchers the argument that the material lacks spontaneity and is therefore suspect. In this technique the use of identical utterances spoken with different expressive content is designed to normalize out the effects of non-expressive meaning in the utterances. It must be remembered, though, that, as pointed out above, if expression relies on small changes in the waveform these may be lost in the statistical data reduction process involved in processing material taken from relatively large sets of data.

10.2.1 *Data provided by actors vs. non-actors*

The problem with using actors is that, although their speech might be reliably perceived as having this or that expressive content, it is not necessarily the case that the perceiver's response was triggered by phenomena in the signal which are the same as those produced by a non-actor. Acting in general, however apparently natural or spontaneous, uses certain conventions which are confined to acting and are not necessarily part of the behaviour of non-actors. These conventions are known to and understood by perceivers—there is hardly anyone, surely, who does not encounter acted speech on a daily basis on TV. At best such conventions might just be exaggerated forms of what would be there in natural speech; at worst they would actually be different, cutting across the phenomena in natural speech. The latter is particularly dangerous because neither actor nor perceiver will be necessarily aware that they have switched to conventions which do not accord completely with what happens under more natural circumstances.

Non-actors are unlikely to be aware of or be practised in the conventions learned by actors. What seems to happen with non-actors is that they do not consistently produce the target expression type or are generally inconsistent. They also find it very difficult sometimes to provide data with this or that expression, particularly if some subtlety is called for: what *is* the difference between mildly irritated, irritated, somewhat angry, and very angry? One of degree or one of type? Often non-actors simply do not know how to 'perform' on demand, and will produce something which even surprises them when they listen to a replay of what they have just said.

Whether using actors or non-actors for producing utterances which are emotive on-demand, experimenters judge the data to be satisfactory if listening tests match up the requested expressive content with the perceived expressive content. This technique for evaluating the appropriateness of the data for the experiment is probably less satisfactory when actors are involved because of the possibility of special coding for acted speech—coding which the listening panel might be subconsciously using. That is, listeners may be judging the satisfactory use of acting conventions rather than natural expressiveness.

10.2.2 Natural databases

In theory it should be possible to assemble databases which contain only natural speech—speech uttered spontaneously by people talking to each other. Careful choice of conversational topic could eventually deliver examples of a wide range of expressive content containing many examples of expression. Such a large database would need to be processed by computer to assemble and categorize its expressive content. Computer processing, however, usually needs the data to be annotated or marked up in a number of ways. In our case, the recordings or a carefully aligned written transcription would need to show the 'flow' of expressive content as the conversations unfolded—we sometimes call this the 'expressive contour', a term which focuses on the changing nature of expression as utterances unfold.

This raises the question of whether the annotation or mark-up should take the form of category labels, 'angry', 'deliberate', or 'authoritative', for example, or whether a more detailed mark-up, indicating degrees of particular expressive attributes and showing how they change and blend into one another, should be applied. The value of such a database to linguists and psychologists alike cannot be overestimated. But there are two difficulties:

- We do not yet have a good theoretical framework within which to characterize blending or shading expressive content—or even to help us mark it up.
- We need to develop automatic methods of mark-up so that large amounts of data do not have to be processed by human researchers.

The techniques for recording natural conversation exist and have been developed by sociolinguists. They can provide databases of high-quality audio material. But the techniques needed for marking up the databases prior to analysis are not yet agreed or in place. Marking up a database is theory-dependent—that is, there are theoretical decisions to be taken before marking up begins. If the wrong decisions are taken the mark-up will not be suitable for processing in particular ways later. In Part IV we discuss the mark-up of expressive speech, and over the next few years it is likely that new methods of mark-up and alignment will be developed as researchers address the dynamic properties of expressive content in speech.

10.2.3 Signal content

The acoustic signal outside the speaker's mouth is the end product of a complex aerodynamic system. In speech production theory we usually identify anatomical objects within the vocal tract, and classify them according to the role they play in producing and influencing the aerodynamics of the vocal tract. The interaction between the respiratory system (responsible for providing airflow), the phonation system (responsible for modulating the airflow at the larynx usually to produce periodic excitation), and articulation (responsible for providing a time-varying resonance system which filters the acoustic signal resulting from phonation and other sources) is fairly well understood. The result of this interaction is the final acoustic signal.

A first approximation model attempting to characterize speech production might regard all elements involved as relatively independent of each other, and to a large extent independently controllable by the speaker. This is not the case, however, and there are many dependent relationships within the overall system. There are a number of good texts which deal with this aspect of speech production theory (e.g. Fant 1960; O'Shaughnessy 1987). What is important from our point of view, as we try to characterize how a speech signal can acquire and manipulate expressive content, is to what extent these dependencies constrain the signal.

Full details are not yet known, but as an example we can cite coarticulation as a time-governed phenomenon constraining how the signal moves from one segment of speech to another. Potential abrupt changes between segments are smoothed—low pass filtered—by predominantly mechanical and aerodynamic inertial or elastic effects. These constraints can be so severe as to remove the perceived identity of a single segment divorced from its linguistic context. Thus formant bending in rapid speech can change the expected relationship between formant frequencies, particularly in short vowels, to the point where without the adjacent consonantal context the vowel becomes transformed into 'another'! To a certain extent speakers can anticipate these constraints and attempt to negate them, sometimes with great success and with good articulatory 'precision', at other times with varying degrees of success. The characterization of precision of articulation and phonation is covered within the Theory of Cognitive Phonetics (Tatham 1990).

Coarticulation and its control, though, are excellent examples of how the situation changes as we add expressive content. If, as coarticulation theory predicts (MacNeilage and DeClerk 1969), blending or overlapping effects are time-governed with smoothing becoming progressively more severe as speaking rate increases, then we would expect the fast speech produced when a speaker experiences a high degree of anger to be heavily smoothed: in fact it is not, and angry speech typically has a level of articulatory precision greater than speech produced under less emotive intensity.

We suspect strongly that a worthwhile and productive research topic in the area of expressive speech would be an investigation of precisely how precision of articulation is governed. There is no doubt that even in placid speaking conditions precision varies, even during the course of very short, word-sized periods of utterance; but it also varies during angry speech. The underlying expressive content of the acoustic signal ebbs and flows as the utterance proceeds. The traditional long-term characterizations of the affected parameters masks these changes. For example, the simplistic statement that in angry speech the range of f0 of an utterance is greater than expected for more neutral speech conceals the fact that there have been f0 range variations *during* the utterance. These variations may be systematic and significant.

One point which must be made strongly is that for the speaker the creation of an acoustic signal has a goal. For those aspects of the signal which are produced deliberately by the speaker we can say that the goal is to cause a listener to experience an appropriate percept. Involuntary aspects of the signal might also cause a listener to react perceptually. The acoustic signal conveys whatever is necessary for these listener reactions—it is not an acoustic signal devoid of intended meaning.

It is for this reason that signal-processing-type measurements made on the waveform have always to be linked with parallel accounts of the signal's function. Thus we find, for example, that changes in f0, say, at the end of an utterance reflect or embody changes of *intonation*. Fundamental frequency is not intonation, it is rather the vehicle by which intonation—and all that this 'means'—is signalled to the listener. An example of contextual reinterpretation of a prosodic signal is given by Ladd et al. (1985, though there are many others): in English the 'preferred' method of asking a question is to invert the subject and its verb, and introduce a slight rising intonation at the end of the question. The preferred method in French is arguably not to invert the subject and verb, but to produce a greater rising intonation. Thus: *Did he go home?* and *Il est rentré?* (alternatively, but perhaps less frequently: *Est-il rentré?*). But note that in English *When did he go home?* usually has a falling intonation, but *Quand est-il rentré?* maintains the rising intonation. *Wh*-questions in English usually have the falling intonation which listeners judge to be 'neutral'—that is, the question element is conveyed by the *wh*-question word rather than by the intonation. Thus interpretation of linguistic phenomena like 'question' depend on the context of the prosodic elements as well as the segmental elements they enclose.

The point of this is that intonation contours *in themselves* do not have expressive content. Interpretation of expression by the listener depends on context—in this case syntactic context. But this means there are two types of context: there is this one—context *external* to the signal, and there is the other type—context *internal* to the signal ('This contour is going up relative to that one', for example).

10.3 Speakers

Researchers attempting to characterize how emotion and attitude are conveyed by speech find that it is essential that descriptions

Linguistics, Phonology, and Phonetics

of the underlying emotions and their manifestations in the speech waveform should be compatible. For this to work there must be a common basis for establishing relationships between the two, which will enable us to see clearly how the parameters of one description link with the parameters of the other—though there is no need for this to be on a one-to-one basis.

10.3.1 Characterizing emotion in speech

We think it unlikely that a single framework for this task will be entirely possible because emotion, at least from the cognitive point of view, is abstract and the parameters of the acoustic signal used to convey expression in general are physical. We would go further, and emphasize that the descriptive framework which deals with listener perception of the expressive content in what is heard, and how the listener reacts cognitively to the soundwave, must also be compatible. So far the clearest and least ambiguous area of the chain of events linking speaker feelings with the listener's perception of these feelings is the acoustic signal itself. Although there are still difficulties in saying just which acoustic parameters are involved and how they correlate precisely with underlying emotions or attitudes, measuring techniques in the acoustics of speech and the statistical treatment of the data are quite robust and not in question.

When it comes, though, to a characterization of underlying emotions the picture is less clear. It depends on the researcher's purpose and why they are building their model or what the basis for their overall theory of expression is. There is no doubt that much progress has been made in recent decades in understanding the nature of emotion and its expression in speech—despite the fact that the work often has niche status. We feel that the time is now right, however, for a proper integrated theory and a robust general framework for the field of study.

10.3.2 Where to start?

Some researchers feel that the place to start is with some major categories of emotion—contentment, sadness, fear, disgust, anger, and surprise—and proceed from these to the subtler, less 'obvious' emotions. They approach emotions from three angles:

1. describe them;
2. explain their causes;
3. characterize their effects.

Each of these tasks is fraught with difficulties.

The *description* of an emotion involves accounting for the nature of something which is essentially an abstraction. An emotion is something a person feels or experiences: it is not a physical object. Its description has to be in terms suitable for characterizing abstractions for which we mostly have data derived only from human responses to these abstractions or reports of their behavioural effects. The techniques involved here usually come from psychology, and address cognitive manifestations of emotion. As such, emotions are usually thought of as discrete objects with separate labels: 'anger', 'joy', etc. In Part IV we discuss how these separate categories might be modelled as part of a continuous multi-dimensional object called 'emotion'.

The *causes* of emotions are just as elusive. The trigger for experiencing an emotion, we can imagine, can be generated within a person, or impinge on a person from outside. In either case the trigger may be cognitive or it may be physical. Some would argue that physical causes are mediated cognitively to produce the trigger responsible for experiencing the emotion. The theoretical problem here is that it is difficult to reconcile frameworks for describing the relationship between physical and cognitive phenomena. Exactly the same problem exists in linguistics in trying to relate phonological (cognitive) and phonetic (mostly physical, but sometimes cognitive) processes.

The *effects* of emotions are often described rather vaguely. If an emotion has physical or somatic correlates in a person the effects can be somatic or motor, voluntary or involuntary, and generate visual or auditory cues for a witness to the person's emotional experience. Cognitive effects might induce a speaker to deliver utterances in particular ways, altering the expected prosodics which then could be said to be 'encoding' the emotion—a cognitively dominated effect. But additionally a *communicated* emotion—one which has been perceived either visually or auditorily by another person—itself may trigger an effect in the perceiver. As a result of perceiving sadness in a speaker, a listener may themselves become sad; for the listener this is clearly an externally caused emotion.

But from a scientific point of view, finding a common framework within which to build an integrated theory of emotion is going to be very hard indeed. The most we have been able to do is characterize parts of the chain of events within the appropriate disciplines—psychology, biology, linguistics, phonetics, sociology, computer science, etc.—and do this with enough care at least to ensure that there is not total incompatibility between these sub-theories or models.

10.3.3 What next?

Much current research emphasizes the discreteness of emotions. But it also recognizes that there seem to be two different levels involved, and distinguishes between discrete 'primary' emotions and 'secondary' emotions. The secondary emotions are sometimes said to be mixes or blends of the primary ones (Plutchik 1994; Oatley and Johnson-Laird 1998). The limit to the number of secondary emotions would be a function of how many discrete mixes could be distinguished by the person experiencing the emotion. On the audio communicative front the limit to the number of secondary emotions would depend on how many discrete mixes could be signalled by the audio signal and what limits there are on perceiving differences in the signal—the 'difference threshold' factor.

An alternative model might suggest a different approach. There might be a number of parameters which come together to enable category identification of an emotion. That is, when certain parameters intersect a particular emotion is identified. The system could be thresholded, and we might say that any identified emotion which rises above a particular level constitutes a primary emotion. So a primary emotion arises when features cluster in particular ways, and different ways are identified as different emotions. So in this model there are 'features' of emotion which underlie particular emotions. Thus it is the way features group which defines basic emotions.

10.3.4 Speaker expression of emotion

Some researchers have noted that it is not necessarily the case that speakers are aware that they are experiencing an emotion, or, if they are, then exactly what that emotion is. This is one of the reasons why spontaneous expressive speech is so difficult to collect for the purposes of analysis. There are several possibilities:

- An emotion is being experienced but the speaker is unaware of this.
- An emotion that the speaker is aware of is not being encoded in the acoustic signal, not being 'expressed'.
- The emotion being experienced is not clear or is very weak and is expressed as an ambiguous acoustic signal.
- The experienced emotion is clear and strong, but the 'wrong' acoustic signal is being produced.

Pinning down speaker emotion is especially difficult for this kind of reason. Some researchers have sought to provide a secondary channel of data which might independently back up a speaker's reported feelings about experience of emotion, or provide a check against the expressive content of the acoustic signal.

The kinds of independent check which have been tried involve, for example, detection and measuring of what are often called 'physiological parameters' which are concomitant with the attempted expression of emotion. As an example of this, researchers have attempted to correlate emotion with parameters such as heart rate, sweating, or the activity of certain muscle groups (Amir and Ron 1998), also breathing rate and blood pressure. With a similar aim in mind other researchers have been tracking hormonal levels (Scarpa and Raine 2000).

10.3.5 Voice quality changes and deliberate prosodic effects

A number of emotions, particularly if felt strongly, appear to produce bodily or somatic reactions. So, for example, amusement is usually accompanied by a smile. And, as in the case of a smile, if the somatic reaction is facial or in some way distorts the speaker's vocal tract it is likely to be the case that a change is made to the acoustic signal. Initially we might think of this change as unintended, but there is no reason why a speaker could not use this as an intentional way of signalling expression, provided its occurrence is systematic. Speakers detect the expressive content in speech and either indirectly (through recognizing the smile) or directly (recognizing the amusement which caused the smile) assign an 'amused' label to the speaker (Tartter and Braun 1994).

There has been some discussion about involuntary vs. voluntary introduction of expressive content into speech. Generally voluntary control means the deliberate use of an acoustic parameter— almost always one associated with signalling prosody—to let a listener know how the speaker feels. Voluntary control either means that the speaker has

- deliberately (by cognitive choice) caused an acoustic effect by altering the motor control of the vocal tract in some way; or
- deliberately not tried to suppress an effect which is caused involuntarily—such as the tremor resulting from 'shaking with anger'.

The second of these is interesting because it means that speakers are aware of involuntary effects and to a certain extent can allow them or not. This is like the control of the involuntary effects of coarticulation, discussed in Cognitive Phonetics.

But in addition there is the possibility of a speaker simulating an otherwise involuntary distortion of the acoustic signal. Speakers know, for example, that listeners can easily 'hear' a smile. This means that they can smile deliberately, even when they are neither amused nor joyous, to give the impression that they are experiencing the emotion. We might associate this effect generally with the extreme case of acted speech—speech from trained and professional actors—but ordinary speakers do the same thing. An interesting question is whether listeners can tell the difference between a genuine smile (the involuntary reaction to amusement) and a faked one (a deliberate attempt to change the acoustic signal or create a visual impression). One or two researchers believe that on the whole listeners can tell the difference (Aubergé and Lemaître 2000).

Earlier Damasio (1994) had claimed that memory of 'somatic states' enables speakers to reproduce at will effects which might usually be associated with involuntary expressive content in speech. The question which is not yet entirely answered is whether the memory of the somatic state enables the state itself to be reproduced or whether it enables the acoustic effect it did produce to be reproduced without necessarily repeating the somatic effect itself. Damasio, and to a certain extent Aubergé and Lemaître, feel that the somatic state is usually what is recreated, but clearly both are possible.

10.3.6 Voicing source and quality changes

A number of researchers have investigated expression-related spectral changes to the vocal cord excitation source. In linguistic terms, sounds which are normally rendered phonetically with vocal cord vibration are called 'voiced sounds'. Changing rate of vocal cord vibration is involved in rendering intonation contours and other prosodic phenomena. What researchers have been looking at, though, is spectral changes in the excitation source. There are two ways in which variations in voice quality play a role in communicating speaker feelings.

1. One involves voluntarily switching on and off various modes of voicing. The categories proposed and described in detail by Laver (1980) are sometimes used as a starting point for this work, and there are several examples in the literature of tables showing the expressive uses of particular voice qualities (Table 10.2), though other researchers have proposed alternative categories—but the principle is the same. Speakers deliberately (consciously or unconsciously) use these voice qualities to communicate their associated expressive content.

It should be noted that for Laver 'expressive content' does not necessarily relate directly to specific types of emotion of the kind generally discussed in the more recent literature. 'Intimacy', for example, is something the listener feels when hearing breathy voice, but it is outside most definitions of emotion, attitude, and

Linguistics, Phonology, and Phonetics

Table 10.2. The relationship between voice quality and associated expressive content (after Laver 1980)

Voice quality	Associated expressive content
Breathy voice	Intimacy
Creak	Boredom
Whisper	Confidentiality
Harsh voice	Anger

expression. This has not detracted from the use many researchers have made of Laver's categories as a starting point for a more constrained approach.

2. The other way in which voice quality plays a role in communicating speaker feelings relates to the changes to the vocal cord sound because the larynx or associated mechanisms are being physically distorted by some external force. An example of this is when a speaker is so angry or excited that they are shaking—causing a tremor in voicing. Strictly this is not switching between different voice qualities, but externally induced changes to whatever voice quality the speaker is attempting to use.

10.3.7 The relationship between prosody and expression: wrappers

The primary linguistic vehicle, it is generally agreed, for conveying expressive content in speech is prosody. However, the question arises as to whether prosody is within expression or expression within prosody—which has the dominant node in the hierarchy? A more technical terminology would speak of either expression wrapping prosody or prosody wrapping expression. Is linguistic prosody (like question intonation) fitted to expressive use of prosodic parameters, or is it the other way round? We are clear that for us expression wraps or dominates linguistic prosody. And it is on this basis that the detail of the supporting speech production model is given in Chapter 16.

Certainly, physical distortion of the signal (as in sobbing with sadness) has an effect on the way the intonation contour is handled in asking questions and signalling other prosodic effects.

In a cognitively dominated expression of the sadness emotion the same is true: a narrowed range of f0 excursion constrains how much f0 can signal questions. In general, partly because expression is a longer-term effect, we feel that expressive content wraps prosodic content—that is, in this case we should see that the acoustic correlates of linguistic prosody are constrained by the expressive acoustics. The range of f0 available for question-asking depends on the mood of the speaker, and it would be a simple matter to examine experimentally whether anger produces wider-range f0 linguistic prosodic effects than, say, sadness. Similarly, it should be possible to establish the relative contribution of predominantly physical origins of expressive content (like intense anger) and predominantly cognitive origins (like politeness).

If the claim is appropriate, expressive content dominates prosodic content just as it dominates segmental rendering in its ability to call for increased (for anger) or decreased (for a 'couldn't care less' attitude) precision of articulation. Using XML notation we would indicate this as:

<expression> <linguistic_prosody> *utterance*
</linguistic_prosody> </expression>

A possible source of confusion here is the fact that the parameters of linguistic prosody and the parameters of the acoustics of expression may be the same. Thus change of f0 is used to signal the presence or absence of a question, and change of f0 is also used to signal some aspects of expressive content. Thus the interaction between the two uses of the parameters must be known both to speaker and listener if successful communication is to take place.

In the case of f0—although the same applies to other parameters—we must be careful of the way abstract linguistic descriptions and abstract emotive descriptions relate to the actual soundwave. Abstract descriptions are likely to omit reference to linguistically or emotively irrelevant detail in the signal—this does not mean that this acoustic detail is irrelevant to the acoustic *model*. A parallel would be the way in which, for phonology, acoustic smoothing caused by real-time constraints on abutting segments (coarticulation) is irrelevant and omitted from phonological characterizations, whereas smoothing which is not time-constrained but which *is* linguistically relevant (assimilation) *is* included in phonological descriptions.

Another example is the way the notion 'sameness' differs at the abstract and physical levels in speech and language. Physically two objects are the same if, within the limits of measurement, no readings or scores differ for the chosen parameters. But at an abstract level sameness refers to functional equivalence—two items are the same if their functioning cannot be distinguished. Because the notion of sameness varies at different levels in the characterization of language—including expressiveness, prosody, and segmental effects—it is necessary to be very clear about the level of detail to be included in characterizations. It is not always the case that researchers have taken this kind of consideration into account, making direct comparison between observations by different researchers difficult.

In characterizing expressive content in the acoustic signal and making comparisons with prosodic content in the signal, care must be taken to compare like with like. Relating generalized expressive contours with intonational contours makes some sense, but relating acoustic details of f0 changes because of expressive content with abstract intonation contours does not make sense and can easily lead to questionable assertions. We must be careful not to imply 'ownership' of acoustic parameters either by prosody or by expression. Prosody and expression *share* their acoustic parameters—though this does not detract from the idea of a hierarchical, wrapped relationship.

Paeschke and Sendlmeier (2000) point out that between the end-point values of f0 at the start and finish of a sentence 'accent' (intonation domain), there are several word accents and 'minima' between these accents. When quantified and expressed as a temporal progression of values, the sentence assumes a characteristic accent time profile—a potential parameter of expressive content. In comparing different expressions for the same utterance, the technique may have important discriminative power. We suggest an explicit link between intonation and rhythm—a potential correlation which could use more investigation. It might well be the case that the relationship between intonation contours and timing could profit from more attention in both prosodics and expression research.

10.4 Listeners

Based on a construct from perceptual psychology, some researchers postulate a perceptual space for emotion, within which the various emotions are to be located (see Eskenazi 1992 for a multi-dimensional space for the acoustics of style, and also Tams and Tatham 1995). We also base aspects of our perceptual work on this concept. This is quite similar to well-established ideas about the perception of speech which go back to the 1960s, and possibly originated with the acoustic vowel spaces of Peterson and Barney (1952). These perceptual spaces are sometimes two-dimensional, but are more likely to be multi-dimensional, reflecting sets of parameters which are used to characterize the perceptual objects which fall within them. Perceptual objects are located within the space, usually at points of intersection of the parameters. Recognizing a certain 'fuzziness' in perception in general, some researchers speak of 'areas' or zones of intersection for the parameters rather than points. Others use points in an abstract way, but speak of actual instantiations in terms of a variability associated with the perceptual fuzziness.

10.4.1 The representation of perceived emotions

It is quite common to try to set up correlations between these perceptual spaces and spaces which can be used to characterize the perceived data on a different level—usually a level prior to the act of perception. For example, phoneticians note a two-dimensional space described by the measured values of the centre frequencies of the first two formants of isolated vowels; these values are measured in Hz, though some transformation may be applied to make the space more manageable. This physical space is correlated with points placed on a two-dimensional perceptual space by listeners—sometimes with the help of a given reference point for a particular vowel. Thus in a typical experiment listeners would be asked to give graphical representation to the positions of heard vowels within the perceptual space. There is a remarkable degree of correlation between these two spaces—and indeed between both of them and the Classical Phonetics vowel charts.

The perception of emotion is certainly more complex than the perception of vowel sounds, but the notion of a perceptual emotional space is very useful in helping understand how emotions are categorized by a listener. Just as in the perceived vowel space, notions of 'distance' between other phonetic objects are easy to elicit from listeners—hence the term 'space'. Distance terms are also used in lay language to relate speech sounds and heard emotions—anger and irritation are 'closer' than anger and happiness, for example.

10.4.2 Listener interpretation of different emotions and attitudes

Many speech researchers report that a few emotions, for example anger, fear, sadness, and contentment, are more unambiguously perceived than others. In most cases what researchers mean by this is that listeners' reports as to which emotions they heard match what the speaker intended. One of the problems here is knowing what the expressed emotion was. There are two ways of finding out:

- Ask the speaker.
- Measure the acoustic signal.

Good matches between perceived and intended expressive content are invariably reported for the 'basic' emotions, less success—expressed as increased confusion or error—with 'secondary' emotions. In speech research the stronger emotions are those which either are said to be felt more strongly by the speaker or provide the least ambiguous acoustic signals as measured. It is often found that when an error does occur, a listener identifies an expression which is close to the intended one rather than distant from it.

Some researchers are trying to discover the extent to which the feeling and consequent acoustic encoding of emotions and other categories of expression are universal—in the sense that they transcend different languages or language groups. The work is still at an early stage, but it seems that non-native speakers of a language are less likely to achieve correct scores when assigning emotion labels to the signal than native speakers. There could be several reasons for this besides the more obvious claim that emotions are signalled subtly differently in different languages. For example, a non-native speaker may be preoccupied with extracting primary semantic content rather than expressive nuance, thus reducing the capacity of their processing channel, so to speak.

Definitions concerning strength of expression are invariably rather informal, and the usual criticisms can be levelled at the use of actors to provide the data. A few researchers have attempted what is known as a semantic analysis of the emotions and tried to correlate this with clear indications in the acoustic signal. Work here is very incomplete, but a study by Paeschke et al. (1999) showed a not unexpected correlation between the intensity of the acoustic signal and stressed syllables; they were thus able to differentiate between emotions semantically assessed as 'excited' and 'non-excited'.

Semantic analysis and establishing correlations between semantic features and acoustic parameters is an area of research which shows promise, provided clear definitions of the semantic features are agreed. One opportunity presented is that it may be possible to assess in a usefully quantifiable way to what extent a listener has 'missed' a correct interpretation of some expressive content.

10.4.3 Perception of expressive content and context-sensitivity

Studies have focused on discovering what it is in the acoustic signal that reflects a *known* emotion or attitude in the speaker. As we have seen, the question arises: How do we know what this speaker emotion is? Earlier we pointed out that the experimental databases used in this kind of research often come from actors asked to produce sets of utterances with particular expressive content, and sometimes come from non-actors also prompted as to what expressions to use during the recording sessions. Judgements of the accuracy of the performers' efforts are made either by the experimenter or better, by panels of listeners who score them for whether the acoustic signal truly reflects the intended expressive content. Very seldom do these researchers discuss the listeners' ability to do the scoring accurately.

However, psychologists and phonetics researchers who have looked at perception in general and at the perception of segmental aspects of speech in particular report that perception is very often context-dependent. Indeed, it may well be the case that perception is always context-dependent, though occasionally context may actually matter little. If this is the case, it follows that unless context is taken into account in evaluating what listeners report they hear, it may be the case that for a given acoustic signal different interpretations may be made on different occasions, or conversely different acoustic signals may give rise to the same interpretation.

With segmental speech the contextual effect is considerable and complex, and depends on several factors including semantic, syntactic, and phonological selection, and phonetic coarticulation. We also know that speakers can and do adjust their speech in anticipation of contextual effects which might tax the perceiver. Certainly at the segmental level the overall effect is such that models which attempt to show a one-to-one correlation between phonological objects (or utterance plans), acoustic signals, and the labels assigned by listeners fail seriously to account for even the most casual of observations.

Figure 10.1 shows a spectrogram of the acoustic signal of a monosyllabic utterance, *dad*, spoken by a speaker of Estuary English, an accent of English spoken by perhaps as many as 10,000,000 people. The phonological plan for this utterance consists of the sequence of extrinsic allophones / d + æ + d /, and this is the plan recovered by a typical listener—by which we mean that this is the allophonic string assigned by a listener in the process of interpreting what they hear. We can note that [d] is planned as a voiced alveolar plosive for speakers of this accent. However, the phonetic rendering, the acoustic signal of which is seen in the

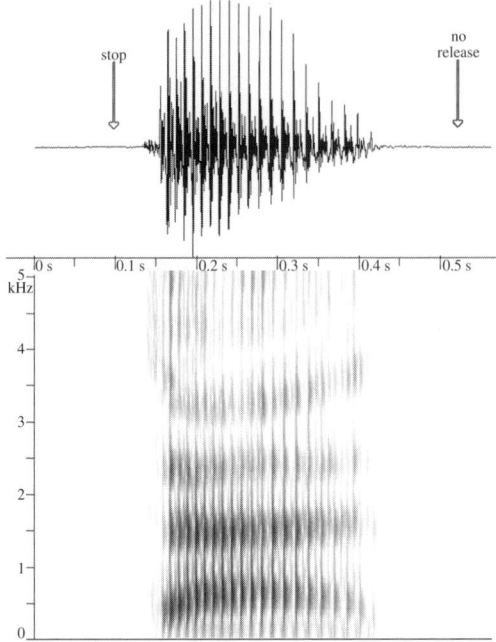

Fig. 10.1. Spectrogram of the word *dad* spoken by a speaker of Estuary English.

spectrogram, has no voicing of the initial plosive prior to its release, and there is no signal present following the vowel; the final plosive was rendered as voiceless and unreleased—so was 'silent'. So, apart from the release of the initial plosive, both have very little or no acoustic signal 'associated' with them. It therefore follows that the burden of triggering a correct labelling by the listener falls almost exclusively on the vowel section of the utterance. This is what we mean when we say that there is no one-to-one correspondence between the plan (as intended by the speaker or as recovered by the listener) and the associated acoustic signal.

The conclusion of the segmental studies is that listeners' labels are not actually to be found *in* the signal—they are *assigned* by the listener in response to what they hear, what they know, and what they feel. The assignment of this or that label is possibly not even mainly determined by the acoustic 'trigger' the listener hears, though of course *something* is necessary in the normal course of things to set the perceptual process working. And if this is true of segmental objects in speech it is probably also true of suprasegmental objects. Diagrammed, the perceptual assignment of labels looks like this:

$$\text{waveform} \rightarrow \text{listener} \rightarrow \text{label}$$
$$\uparrow$$
$$\text{set of labels}$$

Speech researchers lack an agreed research strategy for dealing with and defining the limits of context sensitivity in either the production or the perception of expressive content in speech. Research databases which rely on multiple versions of similar utterances spoken with different types of expressive content contribute to the problem. These short sentences are not at all representative of speech in context, except by accident. They are not, for example, extracted from protracted conversations in which context flows and ebbs in a natural way. These short utterances are untypical of what we get in real conversation, and they tend to have been spoken with unchanging expressive content throughout, whereas expressive content can and does easily change during the course of a single utterance. This point is made very clearly by Cauldwell (2000), though his own experiments are based on an unnatural forced-choice paradigm for listener judgement of the expressive content of utterances.

The observation that such lack of context might be an advantage because contextual effects might be able to be normalized or factored out *automatically* is not helpful either, because there is no way of determining what has been factored out to make this speech unnatural—it was never really known to be there to begin with. The other argument which might be brought is that the assessment of these utterances which apparently lack context might provide some kind of benchmark against which to compare utterance *in* context. This argument has some force, but we must beware of falling into the segmentalist trap of claiming that a standard sound is one uttered in isolation, when nobody actually goes around speaking sounds in isolation! Sounds in 'real' utterance context are so different from these artificial utterances that it is hard to know where to begin relating them. We are aware that not everyone agrees with this viewpoint.

10.4.4 General acoustic correlates

We referred earlier to lists of acoustic correlates. The current feelings about correlates are summed up for the main, strong emotions in Scherer (1995) and Johnstone et al. (1995):

- Anger: increase in mean f0 and mean energy. In 'hot anger' there is some indication of increase in f0 variability and in the range of f0 between successive utterances. These last effects seem not to be found in 'cold anger'. Additional effects: increase in high-frequency energy (perhaps caused by tenser vocal cords during stretches where they are vibrating), downward-directed f0 contours (perhaps as sub-glottal air pressure begins to fail); increase in the rate of articulation.
- Fear: increase in mean f0, increase in f0 range, and increase in high-frequency energy (all correlates of high arousal levels, and these are present in fear). Rate of articulation also increases. An increase in mean f0 also correlates with 'milder forms' of anger such as worry or anxiety.
- Sadness: decrease in mean f0, decrease in f0 range, decrease in mean energy; downward directed f0 contours. High-frequency energy decreases; rate of articulation decreases. A highly aroused (Scherer's term) variant, desperation, might show an increase in both f0 and in energy means.
- Joy (extreme: elation; subdued: enjoyment, happiness): usually involves high arousal, and therefore increases in f0, f0 range, f0 variability, and mean energy. Some researchers have found an increase in high-frequency energy and rate of articulation.

'Vocal parameters' correlate with degree of intensity of different emotions, but also differentiate 'qualities'. Johnstone et al. (1995) report that for actors some emotions, such as 'hot anger' and 'boredom', produce consistent acoustic profiles and are accurately labelled by listeners. Some produce consistent acoustics but are less well recognized—perhaps, they suggest, because the actors used were unable to control completely 'all the aspects of voice or speech relevant to that emotion'. This, they claim, might be explained by involuntary physiological changes which are inaccessible to actors but which come across accurately in the case of real, non-acted emotion—though it is difficult to appreciate what this might mean. Some emotions (such as 'interest', which is more related to attention, perhaps, than to emotion) might be encoded using suprasegmental features 'other than long term average modulation of the speech signal', such as temporal changes in f0. 'Disgust' seems universally badly encoded and decoded alike.

10.4.5 *Acoustic correlates: production and perception*

Johnstone and Scherer (2000) are quite unambiguous in their claim that in speech production there are specific modifications of speech to express the various emotions. The claim is quite prevalent in studies of expressive content in speech, and incorporates a number of interesting points which we construe as constituting hypotheses. Using our terminology we can formulate these hypotheses with our own comments:

- Emotions are 'expressed'—that is, voluntarily or involuntarily a speaker's emotions are directly encoded in the speech waveform (the direct encoding hypothesis).
- These encodings produce properties specific to particular emotions (the uniqueness hypothesis).
- Speech is modified by the encoding (the modulation hypothesis).

The direct encoding hypothesis makes the weak claim that there are properties of the waveform which can be directly associated with emotions felt by the speaker. The implication here is that when it comes to perception, decoding could take the form of detecting the properties of the waveform, discriminating emotions, evaluating them, and concluding the presence of a specific emotion.

- An alternative to the direct encoding hypothesis would claim that there is no a priori reason to assume a linear correlation between any particular emotion and its soundwave encoding. On the contrary, there is scope for hypothesizing a non-linear correlation involving a variety of contextual constraints.

We might call this alternative approach the indirect encoding hypothesis.

The uniqueness hypothesis goes further: properties or combinations of properties in the waveform uniquely identify an emotion irrespective of an act of perception. The emotion is encoded in the waveform and is there for a discriminator (human or otherwise) to find. The uniqueness hypothesis suggests a very simple perceptual model which involves the minimum of interpretation. Under such a hypothesis a label for the emotion thus encoded would be derivable from discovering particular properties in the waveform itself: the listener would bring comparatively little to the discriminating and labelling process.

- Again there is an alternative to the uniqueness hypothesis. It follows from the non-linearity of the indirect encoding hypothesis that in the waveform a single parameter value or particular combinations of parameter values would not uniquely specify an emotion. Discrimination between encoded emotions would require an evaluative perceptual process which at the very least would have to assess the constraints leading to non-linearity in order to *assign* an emotion label to the signal. The perceptual process is one of active assignment rather than a more passive derivation. We might call this alternative the non-uniqueness hypothesis.

The modulation hypothesis amounts to a quite fundamental claim about the speech production process in general. Speech production in this model is essentially a process of generating neutral utterances—either in actual fact or in 'rehearsal' prior to the rendering of a plan. Separately and logically posterior, the potentially neutral utterance is modulated (our term: Johnstone and Scherer refer to 'modification') by an emotion. The modulation is specific since it produces what amounts to a unique distortion of the potential neutral waveform.

- The alternative here for the modulation hypothesis suggests that speech is not planned separately from emotion, but planned within the context of emotion—and that not only the final signal but also the planning process itself varies depending on the emotion being expressed. Emotion is seen as a 'wrapper' for the entire system. We call this the 'wrapper hypothesis'.

In common with other researchers, Johnstone and Scherer note that different emotions are perceived with varying success. We can put forward here several reasons for this:

- The set of discriminating parameters is not optimal: some which are included may not be necessary and may be adding noise or ambiguity to the system; some may have been omitted which should have been included, thus contributing to partial failure to raise discrimination far enough above the noise floor equally for all emotions.
- Emotions may differ either in their intrinsic 'strength' or in the strength of their expression in the speech signal—the idea would assume that stronger emotions or emotive content would be perceived with greater accuracy, so that poor accuracy indicates low strength (not necessarily the only conclusion possible).
- Contextual effects have not been sufficiently controlled in the experimental data, such that the perception of different emotions has varied with respect to 'supporting' context.
- Perception may involve more listener contribution than the writers suggest—and the ability of the listener may have varied in the experiment, or may vary in general, thus resulting in uneven discrimination between emotion candidates.

Chapter 11

The Speech Technology Perspective

Many researchers have attempted synthesis of expressive content in speech, and developed techniques for evaluating the feasibility of using current synthesizers for expressive speech. This work is necessary because there is little doubt that synthesizers have been designed around early models of speech production which have not recognized the importance of synthesizing prosody, and usually completely neglected considerations of accurate synthesis of expressive content. Feasibility studies are designed to discover whether a given synthesizer can simulate expression in speech transparently—that is, without constraints imposed by the device itself. This is particularly important if the synthesis is to be used for testing a model of expression: it is important to know whether errors arise from the model or from an inadequate test-bed—the synthesizer.

11.1 Synthesis feasibility studies

Below we examine the relative merits of different synthesizers when it comes to synthesizing expressiveness, but we must

- first, determine whether particular types of synthesis system are inherently suitable;
- secondly, make sure that any one synthesizer is a reliable and stable implementation of its type.

The two most popular system types are concatenative waveform and parametric synthesizers, with parametric synthesizers subdividing into formant-based systems and linear predictive coding systems. Concatenative systems are usually thought to produce the most natural *neutral* speech (though some would disagree with this), whereas parametric systems are the more manipulable of the two types. Based on contemporary models of expressive content in the acoustic signal, researchers have attempted to evaluate whether particular synthesizers are adequately manipulable. Table 11.1 summarizes the results.

As far as fundamental frequency is concerned, both types of synthesizer can change the actual values on a moment-by-moment basis, and hence can manipulate average f0, f0 floor or baseline (the lowest value, useful in studies of declination), and f0 range (the difference between the lowest and highest values). Both systems can also manipulate timing: overall utterance rate, rhythm, and duration of syllables or smaller elements can all be changed. When it comes to the two other main parameters: formant frequencies and voice quality, changes are usually only possible with parametric synthesis. Hence changing the effect of coarticulation on formant frequency-bending as rate of utterance changes is not possible with waveform concatenation. Similarly, altering the precision of an articulation, which usually also means changing the effects of coarticulation on formant frequencies, is not possible. Altering voice quality, often necessary in expressing

Table 11.1. Synthesized expression parameters compared with their availability in concatenative waveform and parametric synthesis

Synthesized expression parameter	Concatenative waveform synthesis	Parametric synthesis
Fundamental frequency	yes	yes
Formant frequencies	no	yes
Individual formant amplitudes	no	yes
Articulatory precision	no	yes
Overall amplitude	yes	yes
Element timing	yes	yes
Rhythm	yes	yes
Voice quality	no	yes

strong anger, sadness, or boredom, is usually not possible either with concatenative synthesis.

So, to summarize, experiments such as these indicate that the most versatile synthesizers from the point of view of injecting expressive content into speech are the parametric ones. Concatenated waveform systems, while often able to provide the most natural-sounding speech, are less versatile.

11.1.1 Device settings for expressive speech synthesis

There are a number of settings in synthesis systems which are usable for prosodic effects and hence expressive content. These are shown in Table 11.2. For each variable 'speech parameter' there are corresponding variables which can be adjusted in most synthesis systems—particularly those of the parametric type. The table does not show an exhaustive set of parameters or variables, but these are the commonest cited in the literature as being the most appropriate for rendering the least ambiguous types of expression.

In general these are the properties involved in introducing expressive content into speech, and researchers have focused on these. We draw attention to them here because they form the basis of almost all the work so far on the synthesis of expression—and specifically emotion—in speech.

Table 11.2. Correspondence between parameters of the speech signal and their associated variables

Speech parameter	Corresponding variables
Fundamental frequency	Global settings for f0 mean and range
	No. of f0 maxima and minima per time unit
	Duration, 'magnitude', and steepness of f0 rises and falls
Tempo	Duration of pauses
	Articulation tempo (number of rhythmic units per unit time)
Intensity	Global settings for intensity mean and range
	Some index of dynamics: difference between mean intensity for intensity maxima and overall mean intensity
Voice quality	Spectral slope
	Creaky/lax

11.1.2 Recent improvements to formant synthesis

In recent years there have been attempts to improve the naturalness of formant synthesis by incorporating models of how the acoustic signal is produced aerodynamically—that is, the introduction of 'pseudo-articulatory' parameters. Perhaps the most successful implementation of this approach is the HLsyn™ implementation by Sensimetrics Corporation of Somerville, Mass., which is based on the earlier Klatt synthesizer (Klatt 1980). HL here stands for 'high level', but this should not be confused with our use of this term in this book and elsewhere to refer to the underlying linguistics rather than the physical events which give rise to the acoustic signal. In the HLsyn™ interpretation of 'high level' the model adds to a Klatt synthesizer a dozen or so new articulatory parameters.

The results are a clear improvement in naturalness of, in fact, the low-level synthesizer, but this still needs to be driven by high-level (our meaning) information. In the synthesis of expressive content it is fair to say that the current prosodic models are still quite unable to do justice to such improvements in low-level systems. Where synthesizers of the HLsyn™ type will eventually come into their own will be in being able to provide the kinds of subtle variation of the *acoustic* signal demanded by expressive prosodics. These are variations which involve precise adjustment and manipulation of articulatory, aerodynamic, and acoustic parameters in a way which is quite impossible in concatenated waveform systems. The least subtle of these is the ability to vary independently the centre frequencies, bandwidths, and amplitudes of individual formants, but there are several others.

For example, for the purposes of synthesis we commonly model fundamental frequency *contours* as relatively smooth changes in fundamental frequency; but in doing so we risk masking period-to-period variability in the waveform. Such variability might well be involved in the encoding of expression, as in the local introduction of 'breathy voice' for brief periods during 'breathless fear' or 'uncontrollable excitement'. For the moment this is not too important, since our high-level modelling of such expressive content is far from satisfactory, but the time will come when the high-level modelling begins to anticipate the availability of the kind of fineness of control being introduced by this new generation of formant synthesizer. Designers of a new implementation of DECTalk (Bickley et al. 1997; Bickley and Bruckert 2002) claim improved control of voice quality capable of participating in producing 'precise articulation' or 'creaky voice' or even contributing to such expressive content as 'urgency'. How such effects can be obtained without resorting to manual control of the synthesizer parameters ultimately rests squarely on the quality of the controlling high-level prosodic model.

Since the earliest formant synthesizers of the middle twentieth century we have learned much more about the details of the acoustics of speech production, in particular details which go a long way beyond the relatively simple source/filter model (Fant 1960) which formed the basis of these synthesizers. But in addition much more is known about variations between speakers in terms of their anatomy and therefore the characteristics of the speaker-specific waveforms they produce. This knowledge is important in modelling for synthesis purposes the detailed characteristics of different speaking voices. The additional layer of 'articulatory control' goes a long way to enabling the implementation of these recent findings (Stevens and Bickley 1991; Hanson and Stevens 2002).

11.1.3 Formant synthesis with articulatory control

The basis of formant synthesis is the modelling of the acoustics of speech production in terms of a source of sound and a set of filtering processes. Extensions of this idea include using a set of control parameters deriving from models characterizing how subglottal pressure, laryngeal configuration and larynx state, and the configuration of the vocal tract change dynamically during speech. An explicit mapping between these 'underlying' parameters and the more 'surface' acoustic parameters enables control of the synthesizer to originate higher up the chain of events leading to the acoustic signal.

Some researchers claim improved detail in the acoustic signal because of this higher-level control. Stevens (2002), for example, claims advantages to this approach in the areas of segmental, syllabic, and prosodic aspects of the utterance. Early research on this idea includes the work by Werner and Haggard (1969) and by Tatham (1970a,b). These researchers attempted with some measure of success to drive acoustic parametric synthesizers using control data derived from vocal tract configurations.

Provided we are able to construct adequate models of the acoustic and articulatory correlates of expression in speech, it should be possible to incorporate such extensions to the more usual acoustic parametric synthesis to advantage. However, most current ideas of the acoustics of expression adhere closely to the traditional parametric model found in the earlier synthesizers. A reanalysis of the acoustic signal may not be enough to provide the necessary data, however, unless this can be directly inferred from the acoustic data. It is questionable whether we yet understand enough of how these 'articulatory' correlates relate to the traditional synthesis parameters to be able to test our overall models of expression. Clearly the basis of the test-bed must itself be well understood before we can be sure, for example, of the source of errors in the output: do they come from the expression model, or do they come from errors in the mapping between articulation and acoustics?

Much has been written in the last few decades about the mapping from vocal tract configurations and details of larynx states to the raw acoustic signal of human speech, but whether this knowledge transfers well to the parametric characterizations which have usually been developed for their *economy* of representation remains a matter for empirical testing. Extended parameter synthesizers, such as the Klatt model and the more recent HLsyn™ model, subscribe less to the economy approach but, as models, their explicit relationship to human articulation remains a matter for investigation. There is clearly some kind of trade-off relationship between the low-level synthesizer's ability to fine-tune the acoustic output and detail in the high-level specification.

Stevens (2002) suggests that the technique of adding a higher level of articulatory parameters and a mapping between these and the synthesizer parameters can result in improvements in syllabic and prosodic rendering—the syllable is the basic unit of prosody (Tatham and Morton 2002), but it is hard to see how adding an articulatory layer contributes to better modelling of prosody.

11.1.4 Concatenated waveform synthesis and utterance style

Concatenated waveform synthesis is generally unsuited to the prosodic subtleties of expression. This is because of the very limited control over features of the waveform other than fundamental frequency and timing. And even with the best waveform modification techniques, distortions are introduced if f0 and timing are varied beyond certain relatively narrow limits.

Campbell (2000) and others have suggested that since ultimately in waveform concatenation synthesis what is possible is constrained by what prosodic features are available in the system database, it would make sense to introduce several databases into the system, each reflecting a particular style or emotion. Clearly there are serious limitations in the use of such a system:

- Only two or three different styles or emotions would be possible before the amount of data required became unwieldy, especially if there are interactive factors such as f0 and 'voice quality'.
- The use of the different styles would at best be confined to relatively long stretches of speech, with none of the subtle changes human speakers make, even within an utterance, impossible except with great difficulty and perhaps considerable luck.

Johnson et al. (2002) have however demonstrated a limited domain system simulating military commands in four different speaking styles. The synthesis was for animated characters. The appropriate style was called by using XML tags marking the required style for any given utterance within the scope of the domain. This shows that, provided systems are designed around their intrinsic constraints, useful synthetic speech can be achieved. The XML tag system used was very gross, however, and did not permit the kind of subtlety observed in human speech where type and degree of expressive content can vary over very short stretches of speech at sub-utterance levels.

11.1.5 The importance of prosody in concatenated waveform synthesis

Prosody is a term used in speech synthesis systems (particularly in text-to-speech systems) which can refer to one of two different levels in the model: it can refer either to prosody at a linguistic level or to the acoustic correlates of linguistic prosody.

- At the linguistic level we can assign such features as intrinsic word stress without reference to anything more than the textual symbols themselves—that is, the individual objects or units, such as words, without reference to their context. Other features, such as sentence stress or intonation, require assignment based on what can be worked out from the semantics and syntax of textual elements such as words or words in combination. Still other features can be projected as 'interpretations' of the text: intonation, putative rhythm, and abstract expressive features such as 'angry'.
- At the acoustic level we have the various correlates of these linguistic features.

One of the main points to be made is that at the linguistic level many of the features—the 'projected' ones—have to be assigned on the basis of generalizations derived from examining the way texts are typically read aloud. These features are usually either not entered in the textual representation (for example, intonation) or barely represented, such as the full stop or period indicating sentence-final endpoint—which could be taken as signalling a 'final' fall in the intonation curve in English. Terms such as 'angry' are one stage removed from the 'normal' (that is, 'no additional expressive content') in as much as they refer to expression which uses prosody as its carrier. The acoustic correlates, as we have seen elsewhere in this book, have the status of 'proposed' rather than 'agreed', since it is not possible yet to be absolutely certain about the acoustic correlates or the degree of linearity attached to the correlation.

A common starting point for designers of text-to-speech systems is the development of strategies for marking up the text to include a minimum of prosodic textual markers not found in ordinary orthography. The more detail that is added the closer the acoustic signal will be to what is required—provided the algorithms relating the linguistics prosodic mark-up and the acoustic variables are adequate. We have to be careful, though. Increased detail in the mark-up may mean increased linguistic detail: it does not necessarily mean that this translates easily to real-world parameters. Sometimes researchers equate these two more closely than merited, or assume the correlation to be more linear than it actually is.

There are two prevalent methods of using prosodic tags:

- Use the prosodic tags to compute quantitative target values—this is the linguistically well principled method for intonation assignment (Pierrehumbert 1981; Tatham and Lewis 1992).
- Use the prosodic tags as the basis for searching large databases to find a match with units having similar tags; these are then concatenated (and perhaps some signal processing is applied to smooth the output—such processing is not linguistically motivated).

There is evidence to suggest that the acoustic parameters which are usually understood to reflect utterance prosodics—fundamental frequency, duration, and amplitude—are not the only ones influenced by prosody. There are also spectral changes (Epstein 2002; Wouters and Macon 2002a; 2002b). Work in this area is comparatively recent, but it is fairly clear that we do not yet fully understand or perhaps even appreciate the interaction between prosody and the spectrum. It is reasonable to assume that the 'extended' use of the acoustic correlates of prosody to include expressive content will also have to involve considerations of interaction with the spectrum in addition to the three usual acoustic parameters associated with prosody. In formant synthesis models it should not be difficult to implement spectral changes, but the same cannot be said of waveform concatenative low-level techniques. Modifying detail of the spectral *structure* and spectral *dynamics* of a waveform is not easy, although gross spectral tilt and waveform shaping (gross aspects of spectral structure) can be altered by suitable filtering. Filtering of this kind, though, is only usually applied over comparatively long stretches of utterance, and local application would be difficult to accomplish and difficult to control, though they may prove essential for short-term changes in expressive and emotive content.

Strong emotional factors which influence whole sections of speech are the easiest; so, for example, some degree of spectral tilt might be introduced to reflect the laryngeal tension associated with excitement. It is also likely that the spectral composition or balance within stressed syllables is different from that in corresponding unstressed syllables, assuming no 'vowel reduction'. In such circumstances we are likely to find that the rate of change in formant values is greater for the stressed syllable, reflecting the effects of time-governed coarticulation. Despite this, inspection of spectrograms reveals that the change in the rate of formant bending seems not always to correlate in a linear fashion with the durational changes in the syllable, and indeed the changes do not apply equally to all formants. When there is linear correlation then durational adjustments should automatically change the rate of formant bending and this is certainly a good first approximation for all cases.

However, it is very early days to be discussing the detail of such modifications, though some progress is being made. Van Santen and Niu (2002) and particularly Epstein (2002) cite factors such as word stress phrase finality as affecting the spectral content of an utterance, and propose filter-style modifications of the acoustic based on five 'formant frequency range bands'—derived from an ad hoc model of the spectral structure of speech which hypothesizes that

- there are bands in the frequency domain which can be regarded as 'belonging' to particular formants, and
- gross modification of spectral amplitudes within these bands adequately models formant amplitude changes which depend on prosody.

11.1.6 *The role of fundamental frequency*

One or two researchers (e.g. Scherer 1986; Mozziconacci 1995) feel that strong emotions correlate with relatively large f0 excursions. This observation does not rule out the possibility that other factors are also involved. For example, there might be accompanying changes of 'voice quality'—that is, there is at least the possibility, we feel, that controlling f0 in a way which might be unusual could cause distortion of normal glottal function, altering the voice quality itself. In any case, it is attested (Fant 1960) that, for example, high rates of vibration of the vocal cords correlate with greater continuous air leakage (breathy voice) than do low rates; so we could at least begin by generating a hypothesis$_1$ that changes of this kind tend to accompany wide swings in rate of vibration and are inevitable. An alternative hypothesis$_2$ would be that f0 changes and voice quality changes are independent variables—this is Scherer's (1986) suggestion, the implication being that f0 and voice quality are used to signal different aspects of expression, or even different expressions. More recently some extensive data has been collected on this relationship (Epstein 2002), with similar results. It is important that hypothesis$_1$ is correctly understood: f0 might cause voice quality changes as it fluctuates beyond certain limits. This hypothesis$_1$ does not preclude the possibility that, in the absence of wide f0 fluctuation, voice quality may be used to signal expression—that voice quality can be both dependent and independent would be an extension of hypothesis$_1$. An informal observation for our breathy voice example is that it is perfectly possible to use *some* degree of breathy voice at any rate of vibration of the vocal cords. If this is true, then the hypothesis can at least be tested for other types of voice quality, such as whispery, creaky, lax–creaky, modal, tense, and harsh voice, to borrow Laver's early (1980) classification.

Attempts such as Gobl et al. (2002) to establish a mapping between voice quality (when it combines with fundamental frequency correlates of expressive speech) and expression have proved inconclusive, and are perhaps confusing, because they do not usually normalize for correlates between different voice qualities, and between these and fundamental frequency which may exist outside the domain of expressive content. In our view the approach is hard to understand and lacks the persuasive argument of Scherer and the fullness of experimental detail of Epstein.

However, until the classification systems mapping impressionistic categories of voice quality are developed into models enabling us to understand how different qualities are produced and what the aerodynamic and other constraints are on them, it may be the case that little progress will be made in understanding how these qualities interact to trigger perceptual feelings as to a speaker's expression. The problem is one of separating controllable features of the phenomena from their intrinsic constraints.

11.1.7 Timing: rhythm and speaking rate

Researchers examining the expressive content of speech observe that timing is one of the critical parameters. There are two aspects to timing:

- overall speaking rate;
- rhythm.

Speaking rate and rhythm stand in a hierarchical arrangement, with speaking rate dominant. Most synthesizers have comprehensive techniques for determining rhythm, often based on the intrinsic durational properties of individual speech sounds interacting with—in languages like English—the stress patterning of utterances (Taylor et al. 1998; Tatham and Morton 2002; but see also the earlier more localized approach adopted by Klatt 1979). The utterance is divided into feet (Abercrombie 1967) or rhythmic units (Jassem et al. 1984) within which the stress patterns are accommodated. Thus in English a sentence like *The president had a good lunch* might fit this model thus:

> The | pre-si-dent | had a | good | lunch.
> where | stands for a foot or rhythmic unit boundary.

Even with this simple sentence there are alternative places to assign rhythmic boundaries, but from this particular example we can see that, *if* feet are approximately equal in duration, the number of syllables to be fitted into a foot can vary. Equal timing of feet is called 'isochrony', an essentially abstract concept (see Lehiste 1977), which may or may not have correlates in the physical signal.

Take a fragment of the same sentence and change it slightly to ... *a good but quick lunch* and we have

... a | good but | quick | lunch.

in which the time allocated to *good* + *but* is no greater than that allocated to *good* in the previous version, because they both occupy a single foot or rhythmic unit. Usually, various rules forming part of the prosodic sub-system deal with such occurrences.

The assignment of correct rhythm to utterances depends, however, not just on local word, syllable, or segment durations and their stress patterns, but also on the overall rate of an utterance. Rate is often quantified in terms of the number of syllables, or better, the number of rhythmic units per unit time. In general synthesizers are set to speak at a particular rate, but can usually be varied by a global command to such settings as 'fast' or 'slow' which are defined relative to some usual or normal rate. The problem is that rate varies in natural human speech over much shorter periods than the entire utterance; to reflect this we need rate control at a sub-utterance level.

The relationship between overall utterance rate and the rhythmic structure of an utterance has not yet been modelled in the amount of detail needed to provide a convincing rendering of details of expressive content. Work is being done (e.g. Vanner et al. 1999; Tatham and Morton 2002; and Masaki et al. 2002) but it is early days yet. Pausing between and within utterances, discussed by these three teams, presents particular problems, since it depends both on the timing factors cited here and on the syntactic structure of the utterance, and gives rise to incomplete rhythmic units which are difficult to predict.

11.1.8 Prosody and unit selection

In variable or large-unit concatenated waveform systems using unit selection, prosody is usually available as an intrinsic property of the selected units. The smaller the unit—and the smallest is usually the diphone—the less usable the unit's intrinsic prosody. In such cases, or in larger unit systems which 'miss' the required prosodic feature, the prosody needs to be computed by sets of rules or some other technique. A rule-based system often results in superior quality because it is not subject to the hit-and-miss vagaries dependent on corpus size in even the largest of unit selection systems.

It makes sense to run a rule-based system for generating prosodic structures alongside deriving prosody from the intrinsic properties, such as the patterning of stressed vs. unstressed syllables or clear intonational patterns, of a large database unit selection system—if only to check for anomalies due to the selection of small units or awkward concatenations. The cost of such a dual system is high in terms of computational load.

In a system described by Prudon et al. (2002) the prosodic features of a large database system were extracted and transposed onto utterances generated by a diphone system, thus avoiding the need for a large set of complex rules and avoiding other than minimal use of syntactic and other analyses. Although entirely a pragmatic approach with no claims toward reflecting any human rendering strategies, the results were surprisingly good, enabling easy adaptation to new voices (by introducing a new database), and surprisingly simple (no need for much syntactic and other processing). The results were not, however, quite as good as the best rule-based systems.

The approach adopted by Prudon et al. is interesting from our point of view because it has the potential for forming the basis of a semi-automated iterative procedure for modelling the acoustic correlates of prosody. No mention of this is made in the reported work, but we suggest there is room for an experimental setup in which a human listener could make progressive alterations on an iterative basis to a rule set dependent on perceptual judgements of the quality and detail of the recorded corpus. Fragments of the corpus and the rule set would be linked by a common descriptive prosodic model. The experiment would point to convergence of the two by this progressive adjustment of the rules. In effect this would automate what researchers developing rule sets already do—but here the corpus fragments would be controlled, and retrieval would be dependent on the unit selection principles in operation rather than on chance encounter or on contrived script-based utterances.

11.2 Testing models of expression

Researchers have discovered that there are difficulties associated with testing models of expressive content using existing synthesis systems. Unless the basic prosodic rendering is good there are worries that, since expressive content is mostly signalled by prosody, it is not possible to tell whether errors are generated by the system or by the expression model. There is agreement that expressive content is often signalled in subtle ways and that human listeners are very sensitive to these subtleties. An experiment which allowed errors in the underlying prosodic system greater than such subtleties would fail to show the source of the errors because of a masking effect.

11.2.1 Testing the acoustic model using synthetic speech

One way around introducing errors in the synthesis itself is to minimize the role the synthesizer's own procedures might play in testing the model of expression. For example, we might use the fact that a text-to-speech system generally has two conceptually distinct levels—one corresponding to high-level phonological and prosodic processes, and one corresponding to low-level physical and acoustic processes. Most text-to-speech systems produce errors in their high-level processing, and it is sometimes possible to bypass this part of the system by tracking what is actually happening in human speech rather than trying to derive this by rules. So, for example, suppose we have a model of the soundwave produced by angry speech, we could take a recording of a human being speaking with the minimum of expression and manipulate it using a resynthesis technique (Holmes and Holmes 2001). The manipulation would follow the proposed model of the acoustics of angry speech, but would apply these to speech guaranteed otherwise 'correct' simply because it is real and not synthesized.

It can easily be argued that an emotion pervades all aspects of speaking, so to this extent the technique could produce false results; but it is argued that this danger, whilst being very real, is smaller in impact than the danger of errors arising from trying to

The Speech Technology Perspective

synthesize everything. The diagram below illustrates the procedure for resynthesizing speech with a new prosodic contour. The model of expressive content in the soundwave is used to predict the relevant parameters of the soundwave—for example, fundamental frequency. The new curve is then introduced into the recording, replacing the speaker's original f0. Typically a listener panel then scores the result.

real speech → prosodic normalization → prosodically neutral speech → re-synthesized expression
↑
expression model

Some researchers use a complete system (including high-level processes) to generate a 'neutral' prosodic contour—basically one which conforms to the system defaults which would typically not include any attempt to handle expressive content. The output is then manipulated, as with the resynthesized speech above, according to predictions made by the expression model. Best results for this kind of approach are obtained with concatenated waveform synthesizers which have the minimum of processing of the original recordings of the units used in creating the synthetic waveform. This type of synthesizer produces waveforms which, since they are based on recordings of human speech, are the most natural-sounding, and therefore the most like fully resynthesized speech.

11.2.2 Interactive testing

Another approach used for *simultaneously* building and evaluating models of expression. It involves

- using the model of acoustic expressive content to generate synthetic speech or resynthesized speech in the way described above;
- evaluating the results by listener panel;
- manipulating the synthesizer parameters on an interactive basis to further adjust the results: as far as the researcher is concerned, this involves an iterative process of adjustment—listening—adjustment—listening, etc., until the researcher is satisfied that there is a genuine improvement;

- repeating the listener panel evaluation to judge the improvements;
- reviewing the adjustments made during the iterative process to see whether important new information has emerged for improving the basic model.

The technique is not perfect, but it does sometimes provide insights which might otherwise have been overlooked. The main pitfall in using the technique is making adjustments which compensate for synthesizer defects, not knowing whether they have something to say about expressive speech. But with care and a good deal of knowledge of the synthesizer being used the worst experimental errors can be avoided.

11.2.3 Expressive content and current speech synthesis

A number of researchers have used synthetic speech to test models of expressive content in speech (Klatt and Klatt 1990; Carlson et al. 1992; Murray and Arnott 1995), employing a technique relying on published analyses of expressive speech or deriving new analyses from a fresh database and using acoustic models based on this work to resynthesize a new waveform. This is then assessed, usually by panels of listeners, for whether the researchers' intended expression is achieved. As before, there are of course two variables here: one is the expressive model, but the other is the actual quality of the speech synthesizer. This quality itself has several dimensions—it may or may not be a good synthesizer in general, or it may or may not lend itself to control in the way dictated by the models.

However, results vary considerably and this leads us to believe that problems contributed by the synthesizer itself are less significant than those created by the models of expression being tested. Even for the emotions usually cited as being the least ambiguous, like anger or sadness, the results are uneven, perhaps reflecting the variability present in human waveforms. These waveforms have been measured and the parameters of expression 'extracted'—a process which usually involves a certain amount of statistical processing including normalization. These processes by definition abstract away from the actual data, and in doing so help create models of data which has not actually occurred, except as the basis for subsequent statistical processing. Such experiments should perhaps always involve the resynthesis of some human speech which has not been normalized as a check both on the quality of the synthesizer (the result should sound identical to the original in a perfect system) and on whether the normalization procedures have destroyed the discriminatory aspect of the data present in the original.

A technique involving generating a 'neutral' utterance, and then allowing a human user to interact with the system to vary one or two parameters until an utterance with recognizable emotive content is generated, merits further investigation. Rate of utterance, amplitude variation, and fundamental frequency are obvious candidates. A variant on this is not to use a neutral utterance, but to see whether, for example, a given sad utterance can be turned into a happy-sounding utterance. The parallel here would be the attempts to turn one synthetic voice into another by applying some kind of transformation either to the output or at some earlier stage in the system.

Once again researchers have met with limited success, but clearly the technique could be helpful in understanding the thresholds which constrain parameter setting for characterizing different emotions. So, for example, part of turning a neutral-sounding sentence into an angry-sounding one may involve increasing the range of fundamental frequency throughout the utterance. The research question would be how much this has to be done to achieve the objective, and whether going too far detracts from success. Another important use of the interactive manipulation of various parameters known to play a role in characterizing expressive content in speech is to try to establish the way in which they are mutually dependent. So, for example,

- Can one parameter be used to compensate for another, even if this is not usually what most speakers do?
- Is the balance between the settings for different parameters critical from the perceptual viewpoint?

- Can a perceptual effect be achieved by using the 'wrong' parameter—that is, one which human beings do not normally use?

There are many such questions which can be investigated using synthetic speech. As we have said, but it is worth repeating: a prerequisite is, of course, excellent synthesis. That the quality of the synthesis normally produced by the synthesizer is up to reflecting the subtleties of prosody and expressive content needs to be explicitly established before the results of this kind of technique can be usefully incorporated into the body of knowledge in the field. Researchers taking this approach need to establish suitable metrics for enabling a decision on the adequacy of the synthesizer.

11.2.4 Synthesizing natural variability

One of the ways in which synthetic speech does not match real speech is in its failure to take sufficient account of variability in speech. Listeners to human speech expect variability at all the levels in which it occurs: if variability is not present then listeners detect something wrong, though they will not necessarily to able to say *what* is wrong. Variability needs careful inclusion within models of speech production and perception, and in the simulations of these: speech synthesis and automatic speech recognition. Degree of variability is an important consideration—not just variability itself. It is even more important with studies of the expressive content in speech, because the variations imposed by expressive content need to be recognizably different from those inherent in the relatively neutral system. Another way of saying this is to realize that the normal variability present in the speech signal constrains the possibilities for variations due to expressive content. The problem is further compounded by the fact that expressive content itself is subject to variability: that is, however a particular emotion is 'represented' in the acoustic signal it will be subject to a certain degree of variability.

We have incorporated some *segmental* variability in speech at a number of different levels, specifically morpho-phonemic, extrinsic allophonic, intrinsic allophonic, supervised intrinsic, and random:

- morpho-phonemic: variability between elements always results in morpheme change—*unpredictable* underlying elements—dealt with by phonology;
- extrinsic allophonic: voluntary and systematic use of alternative allophones—*unpredictable* surface representations found in the utterance plan—characterized in *phonology*;
- intrinsic allophonic: involuntarily produced time-governed coarticulatory variability—*predictable* from external constraints—dealt with by phonetics (coarticulation theory);
- supervised intrinsic allophonic: voluntarily constrained coarticulatory variability—*predictable* use of the Cognitive Phonetic *Agent* (Tatham 1995; Tatham and Morton 2003);
- random: unpredictable variability due to system stability limitations—uncharacterized for the most part.

However well-executed these segmental variants are in speech synthesis, the result is inevitably machine-like in quality because listeners *expect* expressive content, and within that, prosodic variants. Very early work in Classical Phonetics presented prosodic contours with a phonemic–allophonic style structure, but there has been little characterization of the actual physical signal and how this correlates systematically with underlying abstract representations. If expressive content follows the same pattern there will be variability here too; and although researchers note this and indeed deal with it statistically, the process is generally one of data reduction rather than a detailed study of the nature of the variability.

There is undoubtedly systematic and predictable variation to be found in both prosodic and expressive contours, and at the same time there are surely unpredictable layers of variability. The problem has been noted, but we do not yet have any agreed model of variability comparable to the one we find with the parallel segmental phenomenon. This is a prerequisite to satisfactory synthesis of prosodic and expressive contours. The term 'contour' is a cover term for time-varying acoustic parameters associated with prosody and expression; it is intended to reflect the relatively slow-moving properties of these parameters compared with much shorter-term segmental elements. For example, we speak of a rising intonation contour, abstractly characterizing a slowly increasing fundamental frequency. The relationship is non-linear and is certainly context-sensitive.

11.2.5 What next in synthesis?

At the present time there are a number of important applications for speech synthesis—all of which would benefit from increased naturalness. These include the reading aloud of text-based information, such as fax, email, and brief web pages. But also there are many more interactive applications involving any brief utterance information found in computer databases: bank balances, addresses and phone numbers, GPS-derived information such as street and place names; general information and inquiry services: movie theatre guides, restaurants and their menus, and so on. With improved naturalness, services involving longer spans of utterances can be introduced: talking books, reference books, newspapers, and whole web-based articles. It is clear that the required level of naturalness expected for this last category has not yet been achieved, and that there is still some user resistance based on this fact. The next stage is to introduce a leap in naturalness by incorporating expressiveness into synthetic speech.

In the view of some researchers a text-to-speech system's initial stages should incorporate the means of

- text normalization (expansion of abbreviations and such symbols as numbers);
- pronunciation rules (strategies for coping with non-phonetic orthography);
- phonological rules (characterization of phonological processes);
- rules for arriving at a suitable prosody (overall rate of delivery, rhythm, stress patterning, and intonation) based on grammatical and semantic analyses;
- phonetic rules (characterization of phonetic processes).

Down as far as 'phonetic rules' we ourselves refer to this front end as 'high-level synthesis' since it characterizes variables of linguistic origin rather than external constraints on the lower-level sound production system. For us, 'low-level synthesis' subdivides into phonetic rules (characterized in the linguistic component of phonetics) and other constraints characterized outside linguistics.

The text input and its normalization are responsible for what utterances are to be spoken, and the remaining components are there to determine instructions to that part of the system which shapes how these utterances are to be rendered as speech. Phonological rules describe voluntary variations in the basic characterization of the way utterances are spoken; since the processes are voluntary (though usually subconscious) they are cognitive processes within the human being. Phonetic rules describe any variability which arises as the result of mostly involuntary variations at the motor control, aerodynamic, and acoustic levels in the human being. Phonological rules which are essentially cognitive in origin—though their results require phonetic rendering—are of particular importance because they not only serve in their basic form to signal various syntactic and semantic properties of the utterance, but also are the basis of expressive content decisions. Their place in the cascade of processes listed above varies slightly in different synthesis systems, but in general occurs either immediately after the set of phonological rules or in parallel with them. It is here that processes associated with expressive speech are placed in most of those systems which tackle expression.

The placing of the phonological 'component' in most text-to-speech systems differs from what we are recommending in this book. We feel that in order to implement the idea that expression holds a key and dominant place in the overall planning and rendering of an utterance—or indeed a string of utterances—a characterization of expression should occur right at the top of the hierarchy. Thus if a person is sad this fact will dominate practically everything associated with speaking: it is unlikely to be adequately modelled as a bolt-on process for just prosody. There are consequences of this idea in terms of the placement of basic prosody too. In our model the characterization of prosody is required for utterance planning, and so it is placed immediately after the characterization of expression. We feel that as work proceeds on incorporating expressive naturalness into more and more synthesis models it is likely that expression will become widely regarded as a dominant feature of speech. The 'relegation' of expression to a low level in most current attempts perhaps results from its late arrival on the scene as an important component of the modelling for synthesis; it seemed logical to regard expression as a sub-component peripheral to prosody, especially as theoretical linguistics (usually not concerned—rightly—with emotive and other variation) barely touches on the subject. But as expression becomes increasingly important in creating good speech interfaces between machines and people it is likely that it will take a more central role—not only in research effort, but also in the theory which supports synthesis models.

A further area in the development of speech synthesis is likely to move to a more stage centre position: evaluation. There is little consistency in attempts to evaluate or standardize measures of the quality of synthesis systems, despite one or two research projects devoted to evolving standardization and evaluation procedures. Explicit procedures are needed, not so that we can declare this synthesizer in some trivial way to be better than that one (such evaluations are very dependent on context and projected usage), but so that we can make meaningful comparisons between the different systems.

The reason for wanting to do this is to gain some insight into the usefulness of various techniques and to measure the progress of research. For example, we speak in this book at length about naturalness—but what formal methods shall we use to *measure* naturalness? Up till now most proposed evaluation procedures have centred on developing intelligibility indices, usually using some form of perceptual test. Little work has been done on any formal methods for developing tests or metrics for naturalness—although this is something which listeners seldom have difficulty in commenting on, particularly in the case of long utterances. What work has been done has concentrated on the prosodics of utterances, since this is where expressive content has been modelled as 'added' to speech.

This is because in general it is believed that the synthesis of individual sounds (sometimes called 'segmental synthesis') is no longer a focal issue—although there may still be a long way to go on the detail of segments. This detail is perhaps a key to examining just how prosody and segmental aspects of speech production in human beings interact. Linguistics treats these areas as relatively separate, but acoustic phoneticians have long since sensed a close relationship between the two. It is precisely this kind of detail which needs further investigation, and which also brings us to doubt whether concatenated waveform synthesis is a long term answer to naturalness. In the short term these details are preserved from the database right up to the output sound; but if we wish to manipulate the output (as we do when synthesizing expression), not only is it probably the case that we do not yet have processing access to these details in the waveform, but as we manipulate timing and fundamental frequency (parameters we can manipulate at present) we may in fact be held back by the details.

11.3 Automatic speech recognition: the other side of the coin

Research into the recognition of expression in speech is important for the design of successful systems which interact directly with human users. Such systems include interactive inquiry systems, or any system which needs to respond to human expression and alter its interactive strategy accordingly. The need for emotion-based response in speech-driven computer systems is no less than it is between human beings, where communication is demonstrably more successful if talkers are sensitive to expression in the person they are talking to.

The communication of emotion clearly involves a two-way channel, with users at both ends of the channel sensitive to the expressive content of the acoustic signal they detect and interpret. In the human–human situation, adaptive response to expressive content is readily observable, and much of the way in which human beings develop confidence in others, discuss, argue, etc. depends not just on the normal semantic content of what they hear but also on the expressive content not communicated in the words of the utterances.

11.3.1 *Automatic speech recognition and emotion*

In environments using automatic speech recognition (ASR)—for example, interactive dialogue systems—it is clear that detection of the expressive content of the human user's speech would be useful to the automatic system. For example, detecting the human user's irritation could be used to introduce a calming tone into the system's responses. This type of sensitivity by dialogue systems would greatly enhance user confidence because it gives the feel of dealing with a human being. Users can easily detect whether the person or machine they're speaking to is receptive to their feelings (Morton 1996).

Of less interest, but still very important, is the fact that general detection of prosodic information in speech can be used to assist an ASR system in its more basic task of word recognition. There are occasions, it is claimed, when prosody can help disambiguate the meaning of sentences, as with distinguishing between a statement and question in languages like French which regularly signal the difference prosodically.

Although most of the work on detecting expressive content in speech and using it to assign emotions and attitudes has been done in terms of human listeners there is some research directed toward providing automatic speech recognition systems with this ability. In general the findings have been similar to those found by most researchers: it is possible to say something about expressive content in the speech signal—but the correlations with speakers' emotions or attitudes is not high enough to provide the kind of reliability needed. This fact has triggered researchers in both human perception and ASR to look much more closely at the soundwave itself to refine the acoustic model of expressive content in speech. But so far the necessary levels of reliability have not yet been achieved.

Our own view is that this problem will persist so long as it is felt that the soundwave embodies all the necessary information for reliable decoding of expressive content. We suggest, however, that the alternative approach—using the signal to trigger an active perceptual process—is more likely to succeed. The model may work well with human listeners because, of course, we don't have to programme human beings. But it implies a major change in the usual approach to automatic speech recognition, shifting the burden of recognition from elaborate detection in the soundwave followed by a simple label assignment procedure to using the soundwave simply to activate a complex labelling procedure.

The generalized goal is to achieve what has been called 'affective computing' (Picard 1997), enabling computers to produce and react to signals normally associated with human emotion and other expressions. The approach is usually focused on the acoustic signal; that is, with speech synthesis the goal is the production of an expressive acoustic signal, and with ASR the goal is to appropriately label a waveform known to have expressive content. In general in the area of speech technology there is little focus on actually generating an underlying emotional experience based on the flow of a conversation or in response to some external stimulus, though psychologists are independently interested in this.

In line with the usual acoustic correlates research paradigm, ASR researchers use databases of speech judged by listeners to exhibit particular expressive content to determine reliable acoustic correlates. Apart from being a little more formal than much of the work done by phoneticians and psychologists the conclusions are the same: there are some strong emotions which can be relatively reliably correlated with a set of acoustic parameters (the usual prosodic ones, such as fundamental frequency behaviour), and others which human beings have little difficulty detecting and identifying but which correlate less reliably, introducing ambiguities in the ASR labelling processes.

Most contemporary ASR systems concentrate on recognition at the segmental level, and the commonest approach is based on the use of Hidden Markov modelling (see Holmes and Holmes 2001). This is a statistically based learning approach which proceeds according to 'discovered' probabilities associated with the occurrence of particular sequences of features of the acoustic signal. At the segmental level the technique enjoys a great deal of success, and recognition rates as great as 90% are common for quite large-vocabulary commercially available systems.

In these systems, however, little attention is paid to prosodic effects, so that any disambiguation which is dependent on prosody is likely to fail. The focus distinction between '*Tom* went to Manchester' (as opposed to Bill) and 'Tom went to *Manchester*' (as opposed to Sheffield), important in a dialogue situation, is usually lost. This failure, though, is unimportant if the aim of the system is to operate as a simple dictation system turning speech waveforms into text. An obvious reason for this is that text does not usually encode expressive content; so it is unnecessary for this kind of content to be detected. But now that contemporary success levels are acceptable, attention is turning to further development in interactive, conversationally based systems. Here, information signalled by the prosodics of speech becomes much more significant, and indeed may be critical as far as the acceptability of these systems to their human users is concerned.

So far, however, little progress has been made in incorporating even non-expressive prosodic labelling into ASR systems. It is still early days both in terms of the research and in terms of the demand driving the research. Still less progress has been made in detecting and labelling expressive content in human speech, which is widely regarded as a refinement of prosodic labelling.

11.3.2 Analysis by synthesis

Research at the MIT Multimedia Laboratory (Picard 1997) on enabling machines with emotion is centred on developing a software 'agent' which can assume emotional states analogous to the way a human being assumes emotional states. Once this state is 'recognized' or established it is used to constrain later behaviour. For our purposes this later behaviour would involve speaking in a particular way: that is, injecting expressive content into its speech audio. Thus an analysis—recognition—of the emotive state of the device precedes synthesis of the reaction—speech.

The MIT group refer to synthesizing a number of possibilities from which the best is selected by taking the nearest match to the emotion as analysed. They call this process 'analysis by synthesis', though it differs somewhat from what researchers in the perception of speech have come to mean by this term. In speech perception, analysis by synthesis is a theory which hypothesizes that listeners evaluate what they hear by a process of resynthesizing within their own minds what would underlie their own production of a similar acoustic signal (Stevens and Halle 1967). This process is performed iteratively until the loop is exited consequent on the decision that analysis and resynthesis have optimally converged. At this point the synthesis is inspected for the labels responsible for generating it. These labels are then declared to be the labels appropriate to the analysis of the incoming signal. The signal is then said to have been perceived—the perception being manifest in the set of labels. In the MIT Multimedia group's recognition of emotion the procedure is to synthesize a number of emotions and choose the one which most closely 'resembles what is perceived', an altogether less complex process than Stevens and Halle's analysis by synthesis.

Thus the central feature of the analysis by synthesis perceptual model—convergence of analysed signal and synthesized signal by an exhaustive iterative process—is not what drives the MIT group's emotion recognition procedure: they are looking for closest-match conditions rather than valid convergence. In both cases, however, it could be said that the system 'reasons' toward an answer: the provision of an appropriate label on the one hand for an incoming speech signal and on the other for an experienced emotion.

Chapter 12

The Influence of Emotion Studies

Researchers approach the study of emotion from points of view that stem from approaches that are primarily biological, or cognitive (including social), or a combination of these. They ask:

- Can a reported emotion be unambiguously associated with a specific activity or a particular section of the nervous system or of the brain?
- What is the cognitive experience reported by humans?
- To what extent does language provide the means for expression or shape our reporting of emotion?

12.1 How research into emotion can usefully influence work in speech

For researchers in speech, it is a matter of choice whether they want outside validation for their claims, and if so, whether they wish to proceed from a basic biological or cognitive position. In order to locate emotive content in the acoustic wave, whether the physiology is changed as an initial reaction to events or whether it occurs *after* the event(s) are appraised and evaluated may not matter. In determining relevant characteristics of the acoustic wave it may be enough to assume the speaker's state just prior to speaking is the result *after* everything physiological and/or cognitive has occurred. So the output of the physiological and cognitive processing is the input to whatever module can cope with the changing stance of the speaker and can manage these changes to produce the intended speech waveform. The diagram below shows the arrangement: the production of the final output waveform depends on managed or supervised production. The speech production system and the supervisor are both 'aware' of the output of expressive physiological/cognitive processing.

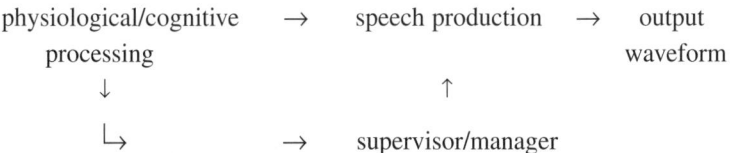

Speech researchers may have to recognize that researching and incorporating expression and emotive content into speech modelling is domain-dependent, and will need to decide what point of view—physiological, cognitive, social, linguistic—could best enable their work to proceed. But the ideal position for speech research would be to have at its disposal:

- a simple biological model of reaction to an event;
- a clear statement of cognitive modification of the biological reaction, perhaps in terms of awareness of an intensity feature related to the biological reaction itself;
- a model, or at least a technique, for relating acoustic features to the basic biological reactions and to the range of modifications brought about by cognitive interpretation;
- a way of interpreting the reliability of self-report and evaluating observed responses of subjects.

In Part IV we present a model for generating expressive speech which is based on the physiological reaction to an outside event as setting the physical parameters for speaking. This choice is on the grounds that our proposed computational model is more coherent if emotive content in speech is considered as part of a larger bodily response to changes in the environment, no matter how small the change might be.

12.2 Emotion and speech synthesis

Turning to emotion and speech synthesis we can ask: why do emotive synthesis? There is an argument from the area of human/computer interface (HCI) that human interaction with machine-based systems have features in common with human–human interaction (Picard 1997; Balkenius and Moren 1998; Polzin and Waibel 2000). Some researchers are quite explicit that the correspondence between humans and machines as partners in communication can be quite high (Reeves and Nass 1996). If this is correct, it would be a significant move forward for speech synthesis systems—particularly when they form part of a dialogue system—to incorporate the ability to produce appropriately emotive speech.

In human–human communication systems involving face-to-face interaction, body language and facial gestures are important; they add to the vocal message. Research on faces has been extensively reported by psychologists (Ekman 1992; Ohman et al. 2001), and the mechanisms for facial change in language use, discussed in linguistic phonetics (Jiang et al. 2002). However, pending much more data and appropriate modelling in the area of facial expression, human computer interaction is likely to remain voice-based and not accompanied by visual imagery.

12.2.1 Application: a simple dialogue example

Suppose we are designing a dialogue system involving the presentation to the user of a series of instructions. The acoustic wave output from the synthesizer needs to contain cues which might reinforce acceptance of the instructions by including features which the perceiver interprets as from a source that is confident, truthful, and reliable. Now, suppose we have a set of acoustic features able to convey the small number of basic emotions. The significant acoustic features we need to include to trigger confidence might be contextually dependent categories providing this fine tuning, and the best result from a set of emotions could be a match between the acoustic feature and the selection of an appropriate *word* in the message. The word and how it is said would interact to generate in the mind of the user the appropriate emotive response.

From the user's point of view when listening to a series of instructions which they cannot follow, the procedure can give rise to the basic emotion of sadness or anger, but modified by the awareness of the true situation, and lead to the cognitive perception of frustration, dismay, or some other labelled emotion. In this case, the voice output of the synthesizer should not trigger more than slight sadness resulting in only mild frustration; too much would result in the user giving up and perhaps getting angry—perceiving the voice as threatening—or possibly giving rise to fear, if the voice seemed too aggressive. The aim of the voice in this case would be to alert the user to mistakes, and suggest trying the procedure again. Notice in these examples the complexity of deriving listener reaction from variable context-sensitivity between the actual words used in a message, the way they are spoken, and the user's state. It is quite possible that user response can be manipulated toward a variety of emotive states if this complex relationship can be adequately modelled and implemented in a dialogue system.

As a further example of complex interactivity or context-sensitivity, we might ask what constitutes *encouraging* emotional content in speech? Can this actually be defined acoustically? Not so far, unfortunately. But by taking the viewpoint which directs the task toward eliciting an appropriate listener response, rather than creating the 'right' waveform, the aim would be to provide an acoustic cue for the basic emotion, and then further modify that emotion by using suitable linguistic context, that is, choice of words, syntax, ellipsis, idioms, short phrases, etc. which are accepted by the community as encouraging and stress-reducing.

This approach assumes that the experience of emotion is a universal, and that linguistic contexts can be precisely specified in this situation. It also assumes that users from different cultural and linguistic backgrounds can function within such a communication system. Such a system would have the advantage that it would be neither culturally nor linguistically specific.

12.3 Prelude to an underlying model of emotion: the inadequacies of the speech model

Let us briefly review the speech acoustics model. Several points can be made:

- It would seem that looking at the waveform is not enough—acoustic information interacts with the semantic content of words and these in turn are combined into phrases and wider

domains. Thus the acoustic signal cannot be uniquely specified for any one underlying emotion.
- Acoustic parameters additional to those normally included in the acoustic model will be needed. These include the means of modelling vowel quality changes correlating with changes in rate of delivery of the speech, voice quality identifiers of expressive content, and so on. Some of these possibilities are being addressed, but we still lack a well-motivated definitive list of acoustic parameters.
- There has been a tendency to specify the values of the acoustic parameters directly in relation to some particular underlying emotion (as identified by an abstract label). That is, the acoustic parameters have been regarded as independently controllable variables. But there is every reason to suppose that if we pull in perceptual considerations it will be necessary to model how these variables interact with each other at the lowest level. That is, each parameter of the acoustic signal has some relationship to the underlying emotion, but in addition has a variable relationship with other acoustic parameters. The acoustic parameters may need to be modelled hierarchically with nested groupings which capture part of the dependency network between them.
- The current technique in concatenated waveform synthesis of modulating a 'neutral' or normalized waveform with new expressive content fails because what constitutes a neutral waveform is not adequately specified at the physical level. It is one thing to imagine in the abstract such a type of speech, but it is quite another to use this concept in the practical environment of synthesis. Because the normalization cannot be guaranteed (since 'normal' cannot be specified, other than by characterizing what has been normalized), the values of acoustic parameters such as f0, amplitude, timing, and so on which are usually derived from a human waveform, when added to the concatenated units, cannot be themselves guaranteed to be correct. At best there is colouration, at worst there are serious listener-detectable errors.
- There are descriptive ambiguities in models of emotion, and there are potential perceptual ambiguities when a listener assigns labels to what they hear. Serious problems arise when these two sources of error come together. For example, some researchers label 'surprise' and 'question' as emotive,

The Influence of Emotion Studies 269

and both are acoustically very similar in many utterances. Disambiguating them relies on other cues, such as question words, surprise words, general linguistic context, or environmental context. If the problem has been anticipated in a text-to-speech system, and if the interactions are adequately modelled, the system can have a shot at disambiguation—creating an appropriate waveform which has unambiguous perception as its goal. In dialogue systems the solution may be more complex.

- There are some identifiable but unaddressed questions, among which is how we implement the idea of cognitive intervention to modify basic emotions. For example: is it reasonable to define a few 'basic' emotions strong enough to change physiological settings, and specify subtle changes brought about cognitive intervention, some of which depends on the words chosen? To what extent does the choice of language structures shape emotion? If this idea is productive, how might basic emotions be identified and replicated in the speech waveform, other than by the simple but possibly inadequate current method of modelling the relationship as linear?

These are just a few of the areas which need further work. In particular, we lack a true unifying perspective on the whole concept of expression in speech—how the underlying emotions relate to the acoustic signal and how they are reassigned labels by the listener. In speech research there is a general lack of understanding of how emotion works *before* it moves to the linguistic encoding processes. Here we attempt the framework of a model of emotion which may fit this general purpose. We know the model will be inadequate, but we hope that it will be couched in such a way that other researchers will be prompted to ask the right questions about its inadequacies. That is, that there is a sufficiently coherent framework presented that hypotheses can be generated which contribute to moving the study forward.

12.4 An integrated physical/cognitive language model

A model that takes into account both physical and cognitive elements as part of spoken language production, and which links with the perception of an expressive or emotive utterance, can be formulated as a set of procedures:

SPEAKER	LISTENER
acoustic trigger →	*reaction* to plain message (physical) AND *recognition* of expressive or emotive content (cognitive)

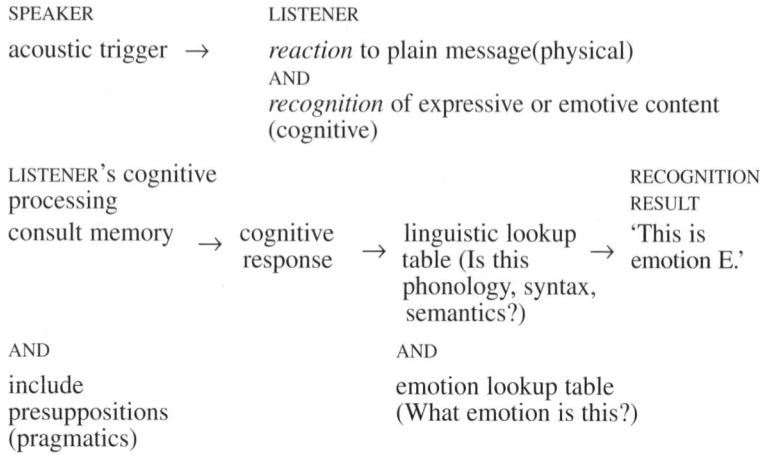

LISTENER's cognitive processing			RECOGNITION RESULT
consult memory →	cognitive response →	linguistic lookup table (Is this phonology, syntax, semantics?) →	'This is emotion E.'
AND		AND	
include presuppositions (pragmatics)		emotion lookup table (What emotion is this?)	

In this very simple model we note that

- the speaker is responsible for producing an acoustic trigger, giving rise to
- listener response, consisting of
- physical reaction to the speaker's encoded plain message AND cognitive recognition of expressive or emotive content in the trigger.

In more detail the listener's cognitive processing

- involves consulting the memory in general AND includes evaluating pragmatic presuppositions in respect of the signal, generating
- cognitive response, which leads to consulting
- the linguistic lookup table AND the emotion lookup table, to identify together
- the speaker's 'intended' emotion—the recognition result.

A simple equation serves to describe how a linguistics module can be added to a basic physical/cognitive model of speaker production:

$$words \: . \: physical\_state \rightarrow spoken\_signal$$

that is

> $W . PS \rightarrow M$
> where *PS* is the physical basis for an emotion state, and *M* is the spoken signal or 'message'.

Consider that the relationship between *W* and *PS* is one of compensation or negative correlation, such that a given message *M* can be produced by the use of a semantically precise word correlated with a low emotive state, or can be produced by using a semantically vague word correlating with a high emotive state.

From this idea it does not necessarily follow that speakers with a large word store and fast access to it can speak with less detectable emotional content, nor that speakers with a limited vocabulary and slow access speak with less expressive/emotive content. The simple relationship between careful choice of word and the physical state of the speaker is a simple practical equation for use in a computational model. In real life, speakers can also add to the communication process facial expression, hand gestures, and other body movements—all providing information to assist the listener process of assigning semantic (plain) meaning and emotive meaning to the detected signal (Massaro and Egan 1996). Listeners are not passive: they actively participate in the assignment process by consulting at least a list of words, general knowledge of the language, and their own memory of 'expression/emotion' and possible physiological settings of self and speaker.

12.4.1 The proposed shift of model focus

Since we can assume that the goal of communication is to exchange information about the world or about our feelings and beliefs, we suggest a change of focus in speech synthesis from simulating a 'standard' emotive waveform—a waveform including some canonical means of adding expression—to asking:

- What behaviour does the message intend to elicit from the listener? That is: What acoustic information, incorporated into a speech waveform, can reliably trigger the perception of the intended emotive content?

This is essentially a non-linear approach which does not assume that there is just one way of manipulating acoustic parameters to guarantee a given expressive content. A catalogue of the traditional kind which associates particular acoustic parameters with particular emotions is not pivotal to such a system; in fact it would be of very limited value, simply because of the inadequacy of a non-context-sensitive paradigm.

- The first task, therefore, is to determine what we want the user to feel or to become aware of.
- The second task is to provide such acoustic information as is sufficient and necessary to apply to the generated waveform, given the semantic context.

This approach focuses on the listener—the user of the synthesis system. The effectiveness is directed not to the emotion the software designer intends the computer to convey, but to the emotional response and the intended behaviour of the user. This is an explicit inclusion of the production-for-perception principle in the production of expressive signals.

The choice of expressive/emotive content in the acoustic signal should be made on a principled basis as to what content will enhance the plain message and carry out the intention of the overall message. In gathering data for establishing which acoustic features might trigger the response from the listener, it must be remembered that the report of emotion is personal and gathering objective evidence is difficult. This means that similar waveforms will often elicit different responses from different people, and different responses from the same person on different occasions.

- Can we determine a suitable human model abstracted from research in physiological and cognitive models of expression and emotion, which might form the basis for good synthesis?

The answer unfortunately is no—but perhaps some general aspects of human expressive/emotive behaviour potentially relevant to speech could be suggested which, if coherent, might enable development of a computer system that eventually could produce expressive/emotive speech. In the following sections we begin suggesting a possible transferable model—that is, a model of expressive or emotive behaviour in human beings, formalized for potential transfer to a speech synthesis environment.

12.5 Introducing a possible transferable model

We need to consider what people actually do in a given situation; that is, how they react to a change in their environment. Then we shall be in a position to make a more formal characterization of the situation.

12.5.1 *The situation: what people do*

Consider the following sequence of events:

- We observe an individual (e.g. a human being) in an environment.
- An event occurs in the environment: attention is directed toward this event.
- A change in the individual may result from a reaction to the change in the environment. This change has a physical element—a physiological reaction to an externally generated event. There may also be a cognitive element—an awareness of the reaction, a recognition of the reaction (e.g. by accessing memory), or some other cognitive effects.
- An observable or detectable behaviour change may follow in response to the initial reaction to the event. There may be self-reports of awareness of the individual's reaction, reports of the event, and other physiological or cognitive activity surrounding the event. We can label some of these behavioural changes 'expression', which can take the form of changes in:

    the body (such as running, dancing, singing);
    artistic creativity;
    facial expressive changes;
    production of language.

The above makes provision, in a simple but clear way, for most of what we observe when a human being reacts to a change in their environment.

Table 12.1. Reactions to environmental changes

Initiating event	An event occurs in the external environment which is a 'potential stimulus'.		An event can also occur internally, but this adds complexity—for example, there would be no reflex action if the triggering event were internally generated. The model here assumes an external event.
Reaction	There is a reaction within the individual.	1. Physical-sensory The sensory system (e.g. hearing) detects an environmental event, and there is: (a) *a reflex reaction*— an automatic physical internal reaction involving only the spinal cord, OR (b) *physiological reaction*—stimulus reaches a threshold triggering a physiological change, OR (c) *no change*—the stimulus does not reach the threshold necessary for generating a reaction.	Sensory activity is logically prior to cognitive activity. That is, sentient mammals cannot be aware of something that does not, for them, exist. There are potentially physiologically measurable changes in body states, such as heart rate, blood pressure, and hormone levels, etc.
		2. Cognitive There is: (a) awareness of the sensory detection of an event, AND/OR awareness of bodily response, OR (b) no awareness of sensory detection, OR (c) no awareness of bodily response, OR (d) no awareness of sensory detection BUT awareness of bodily response.	Cognitive awareness is logically post sensory detection. It can include appraisal of bodily response *after* sensory detection. It is possible to be aware of both sensation and body changes at what appears to be the same time. Some researchers distinguish between an awareness of sensory input, and appraisal as to whether the event is good or bad for the individual. This is followed by an awareness of bodily changes. This awareness of these changes is labelled 'emotion state'. However, much research is based around subjective reporting—and it is difficult if not impossible to subjectively time internal events. What appears to be *prior* may be *parallel processing*, or even *short-circuited* (insertion of an apparent 'delay line'), as in explanations of the 'déjà vu' phenomenon.

Response		
Changes in the individual that can be observed or self-reported, or suppressed.	1. Observed IF there is an observed response AND IF the physical response is labelled 'expression', THEN we can observe AND/OR measure physical/body movements OR verbal output OR both	However, a response can be difficult for an observer to evaluate. Responses can be of many types: fight, flight, etc. But in this book we are concerned with 'expression' and in particular 'emotive content of speech'. We can only infer a response from the speech waveform which is our source of data—a physical event.
	2. Self-report Some responses cannot be observed, so self-reporting is the source of data.	Speakers report that they are aware of the emotion state, and label the emotion. The report can be correlated, although somewhat loosely, with acoustic events in the speech waveform.
	3. Suppression (a) no visible response either physical or verbal, OR (b) a choice of some other response.	Although the speaker intends to suppress an emotion reaction, the listener can sometimes tell if a speaker is suppressing and not expressing emotive content by facial and bodily changes, or an unexpected reaction such as a smile in an argument.

For example:
- If physical, we might see a smile, or frown.
- If verbal, then we might detect speech.
- If both simultaneously, then we might describe a smile and kind words or possibly a smile and harsh words.

12.5.2 A more formal statement of the situation

We posit a context for emotive speech production based on evidence from physiological and cognitive research on expression and emotion. Table 12.1 presents, a more formal statement of the situation described above.

Special conditions may occur in both reaction and response:

- There may be a time delay in reaction, either initially or when trying to identify the event. The response would not immediately be obvious to either the speaker or listener, and a consequence of this could be that the conversation would follow a different path than if there had been an immediate response.
- It is quite clear that many events that may occur in the above sequence might give rise to difficulties in description, setting up experiments, or even in self-reporting. For example, there may be an immediate internal reaction of which the speaker is not aware, but to which they have unknowingly responded. The response in this case is to be quiet, perhaps fearful or tense. The cognitive ability to evaluate might then take over and dictate a suitable response or it might not; it might choose an inappropriate response.
- The observation has been made that people seem to delay sometimes in making a response, but this delay may obscure an unaware response of 'do nothing for the moment'—that is, freezing in fear. So the model that states that there *must* be an immediate physical response is not denied by a delay—and cognitive evaluation is ongoing while the person or animal is in a suspended state as a fear reaction. If verbalized, this reaction might be described as confused, perplexed, or undecided.
- The initiating event could be seen as a stimulus within a particular context. Context arises in conversation, or in teaching or professional consultations, where there is a purpose to the interaction; speech here can be regarded as an event in the environment which asks for a response. The verbal event in speech can be seen as a stimulus requiring a response, but the emotional stance of the speaker (if detectable) can be seen as a context also. The listener can respond to either verbal or emotional stimuli, or can respond only to one or the other. And the listener may not detect the emotional stance, or may detect an emotional stance the speaker does not intend or is not aware of.

What we offer here is a basic framework, directed toward researchers in the speech area, which might provide a foundation on which to build a theory of expression in human speech, and a theory of expression which might enable work in speech synthesis to move toward improved naturalness.

12.6 Building a model for emotive synthesis: the goals

In moving toward a useful model for emotive synthesis we need to take account of two major concepts as our possible goals.

1. An initial goal is to model expression, which we define in this book as:

- a way of externalizing an internal state which may or may not be under conscious control; for example, it is possible to express self though body movements;
- a verbal report of an awareness of an emotion state, related to an event which either occurred in the world or is the impression of a change of state within the speaker.

2. A second goal is to model emotion as a type of expression which may:

- initially consist of a bodily reaction to an event, sensory or sensory + physical, and which is sometimes difficult to separate in time from an awareness of the event, or
- be a clear reporting of an awareness of physiological change, or
- be the result of a reaction to an internal or external event that can be labelled with an emotive word, or
- be the awareness of a reaction formed after evaluating the occurrence of an event of some kind.

12.6.1 The formal statement of the framework: the domain of enquiry

A model is a construct designed to describe, account for, and perhaps explain a phenomenon. Emotion as a type of expression, producing responses to external or internal events, is an undeniable fact of life, a naturally occurring phenomenon. What processes characterize this activity? A simple model of the relation between an event, a physical reaction, awareness, and a response labelled 'expression' might be:

STIMULUS
the 'event' → thresholded physical reaction → awareness [optional] → expression [optional]

There are a number of points where options can occur: 'optional' is a term in the model which does not necessarily mean *choice* is available to the individual. A speaker who is unaware is not aware there is a choice to make; but a speaker who does not express an emotion of which he *is* aware, *has* made a choice. Expression itself is optional in the sense that one can intentionally keep quiet. Awareness is optional in the sense that some reactions are unknown to the speaker/listener. That is, an external or internal stimulus leads to a physical arousal in response to that stimulus event which may lead to an awareness of the arousal and also perhaps to an awareness of the actual event. The individual may express or suppress or be unaware of a response.

In this simple model, there are many unknowns: an external stimulus can lead to physical arousal in response to that stimulus event, which may have an accompanying awareness of the arousal and perhaps also awareness of the actual event, which may result in expressing a response to the initial event.

12.6.2 *The basis of a computational model of expression in speech*

All models start with assumptions. Here we enumerate the main linguistic and physiological/cognitively based assumptions on which our proposed model is based.

1. Linguistic and acoustic phonetic assumptions:

- The speaker and listener share a similar linguistic code.
- The prosodics and pragmatics (the formal characterization of 'expression'), are adequately described, together with how they interrelate.
- The linguistic descriptions are adequate.
- There are discoverable acoustic correlates for the linguistic descriptions.
- The acoustic correlates are identifiable and measurable.

The Influence of Emotion Studies 279

2. *Physiological and cognitively based assumptions:*

- The emotion effect is physiologically based, on the basis of evidence that limits us to a simple small set: *fear, anger, contentment, sadness.*[1]
- The following additional assumptions are suggested in order to link a linguistic acoustic description of speech output with an emotive state; assume:

  a close link with biological substrate;

  a physiological setting for expression—expressing emotion and the awareness of a physiological stance;

  the participation of the entire body in this physiological stance, mediated by the known characteristics of the physiological system;

  that the speech production mechanism takes on a *new basic setting*, depending on the physiological state of the entire person;

  that there is a reflection or manifestation of this bodily physiological *setting* in the acoustic waveform;

  that this physiological setting contributes to what has been called 'variability' in the acoustic waveform, superimposed on the setting;

  that it is possible to tease out *invariances* in the variability that can be associated with changes in physiological setting;

  that these invariances can be isolated from phonological (the plan) and phonetic (rendering) invariances.

In addition, unknown degrees of cognitive intervention and cognitive generation of emotion effects will modify the basic system. If the effect of emotion is initially solely a product of cognitive activity, then these assumptions will not be valid. If cognitive intervention (in the physical event) varies from being a very small part to being a very large contribution, the biological

---

[1] These are simple because there are fewer and the reactions are more clearly defined than for, say, surprise/happiness or woe/despair. There are quite clear biological systems associated with those four. Once these can be simulated, perhaps differences between emotive content and style, and between style and expression—such as authoritative, pleasant, expansive, reflective, or thoughtful—can be attempted.

and linguistic assumptions are unaffected; what *is* affected is the range of variability the non-linguistic and non-biological effects can influence.

12.7 The evidence supporting biological and cognitive models suitable for speech work

We need to address the question of whether there is evidence to put forward from biology and psychology that can support a model which takes into account biological and cognitive activity associated with emotive content in speech.

12.7.1 Biological aspects

Our main basic assumption here is that a reaction to an event will result in a particular biological state in the speaker. For example, if a person is angry or very happy this fact will show itself in their vocal tract configuration as the vocal organs participate in a general bodily reaction. We would expect the speech to show a detectable and specific angry-type tone of voice, unless it is suppressed. If the tone of voice *is* suppressed this might also result in a particular vocal tract configuration which may be reported by a listener as 'suppressed anger'. We expect that the physical reaction may often be virtually undetectable by current instrumentation.

Some fundamental work by MacLean (1990), and later Panksepp (Panksepp and Miller 1996; Panksepp 1998) on emotion systems identified as being organized within sub-cortical circuits reports that there are four distinct neurophysiological systems. These can be regarded as in principle isolatable and definable circuits which can reasonably be related to observed response states when the environment changes (Panksepp 1998):

- *no need to change*—contentment (that is, the homeostasis is returned to, and the biological settings are constant);
- *need to respond* to a threat—anger;
- *need to be aware* of a threat that might not be able to cope with—fear;
- *loss*—leading to depression.

The Influence of Emotion Studies

The general assumptions about the production of an expressive waveform are:

- If the physiological setting can be changed, and if it *is* changed, then the body will be in a different condition from before the event, and the mediating systems for these body changes can be determined.
- To carry this into utterance production, we regard speaking as a neuro-physiological activity.
- The vocal tract settings will change and be observable in speaking.
- The resulting changes in the act of speaking will show up in the speech waveform.
- The acoustic changes (some of them) will be able to be detected, quantified and identified.
- We can therefore expect to find invariances associated with reported emotion and the speech waveform.

The test for the coherence of this model is whether or not the assumptions and the terms of the model are computationally adequate: will it run? If it does, this does not mean that the assumptions and terms are 'good' or 'true', it just means that they are coherent. But, having established coherence, we have a model which provides a sure base for building hypotheses that might result in a 'good' model.

Take a simple model for accounting for emotive content in speech:

- Assume all initial emotional response is biologically based. The initial biological reaction may be clearly manifest, or be damped down, or sometimes even reversed (for example, inhibited by antagonistic systems—chemical and neurological—which have been either automatic or learned). Modifications can also be made within the body chemistry, for example, by surges of adrenalin on occasions specific to the individual. The process of learning through personal experience might well result in varieties of speech waveforms, labelled differently by analogy with the observations of many different dialects of a language. Each word contains shades of nuance—as a colour chart can contain many different colours.

Social custom and personal experience are also considered to be a large part of the experience of detecting emotion and reporting feelings, and thus contribute to expression and, in language, the choice of words. If much of speech contains emotive expression, and emotion is biologically based, then the vocal tract will respond as does the rest of the body to a change in initial emotion state.

This model suggests there are two types of expression to look for in the speech waveform, biologically based and cognitively based—remembering it is difficult to disentangle cognitive contributions to a biologically based initial reaction.

Much of the data in building speech production and perception models is based on measurement of acoustic features in the soundwave. These features are the result of the activity of the articulators which change the shape of the vocal tract. The movement of the articulators may be intended (cognitive) or unintended (automatic physiological response). Since the variation in the occurrence of acoustic features constitutes a stimulus which triggers the perception of expression in the listener, we feel an awareness of the general underlying cognitive and physical models may be useful.

12.7.2 Biological mapping and the dynamic perspective

Ideally we would like to know what actually happens physiologically for each emotion, simply because of the evidence that some physiological changes are reflected in the speech waveform—for example faster or slower breath rate is directly related to production of speech. If we could define the basic physiological changes by a feature set, this could help in showing a direct relation between physiological changes and the speech waveform. Table 12.2 gives an example.

We now need to ask which changes are correlated with the physiological setting, as the individual responds to changes in the environment, and what the implications are for speakers as the emotive content changes during dialogue. This point is important, since emotive content is far from static. We are interested, for

Table 12.2. The relationship between physiological features and the speech waveform

Feature	Possible values or ranges
Heart beats	Faster vs. slower
	Stronger vs. weaker
Breathing	Faster vs. slower
	Deeper vs. shallower
etc.	

example, in change of heart rate, breathing rate, blood pressure, biochemicals and their receptors in correlation with changes in emotional response from, say, anger to contentment.

In this sequence the next step might be to determine if we could model the listener percepts that might be built up from recognizing these physiological changes, just as we assemble and build up phonological percepts on hearing a speech signal. Such percepts are then to be labelled—assigned a symbolic representation.

12.7.3 Cognitive aspects

Features that can be identified as cognitive need to be accounted for in the emotive content of speaking. Again, we need to be clear about definition: does 'cognitive' *imply* awareness, or *require* awareness? In this monograph, we consider linguistic cognitive processing to carry on throughout language production with no constant awareness of monitoring when selecting words, grammatical categories, or sound shapes. Specifically in emotion studies, cognitive activity can also mean assessment and evaluation of information which may be either externally or internally sourced.

One aspect of cognitive control over physiological reaction can be seen in *suppression* of that reaction. For example, if a person living in a particular culture has been taught to overcome anger, to always speak softly, this will be detected by the listener; if the rules are broken, the resulting deviation from the expected is often immediately recognizable. The listener is alerted to a change. But the same speech waveform may be acceptable in other cultures. In this case, speaking with some degree of anger might be useful, since the detection of anger by the listener is a trigger for the speaker to perhaps back off, or a trigger to caution the listener to proceed carefully. However, the same function can occur by choosing the appropriate words such as *I am quite annoyed*, rather than revealing irritation through tone of voice. This is the effect which involves resolution of the concord or discord between the plain semantic content of the utterance and its tone of voice. We often can make a choice as to our behaviour. For example, as applied to speech production, if the model is adequate, an evaluation can be made along the lines: 'Is it better to speak carefully, or express anger, perhaps in a different way on this occasion?' The speaking may be tied in with other styles of bodily response and personality response to some outside stimuli.

12.8 Concluding and summarizing remarks

If an emotion can be said to be both physical and cognitive, we wonder if there are similar problems and pointers toward solutions in linguistics, which also has to deal with these two levels of representation. In linguistics, there are several ways proposed which attempt to relate the phonological (cognitive) pattern and the phonetic (largely physical) rendering of that pattern. However, it is worth signalling a warning: the problem in linguistics of relating two types of representation—the cognitive and the physical—is unresolved. Determining the emotive content of an utterance may well be similarly intractable.

In Chapter 15 we describe a possible synthesis system for incorporating expressive content. One way of building machine systems is to look at human systems which accomplish the same task. The features of the proposed system are based on physiological and cognitive evidence, and the purpose of the model is to trigger appropriate perception in the listener. Since a principal goal of communication is to exchange information about the world or about our feelings and beliefs, we have suggested a change of focus from simulating an existing emotive waveform to asking: What behaviour does the message intend to elicit from the listener? That is, what acoustic information, incorporated into a speech waveform, can reliably trigger the perception of the intended emotive content? This approach focuses on the listener—on the user of the synthesis system. The emphasis is placed not on the emotion the software designer intends the computer to convey, but on the emotional response and the intended behaviour of the user.

A choice of expressive/emotive effect must be made on a principled basis as to what content will enhance the plain message and carry out the intention of the message. In gathering data for establishing which acoustic features might trigger the response from the listener, it must be remembered that the report of emotion is personal, and that gathering objective evidence is difficult. This means, as we have emphasized, that similar waveforms will probably elicit different responses from different people, and different responses from the same person on different occasions.

We must ask ourselves whether we can determine an entirely suitable human model abstracted from research in physiological and cognitive models of expression and emotion. Unfortunately, the answer for the moment is no—but perhaps some general aspects of human expressive/emotive behaviour potentially relevant to speech could be suggested which, if coherent, might enable development of a computer system that could produce expressive/emotive speech.

Part IV

Development of an Integrated Model of Expression

Chapter 13

The Beginnings of a Generalized Model of Expression

In Parts I–III we dealt with the groundwork necessary to understand where researchers are at the present time in terms of modelling expression in speech. In addition we have discussed attempts to simulate expressive speech using synthesis techniques based on the state of the art. Our general conclusion has been that, although much of the current technology can probably handle expressive speech adequately, attempts so far have been more or less inadequate. There have been some demonstrations of excellent expressive speech, but this has been obtained under laboratory conditions, and has usually not been generalizable. We now wish to develop the model further, with a number of aims in mind:

- develop consistent analysis techniques to examine the acoustic detail of expression, however subtle;
- build good models of expression at three levels: speaker production, the acoustic signal itself, and listener perception—these must be fully computational to enable adequate testing;
- develop the necessary computational models for synthesis applications using expressive content, resting on what we can characterize of human production and perception.

As a first step we suggest beginning with a redefinition of terms and goals to enable further development of the work which has already been done. The reason for this is that the terminology used at the moment is very vague. Words like 'emotion', 'attitude', and 'style' reflect the basic abstract nature of expression, so it is not surprising that it is difficult to pin down exactly what we mean by them. But if our acoustic modelling is to be more explicit and tighter, the answers to questions such as: What exactly does this acoustic signal represent? will have also to be more explicit.

In Part IV we outline a possible framework for moving the area forward. It is not our intention to propose answers: the subject area is much too new and continues to give us more questions than answers. But we feel we can move forward by proposing a more integrated approach to what is in effect a difficult multidisciplinary area, and by proposing a more explicit approach lending itself to more formal, computational modelling. There are going to be other ways of tackling the problem: this is our current suggestion.

13.1 Defining expressive speech

The general position which has been taken by most researchers is that expressive speech is speech in which a listener can detect a particular emotion, attitude, or intention. That is, besides what we might call the basic meaning conveyed by the actual words of the utterance and the way they are arranged syntactically, there is an additional element which enables listener reports like: 'spoken angrily', 'the speaker is happy', or even 'they like me'. Comments such as these refer to information separable from the words themselves. If we think of the written version of an utterance, we can see it can clearly be instantiated or read aloud as several different spoken versions conveying different expressive content. The situation is analogous to scripting for drama:

> John: [sincerely] *I love her.*

The actor playing John is to speak the words 'I love her' sincerely, such that Mary (and indeed the audience) is to be in no doubt as to his intentions. The convention makes provision for such alternatives as:

> John: [angrily] *I love her.*

and

> John: [dreamily] *I love her.*

or, in the general case

> Actor: [with_emotion] *utterance*.

This model of production (for that is what this drama scripting convention amounts to) makes a clear distinction between an utterance and the tone of voice in which it is to be produced. It is clear that [with_emotion] is a variable unconstrained by the spoken words, *utterance*, immediately following.

Although the notation does not explicitly allow for constraints, some combinations might be ruled out because of incongruity:

> Richard: [ecstatically] *I die at dawn*.

or at least provide an unexpected or convention-breaking jolt. The implication here is that there is an expected link between the meaning of the basic message and the tone of voice adopted while uttering it. There seem to be rules about which utterances can be spoken with particular expressions. This may well be, and if so the violation of these co-occurrence expectations is what invokes surprise, as in the preceding example. But the very fact that it is possible to violate the rule means that there is an important operational distinction between the two elements, the utterance and the way it is to be spoken—and language users know about this.

In the conventions as to how to set out a drama script, the set of attributes describing the required tone of voice is presumably finite and comprises all possible ways of saying something, though each can receive a modifier of some kind: [very angrily], for example. The model is crude and does not exhaust the possibilities. Nor is it particularly formal, but the fundamental distinction being made between what is to be said and how to say *it* as two independent variables is clear.

13.1.1 The what and how of an utterance

Transferring the drama script analogy to the general speech production perspective we suggest, one can say that both the what (the utterance itself) and the how (the tone of voice to be used) are here represented separately as part of some underlying or abstract plan: they constitute the intention, and the intention is in two parts. What is in the script is a plan which underlies the acoustic signal the actor will produce. We say the plan is abstract because it is not itself an actual acoustic signal. The plan or script captures the *intention*, rather than the actual signal, and intentions are abstractions.

In the dynamic model of speech production we propose, an abstract intention or plan of an utterance has to be 'rendered'. In the drama this is the job of the actor, and it is important to note that the rendering process is deliberately inexplicit: it is part of the actor's art. The rendering of a script—speaking utterances with appropriate tones of voice—requires artistic interpretation of some kind. This is why we can point to the individuality of interpretations by different actors of the same passages in a play. A parallel would be the interpretation (an instantiation) by a musician of the composer's score (the abstract plan). But, of course, speech production modelling is not about characterizing an art. A speech production model must characterize explicitly how the two aspects of the plan are brought together to produce a composite soundwave which integrates the utterance and its expression.

The task of the corresponding *perceptual* model is to input the composite soundwave and, for example, output a label for the utterance (perhaps together with a semantic analysis saying what it means) and a label for the emotion underlying the speaker's tone of voice. In the case of an utterance *I love her* spoken with sincerity the listener will provide the two labels:

- the utterance was: 'I love her' [semantic analysis: ......]
- and the intended expression was: [*sincerely*]

The simple overall general model looks like this:

$$\left\{ \begin{array}{c} utterance \\ + \\ emotion \end{array} \right\} \rightarrow composite\_soundwave \rightarrow \left\{ \begin{array}{c} utterance' \\ + \\ emotion' \end{array} \right\}$$

where *utterance* and *emotion* form part of the speaker's abstract plan for this utterance and *utterance'* and *emotion'* are listener assigned labels; the composite_soundwave

A Generalized Model of Expression 293

produced by the speaker and heard by the listener is a single complex entity.

We shall be discussing later how the perceptual model works in detail, but for the moment we shall say that *utterance′* and *emotion′* are two separate labels assigned by the listener to the speaker's waveform. The justification for this 'separate becomes single becomes separate' approach is the observation that both speaker and listener can and do talk about utterances and the accompanying expression of emotion as though they were distinct entities, despite the fact that the acoustic signal, the medium used to transmit these entities, is a composite *single* entity. We speak of the two entities of utterance and expression as being *encoded* in the composite soundwave. The emotion contributes to the actual meaning of the utterance; for example a sarcastic tone of voice can alter semantic features associated with the words used, and errors can arise in

- encoding;
- production;
- perception;
- assigning the wrong features in decoding.

Consider this fragment of conversational exchange:

> A: *I'm a human being too, you know.*
> B: *Surely not!*
> where *surely not* is said with a tone-of-voice which clearly indicates: *of course you are*

The soundwave prompts the listener to assign two labels which correspond to the two original entities. We have used a diacritic (emotion′ and utterance′) on the labels to indicate that they are not themselves the original entities. They are objects in the listener's reconstruction of the speaker's plan and are differentiated from the two speaker entities because the speaker → medium → listener chain is fraught with constraints on a perfect match between the speaker's intention and the listener's decoding. That is, the system is prone to error, which can result in a mislabelling of the stimulus waveform.

13.2 The simple composite soundwave model

Now that we have a few definitions, we are in a better position to work out what the dominant research paradigm for investigating expressive content in speech is. The focus is on the composite soundwave:

1. It is an acoustic rendering of two distinct underlying or planned 'objects'—the basic utterance and its expression.
2. These are each discoverable and separable (because human beings can derive separate percepts for them).

Furthermore

3. Once each object has been separately acoustically modelled they can be recombined in synthesis.

The first two points are the very simple framework which forms the basis of the majority of research into the nature of expressive content in speech. The third point follows if the research task is to resynthesize expressive speech as opposed to the more usual synthesis of an utterance on its own and without expression.

13.2.1 Unravelling the dangers of the composite soundwave model

There are a number of dangers inherent in the composite soundwave model. Perhaps the most significant is the implication that the soundwave delivers both utterance and plan which have been encoded into it in some way by the speaker. The implication also is that the final stage (perception) consists of decoding the acoustic signal into the same two components mixed when it was created. The problem is that from what we know of perception this interpretation of the model is not correct. Perceivers do not demodulate signals from a carrier acoustic signal—they use the signal to *assign labels*, and this is not the same thing at all.

Put another way, the acoustic signal could be said to be a composite of acoustic signals—mixed as part of the production process. But even if this is true it does not imply that the perceptual system *un*-mixes the composite signal to obtain two acoustic

A Generalized Model of Expression

signals, and then uses these to create its labels. The labelling might be assigned without a reconstruction of its underlying component parts. This would be especially true if the signal were quite simply no more than a set of triggers to promote the labelling procedure and assign the correct labels. This is a rehearsal of the old argument as to whether the acoustic signal contains its own labels or whether these are assigned, from storage in the listener's mind, as part of the perceptual process; we strongly believe the latter to be a more appropriate model.

But if we want to model the acoustic signal as a blend of two components there is another, better way of doing it. If we consider expression to be a comparatively long-term phenomenon and utterances—domains of phonological and syntactic events—to be comparatively short-term events, we can use the analogy of modulation from radio technology to say.

- An expressive carrier is modulated by the planned utterance.

That is, utterance and expression are not objects with equal status: the utterance shows *abrupt* shifts as it moves from word to word (or small unit to small unit), but the expression present shows *fewer* and *slower* shifts or discontinuities. The carrier signal changes relatively slowly, but it is modulated with a signal whose characteristics change relatively quickly.

This is not the usual way of considering the relationship between plain message and tone of voice. The tone of voice is usually thought of as overlaid on the plain message; we are saying very clearly that we feel a more appropriate approach to modelling would be to have the message overlaid on the tone of voice.

Notice how the two objects, expression and utterance, now have different status and that this is based on rate of change: it is useful to think of the slower-moving object as the carrier and the faster-moving object as the modulation of the carrier. But although it may be useful and the usual way (in radio technology, for example) of doing things, it is not the only way: it could be the other way round. So we have to have a principled reason for laying out the model in this way, and in the explanation of our general model of speech production we detail how we see prosodics (and thus expression—since the two converge in the acoustic signal) as being an envelope within which speakers develop their utterances.

How do we choose between the two models: expression first, or message first?—for the choice might affect the way we analyse then resynthesize the acoustic signal. One way of evaluating models is to consider their scope and see whether they account for all the data.

What, then, about lay listener remarks like:

- *That the news had made him happy came across in the way he spoke.*
- *It took a full hour for the anger in her voice to begin to subside.*
- *He may have said he was happy now, but the anger was still coming across in his voice.*

Data of this kind seems to point to the expressiveness element as being long-term, and in addition points to its independence. The independence is such that the last sentence here is reporting that the words and the expressiveness contradict each other: not, in fact, a rare occurrence. The fact that the words say the speaker is happy does not imply that the expressiveness of the utterance correlates with happiness, and the listeners may well *know* that the speaker is really unhappy.

13.3 Short-term and long-term expressiveness

Linguists' attentions have usually been focused on the semantic content of an utterance, because it was thought that the message is primary, with tone of voice being secondary—this is reflected in writing systems which tend to play down tone of voice, but clearly and explicitly convey the message. It seems to be the case that of the two elements expression and sentence semantics (or local variations in basic meaning), expression is a longer-term phenomenon. That is, expression spans changes in local meaning. For this reason it seems to be worth considering that it is the basic utterance that modulates the expression 'carrier'.

But we must also make provision for the fact that expression itself can also vary in span: sometimes long, sometimes short. Another way of saying this is that a particular expression does not necessarily hold for a fixed length of speaking. Expressive

A Generalized Model of Expression

content varies, sometimes within the utterance, sometimes within a sentence, sometimes spanning several sentences. If we think of all possible modes of expression as held within an 'expression space', then movement within the expression space is not at some predetermined fixed or governed speed, or indeed at some predetermined syntactic or other 'linguistic' boundary.

If we think of the space as containing a number of expression 'vectors' (see Fig. 13.1), then movement within the space can be abrupt either along a single vector expressing degree of the same mode of expression—e.g. 'irritable ... angry ... furious'— or between vectors expressing change of expression—e.g. 'happy ... angry'.

A point which we pick up later is the fact that expression can change in type as well as degree during the course of an utterance.

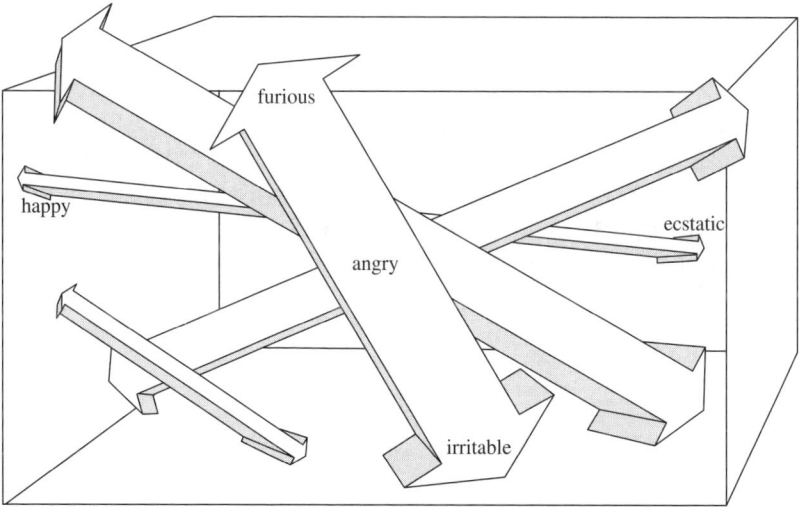

Fig. 13.1. 'Expression space' represented as a cube with five expression vectors located within the space. The space can be thought of as having various dimensions corresponding to some abstract parameters of expression, and the vectors as representing a continuum of degrees or intensity of a particular expression. For example, the heavy vector running almost vertically through the space might be the 'irritable ... angry ... furious' vector or axis, the faint vector at the back might be the 'happy ... ecstatic' vector, and so on. The space is conceptualized to show graphically how various modes of expression relate to one another and how each can vary along its intensity vector.

13.3.1 A single carrier but multiple modes of expression

So far the model we have been suggesting describes an expression *carrier* which is modulated by the actual words of an utterance. This carrier should not be seen as expressing a single vector of expression along which are the various modes of expression, each with its degrees, but as a multi-parametric or multi-vector carrier.

In this particular model each vector is considered as home to a single axis of expression—'irritable' to 'furious', for example. But along each vector there can be recognizable zones or *categories*, each capable of being multi-valued. This is not difficult to imagine. Along the example vector *irritable* ↔ *furious* we find a category 'angry' which itself can be expressed in terms of degrees: 'mildly angry ... very angry'. Figure 13.2 illustrates this vector-based model.

In the upper part of the diagram we see a particular emotion vector showing the *potential* for a number of different categories along its length. In the abstract these categories are equally intense—or rather they just have intensity potential. In the lower part we see how an instantiation of the vector results in an increase of a particular emotional category and a decrease in the others. Speakers and listeners will both think of these categories as distinct, but in reality they are more like zones blending into one another. The apparent distinctness is the result of categorization on the part of the speaker and listener—the well-known effect of categorical perception (Pisoni and Lazarus 1974).

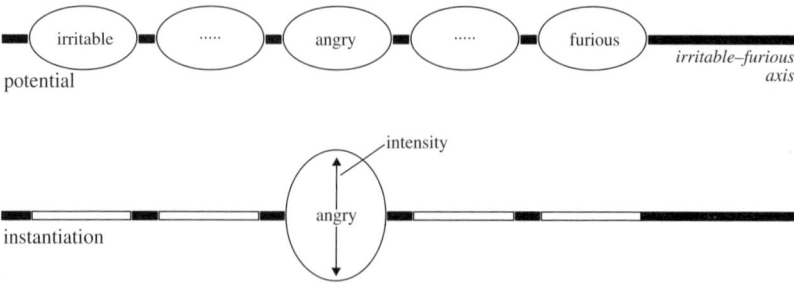

Fig. 13.2. The vector model for characterizing emotion. The upper vector represents abstract potential, whereas the lower vector represents an instantiation of this potential.

A Generalized Model of Expression

Thus we can think of a single carrier which consists of 'strands' of expression—the vectors—along each of which there are various categories of expression. Within each of these, there are various degrees of intensity. Notice in the diagram that the size of the anger zone can vary according to the intensity of the emotion. But furthermore notice that by using this mechanism the model captures the lay differentiation between feelings like 'extremely angry' and 'mildly furious'. These varying degrees of different emotions may converge in the actual acoustic signal, but the terminology of ordinary language shows the strength of the category concept in speakers and listeners.

Chapter 14

All Speech is Expression-Based

If it is hard to identify and define the sources of expressiveness in speech, we can at least separate them out from how they are communicated: it is useful to treat a emotion, for example, and how it is expressed as two different things. Equally, it is useful to treat the perception of an emotion as yet another. This is not to say that these objects and processes are not interrelated, for indeed they are obviously dependent on one another; but unravelling the strands of any complex situation is often helped by separating out the various components which do interact and initially considering them separately.

We need to consider whether it is possible to have speech which does not have some expressive content. Bearing in mind all the while that a model is not the same as the object being modelled, the question of the necessity of expressive content soon develops into another one:

- Is it appropriate to model the expression in speech as though there is always some expressive content present however small?

If the answer turns out to be yes, we then have to find a suitable place in our model for what people might feel is 'neutral speech'—speech apparently without expressive content.

The question is not trivial, because it relates to how we actually go about building a model of expression and what form it will take. As we see repeatedly, researchers very often choose to set up neutral speech as some canonical version of speech against which expressive speech is assessed. Despite the complexity of some of the work, the basis of this research paradigm is the simple idea that if you subtract non-expressive speech from expressive speech you are left with the expression itself.

$$speech_{expressive} - speech_{non\text{-}expressive} \rightarrow expression$$

So within this research paradigm, for example, if we observe and measure that comparatively neutral speech has a fundamental frequency range of r for a given speaker over several samples of utterances and that when this speaker gets excited the range increases by 30%, we say that this extra range *is* the expression of excitement. The paradigm even allows for a simplistic recipe for creating excited speech:

1. Take neutral speech.
2. Increase its fundamental frequency range by 30%.

And at first glance this is exactly what we need if we are to use our description of expression in human speech as the basis for resynthesizing speech with expressive content. 'All' we need is an exhaustive set of such recipes covering all expression. In the emotion subset of such recipes, for example, we would have one for turning neutral speech into angry speech, neutral speech into happy speech, and so on. Via an intermediate stage we could even turn happy speech into sad speech—that is,

1. subtract happiness to derive neutral speech;
2. add sadness to create sad speech.

Following through and still confining ourselves to the soundwave's fundamental frequency parameter, we are in effect saying things like 'Sadness in speech is the narrowing of its fundamental frequency range'. That is, we are defining what is an abstract and essentially *perceived* concept in terms of the quantity of a physical parameter. What this definition should really be saying, though, is: 'If we narrow the fundamental frequency range we will perceive sadness in the speech.' Co-occurrence or correlation can at best be only a weak form of definition. The tables of acoustic correlations are really assertions of this kind—a statement of how physical attributes correlate with abstract terms.

A question which arises directly from this approach to characterizing expressive content in speech is whether there is really such a thing as truly neutral speech—that is, speech without expressive content. Can people actually communicate with no expression? The answer to this question is critical for the research paradigm which measures the difference between an acoustic signal with expressive content and one claimed to have no expressive content.

14.1 Neutral expression

Almost all speech contains some level of expression. There is, however, one way in which we could think of neutral speech as special. We could consider neutral expressive *content* to be an abstraction. It would be almost as though in an abstract way all speech can be characterized at a particular level where its expressive potential has yet to be realized. If we took this line we would be saying that all speech has the potential to have expressive content, and that filling in the actual expression for any one utterance comes later, either logically or temporally. The importance of this approach lies in the way it models expression as part of the prosodic hierarchy, thus fitting in with the widely accepted approach to modelling in general in linguistics. Neutral speech looked at in this way does not exist at one end of a cline but dominates all expression in speech, since it gets instantiated by different expressive content drawn from the cline.

14.1.1 Expression comes before the message

We return in more detail to the question of which comes first, the expression or the message, since this is fundamental to the model framework we propose. We ourselves model expression as dominating the prosodic hierarchy. In terms of the carrier/modulation model we could say that expression is in the form of a carrier for the message. Certainly, in those cases where the speaker's acoustic signal is distorted by facial contortion or tension—as with a smile or the tension associated with strong anger—the expression comes first temporally (it lasts for longer than the message) and logically (it dominates the message). These are examples of physically sourced expression, and this is the clearest type of expression which might be said to exist distinctly from the message and prior to it. But we are confident also that the same is true also for any cognitively sourced expression. For both types of expression, emotion is a longer and more slowly moving element of speech than utterances; emotions and attitudes in a way transcend utterances.

14.2 Listener message sampling

Listeners perceiving messages can be thought of as *sampling* them. We can model listeners' input as proceeding in intervals rather than continuously. This is analogous to the sampling process associated with digitizing analog acoustic signals: the signal is measured or read at particular intervals. 'Slow-moving' signals need less frequent sampling than fast-moving signals because their content changes less rapidly, and nothing is 'lost' with longer measurement intervals—lower sampling rates. We can say that the information content or data rate of a slow-moving signal is less dense than that of a fast-moving signal.

As an example of this idea of fast and slow data rates, but this time on the production side of the equation, let us consider again how drama scripts are marked up. A character in a play is to speak a line thoughtfully:

> Hamlet: [thoughtfully] *To be or not to be—that is the question.*

Thoughtfulness spans the entire utterance and does not change during it, whereas the information content of the actual utterance is in fact changing with the unfolding of each word—a far denser information rate. And just as we argued above, thoughtfulness is a style which envelopes the entire utterance. The actor samples the stage direction once, but samples his line as it changes from word to word. The stage direction is dominant in the hierarchy.

14.2.1 *Expression and message data rates*

Data rate is important in speech production and perception, and applies to a variable or set of variables. Here we are dealing with two main interrelated variables—expression and message content—each with a different data rate. In a hierarchical model implying greater abstraction further up the hierarchy, the data rate tends as a rule to be lower in this kind of instance, and we are capturing the hierarchy by speaking of expressive content as enveloping or wrapping message content from the production point of view. When it comes to listener processing, our model claims a perceptual 'unravelling' of the composite acoustic signal in terms of the variables, back to their hierarchical relationship.

The data rate concept is implicit in much of the literature on the acoustic correlates of emotion. Hence we find excitement characterized as including a widening of the normal range of f0 variation: the implication is that the expressive range for f0 change holds good for as long as excitement prevails in the speaker and is detected by the listener. Part of our objective in this book is to make some of these points already implicit in the literature more obvious and more formal.

The stage direction example above refers to the entire utterance to be produced by the actor. Finer control of the expressive content of the actor's lines is obtained by occasionally including a new direction which focuses on the lines to follow, or until a new direction is included. In other words these stage directions are signalling the point at which expressive content changes, as well as its type. This is a relatively crude system of indicating expression, partly because it leaves the actor scope, for example, to vary the intensity of expression and the control of how different expressions should blend into each other. This scope, of course, is what enables artistic interpretation and the important variation observed between the way different actors will deliver their lines.

Introducing XML, a more formal way of declaring these stage directions as data structures, we can rewrite the initial part of Hamlet's speech like this:

```
<Hamlet>
   <pensively> To be or not to be—that is the question </pensively>
   <musing> Whether 'tis nobler in the mind to suffer the... </musing>
</Hamlet>
```
[1]

---

[1] The notation we use here is XML—extensible mark-up language—(Altova 1998–2002) which provides a formal hierarchical declaration of data relationships. XML, which is most usefully deployed to declare data structures, should not be confused with HTML or its derivatives, which are most commonly used to mark-up

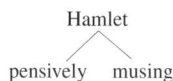

Fig. 14.1. Tree diagram as an alternative to the XML declaration.

In the broadest sense the complete data here is the play itself, together with its internal data structure—the actors, their speeches, etc.

XML declares types of data and their relationships by using tags which surround subsets of the data. Thus the opening and closing tags <pensive> and </pensive> indicate that the data contained within this envelope is assigned to this particular category of element. Although temporally sequential, the sections of Hamlet's speech tagged <pensive>...</pensive> and <musing>...</musing> have equal status—they are both parts of this particular speech. However, both are contained within the <Hamlet>...</Hamlet> declaration, which occupies the next higher dominant node. A more conventional tree diagram of the data is presented in Fig. 14.1.

We can see from the tree diagram that the node *Hamlet* dominates equally the nodes *pensively* and *musing*, which have equal status. A convention places *pensively* logically or temporally prior to *musing* since it is to the left; by linguistic convention in English, adverbs have temporal precedence.

14.2.2 Data rates and perception

Signalling the point of change for expressive content, though, is a concept which matches well with ideas about the perception of slow-moving phenomena. All modalities of perception respond to changing phenomena rather than steady-state phenomena. It is change, particularly abrupt change, which alerts the perceptual system to interpret the signal. Within limits, the more abrupt the change the more sensitive the perceptual system is to it, especially if the change is important; conversely, the closer the

textual material for visual display purposes. We cite Altova's XML development environment because it emphasizes the declarative properties of XML rather than its comparatively trivial display mark-up usage.

phenomenon is to being steady-state—that is, not changing or changing only very slowly—the less sensitive the perceptual system is. Speakers use their knowledge of this property of perception to draw attention to various points in an utterance. Contrastive emphasis is a good example: to signal that one word contrasts with another a speaker may introduce a high fall intonation contour onto the stressed syllable of a word. In physical terms this means that there will be a relatively rapid fall in the fundamental frequency during the syllable which bears the contrastive emphasis. The rapid change in the fundamental frequency will be readily detectable by any listener for the very reason that it *is* rapid change.

With slow-moving phenomena listeners might simply sample the data at intervals; it would not be necessary to have continuous sampling simply to reaffirm the slow rate of change. There are two ways in which the listener might proceed: there could be regular spot sampling at a predetermined rate, just to see if there has been a change, or change itself may trigger sampling. We do not feel that we are in a position to determine which of these is the more appropriate in our model. For the moment we shall simply say that with slow-moving data which may incorporate the odd rapid change, sampling need not be very frequent, and the *expressive content* 'channel' in the data is just such a data stream. The *message* channel is comparatively much more likely to incorporate a rapidly changing data stream needing more frequent sampling.

A parallel in the psychology literature focuses on edge detection as an important strategy in visual perception (Marr 1982). Here we could imagine the perceiver as performing a continuous background scan occasionally brought to the forefront by the detection of a rapid change in the data—the occurrence of an 'edge'. The set of edges in the visual scene being scanned would be the set of pivotal, focus, or reference points for the scene. We do not know whether the perception of speech works in the same way, but it is reasonable to assume that perceptual sensitivity varies in much the same way for slow and fast changes in audio data.

Thus we see that a consideration of data rate is important in the points of view of both production and perception. Our feeling is that higher nodes in the hierarchy carry lower data rates when considered simply as abstractions or labels. Their *inner details* (the details that the higher nodes 'wrap') hang off them and call for higher data rates. As a final example in production, consider the phonemic units which give rise to allophonic instantiation: the data rate associated with the phonemic tier in the hierarchy is lower than that associated with the allophonic tier, where there is much greater representational detail.

14.3 The expression envelope

Neutral speech can be regarded as speech with zero or little intended (production) or detectable (perception) expression. But this special case does not detract from the idea that all speech is wrapped in expressiveness. Each zone on the vector is potentially a wrapper for an utterance or set of utterances. Thus for example the wrappers 'happily', 'angrily', and 'with authority' can dominate any messages the speaker may choose to utter. If a person is happy (a cognitive condition coming prior to actually planning an utterance) happiness will pervade whatever they say within reason. It is in this sense that we speak of the expression as being the *carrier* for the message. So:

```
<expression>
    <happy/>
    <angry/>
    <with-authority/>
</expression>
```

The slash occurs after the element to indicate that an opening and closing pair of brackets is implied, but so far the wrapper or 'container' is empty. A less conventional notation might be <happy>...</happy>, with '...' indicating 'currently empty, but with potential for filling'. The element <expression>... </expression> is not empty of course in the example: it already contains the three potential instantiations.

So, in this model the term 'cline' or, better, 'vector' relates particular instantiations to an abstract expression *node* which points to expression in general rather than any particular expression. Instantiations are to be drawn from what is available on the expression vector, including the far-end special case of neutral expression. All of this is prior to any message generated *within* the expressive wrapper or envelope.

14.3.1 The general prosodic envelope

Developing this hierarchical model further, we use the expression 'node' to wrap general prosody. Utterances have an underlying prosodic structure which initially is just a blank structure with potential. This gets instantiated in particular ways, including the introduction of expression. The hierarchical format of this model and the XML formalism which declares it permit *inheritance*—the handing down of higher properties to dependent nodes. Properties are *attributes* and are inherited as *potential* attributes of an element; they subsequently become instantiated with specific values.

We now have a model which envisages spoken utterances within a specific prosodic framework and dependent on that framework. In this approach a specific prosodic feature—this or that intonation pattern, for example—is not applied to an utterance. Rather, an utterance is fitted within the prosodic framework, along with other utterances which may form a grouping of utterances. With this approach we are able, for example, to discuss the prosodic structure of a paragraph without the difficulties of considering prosody on a sentential basis. Furthermore, we can discuss the entire prosody of a stretch of speech without reference to its meaning. Thus, simply, we can say that all questions of a particular type may have 'question intonation'—an intonation which we might define as a contour of primarily rising intonation without reference to the meaning of any one sentence it may wrap. Or we could speak of phrase boundaries 'resetting' intonation contours and declaring what resetting means in terms of type or 'shape' of contour, without referring to any one particular phrase or sequence of phrases. Any element higher in the hierarchical framework of the model is thus able to capture greater generalization. This framework and the generalization

All Speech is Expression-Based

properties of hierarchically arranged elements is the basis of the particular formalism of linguistics. We are going beyond this conceptually because, as we shall see when we discuss the general speech production model, the static domain of traditional (generative) linguistics is inadequate for our purposes.

We may want to link words to specific features of a prosodic contour but the contour dominates—we do not link *it* to the words of the message. The *domain* of utterances becomes the general prosodic unit, a highly abstract element. We discuss the model based in prosodics in general but a useful way of picturing the approach is to consider a couple of examples of a speaker's strategy in composing an utterance. The speaker says (internally):

- 'Ordinary' prosody example: *I'm going to ask a question—and this is it*, rather than *Here are my words—and I give them to you in the form of a question*, or
- 'Expressive' prosody example: *I'm angry and my words come out like this*, rather than *I've got something to say to you and I'll fit an angry tone of voice to it*.

14.3.2 Prosody as the carrier of messages

Using the analogy we introduced earlier, we can speak of messages as being modulated onto a prosodic carrier. This means that an utterance *is* a modulated carrier: it is not the carrier on its own, nor the message on its own, but a new structure dependent on both. The utterance is less abstract—it eventually derives what we can actually measure in acoustics—but the carrier and message are not measurable in the same ways. We can imagine a blank *un*-modulated prosodic carrier, instantiated perhaps as a hummed intonational tune, but we cannot imagine a spoken message on its own. An abstract message can be dealt with, but no *spoken* message, in this model, can exist without its carrier. It is in *this* sense that we have introduced the idea that all utterances have some expressive content.

The message is modulated onto the prosodic carrier. In other words the prosody and its expressive wrapper constitute the carrier and as such have no meaning—other than what we might call 'prosodic meaning': any information content is conveyed by prosody alone including the communication of emotion. The message comes later, and is modelled as separate from the prosodic carrier. The modulated carrier forms the basis of the utterance and its acoustic waveform.

We are modelling a modulated prosodic structure—adjusted for expressive content. Prosody and message combine in this special way to contribute to the utterance plan. The phonetic stages of the model render the plan, reflecting in the final detail of the rendering as much of the prosodic structure as necessary or required. We say this because it may not be necessary for the system to include all the prosodic information to achieve a satisfactory level of perception. Judgement as to exactly how much detail to include rests with a supervisory 'agent' (Chapter 16).

14.4 Defining neutral speech

We return again to some aspects of the concept of neutral (apparently non-expressive) speech which still need to be defined. We have made this a recurrent theme because the idea is all-pervasive in the literature. But now our intention is to characterize neutrality in the context of our suggested model.

We have just described how the prosodic carrier (with expressiveness marked) and the message come together to provide the system with what we call an 'utterance plan'. A plan is an abstract representation of how the utterance may sound ideally after rendering; it is the basis for rendering to proceed. And rendering is the process of taking the plan and developing from it the necessary articulations which are ultimately the basis for the soundwave required to satisfy the speaker's goal to be perceived. We use the term 'rendering' rather than the more usual 'interpretation' or 'realization' for combined phonetic processes because we treat the process rather differently from other theorists: rendering involves passive and active processes, and within active processes involves also intelligent reasoned choices—the role of the phonetic agent.

At an abstract level—the level of underlying plan or subsequently of the listener's percept—neutral speech is speech which lacks expression; expression is a 'way of speaking' or a 'tone of voice' which gives emotive or attitudinal content to an utterance. The feeling sometimes that an utterance *lacks* expressive content could result from speaker judgement or listener perception: either way both speaker and listener might report that the utterance has no expression and that the meaning of the utterance focuses entirely on its basic semantics. Notice here that we are speaking of judgement and perception rather than physical measurement.

In the model such judgements of 'no expression' result from placing the planned expressive content of the utterance at the end of a vector of degree of expressiveness: the parameter is set to its minimum value. When it comes to rendering the underlying plan to give us a measurable acoustic signal, 'neutral' would mean the absence of any acoustic phenomenon which could be assigned an expressive label. Absence here means unmeasurable, but present. The problem is that if the claim that there is always some expressive content in an utterance is valid it follows that we never find an utterance to measure which does not have expressive content—so we cannot measure expression-free speech.

A similar problem arose in the context of developing the model of coarticulation in the 1960s. It was quickly realized, once the idea of coarticulation between segments had taken hold, that the chances of finding a segment without some degree of coarticulation in a normal speed utterance stream were low. Spectrograms show the point clearly. For example (see Fig. 14.2), in a monosyllabic utterance such as *tart* [tɑt] formant bending at the start of the vowel nucleus will suggest a high locus for F2, and return to a high locus at the end of the vowel nucleus. It is questionable—even when, as here, the vowel is comparatively long—whether there is time in the 'centre' of the vowel for the 'true' or canonical frequency of F2 to be reached. This means that it is difficult or impossible to answer, from this example or similar ones, the question: What is the F2 centre frequency value of the [ɑ] vowel nucleus?

Still relevant to our own dilemma, there were two ways of solving the problem of determining the acoustic specification of

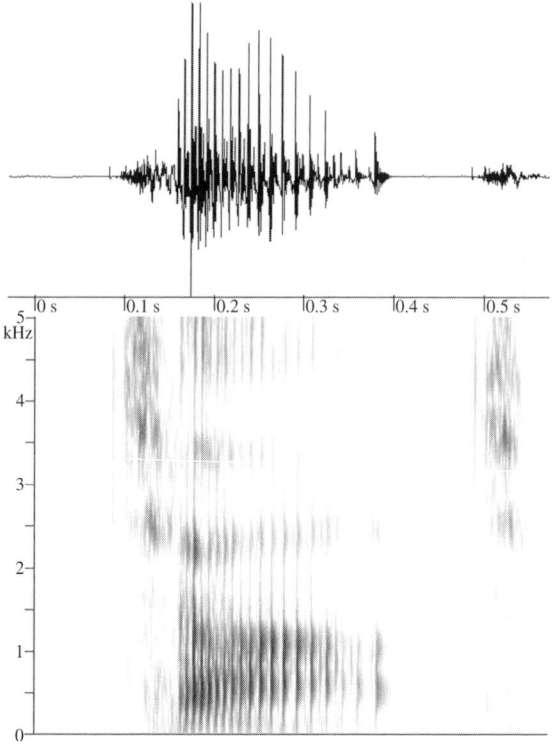

Fig. 14.2. Spectrogram of a spoken instantiation of *tart* [tɑt]. Note the formant bending (especially of F2) following the initial plosive release and preceding the release of the final plosive.

a canonical segment:

1. One was to measure, in our example, the F2 value for the vowel [ɑ] (defined abstractly as the 'target' vowel) in many different contexts and take some kind of average of the observed values—itself therefore an abstraction.
2. The other was to try to devise an experimental paradigm which provided a non-coarticulated version of the vowel for direct measurement. Attempts here ranged from simply getting a native speaker to utter the vowel in complete isolation (something native speakers almost never *actually* do, yet curiously, always *can* do!), to deliberately setting up a 'neutral' coarticulatory environment unlikely to influence the canonical

or target of the vowel in question—by using, for example, a specially devised frame for the sound.

Neither of these solutions is theoretically satisfactory, for both attempt in some way to provide a physical measurement of something which is essentially abstract. Researchers were trying to assign physical values to an abstract label by measuring physical objects to which they had applied the label. The way out of the dilemma is to recognize that abstract objects cannot be assigned physical values: these are reserved for their physical instantiations.

In the case of expressive content, there is no point in trying to assign physical values to an object like 'sadness'. All we can do is say that when sadness is present we observe certain physical values. These physical values always vary with utterance context, just as coarticulated allophones always vary with segmental context. They *relate* to underlying abstract constructs like emotions or, in the case of coarticulation, extrinsic allophones, but they are not *measurements* of emotions or extrinsic allophones.

There is no doubt that defining neutral speech is difficult, and is all the harder for the fact that neutral speech is arguably an abstract concept with no physical manifestation. The nearest we come to relating neutral expression to physical measurements is to offer measurements of some other non-neutral expression with parameter values set to a minimum.

14.5 Parametric representations

By modelling the range of different emotions experienced by a speaker as combinations of a small number of basic emotions some researchers (Lewis 1993; Plutchik 1994) have moved towards a simple type of parametric representation. The property of parametric representations which is significant from our point of view is that they show transparently how a set of objects relate to one another by indicating how each is represented by a unique combination of basic properties. For example, in Classical Phonetics the set of sounds we label [p, t, k] share the properties

Table 14.1. Diagram illustrating how three features distribute among six phonetic elements

	p	t	k	b	d	g
Plosive	*	*	*	*	*	*
Voiceless	*	*	*			
Voiced				*	*	*

of being plosives and voiceless, whereas the set [b, d, g], while still sharing the plosive property, are not voiceless but voiced. In tabular form this representation looks like Table 14.1.

The table or matrix shows how it is easy to group elements according to classes which are identified by means of their features. Thus all six sounds share the 'plosive' property and belong to the class of plosives. But only [b, d, g] belong to the class of voiced sounds and only [p, t, k] belong to the class of voiceless sounds.

In a parametric representation of a set of objects it is usually helpful to choose a set of parameters which are shared by all the objects to be described, even if the values of some of them are set to zero, perhaps indicating non-applicability. But it is important to notice that in the representation of plosives the properties or features used are combined to describe an object which transcends the individual features. Another way of saying this is that [t] is a different *kind* of object from 'plosive'. But this is not something we can easily say of the characterization of subtle emotions, or shades of emotion, by referring to half a dozen or so 'basic' emotions. 'Plosive', 'voiceless', and 'voiced' are properties or *attributes* of sound *elements*, but we cannot say in the same way that 'anger' is an attribute of 'irritation'. The proposal that all emotions can be 'represented' by combinations of six basic emotions is an interesting one, but does not constitute a proposal for a true parametric representation because in a sense what is being represented is on the same 'level' as the elements used to do the representing.

However, when it comes to the acoustic representation of expression we want to be in a position to adopt a true parametric representation by using features such as 'fundamental frequency range' to characterize expressions such as 'anger'. It is obvious that f0 range is not an expression: it is an attribute of expression at the acoustic level.

Table 14.2. Matrix showing the relationship between a set of derived emotions and underlying basic emotions

	e_1	e_2	e_3	e_4	e_5	e_6	e_7	...	e_n
b_1	+	+			+	+	+		+
b_2	+		+	+	+				+
b_3		+		+		+			
b_4	+		+	+			+		

Nevertheless some researchers in the field of emotion (not its acoustic representation) feel they have identified a number of basic emotions which can be characterized in terms of a small number of biological states. Since biological states are not emotions, but simply correlated with emotions, especially if by 'emotion' we mean something essentially cognitive in nature, a characterization of emotions in terms of these underlying biological states is more like the true parametric representations we are discussing (Plutchik 1994; Lewis et al. 1998; Panksepp 1998). So, in the abstract, we can illustrate this by Table 14.2.

Each row represents a different basic emotion, b_j, and each column a derived emotion, e_i. Some derived emotions are represented by two basic emotions and some by three, but clearly there are limits to the number of derived emotions which can be represented. Assuming the basic emotion contributes in a binary way (i.e. it is either 'present' or 'absent') then, if we use just one basic emotion we can represent two derived emotions; if we use two we can represent four derived emotions; three gives us eight, and four give us sixteen. Obviously we can have many more derived representations if we allow an *n*-ary value for each basic emotion. The division of each basic emotion into *n* values would have to ensure that *n* was not so 'fine' as to be unable to be made reliably by the speaker or detected by an observer. The general equation is that there are n^j possibilities, where *j* is the number of basic emotions and *n* is the number of discriminable 'levels' for each.

14.5.1 Relating the features of underlying emotion to acoustic features

In the speech literature the characterization of expressive effects is by acoustic parameters (like f0, amplitude, timing), and so it would be useful if the underlying emotions themselves were represented parametrically. This would enable at least the same *type* of representation to be carried through a complete model, beginning with the source of the expression and ending with the way it comes across in the acoustic signal. So, we could either say that 'anger', 'happiness', etc. are parameters of all emotions (including themselves) or we have to have a different set, which are really just features. The formal problem is that if an emotion is a combination of features it cannot usefully be a feature itself.

So the actual use of physical features in the human being (candidates might be a set of contributing hormones, or neural activity, for example) or the use of features in the scientist's representation depend on how many discrete values each feature can be given. What we cannot have is a *continuous* vector for each feature—since this would imply an infinite set of values for each feature and therefore an infinite set of emotions. It is probably the case that the vector needs to be expressed in a categorical way—and the constraints on the number of categories would need justifying physically or cognitively as mentioned above. Hence, we say that each feature, f, has a certain number of distinct values, say n, on a single vector. It is possible, of course, that the n possible values for each feature do not themselves turn up with equal probability—in which case there is a further constraint on how many different emotions are possible. In principle, the mapping from underlying feature set to external acoustic features set would be simple:

biological or cognitive feature set → expressive acoustic feature set

Any one particular combination of biological or cognitive features each assuming particular values would be the characterization of a particular emotion or attitude in the speaker; similarly, a particular combination of acoustic features would cue the identification, by a listener, of the speaker's emotive state. There would not necessarily be any one-to-one correlation between features in the underlying (biological/cognitive) and surface (acoustic) sets. That is, there would not necessarily be a predictable linear relationship between some biological features and, say, range of fundamental frequency, though it is conceivable that there *is*.

14.5.2 Correlating underlying and surface feature sets with the perception of a signal's expressive content

Ideally the underlying feature set would match in some linear fashion the acoustic feature set used to represent it. By examining the acoustic signal (in a parametric representation) we should be able to determine which parameters are involved in the expression of emotion and how that representation is accomplished. We should be able to identify the relationship between each emotion—that is, the label on each emotion—and distinct combinations of parameters.

Unfortunately when it comes to the final part of the equation—relating the acoustic signal to the expressive content as identified by a listener—things are far from simple. The elementary parametric model we have just outlined assumes that the emotion itself is represented in the acoustic signal; each stage in the model is a re-representation of what is basically the same information. But this may not be the case. What is represented by the acoustic signal may be just a simple trigger for prompting the listener to assign an emotion label to a stretch of utterance where a particular combination of features occur. This illustrates what is almost certainly the probability of a non-one-to-one correspondence between the acoustic features and the assigned label. Any non-linearity here is crucial because it means that a label L_i, which any one set of acoustic features F may trigger in the listener on one occasion, may become L_j on some other occasion, triggered by the same F.

An analogous event in segmental speech perception would be how in American English the acoustic event corresponding to a voiced alveolar flap is sometimes assigned by a listener the label /t/ (as in the word *writer*) and sometimes the label /d/ (as in the word *rider*).

So we have features describing an underlying emotion, features describing the waveform, and features which are detected by the listener for the purposes of label assignment. Only as an unlikely first approximation should we assume a linear relationship between these sets of features and the underlying and perceptual labels.

14.5.3 The acoustic parameters of expressive content

Dealing with expressive speech involves assignment of abstract labels to the intended or underlying expression, 'happy', 'angry', 'purposeful', etc. These are analogous to the target segments in the coarticulation example used above. And we have analogous soundwaves to measure. Except that with expressive speech we begin by having little idea of what it is that we are to measure. Initially we are constrained by the traditional acoustic parameters associated with prosodic phenomena like stress, rhythm, and intonation, since it is widely believed that these are the basis of expressiveness. Most researchers cite the physical correlates of prosodics as being *further* manipulable to convey expression. Thus intonation, as a prosodic feature, has for a given speaker a certain range of correlating fundamental frequency: widen this and the speaker is perceived as conveying excitement. This is the basic and most accepted working model: expression is 'prosody plus' as far as the acoustic signal is concerned.

Table 3.2 in Chapter 3 reveals what researchers consider to be the main physical correlating parameters of expression. The problem is that this approach can sometimes be a little misleading since it implies: 'once a parameter always *the* parameter'. Other aspects of the signal are also affected and may well come into play in listener identification of particular expressions. For instance, supposing for prosodics in general we choose to focus on timing as the parameter involved in rhythm. Our characterization will necessarily be in terms of how the timing of various segment of speech correlates with the speaker's intended rhythm or the listener's perceived rhythm.

But as the rhythm slows toward the end of a declarative statement, for example, not only does the timing change but also the formant structure of the signal—the point being that time is a constraint on coarticulation the effects of which are being progressively 'reduced' as the rhythm slows. So, in this example, the prosodic parameter of rhythm as a suprasegmental exponent relates also to identifiable correlates in the segmental representation of the utterance. Put another way, the changing parameters of coarticulation correlate with a changing parameter of rhythm.

All Speech is Expression-Based

There are many interrelating factors of this kind in dynamic speech, and it quickly becomes clear that simple models of phenomena like coarticulation or the acoustics of expression which have an essentially static foundation are not really adequate.

Models of the acoustics of expression, like the models of segment coarticulation, fail to take into account the dynamically changing relationship between the parameters involved. They tell us the correlates of this or that mode of expression, but they do not tell us under what circumstances the values assigned to these correlates change. So, excitement tends to widen the range of fundamental frequency, but by how much? And does this widening always take place, and always by the same amount? Does varying rhythm, to name just one possibility, change the amount by which the range tends to widen? And so on; the list of detailed questions is not short.

As a rule parametric representations should not assume that no other aspect of the signal is affected or that there are no dynamic changes involved. Parameters are chosen because they represent the major contributing features for characterizing phenomena in a way useful to our science: that we select a particular set of features does not imply that other aspects of the signal are not also involved, it simply implies that other features are less significant for our purposes. A truly dynamic model, though, will take into account that this very significance might itself change over time as other factors change during an utterance or between utterances.

As a final example of this problem of interrelating parameters and how the significance of parameters alters dynamically as utterances unfold, consider speech conveying anger. An often-hypothesized property of angry speech is increased precision of articulation; this is not strictly a prosodic correlate but one which affects segments. Some of the acoustic correlates of anger derive from the way heightened neck and facial tension associated with the emotion distorts vocal tract performance, but the increase in precision is unlikely to be caused in this way.

Increased precision of articulation entails a reduction of coarticulatory effects. But how could this be, especially as angry speech is often delivered faster than usual—precisely the condition which would normally result in *increased* coarticulation? It can

320 An Integrated Model of Expression

only be that coarticulation—often modelled as automatic processes which are independent of linguistic considerations—has somehow been interfered with. In this example a segmental correlate (increased coarticulation) of a prosodic effect (increased rate of utterance) has been *reversed*. How this kind of effect is to be handled in speech production theory is a focal point of our general model of speech production, and plays a major role in how expressive content is managed. We discuss cognitive control of phonetic processes like coarticulation in Chapter 4.

14.6 Data collection

The approach usually taken in experiments designed to determine the acoustic correlates of various modes of expression is similar to that taken in many contemporary coarticulation studies. Assemble a data set which the speaker judges to have been spoken with a particular mode of expression as part of their intentions, and which a panel of listeners in standard listening tests agree consistently triggers a particular expressive percept; then measure, at least at first, the parameters of prosody (timing, amplitude, fundamental frequency) and compare the statistically processed results with results from a yardstick data set judged in listening tests to be 'neutral' or conveying some other mode of expression. The diagram below shows the general experimental procedure.

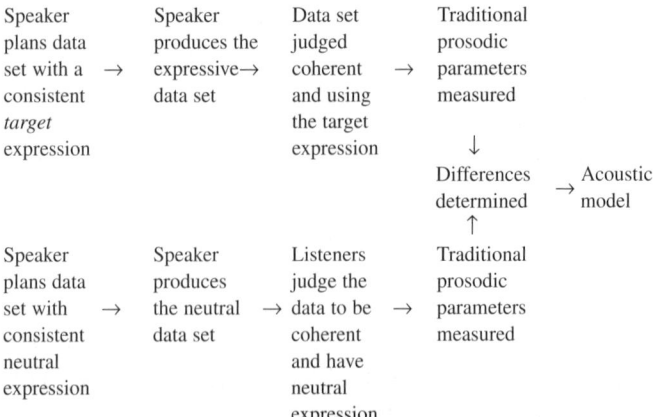

All Speech is Expression-Based

The data must be statistically processed to overcome the variability problem. If, because of the variability inherent in speech, statistical processing includes averaging, then by including some measure like the coefficient of variation ensures that the averaging procedure does not completely obscure the variability: it might be important. A carelessly chosen statistical technique might obscure the very feature we are trying to highlight.

So, if we want to characterize acoustically five different modes of expression we measure examples of all five and compare them either with a sixth standard set or with each other. Just as with coarticulation studies, the extraction of the canonical or neutral form from the data set is problematical.

14.6.1 Determining the universals in speech: a parallel problem

There is another way of doing this experiment—and we are reminded of early discussions (Chomsky 1972) in the area of universals in language and speech. There are two main ways of determining the universals of speech:

1. Observe all the world's languages and note the commonalities.
2. Work out the properties of the human speech production system which all people have, and deduce the universals from this.

The first method does not guarantee success because it is not possible to observe all the world's languages—especially those which have not yet occurred. A model based on this data will have only weak predictive power. So, if we say that we observe sound [s] to have certain characteristics in all 200, so to speak, languages we have looked at which have the sound, we are *not* able to predict absolutely that this sound will have the same characteristics if it occurs in the *next* language. At best we can give a probability index for its occurrence. An example of this method of approaching a discussion of universality can be found in Ladefoged and Maddieson (1996). This method is effective if the resultant model's level of predictive power is sufficient for the researchers' purposes. In particular, the method is useful in backing up an explanation as to why certain expected sounds may *not* occur in some languages. This is the key to the strategy: it is *linguistically* based.

On the other hand, the second method does guarantee success for all current languages and for all future languages so long as the design of human beings does not change. Because the second method is based on what underlies the sound, concentrating on what it is about human beings in general which has given the sound its characteristics, it enables a true predictive model enabling the characterization with a high degree of certainty of the properties of the sound if it occurs in as yet unobserved languages. This does not say that a particular sound *will* occur (a linguistically motivated observation) but it does predict accurately that when it *does* occur it will have the specified universal characteristics.

An advantage with the first—data collection—method is that, in the early stages of scientific investigation, it enables a fairly systematic discovery of just what the human vocal system is capable of in practical linguistically usable terms. This first method is equivalent to an enumeration of the objects. The second method can only predict the range of capabilities in a rather abstract way not necessarily related to linguistics, and assumes either that there are no constraints on the system or that the constraints are fully known—in other words the second method assumes the availability of a complete or near-complete general model, which is not available at the *start* of scientific research in an area. We look now at the possibility of using this second approach in the investigation of expressive content.

14.6.2 Universal parameters for expressive content in speech?

In terms of determining the possibilities for communicating expressive content it should be possible to investigate just exactly what the capabilities of the system actually are, thus predicting the characteristics that the data collection type of experiment (the first type above) sought to discover. The assumption here is that the speech production system's universal capabilities define its capacity for communicating expression and that this is reflected in the basic neutral case. This idea puts aside for the moment the possibility that involuntarily and physically determined expression might distort the vocal tract, and hence the acoustic signal.

So, if we have a good abstract model of the general prosodic structure of speech, and if we assume that expression is for the most part communicated by varying this prosodic structure in systematic ways, it should be possible to predict the range of variations which are possible and which can be assigned to particular expressive modes. It is as though we were designing an expressive content communication system: Just what acoustic possibilities do we have? Let's assign them systematically to particular expressive modes.

With this method we can also predict when we shall run out of possibilities—and therefore constrain the number of expressions, or the subtlety of expression, possible with the system. We might predict, for example, that there are only twenty possible expressive modes, given the constraints of the acoustic system—just as a universal sounds project might predict that there are only 250 possible sounds in human language (without ever having measured them).

There is a serious problem with this technique—working out what the possibilities of the *system* are in advance of ever having discovered them—and that is that we are assuming a one-to-one and invariant operation of the human perceptual system which is going to use the acoustic data. The problem arises, as it did with predictive models of coarticulation in the 1960s, because production is being considered independently of perception. If there *is* one-to-one correlation there is no problem, and the predictions of the production model are mirrored in the perceptual system: everything matching up perfectly. But with even rudimentary knowledge of how human perception works we should have our suspicions that one-to-one correlation is not likely—in lay terms, the so-called 'subjectivity' element kicks in—and we already know, partly because of the coarticulation studies just mentioned, that perception does not in fact work on a one-to-one basis.

Suppose the perceptual system assigns category labels to zones of analog stimulus continuously varying along a cline. The perceptual identification of these zones along the cline varies according to a number of factors, but one factor is the speaker's use of the cline to place a number of 'target' positions. So, if we take a vector described for a single tongue point running between an average position for [i] in French to an average position for [a] we plot a line as shown in Fig. 14.3(a). This vector describes the domain available for placing a speaker's targets. Fig. 14.3(b) marks the abstract targets used for the four un-rounded front vowels in French [i, e, ɛ, a], and Fig. 14.3(c) shows measured instantiation zones of 'missed' targets during a number of repetitions of these vowels in similar phonological contexts. We observe that precise targets are only infrequently hit, and, more importantly, that the zones barely overlap. Fig. 14.3(d) shows the same data for the English vowels [i, ɪ, e, æ]. Note that this is not a representation of part of the Classical Phoneticians' vowel chart: vowel charts do not indicate positions of the *same* tongue point. Thus on a vowel chart [ɪ] in English would be further back, as would [a] in French. Returning to the figures, we see that although the target zones do not overlap within each language, they do overlap if we combine the languages. We can find points on the vector which are therefore ambiguous if we do not name the language.

Furthermore, neglecting the possibility of varying degrees of freedom for this tongue point at different places along the vector we observe that closer targets imply smaller zones of missed targets.

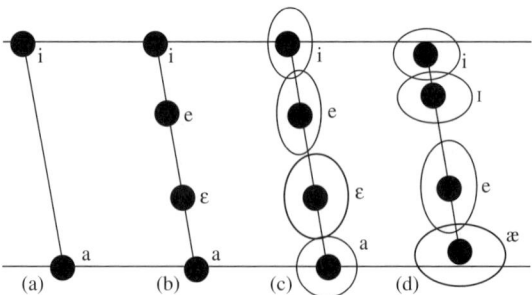

Fig. 14.3. Vowel 'vectors', abstract targets and instantiation zones: (a) a vector running between the position of a tongue point involved in [i] in French and the position of the same point during [a]; (b) targets along this vector associated with the unrounded French vowels [i, e, ɛ, a]; (c) zones of missed targets during a number of repetitions of these vowels; (d) similar zone data for the English vowels [i, ɪ, e, æ].

All Speech is Expression-Based

The fact that these zones vary in size for the different languages means that their size is not dependent on their position—rather it is dependent on the way the *language* is partitioning the vector. It follows that zone size is under control and correlates with the spacing of vowel targets. The range of variability found in the motor control of tongue positioning for vowels is not solely dependent on the motor control system's intrinsic limitations, but also on the way it is being used for creating sounds within a particular language.

There is a parallel on the perceptual side. There are limits to perceptual discrimination. And no language would attempt to place more target points on one of these vectors than could safely and repeatedly be discriminated by the average listener. It seems to us that there is an all-pervasive collaboration between speaker and listener, and that the constraints on each are known to the other. This overall approach enables us to begin to understand why some acoustic phenomena are interpreted by listeners in different ways on different occasions. We suspect that for this kind of reason it is going to prove hard to fix tables which list 'the acoustic correlates' of this or that expression, just as it is hard to list phonetic features for sections of running speech. Listing basic features for *abstractions* from running speech is proving easier, but such specifications need to be accompanied by a statement of how we get from abstraction to physical instantiation. All these difficulties normally associated with the segmental viewpoint on speech are also true of the prosodic viewpoint.

We have dwelt on this example, showing how there is collaboration between production and perception systems during an act of communication and how the production and perceptual systems' intrinsic constraints are further limited in use in language—but in different ways for different languages. The phenomenon with individual sounds and sounds in context is well attested in the phonetics and psychology literature. We are extending the idea to cover prosodic and expressive effects also. A full model would specify the range of effects possible for general prosody and expression according to how the parameters of these effects are varied. What we are looking at, then, is a comprehensive production/perception system in which detailed observations of the data make sense only in the context of the overall system. There are constraints on production which might contribute toward the idea of universals in all aspects of speaking, segmental, and suprasegmental including expression, but there are also constraints on perception which interact with the production constraints.

Chapter 15

Expressive Synthesis: The Longer Term

We saw in Chapter 11 that part of the process of creating a comprehensive model for synthesis, given the state of what we know of speech production and perception in human beings, would be to prepare the specification for a synthesizer based on this knowledge. Such an approach means that the synthesizer will be built from the speech production perspective: in effect it becomes a framework for a computational model of speech production, though without the detail of the motor control aspects of production, unless the synthesizer is to be of the articulatory type. We want a synthesis device that is a practical speaking machine, but that can also provide us with the means of testing our general theory of speech production.

15.1 What does the synthesizer need to do?

There are two main groups of questions we need to ask at the outset; the answers to these questions define how we proceed with a synthesis-oriented computational model of speech production.

1. What does a speech synthesizer need to do, and how does our knowledge of human speech production fit into this? What is the device capable of, and what are its limits? Here the perspective is from the synthesis viewpoint—we need good synthesis, and will incorporate all we know that is useful from our understanding of the speech production and perception processes.
2. What data do we have from speech production and how can we build a computational model of this data? Here the

perspective is from the production modelling viewpoint—we have data and ideas about how this all fits together—enough for us to build a computational model of speech production which can itself *be* a speech synthesizer. We give an example of declarative coding for a computational speech production model.

We base this model on a theory of speech production. In general, theories *explain* data and models *exemplify* the system from which the data is derived: a model is often more complete, hypothesizing how gaps in the knowledge might be filled for the sake of completeness. 'Explain' is a powerful word, and ideally a theory would attempt to say why some particular patterning of the data is the way it is, rather than some other way. But in a weaker form, explanation often entails simple, yet clear, transparent, and coherent characterization of the phenomena and their patterns. The word is used rather freely: what we aim for in a theory is as full as possible an understanding of why the system under investigation and its component sub-processes are the way they are. It is not sufficient to know that the data has been gathered and can be processed to reveal patterning. This is partly why a database on its own is of little theoretical value.

15.1.1 Alternative inputs to the synthesizer

For the purpose of testing a model of speech production, we need a synthesizer which

- has alternative inputs: plain text, marked or annotated text, and perhaps other symbolic representations.

Human beings can read plain text aloud, though to do so optimally they need to be able to understand the text; they need to interpret it semantically. The reason for this is that plain text does not include symbolic representation of much of its meaning or exactly how it is to be spoken. Semantic and phonological interpretations of the text have to be supplied by the reader, and ideally our synthesizer would be able to simulate both these processes. In practice we can include good phonological processing of text, but our ability to include good semantic interpretation is very limited. The semantic and phonological interpretations of the text are indispensable if we are to include natural expression as part of the specification. Nuance of meaning (such as emotion, to be expressed as tone of voice) will ultimately be encoded as variations of prosody, and clear semantic and phonological interpretation is necessary for generating the intended prosody of an utterance.

For example, we could approach *plain text* (that is, text with no markings additional to the normal orthography) by setting up a default prosodic scenario. A human reader might modify this according to how some semantic and expressive interpretation is assigned. In such an approach we might speak of the default prosodic structure (scenario) for speech synthesis onto which the input message is modulated (dropped).

We need the option of inputting *marked or annotated text* to get around the fact that ordinary orthography is really nothing more than a prompt to a linguistically knowledgeable reader—it certainly is not an exhaustive encoding enabling direct phonetic rendering. We can either include at the high end of the synthesizer sets of processes which can interpret the text ready for rendering, or we can devise a system of marking the input text with the results of such processes or the results of *some* of these processes.

15.1.2 Text mark-up

One form of annotation often applied to input text in a text-to-speech system is *prosodic* marking. This marking is not to annotate the segmental text, but to provide a default prosodic background—the 'wrapper' within which to render a speech version of the text. In orthography a mark, like *!* will add information indicating a departure from the default prosody. But the degree to which such punctuation marks achieve prosodic or expressive mark-up is tiny.

Take intonation as an example: assigning a good intonation pattern to plain text is very difficult, and in some circumstances the time and effort of including a necessarily inadequate process built into the system to assign intonation results is a less satisfactory achievement than marking the text in advance. So, if we are in a position to use text annotation, a marking system analogous to XML will help illustrate the kind of mark-up which might be applied:

<statement_intonation> *John went home.* </statement_intonation>
<question_intonation> *John went home.* </question_intonation>

where

statement_intonation means 'apply statement intonation rules'
question_intonation means 'apply question intonation rules'

In this very simple example our high-level synthesizer has a set of rules or processes for statement intonation rendering and another for question intonation rendering—but does not have the ability to decide which to apply: a semantic interpretation of the sentence in the context of other sentences around it could supply this, but we do not have the necessary processes in the system, say, for such an interpretation. Accordingly, the need to make the decision between statement and question is pre-empted using text marking.[1]

We chose this particular example because, in a less formal way, normal English orthography already supplies the marking need here in the form of two punctuation marks . and *?* respectively— most synthesis systems designed for plain text input make the most of these informal punctuation marks. One or two languages are just a little more explicit. Spanish, for example, is more formal in its marking, using a symbol to open question intonation text and another to close it: ¿ *Juan's gone home?* But this is the exception rather than the rule: normal orthographic marking is very scant indeed compared with what is needed for a fully explicit mark-up of prosody or expressive use of prosody.

So text marking is used either to supply full information where none is available for a particular effect in the synthesizer itself, or

---

[1] The mark-up idea is important because it allows for 'enclosure' of the text—it indicates that the prosody is 'wider' than the text, that it exists as a dominant domain, rather than something 'put onto' the text. This echoes the idea of a prosodic 'scenario' mentioned above, and in addition draws on the idea of 'inheritance' by which lower levels in the explicit hierarchy of nested domains bring forward properties of their higher-level wrappers.

Expressive Synthesis: The Longer Term   331

to supply a decision-based trigger for processes already included in the device. It is also possible to negate the application of processes which have been pre-included—we could switch off a particular prosodic rendering rule if needed. A simple example of switching on or off a phonological rule in the segmental rather than prosodic domain might be the English rule which assigns a palatalized /l/ before vowels and a velarized /l/ following vowels or before consonants—an uncomplicated phonological rule included in almost every system to include a text-to-speech (high-level) set of processes. We could switch off the rule by text marking and fall back to a default palatalized /l/ in all circumstances if we wanted our synthesizer to speak with a French accent—French has only palatalized /l/ in all phonological environments.

Another form of symbolic marking of the text input might take the form of concept labels (Young and Fallside 1979), and this would be typical of a putative high-quality system designed to interact with a human user to supply specialized information, for example. Such an input would need to be followed by an interpretive inter-level before the synthesizer could convert the symbolic concept marking into properly formed sentences of English or some other language. The detail here is outside the scope of this book, but it is interesting to note that the sentences output from this interpretive inter-level would probably not take the form of normal text, but would be a fully marked-up phonological representation (thus avoiding all the pitfalls of plain text—its phonologically unhelpful morphemic spelling, its failure to include semantic symbols, etc.). In other words the mark-up would be similar to a full XML style semantic mark-up which might otherwise either be supplied by hand, or perhaps less successfully by rules.

15.2 Phonology in the high-level system

A high-level speech synthesis system is that part of the system which deals with processes analogous to cognitive processes in a human speaker. It does not include acoustic physical phonetic processes therefore: these form part of the accompanying low-level system. Traditionally in a post-Classical Phonetics computational speech production model, phonology is concerned with computing a plan for producing a particular utterance to be placed into the appropriate prosodic context. The kinds of phonological rule we see in high-level systems fall into two categories: those concerned with segmental processes and those concerned with prosodic processes.

15.2.1 *Segmental processes in synthesis*

One of the dominant phonological processes in speech production theory is the context-sensitive assimilation process. Assimilation is a process whereby a particular segment takes on some or all of the characteristics of an adjacent segment, hence its sensitivity to context.

It is extremely important not to confuse assimilatory processes with coarticulatory processes—though such confusion is rife.

- Coarticulatory processes are phonetic and arise because of physical constraints intrinsic to the phonetic rendering system; their occurrence is not optional, though sometimes the extent of their effect can be manipulated.
- Assimilatory processes are phonological and are cognitively dominated; their occurrence is optional and subject to decision by the speaker.

The confusion arises because so often a phonological assimilatory process derives from, or is dominated by, an associated phonetic process; such phonological processes are said, for this reason to be 'natural' (Stampe 1979). But the real distinction lies in whether or not the process is linguistically productive—that is, does the process give rise to a property of the language which distinguishes it from some other language or accent? The diagnostic which decides if a rule is phonological is that the speaker can do otherwise; the diagnostic for a non-cognitive phonetic rule is that the speaker cannot do otherwise—so the decision between the two rests on whether or not the process is optional.

Let us take as an example the voicing of an intervocalic voiceless stop/flap in American English. This occurs in words like *writer*, which in its underlying representation opposes the voiced stop/flap in a work like *rider*. These two words, in their underlying representations, are identical apart from this intervocalic stop/flap. In the intervocalic environment the voiceless stop voices (thus becoming like the normally opposing voiced counterpart), but not before the operation of a rule which has made sure that stressed vowels preceding voiced stops are lengthened, and that stressed vowels preceding voiceless stops are not. Thus the opposition on the stops is said to be neutralized, although the contrast between the two words is still maintained, but by reason of the length of the preceding vowel. We call this phenomenon 'opposing feature transference'.[2]

A slightly different type of phonological rule concerns the distribution of extrinsic allophones. Allophones are members of a set of variants traceable back to a single underlying phonological object. In Classical Phonetics (1880s–1960s), however, this phonological object was not 'underlying' since the model did not focus on any hierarchy in the phonetics system: it was the abstract label applied to the set. However, modern speech production models are hierarchical, and the relationship between underlying object and more surface variants is a vertical one.

Classical Phoneticians sensed that these variants subdivided into two types, but only in modern phonetics has the distinction been formalized into 'extrinsic allophones' and 'intrinsic allophones' (Tatham 1971). These, it must be stressed, are terms from phonetics, not phonology.

An extrinsic allophone is one which is cognitively determined within the domain of phonology: it is a variant rendering of an underlying object which is optionally decided—optional in the

---

[2] The previous paragraph illustrates one of the major problems associated with expounding linguistics in a computational setting. Words like *vowel, stop, flap, length, opposing, contrasting*, etc. are virtually meaningless in the computational setting, and engineers or computer scientists will sometimes despair accordingly. They are wrong to do so, however, because linguistics is displaying here *not* a lack of explicitness, as is sometimes claimed, but an explicitness within a different reference domain. The question would be whether that linguistic explicitness falls apart when translated into computational explicitness. It is a scientific philosophical point, but the correlation between different 'explicitnesses' can be a real problem, since the required one-to-one relationship is frequently not found.

sense that it need not be used for any reason other than whim or fashion or that the language just wants to use it—not optional in the sense that a speaker can choose whether to use it or not in any given context: that is not the case, since the language has decided that it shall be used. The palatalized and velarized /l/s above are examples of this.

An intrinsic allophone is a pronounced or surface variant of an extrinsic allophone. If extrinsic allophones are the equivalent of a surface phonological element, then intrinsic allophones are derived in an extension of the hierarchy into phonetics: they are phonetic allophones. They are not optional—they cannot be determined cognitively and are subject to laws of neurophysiology, mechanics, and aerodynamics.

Note that original conceptions of different types of allophone (Ladefoged 1971) did not have them arranged strictly hierarchically: this arrangement was first proposed in Tatham (1971). Later we shall see that intrinsic allophones, while inevitable, are also controllable with respect to degree. This control, since it is a matter of choice, *is* cognitive in origin and it is this idea which forms the basis of the Theory of Cognitive Phonetics.

15.2.2 Prosodic processes in synthesis

The second type of phonological process included in high-level synthesis involves prosodics—the processing of the three suprasegmental properties of stress, rhythm, and intonation. All three of these are, as with any other phonological object, cognitive in origin, as are the processes associated with them. All have correlates eventually in the physical world, which means in the case of speech synthesis in the acoustic world. Again, it is very important not to confuse the abstract and physical worlds here: the physical correlates lie among the acoustic parameters of timing, amplitude, and fundamental *frequency*, though mostly not on a linear one-to-one basis. It is for this reason that prosodics has been regarded as one of the most difficult areas in synthesis, and indeed contemporary models still leave very much to be desired: their characterizations of acoustic signals are far from satisfactory.

What is described here relates to the usual approach which separates segmental and prosodic processes, and imposes the suprasegmental elements onto an utterance specified segmentally. We want later to turn this around to make the prosodic framework, or scenario, central to the entire process, with the segmental element completely 'wrapped' by it. We shall be claiming in the next chapter that a prosodically based model is more productive than a segmentally based model.

The prosodic elements are important to us in this book because they are for the most part the medium of expression in speech; so how they are handled becomes central to any discussion of how to include an expressive element in speech synthesis. Hence the dominance of prosodics in the speech production model, and the relevance of establishing prosodics as the vehicle for expressive content in an utterance.

15.2.3 Stress

There are at least three acoustic parameters which prompt a listener to assert that the speaker has intended stress. It follows that these are the acoustic parameters at the disposal of a speaker if stress is intended. Perceptually, stress is assigned by the listener when there is a feeling of 'prominence' to an element—that is, when the listener detects the appropriate acoustic signal. But stress can also be assigned without there being any acoustic signal cue. In this case, and perhaps additionally in the other case as well, stress has been assigned according to other prompts, for example the stress pattern associated with the particular word, or a rule which fits this particular word (in the case of word stress). The early Chomsky–Halle rules (Chomsky and Halle 1968), for example, were about the assignment of stress and apply in particular to the perception of speech—that is, they characterize the results of listener assignment of stress to the acoustic signal heard. The implication here, of course, is that stress, an abstract property, is not *in* the signal, but is assigned depending on certain triggers in the signal.

There are two types of stress: word stress (which is not prosodic in our sense) and sentence stress (which *is* prosodic). In synthesis systems, and also in automatic speech recognition systems, it makes sense to assign word stress in the system dictionary or by rule, since for the most part it is predictable. Stress marking is on syllables within words. However, stress takes on a different dimension—a prosodic one—when it comes to combining words within a sentence or phrase. Sentence stress—a stress pattern over units of utterance greater than words—takes over, and modifications are made dependent on a number of different factors. Chomsky and Halle's approach is a good starting point for synthesis systems, particularly as it constitutes a model which meets the criterion of computational adequacy—that is, it is explicit and computable—and if the goal is reliable perception of what is being synthesized.

15.2.4 Rhythm

The assignment of rhythm in high-level synthesis has been researched widely, and is closely linked with stress patterns in language. Different rhythm and stress patterns correlate in different languages, but all seem agreed that the feeling of rhythm is closely tied to the patterning of stressed syllables within sentences. In those languages, such as English, where there are both stressed and unstressed syllables the latter have to be accommodated within a *perceived* relatively equidistant timing between the stressed syllables. In languages which appear to have all syllables equally stressed, such as standard Metropolitan French, such an accommodation with unstressed syllables does not arise.[3]

Just as with other features of synthesis, rhythm can be assigned by rule or some of it can be built into dictionary specifications. In our favoured synthesis model, stress is assigned in the dictionary—so matters of morphemic boundaries, and the way in which they affect the stress and hence rhythmic patterns, become irrelevant

---

[3] Just as with the other prosodic features of speech, there is enormous room for confusion and ambiguity when speaking of rhythm. The hierarchical focus of the present model suggests a 'dominant' and planned level which is concerned with speakers' and listeners' *feelings* about rhythm—and this is what we are discussing here. The fact that most researchers who have tried to transfer these ideas to an analysis of the acoustic signal have failed to find one-to-one correlation with these ideas does not detract from modelling what people *feel* about prosodics. Prosodics is an abstract concept.

Expressive Synthesis: The Longer Term 337

except where we choose to assign stress and rhythm by rule. Thus the fact that phonological sequences such as / p i s t ɔː k s /, which parses morphologically as either

/ p i s + t ɔː k s / (*peace talks*), or
/ p i + s t ɔː k s / (*pea stalks*)

is not relevant, because we are not doing an analysis of the phonological sequence, we are doing a synthesis of it. The point here, from the phonological/phonetic analysis point of view, is that the placement of the morpheme boundary affects a number of different factors, such as rhythm and intonation, and indeed some segmental factors such as whether or not the [t] in the phonetic rendering of this sentence has aspiration or not. In a pre-marked system such matters are sidestepped. We are not saying that they are irrelevant to an understanding of the how the phonology of a language works with respect to rhythm and stress, but we are saying that the modelling process is one which is greatly sensitive to the purpose for which the model is intended. We suggest a synthesis approach which is complementary to the analysis approach—it does not argue with it.

15.2.5 Isochrony

The basic rhythmic pattern of speech in any language is quite simple: the rhythmic beat follows an impression of equal timing between sequential stressed syllables. The phenomenon is known as isochrony. However, this basic rhythmic pattern is a cognitive rather than physical effect: people feel speech to have a regular beat but, unlike a similar feeling in music, the beat is not obviously physically regular. The feeling is so strong that researchers repeatedly come back to the acoustic signal to see if this or that way of looking at the data will reveal some constant element that the perceptual system is latching onto (Lehiste 1977; Tatham and Morton 2002). Physical isochrony remains elusive, but it is clear that speakers and hearers alike *feel* speech to be isochronic.

There are indicators, however, that the physical signal and cognitive isochrony are not completely uncorrelated, even if the correlation is not what disappointed earlier researchers expected.

Listeners to any current text-to-speech synthesis system report unease over its rhythm, irrespective of how successful the synthesis is in general. The fact that listeners perceive incorrect physical rhythm means that they are sensitive to physical rhythm and that they *are* able to relate it to subjective rhythm, even though simple isochrony may not be the basis of the perceived correlation.

Rhythm in speech synthesis is not just important because it still eludes us. It is important because it is one of the parameters of expression. Both long-term and short-term variations of rhythmic pattern signal varying expressive content. Being able to predict and simulate rhythm which is acceptable to listeners is important because it means that we then have a general model which can have its terms modified to reflect particular expressive content, such as particular emotions.

15.2.6 Intonation

The third prosodic feature for processing in high-level synthesis is intonation. Intonation is a cognitive phenomenon shared by speaker and listener as a feature of the original (speaker) and recovered (listener) plans for an utterance. It is therefore not a parameter of the acoustic signal though, as with all similar phenomena, there are acoustic correlates to be determined. The physical parameter which most correlates with intonation is the utterance's fundamental frequency—usually corresponding to the rate of vibration of the speaker's vocal cords. The correlate is only measurable therefore during vocal cord vibration, although perceived intonation may 'bridge' vocal cord vibration gaps in the physical signals.

Perceptual bridging of gaps in vocal cord vibration is most likely to occur if the gaps were not part of the speaker's plan—that is, if they are the result of coarticulation. In the word *leader*, for example, in the utterance *The leader of the pack*, for many speakers of English vocal cord vibration will lapse due to unplanned aerodynamic constraints during the period of oral constriction associated with the [d] (Fig. 15.1). Listeners are not aware of this lapse, and track the perceived intonation pattern

Expressive Synthesis: The Longer Term 339

throughout the word sentence, thus bridging the effect. In the same utterance there is absence of vocal cord vibration associated with the [p] of *pack*. This gap *is* planned however, since the segment is not intended to have a periodic waveform (functionally in contrast with [b], which does have an intended periodic waveform). The listener clearly does 'notice' (perhaps not consciously) the period during which periodic sound has stopped, but continues to track the intonation pattern to bridge the gap. This simply means, of course, that suprasegmental phenomena are exactly that—phenomena which transcend the segmental patterning and rendering of speech—and planning and perceptual focus is therefore on long-term continuity rather than short-term changes. This is part of the reason why we say that prosody *wraps* utterances.

The standard way of dealing with intonation in high-level synthesis systems is to incorporate a set of processes (a processing 'module') which begins by assigning to sentences an abstract marking corresponding to a speaker's planned intonation for that sentence. There are several such marking systems (Pierrehumbert 1980; Silverman et al. 1992 in phonology, and Tatham and Lewis 1992 in text-to-speech synthesis), but they generally share the fact that they have been derived from perceiver reactions to speech—that is, they characterize the perceiver's recovered plan, rather than the actual speaker's intended plan. The implicit claim here is that the recovered and intended plans are similar or identical. This approach is common throughout the synthesis model, and if there is a difference between intended and recovered plans then that difference is negligible. (In fact there must be some difference in principle, since distortion and noise must be introduced into the encoding/decoding processes.)

Thus, the input phonological string is marked up with respect to abstract intonation. The next stage involves rendering this abstract marking using a model of the relationship between intonation and fundamental frequency. Intonation in synthetic speech probably does not fail in the abstract mark-up phase of prosodic processing: it fails in converting this to a putative fundamental frequency. The reason for failure at this point is the non-linear relationship between the two and the fact that this relationship has not yet

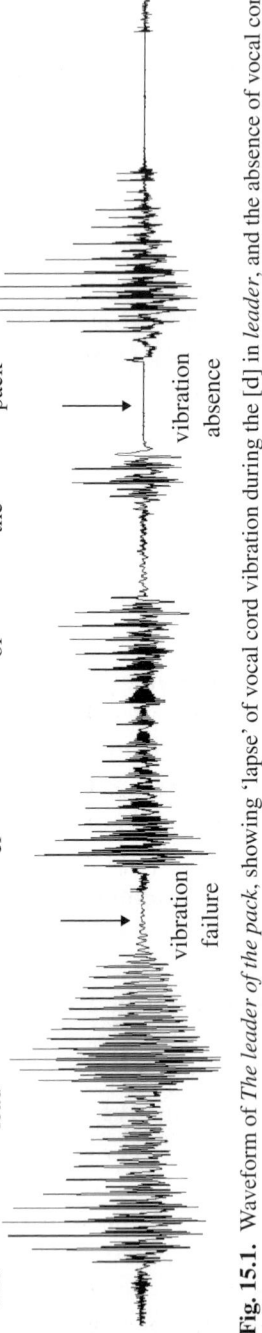

Fig. 15.1. Waveform of *The leader of the pack*, showing 'lapse' of vocal cord vibration during the [d] in *leader*, and the absence of vocal cord vibration associated with the stop phase of [p] in *pack*.

Expressive Synthesis: The Longer Term

been adequately modelled. All synthesis systems fail more or less on this point, and listeners report dissatisfaction with all systems—though, of course, there is a great deal of variation between systems, and occasionally even the worst system gets it right by luck rather than by the application of a sophisticated model.

15.2.7 Segments and prosody

These two aspects of high-level processing in speech synthesis—segmental and prosodic—corresponding to the characterization of segmental and prosodic aspects of phonology in linguistics, are the central areas of this stage of converting input text to speech. In this book the more important of the two is the prosodic processing, since most of the expressive content of an utterance is carried by an utterance's prosody.

However, segmental phenomena are also part of expressiveness. Increased stress on a syllable will result in changes to the final rendering of individual segments within that syllable, as will rhythm effects. The separation of segmental and suprasegmental processes in synthesis systems implies independence, but this is not the case. Systems which separate these processes pass the output of both through an 'integration' process which combines them. It is probably true, though, of most systems that this process of combination is a theoretically unmotivated ad hoc clearing-up operation, rather than principled.

15.3 Defining expression and transferring results from psychology

A major application of synthesis is as the speaking part of an interactive dialogue system. When human beings interact they are constantly adjusting their tone of voice according to the behaviour of the person they are talking to. Current synthesis, however, is not sensitive to perception or how to deal with feedback from the human user of an interactive system. We need to ask if research results from psychology—the field investigating perception—can be usefully applied to model-building in synthesis. We do not presume to contribute directly to building psychology models: it is a question of investigating to what extent work in psychology bears on our area of study.

15.3.1 Introducing a perceptually derived element into synthesis

We know that speakers vary the precision of the acoustic signal they produce dependent on a number of factors. Among these are considerations such as ambiguity (which could arise in any of the linguistically identified components—semantics, syntax, or phonology), rendering constraints (coarticulatory phenomena), and general environmental constraints such as ambient noise. In general, speakers vary the precision of the utterances on a continuous basis, consistent with environmental pressure: if the listener is not experiencing difficulty speaker precision is degraded; if perceptual difficulty increases, then speaker precision improves. With one or two notable exceptions this is not true of speech synthesizers. The exceptions include SPRUCE (Lewis and Tatham 1991) whose high-level model has a production-for-perception element, and Festival (Taylor et al. 1998) which has the potential to produce alternative outputs for the same input via a unit selection approach to composing its output signal.

What would constitute a specification of production-for-perception elements to be incorporated in a synthesis system?

- Sensitivity to potential ambiguity. Ambiguity can arise during the linguistic planning of an utterance at any stage: semantic, syntactic, or phonological. Speakers are usually, though not always, aware of the perceptual consequences of potential ambiguity.
- Sensitivity to ambient noise. Speakers monitor ambient noise. Long-term noise can result in speech phenomena such as increased amplitude to the point of shouting, or speaking quietly in particularly quiet environments (an anechoic chamber, a library or well-damped room). Short-term changes in ambient noise are also sensed by speakers.
- Sensitivity to the listener's special circumstances. Speakers regularly assess their listeners with respect to how difficult it

Expressive Synthesis: The Longer Term 343

will be for them to perceive the planned speech. The parameters of this assessment will vary in their importance, but speakers do develop views as to the causes of listener difficulty.

Adjustment processes designed to alter the basic intended acoustic signal must be in place to take advantage of the results of this sensitivity to different constraints on perceiver performance. Human speakers react to these constraints by making appropriate adjustments to their acoustic output, apparently to anticipate listener error and negate it wherever possible. If a speaker's ultimate goal is successful communication, it is in their interest to make sure that they are producing a suitable signal for optimal perceiver performance. If human beings do this, then so must a synthesizer—because the listener is expecting it.

15.3.2 What do expressive words actually refer to?

We use words like 'happy' and 'sad' to describe people's feelings; we are attempting to model how they communicate this using speech. But we need to consider what exactly it is that these words describe. For example, they could be describing:

- How speakers feel at the time in general; what might they report as their internal state, without particular reference to what they are saying at the moment. How a speaker feels at the time of speaking can possibly colour their speech, irrespective of the message content and perhaps irrespective also of intended expressive content. But discounting the latter for the moment, listeners seem able to detect how a speaker feels by the way they talk. This general feeling we could refer to as 'background expression'; it can be defined as unrelated to the message content of what is being spoken.
- What speakers feel about the content of the message they are communicating. That is, are they happy about what they are saying, even if they themselves are not particularly happy, or not at the time? Against the background expression just referred to can be overlaid expressiveness related to the speaker's feeling (explicit or implicit) about the message content. Because it seems possible to be happy about a message, yet at the same

time be unhappy in the background, it seems necessary to keep these two levels of expressiveness disjoint for the moment—they surely influence each other because they are ultimately to be communicated simultaneously via the same acoustic medium. It would be interesting to experiment, though, to see if a listener can unravel the two different types of expressive content even though they are mixed in the same signal.
- How the listener deals with the incoming message: how might the listener's reception be modelled? For example, can we assume the listener can evaluate the message, and/or the speaker? This is an important problem to come to grips with: *since* there is no point in developing a voice output system with expression if the listener cannot be said to detect it, or if some unpredicted expression is decoded.

Detection of expressive content in an acoustic signal is one thing; acting on it is another. We need a model of detection and a model of how any subsequent action is set in motion, partly because generating the appropriate expressiveness in synthetic speech may need to take both into account.

Thus, we need to consider whether expression should be modelled from both the production and perception viewpoints simultaneously, and whether there would be any gain from doing this. We might model these abstract notions by looking at ways of categorizing them. Researchers in both linguistics and psychology have used the categorical model successfully in several areas of human perception (Strange and Jenkins 1978): there may be potential for modelling emotion along these lines.

Listeners are said to 'repair' or 'normalize' the variability as part of the perceptual process of data reduction; that is, the repair process reduces the variable data to a much simpler but abstract invariant data. Various verbs are used in this connection:

- *The data is 'reduced'*—implying that in its variable state it is too much for perception and needs some reduction in a pre-processing stage.
- *The variability is 'filtered out'*—implying that among the data are examples of the unvaried signal.

- *It is 'repaired'*—implying that somehow the introduction of variability by the physical system is a process of damaging an ideal representation.
- *It is categorized*—implying that the zones along a vector are both significant and able to be identified and isolated.

In terms of modelling the acoustics of expression in such a way that we can accurately synthesize the acoustic signal, we are therefore obliged to bear in mind, as are researchers looking at 'plain' prosodic effects or segmental objects, that we are dealing certainly with a system which takes an object which is abstract and invariant, renders it as a variable object, and then perceives it as an abstract and invariant object again. The perceiver's task is to locate the variables and assign them to the correct invariant label. Just as we make the assumption that in the segmental system the speaker's and listener's invariant objects are the same, so we make the assumption that this is true also in the prosodic system. The variables of expressiveness will, we hope cluster along vectors in the case of pairs of dichotomous expressions, or around points in the overall multi-dimensional expression space.

15.3.3 *The expression space*

We imagine an expression 'space' created by the set of vectors associated with the acoustic parameters which encode expression. Within this space we can plot measured values and statistically locate their 'centres of gravity'. These centres of gravity have been derived from *variable* data—it may be the only way, but if we treat them as abstractions we can only *associate* them with the abstractions of the speaker and hearer: they may not actually be the same as (have identical relational values along the vectors to) the speaker/hearer abstractions. This is the precise problem mentioned earlier about determining the 'neutral' state: we can arrive at a value statistically, but this is not guaranteed to be 'right'; it depends on the sample size, the environmental conditions surrounding the data, and the statistical technique used.

Now, using this space and our statistical information, we should be in a position to reconstruct, or run a predictive model, of the data for the purposes of resynthesis. Data clusters will not occupy comparable volumes of space (just as the early two-dimensional acoustic maps of vowels show varying areas or degrees of variability), and this will tell us something about crowding in the space: it is 'overcrowding' which introduces ambiguity into the system.

15.4 The supervisor model applied to expression

Our general model of speech production introduces the notion 'supervisor'—a cognitive agent responsible for managing the phonetic rendering of an utterance plan. By altering the detail of the *domain*, the general model can be used for supervising the rendering of expressiveness in speech. The domain is the length of utterance over which the settings operate: in the case of the segmental aspects of speech in the general model, we are concerned with the segment within the syllable as our basic unit. In prosodics the units are still the syllables, but it is the syllable-to-syllable or longer-term behaviour which we are concerned with. The modelling strategy can, however, remain the same, within a hierarchical arrangement of processes:

↓ <general settings>—overall expression;

↓ <global enhancements>—the overall basic prosodic setting (neutral to expression);

↓ <base plan>—setting adjustments for *particular* long-term expressions;

↓ <local enhancements>—setting adjustments for short-term modifications of the base plan.

As before, the function of the supervisor is to manage the overall rendering process, correcting as necessary. The supervisor agent is also responsible for ensuring the local enhancements get properly enacted.

The short-term variations we have in mind are changes to goals which may be needed for 'immediate' expressive effect. For example, news broadcasters often introduce a pause before and after a word to highlight it for the listener.

15.5 Is it critical how the goal of good synthesis is achieved?

The acoustic signal need not contain the entire description of the emotion to be conveyed: it need only contain the elements of a trigger to spark within the listener an active creation of the percept. The model which emphasizes that speech production is intended for perception incorporates the means to evaluate how much a speech signal needs to contain to trigger a percept. And this amount varies depending on context and expectation. A human production model based on the results of experiments to determine the acoustic correlates of expressive speech is not necessarily the best basis for developing a synthesis production model, especially if our goal is to generate in the listener the correct percept.

Research into what the acoustic correlates of this or that emotion are may fail to provide conclusive answers because it assumes that the correlates are a constant; they may in fact be a variable, and the production-for-perception model would predict that they are indeed a variable. Thus the problem can be redefined from finding out what the acoustic correlates of expression are, to:

- What variables in the acoustic waveform of the plain message can be manipulated to produce the percept of emotive speech in the listener?

The correlates are new variables, and to use them correctly we need to understand the basis of their variability. The statement 'X is an/the acoustic correlate of Y' is dangerous. We have been aware of this for some time in segmental modelling. So, 'vocal cord vibration is an/the acoustic correlate of voicing' is not particularly helpful if listeners identify a voiced consonant at the end of an isolated word like *bid* in English where the vocal cord vibration rarely continues into the stop phase of the final consonant.

15.5.1 What to look for in the acoustic signal

The basic questions to ask of the acoustic signal are:

- What are the acoustic correlates which satisfy the *speaker* on a particular occasion? The speaker can assert: 'I have done what

I set out to do: I have spoken with confidence and communicated that fact.'

Speakers seem to monitor their speech, because they often know when they make a mistake. The concept of the supervisor agent models a means for continuous monitoring and correction of the way the physical rendering system is responding to the goals of the original plan. For the most part it seems clear that speakers can be confident that they have succeeded in rendering the plan into a satisfactory acoustic signal. The acoustic signal in that sense, then, is the *composite acoustic correlate* of the plan. Our task is to determine the acoustic correlates of some aspects of the plan.

- What are the acoustic correlates which satisfy the *listener*? The listener can assert: 'I have decoded that this person has been speaking with confidence, and wishes to convey that to me.'

Listeners perhaps monitor their own performance, in the sense that they are aware whether or not their hypotheses as to what the speaker's plan was are confirmed. If a listener is clear that they have correctly decoded a speaker's intended plan, we are in a position to ask what it was in the acoustic signal that enable the decoding to take place. Not all aspects or parameters of the acoustic signal are going to be equally relevant—there will perhaps be a hierarchy of relevance of particular acoustic parameters corresponding to particular perceived parameters of the speaker's plan.

- What are the *parameters of variability* which result in the trade-off between the two participants in a conversation? And what are the acoustic parameters which figure in this trade-off?

Even if both speaker and listener are confident that the communicative goal has been satisfactorily achieved, we still have to account for the variability in both processes of production and perception. The production-for-perception concept means there is a trade-off in variables, and this may be critical to either speaker or listener, or both.

15.6 Implications of utterance planning and supervision

The general position with respect to the ideas described in the previous sections is that to be accurate, or even to sound accurate, a synthesis system probably has to take all this into account. It must be able to synthesize speech with variability, since variability is detectable and expected by both speaker and listener. Variability plays a significant role in both the production and perception processes; to omit it altogether will result in the detection of error in the synthesized signal.

One particularly important point is that both production and perception seem to have knowledge of each other: so a synthesis system must be able to consult a model of perception and an ASR device must be able to consult a model of production. Each component's sensitivity to the other side of the coin has significant value in the case of human speech; so if synthesis and ASR are to be successful this problem should be taken into account in their designs.

The consequence is the suggestion that synthesis systems should not stand alone. If aspects of speech production like goal, supervision, and expression can be productively defined in terms of *perceptual* goals, then synthesis systems (like human production systems) need to have access to a model of perception. In practice they need to be linked to a real (in a dialogue system) or virtual (in an apparent stand-alone system) automatic recognition system. This is so that the production system can trial its proposed output—that is, synthesizers must acquire sensitivity to perception.

15.7 Are synthesis systems up to the job?

For the purposes of moving forward in the synthesis of expressive content in speech, we need to reconsider whether systems are really up to the job: to what extent are we able to extend current achievements? We examine the position taking low-level and high-level synthesis separately to begin with, before moving to a full model of speech production in Chapter 16.

15.7.1 The low-level system

In the most versatile synthesis systems the low-level system does not interact with the high-level system; its job is to perform a phonetic or physical rendering of the phonological plan of an utterance. In terms of a supervisory model of rendering it is able to respond to short-term commands to change its normal built-in procedures. This is equivalent to short-term interference with physical coarticulatory processes in human beings. So our question is:

- Is the low-level system able to respond to a plan which includes expressiveness, and which might also include, as part of the rendering process, short-term changes to any built-in procedures?

The answer to this question will depend to what extent the parameters of the expression plan correlate with the manipulable parameters of the synthesiser's rendering processes. There are basically two types of synthesizer in use at the present time: parametric synthesizers and concatenated waveform synthesizers. Both these types can respond to requests to alter fundamental frequency, timing or rate of delivery of the acoustic output, and overall amplitude—all needed in expression synthesis. However, only the parametric approach enables independent control of parameters such as the frequencies, amplitudes, and bandwidths of individual formants or the adjustment of frication bandwidth, etc.

If expressiveness can be characterized in terms of modifications to just the fundamental frequency, timing, and amplitude of the signal, then both systems will respond equally well, so long as there are no interactive elements which produce spurious artefacts. And in general expressiveness is described in terms of these 'prosodic parameters', thus apparently presenting no problems to either type of system.

But it would be wrong to stop there: there are, in fact, knock-on effects which the normal concatenated waveform systems cannot handle. These are to do with rate-dependent spectral variations, and here the unit selection approach to concatenated waveform synthesis will be superior to other techniques. The example we give here is the normal prosodic effect of rate of delivery reduction as the speaker approaches the end of a sentence, particularly if this is also utterance-final ('paragraph' final in some models of production). Consider the following examples of the word *dogs* in various contexts:

1. *Dogs make good pets.*
2. *It was the dogs that dug the hole, not the badgers!*
3. *I like cats, but I much prefer dogs.*

Figure 15.2 shows the waveforms and spectrograms of the word *dogs* for each of the three examples—just one example of each, but the point is made and is consistent within and across speakers.

Notice that the monosyllabic *dogs* is progressively longer in these successive sentences, and notice in the spectrograms how the proportion of vowel nucleus spent on coarticulation with the adjacent consonants lessens. In other words, the spectral properties of the second two versions of *dogs* are not simple stretched versions of the first example—even if the stretching is non-linear. In the final version, in this speaker on this occasion, the vowel is so long as to have a clear 'steady-state' section which cannot be obtained from stretching the first example. Concatenated waveform synthesis based on one example of each word or syllable will fail here. Parametric synthesis enabling alteration of formant frequencies will, on the other hand, succeed if the differences between the examples are properly modelled.

Concatenated waveform synthesis using unit selection stands a better chance than systems relying on relatively small inventories of diphones, syllables, or words because the chance of finding a unit with the correct spectral properties is greater—though huge databases are required to ensure even and exhaustive coverage.

So it is not necessarily the case that all synthesis systems will be able adequately to handle expressive content, even if variation of the three prosodic parameters is all that is needed. But what of the high-level system?

15.7.2 The high-level system

It is in the high-level area of synthesis that the utterance plan is formulated. In the human being we are not dealing with a

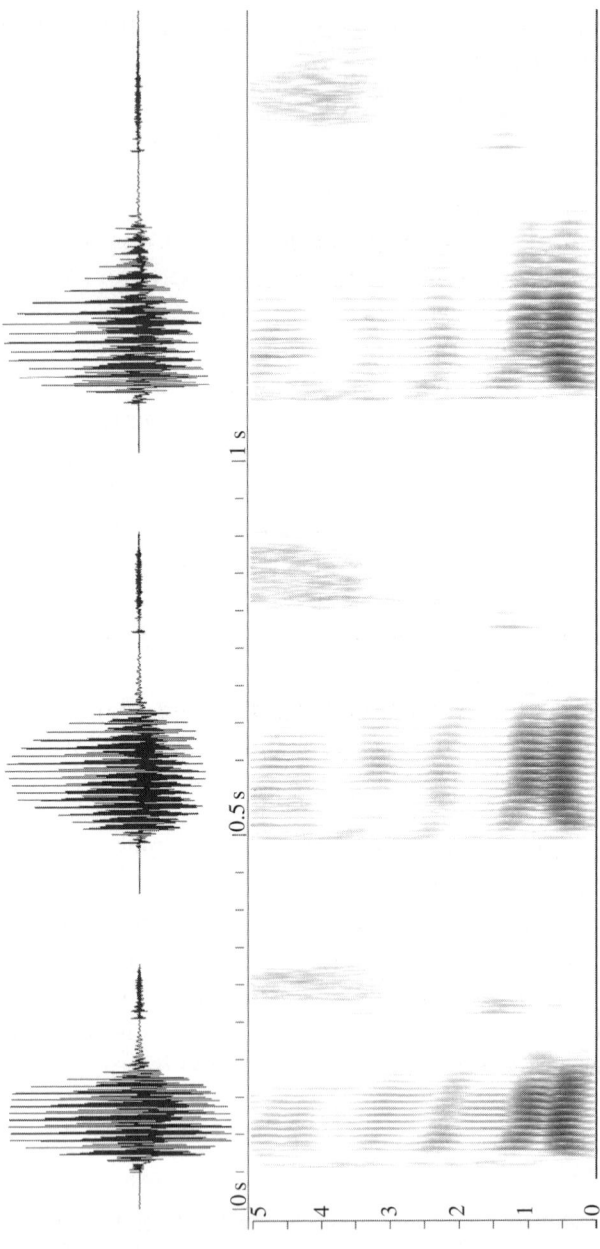

Fig. 15.2. Waveforms and spectrograms of three versions of the word *dogs*, excised from recordings of the utterances: (a) *Dogs make good pets*; (b) *It was the dogs that dug the hole, not the badgers!* (c) *I like cats, but I much prefer dogs.*

Expressive Synthesis: The Longer Term 353

physical system: this is cognitive behaviour, and there are many fewer constraints on what is possible. The same is true of our synthesis analogue. The constraints of the lower-level systems just described are not there to limit the possibilities of simulated cognitive processing involved in formulating the utterance plan. However, in practice both in the human being and in the simulation there are constraints determined by what is possible in the subsequent rendering stage: there is little point in generating a plan which it is impossible to render.

It follows that even high-level processes, while in principle unconstrained by physical limitations, are indeed, in the end, subject to constraints. What is interesting is that these constraints are cognitively imposed and mimic the physical rendering constraints—in other words, this high-level system trials a 'software' copy of the real physical constraints to be encountered later. There is nothing remarkable about this: it is possible that all voluntary motor control (unlike autonomic control) is trialled by copy software at the cognitive level. Put another way, a model of the rendering process is kept at the higher, cognitive level, and can be used to try out plans before any attempt to execute them in the physical world.

Trialling this way, using the cognitively held model of physical rendering, would result in failure of any plan which would not pass the physical process. There is plenty of lay or anecdotal evidence of such a procedure: in the gym we find *That weight's too heavy for me to lift*, or outside *I can't cycle as fast as he does*, or in speech *I'll never get my tongue round that*. These are all, in the scientist's terminology, hypotheses based on the experience of building an internal model of physical processes and using it to trial a plan. So, with the exception, implicit in the above statements, that we can at least try to push the system beyond experienced limits, cognitive processing at the phonological level in human beings or at the high level in speech synthesis is voluntarily limited by a model of subsequent rendering processes: we do not normally devise plans which we know cannot be rendered.

But because the results of the trialling process are obviously optional as far as heeding them is concerned, the rendering model can be used to assist pushing the system to include effects—and these could be expression effects—*previously not used*. An English speaker can mentally practise, and eventually achieve, a physical rendering of tones when learning Chinese—effects of short-term changes in vocal-cord rate of vibration hitherto unused. A Spanish or Greek speaker can eventually push their precision of tongue positioning to accommodate the English distinction between [s] and [ʃ] not made phonologically in their language. An English speaker can cognitively control the precision of lip rounding/spreading needed to make the [i]/[y] distinction in French. If the synthesis model is designed in the same kind of way, it can in principle be taught to make the special control of rendering effects necessary to create speech *with expressive content*.

To summarize: there are unlikely to be constraints at the high level of speech synthesis which cannot be altered to allow the planning of future acoustic correlates of expression. However, the trialling procedures, if present in the system, will need restraining or they may reject some plans. Trialling procedures in high-level systems which are followed by concatenative waveform low-level synthesis will reject calls to change things like the spectral content of vowels, and may limit the system to changes of frequency, overall amplitude, and timing. Special selection procedures may need to be added to unit selection systems to enable these effects (like spectral change correlating with unit durational changes) to be included.

Chapter 16

A Model of Speech Production Based on Expression and Prosody

In this chapter we present a model of speech production in some detail. Since so many of the phonetic features of utterances depend on their prosodic structure, including their expressive content, we feel it makes sense to make prosody the basis of the entire model (see also Keating and Shattuck-Hufnagel 2002).

The focus of the underlying speech production theory is how the data available to speakers is organized for the purposes of producing utterances designed to be *perceived* by listeners. The model exemplifies the theory, and we bring forward illustrations within the presentation of the model using a declarative approach consistent with what we find in linguistics, in particular phonological theory. The viewpoint, though, is distinctly phonetic, and for this reason emphasizes the dynamic aspect of speech. Thus from time to time we consider how the declared data structures of speech production become involved in the running dynamic creation of actual utterances.

16.1 The prosodic framework

The prosodic framework approach

- takes the form of a computational model;
- incorporates hooks enabling us to capture phonetic rendering with expressive content.

The model is designed to tightly integrate prosodic and segmental properties of speech in a well-defined and well-motivated binding process. Prosody provides an envelope for segmental phonology and phonetics, meaning in principle that it dominates all aspects of speech production. We shall discuss how this works as we go along.

16.1.1 The data structures

Clear definition and exposition of the various data structures involved is important for successful computational modelling. For this reason we focus on defining the data structures of one or two key areas of speech production. Sometimes we find that different computational paradigms are appropriate for different areas of the model. For example,

- The deeply hierarchically organized prosodic/phonological framework of the model is most appropriately characterized using a declarative approach, and this is the case throughout traditional approaches. We have adopted here a relatively advanced use of the XML paradigm (Altova 1998–2002).

Whereas

- The declarative (rather than procedural) parts of a generalized object-oriented paradigm (OOP) are used to characterize low-level gestural structures; these have a much flatter low-level hierarchical organization than the overall model.
- The more abstract characterization of an extrinsic allophone calls for a traditional distinctive feature approach, expressed using a simple XML declarative structure.
- The procedures manipulating the data structures, using a procedural paradigm like C, Pascal, or Java, depend on appropriate analyses or parses of the data structures using comparatively simple tree-searching algorithms to bring the information they contain into the mainstream computation.

16.1.2 The overall model

The model comprises a set of hierarchically organized data structures, as in traditional linguistics. But unlike linguistics a dynamic approach is taken, so that for any one utterance manipulation of

A Model Based on Expression and Prosody

the data structures, using a procedural language like C, requires the use of comparatively simple tree-searching techniques to bring the information they contain into the mainstream computation. Tree-searching for verifying or parsing data structures is built into the XML paradigm.

Our object is to present a model which packages the data in a well-motivated way, helping us understand the nature of speech production as a whole. In principle this is no different from more traditional approaches in phonology and phonetics, though we have adopted a more computational focus. But continuing that tradition, we spotlight the data structures as being central to our understanding of the production and perception of speech. The dominance of prosody in the overall model makes it easier to characterize expressive content in speech, and takes a somewhat different approach to traditional treatments of speech production and perception.

16.2 Planning and rendering

The model of speech production distinguishes between two phases, each focusing on the utterance plan. The first is concerned with building the plan and the second with rendering it. In traditional terms these can be thought of as a dynamic phonological phase followed by a dynamic phonetic phase. The first phase of building the utterance plan is carried out by the dynamic phonological phase. We shall see later that this is carried out under the control of the Cognitive Phonetics Agent (CPA). The CPA is the device responsible for monitoring and supervising how rendering unfolds. It is sensitive to both internally and externally generated feedback, and is capable of rapid intervention in the rendering process to optimize it (Tatham and Morton 2003).

We speak of phonetic *rendering* of an utterance or utterance plan, choosing to use a word not normally found in the phonetics literature, because we want to broaden what phonetics does, and focus on the data structures needed for the dynamic active processes involved in developing an actual articulation or soundwave.

358   *An Integrated Model of Expression*

16.2.1 Inputs to the rendering process

Rendering is an active dynamic process which brings something new to developing an articulation from the utterance plan. One input to the rendering process is the plan itself, but an additional input is necessary. The diagram below shows two sources of input: the utterance plan and a supervisory input which is controlled by the CPA. This supervisory input brings to the rendering process information about, among other things, expressive content. The supervisory input is able to modify the way in which the utterance plan is to be rendered on a particular occasion.

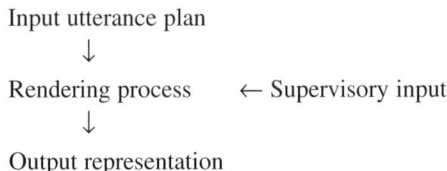

Input utterance plan
↓
Rendering process   ← Supervisory input
↓
Output representation

The flow diagram shows how phonetic rendering is driven by two different inputs: (a) a representation of the utterance plan, and (b) control information concerned with how the plan is to be rendered from the point of view of any pragmatic or similar considerations.

Phonetic rendering works on the utterance plan in the light of pragmatic and other expressive considerations, carefully supervised by the CPA. As we have said, the CPA is responsible for ensuring that the best output is rendered from the plan in the light of expressive and other requests. Rendering is thus a very active and carefully controlled process which is more complex than any of the alternatives such as 'realization' imply, including the means to add expression.

The model needs to identify two separate inputs to the rendering process (the plan and the proposed expressive content) because they are different in type and come from different sources. Thus the inputs themselves need separate modelling in the form of distinct data structures. As a first approximation we could equate the primary data source—the utterance plan—with a plain phonological representation. The control the CPA has over further input information is designed to ensure that rendering is performed in a particular way—for example, with expression.

One way of imagining supervision is to think of it as being equivalent to a control signal setting variables in the derivational process which would otherwise be left in some neutral state deriving a standard or canonical output. The utterance plan is formulated as a data structure devoid of expressive content, but in which certain default values can be appropriately modified under CPA control to bring about an *expressive* rendering. In the model there are no rendering operations which the CPA ignores: the minimum intervention is to assert explicitly that there is no change to the default values. The utterance plan data structure is said to incorporate 'hooks' the CPA can use to render the utterance within the requirement for particular expressive content.

The reason for wanting to confirm explicitly if default values are to be retained is to enable the model to characterize 'neutral' speech or minimally expressive speech—something speakers and listeners alike can identify. They sometimes report that they feel expressive speech to be neutral speech to which something has been added: we don't model it in quite this way (see the discussion on neutral speech, in Chapter 3), but we do want to preserve the observation that there is a representation—the plan—which can exist, at least in the abstract, independently of expressive content. Notice that the requirements for expressive content dominate the rendering and 'infiltrate' the plain utterance plan.

In XML we say that:

`<prosodics>`		`<expression>`
`  <segmental_utterance/>`		`  <prosodics>`
`</prosodics>`	becomes	`    <segmental_utterance/>`
		`  </prosodics>`
		`</expression>`[1]

---

[1] In the XML declarations there are three elements declared: `<expression/>`, `<prosody/>`, and `<segmental_utterance/>`. A bracketed label without a slash means that this is the opening marker of the element to be followed by a later closing marker—the bracketed label including a preceding slash. A label followed by a slash and enclosed within brackets is an 'empty' element which can potentially be a wrapper for more elements. That is, `<segmental_utterance/>` is notationally equivalent to `<segmental_utterance>`...`</segmental_utterance>`.

That is, an utterance wrapped by prosodics becomes, as a result of CPA input, itself wrapped by the expression element.

16.3 Phonetics as a dynamic reasoning device

In our model, phonetics involves dynamic reasoning; this is why we characterize it within the Theory of *Cognitive* Phonetics (Morton 1986; Tatham 1986a, 1986b). Its main purpose is to work out in principle how to render the intended phonological plan, and to monitor and supervise the process. Monitoring involves receiving and acting upon information about how the rendering is progressing, and supervision involves outputting management directions to control the processing.

A number of observations of human behaviour have led us to model the process in this way, rather than continue with other more traditional *static* models. Here are some of the main ones:

1. Speakers can report that they plan what to say—e.g. *I know what I'm going to say*, or *I've thought of a good way to put it*.
2. They can tell us how they intend to say something in terms of expression—e.g. *I know what tone I'll use*, or *A bit of sarcasm wouldn't go amiss*.
3. They can try to set up articulator placement and movement depending on (1) and (2) to derive a sequence of apparently canonical acoustic representations, constrained only by co-articulation. This is normal articulation leading to normal, unmodified acoustic signals when there is no instruction as to how the utterance is to be spoken. Note that in real life the canonical form never actually occurs, since in this context canonical means 'completely unmodified expressively'—a state which only exists in the abstract since real speech is always expressive in some way. This is one reason why in this model expression wraps all other aspects of the utterance.
4. They regularly alter articulation and depart from canonical gestures and acoustics if necessary. Rapid or slow deliberate speech is an example of this kind of modification of the plan. Another is to convey anger in an utterance in which the plain semantic and syntactic content is neutral with respect to emotion.

5. They can vary articulatory precision depending on semantic, pragmatic, and phonological loading, resulting in modified acoustics—e.g. *He doesn't speak much English, so I have to speak carefully* (semantic loading evoked), and *No, I said cat*, not *cap* (phonological loading evoked).
6. They readily constrain and enhance intrinsic coarticulatory effects in correlation with variations in articulatory precision, including systematic accent variation—e.g. *D'ya get that, man?* [dʒ ə g ɪ t ð æ t m æ̃ː n] in which the vowel in *man* is lengthened and has its coarticulated nasalization quite deliberately enhanced.

We model these observations in terms of controlled manipulation of phonetic rendering, not as phonological processes. For us, a phonological process belongs entirely to the cognitive domain, whereas modification—constraining, enhancing—of physical coarticulatory processes *at will* is a cognitively dominated interference with phenomena in the physical domain, to be modelled as cognitive *phonetic* processes.

These and other observations of speaker behaviour and speaker reporting point to a sophisticated device which contributes considerably to the detail observable in the acoustic signal or in articulatory gestures and to much of the systematic variability which researchers report.

The sheer variety of different acoustic signals possible as instantiations of any one sentence plan defies explanation within the current theoretical framework. It is clear that some of the processes involved call for extending the model beyond the simple physical domain which we have usually associated with phonetics. Processes such as prediction, choice, decision, estimation, and evaluation all seem to play a role within phonetics (as well as within phonology). In the 1980s Cognitive Phonetic model they are under the control of the CPA.

This sample of extralinguistic factors alone points toward a phonetic system more associated with cognitive processing than with the physical processing of neurophysiology, mechanics, aerodynamics, or acoustics. The whole system is dominated by the linguistics of speaker/hearer interaction and message exchange, and this ensures that the system should and does cope, in the sense that so long as the speaker stays within limits known to both speaker and listener then communication will not fail.

But it is one thing simply to assert this; it is another to establish the nature of such processes and how they relate, or to invoke known or postulated mechanisms which could fulfil such tasks. This model comes about from observing speech production behaviour—it is therefore data-driven, but seeks verification of the *plausibility* of its components. Initially: are there mechanisms which could do all this, or, if they are not obvious, is it reasonable to hypothesize such mechanisms, thus pointing the way toward empirical verification?

16.4 Phonological and Cognitive Phonetic processes

We need to make a clear distinction between phonological processes and Cognitive Phonetic processes. Neither category *needs* to be executed—that is, in an abstract way they are optional—though in the case of a phonological process failure to execute might violate the language's phonological structure, and in the case of a cognitive phonetic process might disturb the subsequent perceptual process. But they do differ crucially in a number of respects.

A phonological process

- is purely cognitive or abstract and usually operates on the output of other phonological processes—that is, the phonology is a cascade of phonological processes;
- may have phonetic motivation, as in the case of many assimilatory or otherwise 'natural' processes (Stampe 1979);
- occurs (logically) prior to any phonetic process.

A Cognitive Phonetic process

- is cognitive, but always operates on or is bound to a particular physical process, which may or may not occur according to the phonological plan—for example, it might operate on a purely phonetic process like coarticulation—such processes are not in the phonological plan;
- can enhance or constrain the bound physical process (those which are necessary or inevitable);

- may have phonological implications or motivation, as in the case of consistently enhancing a coarticulatory process in a particular accent (Morton and Tatham 1980).

16.4.1 Phonetic rendering adjustment

The present model has phonological and phonetic tiers in the traditional way, but embodies also a Cognitive Phonetics level where the CPA operates and is responsible for the continuous management or supervision of how a particular utterance is rendered. This depends on a very active and carefully managed reasoning process carried out by the CPA. So,

- for any one segmental gesture based on an utterance plan there is a range of degrees of precision from which one is targeted and supervised depending on a reasoned balance between pragmatic, attitudinal, emotional, and other factors—overall environmental or enveloping constraints.

The constraints are referred to as environmental or enveloping because they set up the overall context in which the plan is rendered. In our model it is impossible to disregard the environment, and formally this is declared as wrapper nodes in the hierarchy. This is where the prosody and expression elements are declared.

16.4.2 Phonological planning adjustment

But such decisions and choices are not confined to phonetics. It is also clear that there are similar choices to be made during the dynamic phonological planning of utterances. So, an attitudinal decision to impress may result in some phonological preferences being exercised rather than others. An example here might be a Cockney speaker's reasoned hypercorrection of deleted word- or syllable-initial /h/—not a phonetic decision but a higher-level phonological choice. Some Cockney speakers have been made so conscious of the 'error' of deleting initial /h/ that they sometimes insert /h/ where there 'should' not be one (Wells 1982).

Another, more general example might be the way speakers adjust their accents to the social environment, just as they adjust lexical selection when switching between formal and informal communication.

- For any one utterance there is a range of accents (systematic and accentually coherent phonological choices) from which one is selected depending on a reasoned balance between environmental constraints. The choice may be long-term and the accent may pervade an entire conversation, or it may be short-term and span just a single utterance or part of an utterance.

Furthermore,

- For any one utterance the selection of sub-utterance units and subsequent rendering is a continuously variable reasoning and supervision process, such that, to the listener, factors such as speaker attitude and expression can be felt to change during the utterance.

'Environment' has a broad meaning here, which ranges from the background noise on a phone circuit which causes a speaker to slow down and articulate gestures more precisely under phonetic supervision, through emotive and attitudinal factors which colour phonetic rendering, to considerations of style which promote supervision of phonological choices. All are constraints brought from sources external to the main flow of the production process, and all pass through a reasoning system responsible for their evaluation in terms of a weighted balance. Accent, style, attitudinal and emotive content switching, and variation of precision are all normal phenomena associated with close supervision of speech production, whether at the phonological or phonetic levels. In this descriptive model it is hard to imagine any stretch of natural speech which has not been carefully managed with respect to its phonetic rendering.

16.5 The speech production model's architecture

We presented details of the proposed speech production model in Tatham and Morton (2003). We summarize the model, in Fig. 16.1.

16.5.1 Planes and tiers

Figure 16.1 shows the generalized model of speech production. The first point is that the model is arranged on *two planes*—the

A Model Based on Expression and Prosody

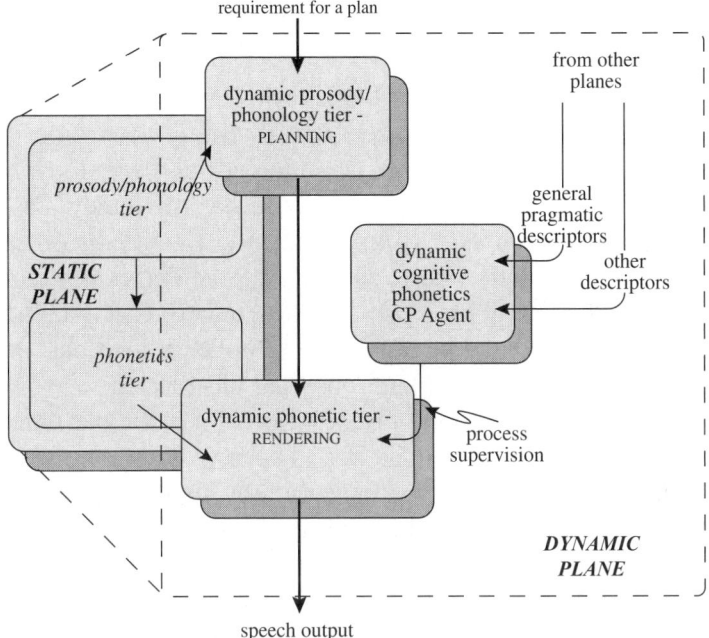

Fig. 16.1. The main components of the speech production model (after Tatham and Morton 2003). Two planes are visible: to the back is the static plane, which holds tiers on which are characterizations of prosody/phonology and phonetics; to the front is the dynamic plane, where we find the 'flow pathway' (indicated by the bold vertical arrows) from dynamic prosody/phonology to phonetics to the final speech output. The rendering process on the phonetic tier is managed by dynamic cognitive phonetic processes which are mediated by supplementary descriptor inputs.

static plane and the dynamic plane, with the static plane shown behind the dynamic one. On the static plan we have characterizations of everything a speaker knows about prosody/phonology and phonetics. The static plane is equivalent to the grammar in traditional linguistics. Conventionally the components of the static plane are arranged in two tiers, one for prosodic and phonological processes and the other for phonetic processes. As with traditional grammars, these processes are not dynamic procedures or functions but static descriptions. In fact they are characterizations of data structures and their internal relationships.

These data structures are capable of two types of instantiation:

1. The first is the traditional 'derivation', an exemplar utterance or fragment of an utterance derived strictly according to the grammar and showing no deviation at all from the plane's processes. These exemplar derivations obviously call for selection of processes from among the totality of processes found on the static plane: clearly any one derivation requires only a subset of all processes. Although there is a dynamic element to this selection process, exemplar derivations do not occur on the dynamic plane: they are abstractions.
2. The second is a dynamic instantiation of a particular utterance on a particular occasion, as in real speech. This is not the rendering of an exemplar utterance, but the characterization of an actual utterance in real time, complete with the considerations which need to accompany 'performance' (for want of a better word). Instantiations of this kind take place on the dynamic plane and draw on information from the static grammar, but also inevitably include information from elsewhere, including pragmatic and expressive information. In an extreme case it is possible for a dynamic instantiation to proceed with minimal external information—in which case such an utterance would mimic one of the static plane's abstract and 'ideal' derivations.

The justification for having two planes is the same as in traditional linguistics, and hangs on a speaker's ability to reveal knowledge of the language held separately from any one example of an utterance. The justification for shifting focus from the static plane of linguistics to the dynamic plane is that the kinds of behaviour we wish to characterize in our speech production model do not appear on the static plane. They involve clock time, active dynamic choice, monitoring and control-balancing incoming channels of information to obtain a suitable final acoustic signal for the required level of listener decoding.

Thus the static plane characterizes all utterances, and little or nothing of the uniqueness or dynamism of individual utterances. If an utterance is ever created on the static plane it is simply an exemplar derivation, *not* an actual utterance the speaker is producing. We believe that the 'neutral' speech of so many

A Model Based on Expression and Prosody

expression studies relates very well to this notion of exemplar derivations and how they can be mimicked by speakers.

Individual utterances are planned (in the prosodic/phonological tier) and rendered (in the phonetic tier) on the dynamic plane. There is a flow of information between the two planes in the sense that to plan an utterance and to render it, it is necessary to draw on the how utterances are planned and rendered *in general* to select what is necessary for an individual utterance. The dynamic planning of an utterance and its subsequent rendering also need information from other parts of the model (not shown) which introduces constraints from areas such as pragmatics.

16.5.2 Contributing evidence

A number of theoretical claims contribute to the architecture of the proposed model. Some are relevant to a discussion of expression in speech, including:

- All utterances are planned and rendered within a prosodic framework (Lewis and Tatham 1991); this framework is not optional, so is always reflected in the acoustic signal.
- The prosodic framework for utterances is hierarchically organized (Morton and Tatham 1995).
- Phonetic rendering is dependent on a simultaneous review of the entire underlying linguistic structure (Tatham and Lewis 1992; Morton et al. 1999).
- The rendering process is managed within a wider 'semantic delivery system' (Tatham and Morton 1995), operating within a specific scenario, a supervisory process overseeing critical areas of the rendering (Tatham 1994, 1995).

Prosody wraps the segmental utterance because

- Prosodic features often extend beyond the bounds of utterances, particularly if the features are being used to signal expressive content. A speaker's mood, for example, can carry through a sequence of utterances and through a conversation in which their utterances are interspersed by utterances from another speaker.
- They can be evoked by speakers without reference to particular utterances: they can sing or hum a rhythm or intonation pattern, but cannot speak an utterance without using some prosody.

Expression, then, wraps the prosodically dominated utterance. So, for example, if someone is angry, any utterance they produce is likely to show a wide fundamental frequency range, a higher than usual rate of delivery and enhanced articulatory precision. These are the main prosodic features which signal angry expressive content in the acoustic signal.

- If expression and prosody do *not* dominate in the model, the utterance would be planned segmentally in advance of adding prosodic and expressive content, and will potentially have a normal f0 range, rate of delivery, and articulatory precision. Increasing the rate of delivery (because of anger) will worsen articulatory precision since the effects of coarticulation are greater as speed increases. The speaker would then have to go back and revise the plan for this utterance, always assuming that they could predict the results of adding an angry expression, because part of the fact that angry speech is expressed is through increased, not decreased precision. If we do not take prosody and expression into account before and during segmental rendering we have to introduce an iterative loop into the rendering process.
- If expression and prosody are allowed to dominate the utterance plan, however the utterance will be planned and rendered in the context of the predicted effects of anger and will come out right without the need for revision.

For us this is one of the clinching arguments in favour of seeing dynamic utterance planning and rendering as taking place within the prosodic and expression wrapper, rather than the other way round.

16.5.3 *A sample declaration (after Tatham and Morton 2003)*

To illustrate with an actual utterance, here is a fragment of the prosodic mark-up of the utterance *Better be safe than sorry*. A traditional phonetic transcription with some prosodic marking:

[|'be.tə.bɪ|"seɪf.ðən|'sɒ.ri|]

shows some allophonic detail, and includes marking of rhythmic unit boundaries [...ðən|'sɒ...], syllable boundaries within rhythmic units [....tə·bɪ...], primary-stressed syllables [...'sɒ...], and nuclear sentence stress on one syllable [..."seɪf ...]. The prosodic markers used here focus on rhythm rather than intonation. Word boundaries are not explicitly marked, though they may correspond to other boundaries; thus in [...ˈbe.tə.bɪ...] the syllable boundary [... tə.bɪ...] also corresponds to a word boundary, as does the rhythmic unit boundary in [... ðən|ˈsɒ...]. Other symbols explicitly include lower-level marks; thus '|' includes '.'.

There are two possible ways of marking this particular sentence for accent groups (AG, the domains of pitch accents):

1. <AG> *Better be safe than sorry* </AG>
2. <AG> *Better be safe* </AG>   <AG> *than sorry* </AG>

And these might correspond to alternative versions in ordinary orthography:

1. *Better be safe than sorry.*
2. *Better be safe, than sorry.*

The second version splits a rhythmic unit and probably introduces a pause between ... *safe* ... and ... *sorry* .... We'll stay with the first version and the single-accent group; this occurs within an intonational phrase—the widest domain of sentence-based intonation patterns. In the system used in this book we would mark up the sentence like this:

<IP><AG> ˈbe.tə.bɪ|"seɪf.ðən|ˈsɒ.ri| </AG> </IP>

Intonational phrases and accent groups are part of the prosodic hierarchy, as explained above, we include within an expression framework:

```
<expression> <prosody> <IP> <AG/+>
  </IP> </prosody> </expression>
```

(The notation shows that there can be a number of concatenated accent groups within each intonational phrases: the '+' means 'one or more'.)

The illustrations above are a mixture of XML mark-up and phonetic transcription.

We now extend this framework declaration to include the syllabic detail of the example. The XML declaration for *Better be safe than sorry* conforms to the generalized schema for expression and, down to the syllable level, is as follows:

```
<expression>
    <prosody>
        <IP>
            <AG>
                <rhythmic_unit unstressed="2">
                    <syllable stress="1"> be </syllable>
                    <syllable stress="0"> tə </syllable>
                    <syllable stress="0"> bɪ </syllable>
                </rhythmic_unit>
                <rhythmic_unit unstressed="1">
                    <syllable stress="2"> seɪf </syllable>
                    <syllable stress="0"> ðən </syllable>
                </rhythmic_unit>
                <rhythmic_unit unstressed="1">
                    <syllable stress="1"> sɒ </syllable>
                    <syllable stress="0"> ri </syllable>
                </rhythmic_unit>
            </AG>
        </IP>
    </prosody>
</expression>
```

The element `<rhythmic_unit>` is qualified by an attribute 'unstressed' which here can take values of either 2 or 1, indicating the number of unstressed syllables following the initial stressed syllable element. Syllables in their turn take an attribute 'stress' which can have one of three values: 2 means sentence nuclear stress, 1 means primary stress, and 0 means unstressed; 2 includes 1—that is, all syllable elements with the attribute 'nuclear stress' also have the attribute 'primary stress'.

IP (the intonational phrase) is the widest intonational domain, and may often correspond to the syntactic domain 'sentence'. Within the IP domain are sub-domains of accent group (AG)—the domains of pitch accents. From the basic syntactic structure of utterances there are no fully predictable IP or AG instantiation types—this means; no particular intonation contours—except on a statistical basis and showing wide variation. Rather, prediction comes from the larger framework of 'expression' and takes in communicative aspects of language extending in principle beyond the utterance.

<expression> can be instantiated in many different ways in this basic model, though we can define it into types like 'style', 'emotion', or 'attitude'. It seems reasonable to us to assume that any of these aspects of expression would have a major influence on intonational contour type associated with how any particular utterance is to be rendered. Because expression seems to pervade all nodal processes of the utterance right down to fine phonetic detail, it is appropriate that it should be located on a dominant wrapper node. Of course, expression as a 'way of talking' often changes during a communicative exchange, and our data structure must take care of this—enabling the node's varying content to influence intonation contour type and any moment of change which might appear lower in the structure such as segment articulation. For example, a changing rate of delivery associated with 'becoming sad', for example, would cause a progressive change in the extent to which coarticulatory influences occur—slower speech would tend to lessen coarticulatory effects, whereas faster speech would tend to increase them.

16.5.4 Summary of the planning stage

Before we move on to describing dynamic rendering of utterance plans let us summarize the position so far. We have two formal declarative models for utterance plans, both captured in XML format.

1. A general statement of the structure of utterance plans from a prosodic/phonological perspective; it is static and appears on the static plane of the model. The declaration of the structure is equivalent to the grammar of a traditional generative grammar. The grammar can be instantiated as exemplar derivations of utterance plans, but these are not utterances to be rendered for actually speaking. An overall expression element is included as a place marker for later detailed expressive rendering, and to indicate that all utterances are rendered within the expressive and prosodic frameworks.

2. An instantiation of the static utterance structure: this plan appears on the model's dynamic plane and captures in principle what is planned about a particular utterance to be spoken. It is important to distinguish the plan for a particular utterance which will actually be spoken after rendering from an exemplar derivation. In particular, expression which is part of the rendering process with not appear in exemplar (statically derived) derivations at this stage.

In our XML formalism, the general description of utterances takes the form of a W3C (World Wide Web Consortium, *www.w3c.org/xml*) XML schema; the schema can be recognized as a file of type *.xsd*. Our first illustration from the static plane is the XML schema, *syllable.xsd*, which declares the grammar of syllables

```
<?xml version="1.0" encoding="UTF-16"?> [this is the XML version, for reference]
   <xs:element name5"syllable">
     <xs:complexType>
       <xs:sequence>
         <xs:element name="onset" type="xs:string" minOccurs="0"
           maxOccurs="3"/>
         <xs:element name="rhyme">
           <xs:complexType>
             <xs:sequence>
               <xs:element name="vocalic_nucleus" type="xs:string"/>
               <xs:element name="coda" type="xs:string" minOccurs="0"
                 maxOccurs="4"/>
             </xs:sequence>
           </xs:complexType>
         </xs:element>
       </xs:sequence>
       <xs:attribute name="stress" type="xs:anySimpleType" use="required"/>
     </xs:complexType>
   </xs:element>
</xs:schema>
```

This is easier to understand alongside its graphical representation see (Fig. 16.2). The declaration shows the root element to be *syllable* followed by a 'sequence' of two elements: *onset* and *rhyme*. Sequencing (indicated by the box with three filled squares) means that both elements will be instantiated (logical AND); an alternative to sequencing is 'choice', meaning that just one of the elements must be chosen (logical OR). Onset is shown as with a dotted outline because it is optional—the number of string objects (of type *consonant*) can be up to three (shown under the onset box), optionality being signalled by the zero possibility.

A Model Based on Expression and Prosody

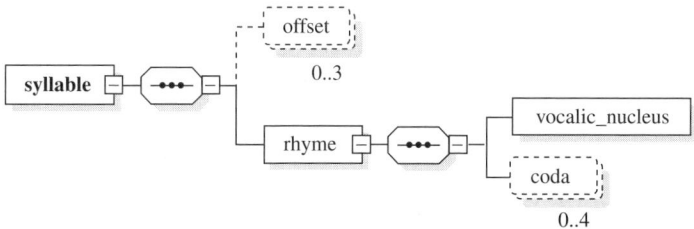

Fig. 16.2. Graphical representation of the XML declaration of the internal structure of a syllable.

There must be rhyme, however, because there must be a sequence of two elements of rhyme, one of which is a non-optional single element, vocalic_nucleus. There is an optional coda with from zero to four string objects of type consonant (shown under the coda box). Thus the only non-optional element at the surface is a vocalic nucleus; this can be preceded by up to three consonants and followed by up to four. Phonotactic rules constrain the sequences of consonants within the onset and coda strings. The detailed schema also shows that the element *syllable* must have an assigned attribute: *stress*. This is separately constrained: 2 means sentence nuclear stress, 1 means primary stress, and 0 means unstressed. Other references in the text version of the schema are necessary for completeness, but need not concern us here.

The grammar represented by the schema can be instantiated on the static plane as a *derivation*. A derivation is an abstract exemplar instantiation which retains all the ideal characteristics of the grammar—it is not an actual utterance. Actual utterances are derived on the dynamic plane. Here is a typical derivation illustrating the syllable *strict* [strɪkt]:

```
<?xml version="1.0" encoding="UTF-16"?>
<syllable stress="1" >
  <onset> str </onset>
  <rhyme>
    <vocalic_nucleus> ɪ </vocalic_nucleus>
    <coda> kt </coda>
  </rhyme>
</syllable>
```

The derivation shows that the syllable bears primary stress (*stress = 1*) and is an instance of the grammar or schema for *syllable* found in file *syllable.xsd*. The root node *syllable* derives two sub-nodes *onset* and *rhyme*, with onset instantiated as [str]. The node rhyme derives *vocalic_nucleus*, instantiated as [ɪ], and *a coda*, instantiated as [kt]. The first line of the declaration simply means that we are using version 1.0 of XML, and the character encoding uses sixteen bits—a unicode font needed for phonetic symbols.

What is confusing about derivations is that under extreme conditions they could look like actual utterance instantiations created on the dynamic plane as careful precise speech, with no departure from the ideal characterized by the schema. In principle we retain the distinction because an actual utterance *must* depart from the schema because it is not abstract and has been constrained by phenomena *external* to the grammar even if these have had minimal impact. Such phenomena include those concerned with expression—the subject of our study. This is partly why our fragment shows a surface representation in phonetic symbols—themselves idealizations away from the actual soundwave—rather than a waveform. Although an actual utterance must depart from the declaration found in a schema, the schema itself always remains the basis of any utterance—this is the foundation for both the speaker's utterances and the listener's percepts.

It is important as well not to confuse exemplar derivations with instantiations which are deliberately precise in articulation and created on the dynamic plane. When a speaker opts for increased precision this means that the usual constraints on precision are managed by the CPA for minimal influence; this is not the same as avoiding constraints by invoking an exemplar derivation. In principle a derivation of this kind cannot exist outside the speaker's mind, or the linguist's characterization. To arrive in the physical world an utterance must have come via the dynamic plane.

16.6 Prosodic and expressive detail

The utterance plan is created within a prosodic framework, and for this reason all prosody is available in principle to all utterances. The plan for a particular utterance (not an exemplar derivation on the static plane) is created on the dynamic plane, and whatever is needed for this process is drawn from the full grammar held on the static plane, so that prosodic and segmental information is transferred between planes whenever necessary. When the plan is finished in the prosodic/phonological tier it is transferred to the phonetic tier of the dynamic plane for detailed rendering. The segmental plan will continue to be wrapped within its prosody all the way to the final soundwave; but included in the rendering process is a rewrapping of the plan for expression, replacing the static plane's place marker <expression/> with an actual call for a particular expression.[2]

16.6.1 Dynamically varying expression

Talking calmly or authoritatively is something a speaker would probably do over the longer term, perhaps throughout a conversation of which any example utterance plan would be just a fragment. There will be traces of, say, the authoritative attitude over quite long stretches of speech, perhaps encompassing several concatenated utterance plans. During a conversation there would be another speaker's plans intervening. In trying to characterize the situation it would be less transparent to have to keep repeating the attitude contribution to the final speech. The authoritative expressive content is not a segmental (allophonic or syllabic) property, or even an utterance property: the speaker's authoritative characteristic is almost disassociated from any speech. Put another way: the speaker is authoritative *and* they are speaking, not: the speech is authoritative. The speaker is communicating their authority via speech. There is a fine line here separating

---

[2] The overall physical stance contributes to phonetic rendering because part of the vocal tract configuration is in response to the speaker's overall physical stance. In this sense we can speak of the prosodic and segmental requirements feeding into the vocal tract which has been 'set'. This is difficult to capture in the model, but is perhaps best treated as a constraint, a variable one according to speaker and perhaps also variable within any one speaker. Extreme anger, as we have mentioned, distorts the vocal tract and hence the acoustic signal: this kind of expression affects the rendering of the plan in a different way from expression, which is cognitively sourced. These physical settings are perhaps usefully treated as though they were a phenomenon akin to variable coarticulation.

authority and speaking. We feel that it is useful to invoke this line, giving the expression the dominant role, and placing the utterance within the speaker's psychology. We want to combine a general psychological approach with individual acts of utterance—and our framework must reflect this. So:

```
<expression>
  <attitude type="authoritative">
    <prosody>
      <utterance/>
    </prosody>
  </attitude>
</expression>
```

This means that within the general psychological framework of an authoritative attitude there will be prosody and an utterance. We are saying that an authoritative attitude is part of the psychology of the speaker or their situation, that is, something which needs a bio-psychological characterization, not a linguistic one. What we need to know in terms of speech production is that this is going to affect the prosody of the utterance. In our notation, lower or child nodes (for example, prosody is lower than expression and attitude, and is bracketed within both) are said to inherit the properties of their parent nodes. Thus the prosody for this utterance will have the attitudinal expressive properties associated with being authoritative, and this information is inherited.

```
<expression>
  <attitude type="authoritative" degree="0.2">
    <prosody>
      <utterance/>
      <utterance/>
      <utterance/>
    </prosody>
  </attitude>
</expression>
```

A Model Based on Expression and Prosody

In this mark-up we find a sequence of three distinct utterances all to be spoken with the same authoritative attitude, though this time we have introduced a degree attribute, giving it a value of 0.2 on a notional ten-point scale from 0 to 1 in steps of 0.1. This is equivalent to switching on a low level of authoritative attitude and proceeding to speak three utterances—all with the same expressive content in the acoustic signal, of course. A listener would perceive unvarying authority coming across throughout. We speak of this as being a 'global' indication of expression.

But we need the framework to be able also to reflect local changes in degree of expression. So, altering the mark-up to show increasing authoritative tone from utterance to utterance:

```
<expression>
    <attitude type="authoritative" degree="0.2">
        <prosody>
            <utterance/>
        </prosody>
    </attitude>
    <attitude type="authoritative" degree="0.5">
        <prosody>
            <utterance/>
        </prosody>
    </attitude>
    <attitude type="authoritative" degree="0.7">
        <prosody>
            <utterance/>
        </prosody>
    </attitude>
</expression>
```

What the mark-up now says is that the general expressive wrapper calls for attitude of type authoritative on each of a sequence of three sentences, with the degree of authoritative expression progressively increasing from utterance to utterance.

But suppose we want to have simultaneous or overlapping expression. Here is an example of a speaker who begins with a high level of sympathetic tone and some authoritative tone, but over the three sentences the sympathetic tone disappears and the authoritative tone progressively increases.

```
<expression>
  <attitude type1="sympathetic" degree1="0>6" type2=
  "authoritative" degree2="0.2">
    <prosody>
      <utterance/>
    </prosody>
  </attitude>
  <attitude type1="sympathetic" degree1="0.3" type2=
  "authoritative" degree2="0.4">
    <prosody>
      <utterance/>
    </prosody>
  </attitude>
  <attitude type1="sympathetic" degree1="0" type2=
  "authoritative" degree2="0.7">
    <prosody>
      <utterance/>
    </prosody>
  </attitude>
</expression>
```

There are a number of different ways of representing elements with increasing and decreasing attribute values in our notation, but the one used here is perhaps the easiest to understand from the point of view of how the idea works. What we have done is set up an element *attitude* which can have type attributes corresponding to different attitudes—we have used *sympathetic* and *authoritative* for our example, but clearly we could have more. An external convention on the XML mark-up might say something like

- Smooth the transitions between degree values across successive utterances.

and would provide a notional dynamic element to the mark-up, but would be a crude representation of simple linear change. We have not found data in the literature which might help us indicate *non*-linear changes. For example, there are research questions to be answered like:

- Is there a predictable pivotal point in an utterance where changes of expression can be detected?
- What are the possible candidates for such utterance points—phonological (e.g. the syllable bearing sentential nuclear

stress), syntactic (e.g. a particular type of syntactic boundary), semantic (e.g. a significant point where meaning or intention 'turns'), etc.?
- Is there a predictable sequence within expression types—attitudes, styles, emotions, etc. (e.g. is it the case that an angry emotion cannot suddenly become an ecstatic emotion, and must there be a transition through happy—or can there be category jumps?)?

The XML mark-up in the examples deals only with attitude, but there are clearly nodes for other expression types. Mood, style, and emotion each have their own node in the expressive system. The nesting of these nodes in the hierarchy is discussed below, but here we illustrate emotion expressed within attitude.

```
<expression>
   <attitude type1="sympathetic" degree1="0.6"
   type2="authoritative" degree2="0.2">
      <emotion type1="angry" degree1="0" type2="happy"
      degree2="0">
         <prosody>
            <utterance/>
         </prosody>
      </emotion>
   </attitude>
   <attitude type1="sympathetic" degree1= "0.3" type2=
   "authoritative" degree2="0.4">
      <emotion type1="angry" degree1="0.1" type2="happy"
      degree2="0">
         <prosody>
            <utterance/>
         </prosody>
      </emotion>
   </attitude>
   <attitude type1="sympathetic" degree1="0" type2=
   "authoritative" degree2="0.7">
      <emotion type1="angry" degree1="0.2" type2="happy"
      degree2="0">
         <prosody>
            <utterance/>
         </prosody>
      </emotion>
   </attitude>
</expression>
```

The above extension of the mark-up of three consecutive utterances adds emotion nested within attitude, both wrapping prosody and the utterances hanging beneath. Two emotions are illustrated, angry increasing slightly and happy staying low.

The notation and the idea of a dominance relationship *between* expressive types (mood dominates attitude, for example) also raises another research issue:

- Is there a dominance relationship *within* expressive types?

The literature is clear in recognizing a few basic emotions, and degrees of basic emotions have also been suggested: happy—joyful—ecstatic, for example. But within the basic emotion type should anger be characterized as dominating sadness?—or are they 'equal' in some sense? This is the kind of question which is thrown up as soon as we start trying to build a formal model linking what data we have, and is typical of the way a science develops. For all sorts of reasons, such as the 'span' of expression (e.g. 'attitude' spanning 'emotion'), the hierarchical framework seems appropriate in general for modelling expressive content and how it arises in speech. And this raises the question: should the hierarchical framework pervade even those areas where hierarchy has not even been considered before? The decision to use a particular formalism has raised additional hypotheses.

16.7 Evaluating competing demands for expressive content: a task for the CPA

One of the ways in which the CPA is active is in evaluating and resolving any conflicting expressive content. This is an important point because most research into the acoustic correlates of expression has assumed lack of conflict or simply not addressed the problem; the position taken is that at any one moment there is either this or that expressive tone. However, it is clearly the case that human speech can convey mixed and varying expressive content. There must be a mechanism within the model, therefore, which is able to handle this observation, even if for the moment this is just another research question.

We suggest that the static plane and its tiers where the 'grammar' resides are neutral with respect to expression—that is, expression is not a valid concept on this plane. In our model, expression is brought in on the dynamic plane as part of the general task of formulating detailed utterance specifications in the prosodic/phonological or phonetic tiers. Our data structure

A Model Based on Expression and Prosody

approach has required the addition of the root element to the XML hierarchy: 'expression'.

`<expression> <prosody> <utterance/> </prosody> </expression>`

There are two questions:

1. Where in the model is this element added—on the prosodic/phonological tier or the phonetic tier?
2. How is the element added—that is, what contributes to the decision to add an element?

It seems that the best place to introduce the overarching expression element into the data structure is before the final version of the plan is produced—that is, before the plan is finalized, and on the prosodic/phonological tier. The test is whether there are details of the utterance plan which depend on expression, or whether expression is only apparent in phonetic detail.

Let us take as an example the expressive desire on the part of the speaker to enunciate carefully (though this is not necessarily emotion-driven). Careful speech implies a reduction of phonological assimilation and phonetic coarticulation. Assimilation is a phonological phenomenon distinguished from its phonetic counterpart, coarticulation, by whether the 'overlap' processes described under these headings are avoidable. In general, if they can be avoided the processes belong on the phonological tier, but if they are unavoidable they belong on the phonetic tier. If we instantiate expression as 'speak carefully', we find speakers adjusting both phonological and phonetic processes. So, a speaker who normally pronounces the word *writer* with a voiced alveolar flap for the /t/ may use a voiceless alveolar plosive under the influence of the decision to speak carefully: this is a phonological adjustment made by not applying the assimilation rule which, for this speaker, normally changes the voiceless plosive into a voiced one and turns it into a flap. The same expressive element, speak carefully, applied to articulation in general results in a measurable increase in the precision of segment rendering—apparent as a reduction in phonetic variability. This is an effect clearly on the phonetic tier since it involves manipulation of physically determined effects. This example suggests that expression wraps both phonological and phonetic processes.

On the phonetic tier there is more support for the 'reasoning CPA' solution. There is evidence that the acoustic parameters of expression are not great in number: average f0, range of f0, and tempo are the most usually cited. There are those, for instance, who believe that all emotive expressive content (to name just one type of expression) boils down to varying combining amounts of half a dozen or so basic emotions. Perhaps surprisingly, then, what we call the 'perceptual resolution' of expressive content is high. What this means is that listeners can recognize a wide range of expression, and grade degrees of expression quite finely. It would seem to follow that if only a small number of acoustic parameters are used for the encoding of all this, it must be the case that the actual encoding is quite finely achieved or managed.

We believe that to achieve this we need a device which can balance the multiple requirements of a cascade of expressive elements, dynamically changing as the utterances unfold. Hence the CPA, which takes in competing demands on a relatively small number of acoustic parameters, juggles with these demands to achieve the best mix possible to satisfy the goal of speech: satisfactory perception. Reasoning of this kind is complex and would seem to involve a predictive element constantly addressing the question: 'What will happen if I do such-and-such?'—where 'what will happen' refers to how the utterance will be *perceived*. In more formal terms the CPA seems to set up a trial solution which is passed before a model of perception to test the adequacy of the results. Perhaps extreme cases result in an iterative process of adjustment to get the perception as near the desired goal as possible.

To summarize: there would seem to be competition for the *means* of expression—the available acoustic parameters. Expression is capable of very fine gradation, yet the acoustic parameters are few in number. Each must be finely used, therefore and the perceptual system must be very finely tuned to tiny variations, all occurring, as we have seen, in a context-sensitive environment.

Because of contextual variation and because of the dynamics of various modes of expressive content shading into one another as utterances and sequences of utterances unfold we find it difficult to imagine that the production process for expression is passive. We hypothesize this very active *agent*, constantly evaluating competing demands on the available parameters and constantly evaluating the perceptual reliability of this or that combination. If we repeat ourselves on this point, it serves to underline the complexity and comparative novelty of this approach to how speech is controlled. At the segmental level the process, though similar, is comparatively simple (Tatham 1994; 1995), but at the expressive and prosodics levels the position grows in complexity. Parametric speech synthesis has taught us just how little of the speech waveform is used in communication, but linguistics and psychology teach us just how much information content is being conveyed to the listener by this same waveform. There can be no doubt that the challenge of this apparent paradox is enormous.

16.8 Spectral and articulatory detail

Some phonetic details appear to correlate with prosodic features, suggesting their dependence on the prosodic framework envelope. Sometimes this is not too surprising: transitions between segments, for example, are usually dependent for their rate on overall utterance tempo. At a somewhat finer level we find that segment-to-segment transition features within the syllable depend on assigned prosodic features of the syllable, for example how timing works out within the rhythmic unit. Ambisyllabicity also plays a role in determining some of the detail of phonetic rendering (Kahn 1976; Gussenhoven 1986).

Examples of detailed phonetic rendering which is directly dependent on the utterance's prosodic framework often occur where adjacent segments differ on the glottal parameter—that is, whether or not they are voiced. For example, intended vocal cord vibration often fails if there is airflow impedance in the oral cavity during voiced stops or fricatives; this occurs particularly if the tempo is relatively slow, and seems more likely to occur if the impedance is over a certain threshold. This is a phonetic coarticulatory effect due to supra-glottal air pressure increases not matched by corresponding sub-glottal pressure increases. As the supra-glottal air pressure increases over time and in correlation with the degree of constriction, so the balance between supra-glottal and sub-glottal air pressures, together with vocal cord tension, moves outside the critical range, leading to failure of spontaneous vocal cord vibration.

The prosodic framework enables generalization of such effects, whereas without it there would have to be local ad hoc solutions. Thus we say that under prosodic conditions resulting in decreasing tempo, or others resulting in particular patterns of stress, vocal cord vibration failure will result. The enhanced generalization introduced by the enveloping framework dominating all utterances also leads to wider predictability and more formal explanation of such phenomena.

16.9 Planning and rendering utterances within prosodic wrappers

This is not the usual relationship we find between utterances and their prosody. For the most part the traditional focus is on planning and realizing the segmental aspects of an utterance first, and then fitting a prosodic representation to them. When phoneticians speak of the possibility of realizing utterances with different prosodic contours this is usually what they mean. So we come across remarks like: '*John took the dog out* can be spoken either with a rising or a falling intonation contour to indicate question or statement respectively.' Here the clear implication is that there are alternative prosodies to be chosen and fitted to segmental plan for the utterance.

Within this approach (call it A) there are two possibilities:

- There are phrase- or utterance-level prosodic contours which express some grammatical meaning (like statement or question) overlaid on which are modifications brought about by effects such as emphasis or emotion. Such *accents* interact with or modify the overall tune assigned. Ladd (1984) has called this the Contour Interaction Theory. It is the more traditional of the two possibilities, and originates in a phonetics perspective on the process.
- There are simple tonal elements or pitch accents which are sequenced movements of pitch, which concatenate to form the

A Model Based on Expression and Prosody

overall intonation contour. The intonational contour of a sentence is simply this sequence and is not some higher or more abstract level (Ladd et al. 1985). This Tone Sequence Theory is a more recent view, and originates in a more abstract, phonological perspective on speech.

Our approach (call it B) is different. A prosodic framework wraps utterances. And although the sub-elements of the alternative theory (in either of its two approaches above) are there and can be characterized from an external viewpoint (that is, descriptively and independently of our theory) they are simply elements of the prosodic framework *visible* for any one utterance. The point is best made perhaps with an example from French where the falling vs. rising sentence intonation is used more consistently than in English. The sentence used is: *Il est déjà midi à Paris* ('It is already midday in Paris').

Approach A
Segmental level   Utterance
                                              ↓
                                  Il est déjà midi à Paris
                                              ↓
Prosodic rendering   Add statement
                                        or question
                                          contour

Utterance with added prosodic   ↵ ↳   *Il est déjà ↗midi ↗à Paris?*
contour *Il est déjà ↘midi ↘à Paris.*

The diagram shows that we start with formulating the utterance at the segmental level. Then we decide whether it is going to be a statement or a question, and put on it the appropriate intonation contour—falling for a statement, rising for a question. Essentially the contour is *added* to the utterance.

Approach B
Decide prosodic wrapper   Statement contour   Question contour
                                       ↓   ↓
                                 Get utterance   Get utterance
                                       ↓   ↓
Generate utterance   *Il est déjà ↘midi ↘à*   *Il est déjà ↗midi*
plan   *Paris.*   *↗à Paris?*

Here we see that the first thing to be decided is what the prosodic contour shall be—statement or question. This depends, of course, on factors outside the speech production model. The model then gets the utterance and formulates it as an utterance plan within the wrapper to produce either a plan with falling contour or a plan with rising contour. Here the plan is formulated *within* the intonation contour.

16.10 Speaking a specific utterance with expression

The input to the phonological tier is the call for a plan for a specific utterance. The call has been generated elsewhere, and we can assume it takes the form of a syntactically and semantically appropriately formulated sentence. Such a sentence triggers a reasoning process in the dynamic phonology—performed by the *phonological agent*—which seeks the information necessary to plan this utterance by going to the phonological tier on the static plane, selecting elements in the form of objects and processes (consulting exemplar derivations if necessary), brings them back to the dynamic plane, and proceeds to formulate the dynamic plan.

It is important to distinguish between the sentence—a grammatical object generated before speech production is required, and the utterance plan—a statement of how the utterance is to be spoken. The utterance may or may not correspond to a sentence; it could be longer or shorter, but can be regarded as a speech production unit. Notice that the dynamic tiers presuppose nothing about what is to be spoken except that it is capable of undergoing phonological planning—that is, that it is a regular utterance of the language. The dynamic prosodic/phonological tier is a planning system, but in principle it knows nothing of the detail of the specific utterance it is to plan: phonological planning calls for reasoning, performed by the phonological agent, which knows how to run the planning process on demand and reason as to its optimal outcome.

So what do we know about phonological planning? There are two input streams to the prosodic/phonological tier:

1. from a higher dynamic, syntactically and semantically connected tier, which is responsible for formulating individual

sentences to be planned for speaking; some of the constraints on the prosodic wrapper will come from here—things like *I need to ask a question* (prompts rising intonation), *Here is my main point* (prompts focal stress);

2. from tiers on parallel planes which exploit channels to convey constraining information relevant to phonological choices about 'expression', etc., to be incorporated into the utterance being planned; some details of the expressive wrapper will come from this source—things like *I want to sound in control* (prompts authoritative speech) or *I'm very scared* (prompts fearful speech); these additional inputs pass through the phonological agent.

Thus an input from (1) might take the form of the sentence *Why shouldn't I study phonetics?* Turning this into a plan for speaking involves specific calls to the prosodic/phonological tier on the static plan to bring across elements such as phonological objects (syllables, segments, etc.) and details of processes relating to combining them. But since there is no one way of speaking a sentence, such information might well contain alternatives with an attached probability index. This paves the way for the 'requirements' stream (2), from planes relating to considerations such as those of a pragmatic nature. One such simple marker might be: <speak with irritation>. Thus:

- For any utterance plan there exists an input sentence and a set of incoming prosodic/phonological constraints which interact to generate that plan. The reasoning needed to create the optimum utterance plan is performed by the phonological agent.

With the dynamic completion of the plan, the model is now ready for rendering, that is: 'speaking'.

16.11 The proposed model of speech production

This, then, is our proposed speech production model, which attempts to integrate expressive, general prosodic, and segmental factors in a planning/rendering framework. We argue that all of the detail is necessary for characterizing what we observe of human behaviour. We also point out that the model has serious gaps, which we hope arise in such a way as to generate research hypotheses. The model is explicit enough to be called computational, and can be tested in an appropriate synthesizer environment. At the same time practical synthesis—the engineering implementation of the model—while not needing to accommodate every detail, will at least have the framework necessary for, we believe, significantly improving naturalness in synthesized waveforms.

Conclusion

Part of the objective of this book has been to make proposals for the development of a model of how expression is encoded in the acoustics of speech as part of a general theory of expression in speech. Much of the research into expression in speech has centred round discovering the acoustic correlates of this or that *emotion* rather than expression in general.

The input to the model

We have stressed that it is not enough to characterize the acoustic correlates of this or that emotion in speech. We want a suitable model of how emotion is represented in the acoustic signal such that a perceiver is able to decide what the speaker is feeling. A statement of the acoustic correlates *is* pivotal to the model, but is a kind of static descriptive model with quite limited use. We needed to build on this to develop a more dynamic model of how expressive content in speech is encoded, a model that predicts what the acoustic signal will be.

Nor has it been enough to speak of a particular emotion as the model's expressive input. Emotions are often just labels put on the speaker's feelings, and what we really need is a descriptive model of what it is that is being labelled. The reason for this is that speakers do not encode a label as an acoustic signal: the encoding process is triggered by the object bearing the label. The object and its label are two different things altogether, and confusion between the two will result in an unsatisfactory account of expression. This point cannot be overemphasized, in our view.

The model's output

Perception is not just the detection of something in an incoming signal. If perception were like this it would imply that the signal itself included an expressive content label, and that the task of perception is simply to find this label. For us, though, perception is a much more active process involving the assignment of a label to the signal. The listener draws the appropriate label from a set of labels they already know. The acoustic signal itself need be nothing more than a trigger to prompt this action. Moreover, we feel that the label is often assigned on a context-sensitive basis; that is, in one context a given signal will cause a listener to assign one label and in another a different label. Arguably there are 'cues' in the acoustic signal for identifying an appropriate label, but we feel the main task is much more active.

For this kind of reason, characterizations of speakers' acoustic signals which contain such triggers need to be in terms relating to how perception works, not just be plain statements of what the signal is like in pure acoustic terms. Just as the input to the expression model needs to take the form of a proper characterization of what is to be acoustically encoded, so its output needs to be a characterization appropriate to how the perceptual system is going to deal with it; and what the listener is going to do is *assign a label to the signal*.

The overall model

We have summarized the three main areas of the model in terms of the parent discipline able to throw the most light on the processes involved.

1. Psychology or bio-psychology characterizes what the emotion is and how it arises, and gives us a label to use; the discipline defines the expression which is going to get encoded in the acoustic signal.
2. Phonology and phonetics examine the acoustic signal and how it is created; they characterize the properties which correlate with the underlying emotion *and* which lead to the correct perception; the characterization of the waveform properties takes the form of a parametric representation;
3. Psychology describes the perceptual process in which an appropriate label is assigned to what the listener has heard.

The discovery of how the acoustic signal represents any form of expression is not a simple quest for correlation between the psychological or bio-psychological label and a set of measured acoustic parameter values, because the acoustic correlates only mean this or that emotion, for example, in the context both of the speaker's felt emotion and of the listener's assigned label. Most researchers tacitly recognize this, and a few refer directly to problems of ambiguity and mismatches between the acoustic correlates and the underlying emotion. This is usually expressed in terms of the range of acoustic correlates which can be called 'identifiers' of any one particular emotion.

We have tried to resolve the problem by building a model of the complete system showing how *later* levels in the model in fact constrain earlier levels. How we deal with the acoustic signal, for example, depends not just on how it is spoken and what it correlates with in terms of speaker psychology, but also on how it is to be perceived. At first glance this looks like a paradox: how could something (the acoustic signal) depend on an event which has not yet occurred (its perception)? We attempt to resolve the paradox by proposing that the speaker has produced a signal dependent on their own estimation of how the listener *will* perceive the signal; the speaker has predicted the perceptual process and its results, and tailored the signal accordingly.

- Speech production involves constant monitoring of a prediction of how its acoustic output will be perceived—that is, how it will be assigned labels.

Note, however, that labels themselves do not figure in the actual encoding process—it is not possible to encode a label, in much the same way as in segmental phonetics a phoneme cannot be spoken.

The prosodic framework

Overall the speech production model has a characterization of prosody as its basic framework. All speech is seen as being processed within this framework—and for this reason much prosodic detail is available in advance of segmental detail. It is as though a speaker says *I am going to ask a question—and this is it*, rather than *Here are my words—and I give them to you in the form of a question*. We have hypothesized that in a dialogue, for example, the major interplay is between prosodic objects, and the entire dialogue can be charted as a flow of prosodic objects or units within a dynamic space which forms the dialogue scenario. We use terms designed to emphasize the dynamic nature of speech and the hypothesis that prosody is playing the major role in these dynamics. It is almost as if the actual utterances were secondary.

Prosodic objects are hierarchically organized around the domain or 'span' of the utterance they envelop. It is only at the lowest levels—the narrowest of the domains—that we encounter lexical objects and their own sub-domains like syllables and speech sounds. This is the organizational structure, the framework, of utterances. For this reason we refer frequently to an utterance's prosodic 'wrapper' or 'envelope'. Instantiation of a particular utterance involves working within the hierarchically organized prosodic framework. The non-prosodic phonological and phonetic properties of an utterance are *fitted to* the framework.

References

ABERCROMBIE, D. (1967). *Elements of General Phonetics*. Edinburgh: Edinburgh University Press.

ADOLPHS, R., AND DAMASIO, A. (2000). 'Neurobiology of Emotion at a Systems Level', in J. Borod (ed.), *The Neuropsychology of Emotion*. Oxford: Oxford University Press, 194–213.

AITCHISON, J. (1998). *The Articulate Mammal*, 4th edn. London: Routledge.

ALLEN, J., HUNNICUT, S., AND KLATT, D. (1987). *From Text to Speech: The MITalk System*. Cambridge: Cambridge University Press.

Altova GmbH and Altova Inc. (1998–2002). *XML-Spy Integrated Development Environment*. Address: Vienna, Rodolfplatz 13a/9.

AMIR N., AND RON, S. (1998). 'Towards an Automatic Classification of Emotions in Speech', *Proceedings of ICSLP*, Sydney: 555–8.

ATAL, B., AND HANAUER, S. (1971). 'Speech Analysis and Synthesis by Linear Prediction of the Speech Wave', *Journal of the Acoustical Society of America* 50: 637–55.

AUBERGÉ, V., AND LEMAÎTRE, L. (2000). 'The Prosody of Smile', *Proceedings of the European Speech Communication Association Workshop on Speech and Emotion,* Belfast: CD-rom. Rev. as 'Can We Hear the Prosody of Smile?', *Speech Communication* 40 (2003): 87–98.

AVERILL, J. (1980). 'A Constructivist View of Emotion', in R. Plutchik and H. Kellerman (eds.), *Emotion: Theory, Research and Experience* 1. New York: Academic Press, 305–39.

——(1994). 'In the Eyes of the Beholder', in P. Ekman and R. Davidson (eds.), *The Nature of Emotion: Fundamental Questions*. Oxford: Oxford University Press, 7–19.

BALKENIUS, C., AND MOREN, J. (1998). 'A Computational Model of Emotional Conditioning in the Brain', in *Grounding Emotions in Adaptive Systems, 5th International Conference for Adaptive Behavior* (SAB '98) Workshop: Paper 04.

BECHTEL, W., AND MUNDALE, J. (1999). 'Multiple Realizability Revisited: Linking Cognitive and Neural States', *Philosophy of Science* 66: 175–207.

BICKLEY, C., STEVENS, K., AND WILLIAMS, D. (1997). 'A Framework for Synthesis of Segments Based on Pseudoarticulatory Parameters', in

J. van Santen, R. Sproat, J. Olive, and J. Hirschberg (eds.), *Progress in Speech Synthesis*. New York: Springer.

BICKLEY, C., AND BRUCKERT, E. (2002). 'Improvements in the Voice Quality of DecTalk', *Proceedings of the IEEE Workshop on Speech Synthesis*, Santa Monica: CD-rom.

BLACK, A., AND CAMPBELL, N. (1995). 'Optimising Selection of Units from Speech Databases for Concatenative Synthesis', *Proceedings of Eurospeech*, Madrid: 581–4.

BORDEN, G., HARRIS, K., AND RAPHAEL, L. (1994). *Speech Science Primer: Physiology, Acoustics, and Perception of speech*, 3rd edn. Baltimore: Williams & Wilkins.

BOROD, J. (1993). 'Cerebral Mechanisms Underlying Facial, Prosodic, and Lexical Emotional Expression', *Neuropsychology* 7: 445–63.

—— TABERT, M., SANTSCHI, C., AND STRAUSS, E. (2000). 'Neuropsychological Assessment of Emotional Processing in Brain-Damaged Patients', in J. Borod (ed.), *The Neuropsychology of Emotion*. Oxford: Oxford University Press, 80–105.

BREGMAN, A. (1990). *Auditory Scene Analysis: The Perceptual Organization of Sound*. Cambridge, Mass.: MIT Press.

BROWMAN, C., AND GOLDSTEIN, L. (1986). 'Towards an Articulatory Phonology', in C. Ewan and J. Anderson (eds.), *Phonology Yearbook* 3. Cambridge: Cambridge University Press, 219–53.

CACIOPPO, J., BERNTSON, G., LARSEN, J., POEHLMANN, K., AND ITO, T. (2000). 'The Psychophysiology of Emotion', in M. Lewis and J. Haviland-Jones (eds.), *Handbook of Emotions*. New York: Guilford Press, 173–91.

—— AND TASSINARY, L. (1992). 'Inferring Psychological Significance from Physiological Signals', *American Psychologist* 45, (1): 16–28.

CAMPBELL, N. (2000). 'Databases of Emotional Speech', *Proceedings of the International Speech Communication Association Workshop on Speech and Emotion*, Belfast: CD-rom.

CARLSON, R., GRANSTRÖM, G., AND NORD, L. (1992). 'Experiments with Emotive Speech, Acted Utterances and Synthesized Replicas', *Speech Communication* 11: 347–55.

CAULDWELL, R. (2000). 'Where Did the Anger Go? The Role of Context in Interpreting Emotion in Speech', in R. Cowie, E. Douglas-Cowie, and M. Schröder (eds.), *Proceedings of the European Speech Communication Association Workshop on Speech and Emotion*, Belfast: CD-rom.

CAWLEY, G., AND GREEN, A. (1991). 'The Application of Neural Networks to Cognitive Phonetic Modelling', *Proceedings of the*

IEE. *International Conference on Artificial Neural Networks*, Bournemouth: 280–4.

CHARPENTIER, J., AND MOULINES, E. (1989). 'Pitch-Synchronous Waveform Processing Techniques for Text-to-Speech Synthesis Using Diphones', *Proceedings of Eurospeech*, Paris: 13–19.

CHILDERS, D. (2000). *Speech Processing and Synthesis Toolboxes*. New York: Wiley.

CHOMSKY, N. (1965). *Aspects of the Theory of Syntax*. Cambridge, Mass.: MIT Press.

—— (1972). *Language and Mind*, enlarged edn. New York: Harcourt Brace Jovanovich.

—— AND HALLE, M. (1968). *The Sound Pattern of English*. New York: Harper & Row.

CLORE, G. (1994a). 'Why Emotions are Felt', in P. Ekman and R. Davidson (eds.), *The Nature of Emotion: Fundamental Questions*. Oxford: Oxford University Press, 103–11.

—— (1994b). 'Why Emotions Require Cognition', in P. Ekman and R. Davidson (eds.), *The Nature of Emotion: Fundamental Questions*. Oxford: Oxford University Press, 181–91.

—— AND ORTONY, A. (2000). 'Cognition in Emotion: Always, Sometimes, or Never?', in R. Lane and L. Nadel (eds.), *Cognitive Neuroscience of Emotion*. Oxford: Oxford University Press, 24–61.

—— —— AND FOSS, M. (1987). 'The Psychological Foundations of the Affective Lexicon', *Journal of Personality and Social Psychology* 53: 751–65.

COOKE, M., AND ELLIS, D. (2001). 'The Auditory Organization of Speech and Other Sources in Listeners and Computational Models', *Speech Communication* 35: 141–77.

COWIE, R., DOUGLAS-COWIE, E., SAVVIDOU, S., MCMAHON, E., SAWEY, M., AND SCHRÖDER, M. (2000). 'FEELTRACE: An Instrument for Recording Perceived Emotion in Real Time', *Proceedings of the European Speech Communication Association Workshop on Speech and Emotion*, Belfast: CD-rom.

CRUTTENDEN, A. (2001). *Gimson's 'Pronunciation of English'*. London: Arnold.

DALGLEISH, T., AND POWER, M. (1999). 'Cognition and Emotion: Future Directions', in T. Dalgleish and M. Power (eds.), *Handbook of Cognition and Emotion*. Chichester: Wiley, 799–805.

DAMASIO, A. (1994). *Descartes' Error: Emotion, Reason, and the Human Brain*. New York: Penguin Putnam.

DANILOFF, R., SCHUCKERS, G., AND FETH, L. (1980). *The Physiology of Speech and Hearing*. Englewood Cliffs: Prentice-Hall.

DARWIN, C. (1872). *The Expression of the Emotions in Man and Animals*. London: Murray. Repr. Chicago: University of Chicago Press, 1965.

DAVIDSON, R. (1993a). 'Parsing Affective Space: Perspectives from Neuropsychology and Psychophysiology', *Neuropsychology* 7: 464–75.

—— (1993b). 'The Neuropsychology of Emotion and Affective Style', in M. Lewis and J. Haviland-Jones (eds.), *Handbook of Emotions*. New York: Guilford Press, 143–54.

—— AND HENRIQUES, J. (2000). 'Regional Brain Function in Sadness and Depression', in J. Borod (ed.), *The Neuropsychology of Emotion*. Oxford: Oxford University Press, 269–97.

DAVITZ, J. (1964). 'Auditory Correlates of Vocal Expressions of Emotional Meanings', in J. Davitz (ed.), *The Communication of Emotional Meaning*. New York: McGraw-Hill, 101–12.

DEIGH, J. (2001). 'Emotions: the Legacy of James and Freud', *International Journal of Psychoanalysis* 82: 1247–56.

DESCARTES, R. (1649). *The Philosophical Writings of Descartes*, trans. J. Cottingham, R. Stoothoff, and D. Murdoch. Cambridge: Cambridge University Press, 1984–91.

EDGINGTON, M. (1997). 'Investigating the Limitations of Concatenative Synthesis', *Proceedings of Eurospeech*, Rhodes: CD-rom.

EKMAN, P. (1992). 'An Argument for Basic Emotions', *Cognition and Emotion* 6 (3/4): 169–200.

—— (1999). 'Basic Emotions', in T. Dalgleish and M. Power (eds.), *Handbook of Cognition and Emotion*. Chichester: Wiley, 45–60.

—— AND DAVIDSON, R. (1994). 'Afterword: Are There Basic Emotions?', in P. Ekman and R. Davidson (eds.), *The Nature of Emotion: Fundamental Questions*. Oxford: Oxford University Press, 45–7.

—— AND FRIESEN, W. (1998). 'Constants across Culture in the Face and Emotion', in J. Jenkins, K. Oatley, and N. Stein (eds.), *Human Emotions: A Reader*. Oxford: Blackwell, 63–72. Originally Pub. in *Journal of Personality and Social Psychology* 17 (1971): 124–9.

EPSTEIN, M. (2002). 'Voice Quality and Prosody in English.' Ph.D. thesis, University of California at Los Angeles.

ESKENAZI, M. (1992). 'Changing Speech Styles: Strategies in Read Speech and Careful Spontaneous Speech', *Proceedings of the International Congress on Spoken Language Processing*, Banff: 755–8.

FANT, G. (1960). *Acoustic Theory of Speech Production*. The Hague: Mouton.

FIRTH, J. (1948). 'Sounds and Prosodies', *Transactions of the Philological Society*, 127–52. Repr. in W. Jones and J. Laver (eds.), *Phonetics in Linguistics: A Book of Readings*. London: Longman.

FLANAGAN, J. (1956). 'Bandwidth and Channel Capacity Necessary to Transmit the Formant Information of Speech', *Journal of the Acoustical Society of America* 28: 592–6.

——(1957). 'Estimates of the Maximum Precision Necessary in Quantizing Certain "Dimensions" of Vowel Sounds', *Journal of the Acoustical Society of America* 24: 533–4.

FOWLER, C. (1980). 'Coarticulation and Theories of Extrinsic Timing Control', *Journal of Phonetics* 8: 113–33.

FRIJDA, N. (1986). *The Emotions*. London: Cambridge University Press.

——(1988). 'The Laws of Emotion', *American Psychologist* 43: 349–58.

——(1993). 'Moods, Emotion Episodes, and Emotions', in M. Lewis and J. Haviland-Jones (eds.), *Handbook of Emotions*. New York: Guilford Press, 381–403.

——(2000). 'The Psychologists' Point of View', in M. Lewis and J. Haviland-Jones (eds.), *Handbook of Emotions*. New York: Guilford Press, 59–74.

——MANSTEAD, S., AND BENN, S. (2000). 'The Influence of Emotions on Beliefs', in N. Frijda, S. Manstead, and S. Benn (eds.), *Emotions and Beliefs*. Paris: Cambridge University Press, 144–70.

FRY, D. (1955). 'Duration and Intensity as Physical Correlates of Linguistic Stress', *Journal of the Acoustical Society of America* 27: 765–8.

——(1958). 'Experiments in the Perception of Stress', *Language and Speech* 1: 126–52.

GAINOTTI, G. (2000). 'Neuropsychological Theories of Emotion', in J. Borod (ed.), *The Neuropsychology of Emotion*. Oxford: Oxford University Press, 214–35.

GEORGE, M., KETTER, T., KIMBRELL, T., SPEER, A., LORBERBAUM, J., LIBERATORS, C., NAHAS, Z., AND POST, R. (2000). 'Neuroimaging Approaches to the Study of Emotion', in J. Borod (ed.), *The Neuropsychology of Emotion*. Oxford: Oxford University Press, 106–34.

GIMSON, A. C. (1967). *An Introduction to the Pronunciation of English*. London: Arnold.

GOBL, C., BENNETT, E., AND NÍ CHASAIDE, A. (2002). 'Expressive Synthesis: How Crucial is Voice Quality?', *Proceedings of the IEEE Workshop on Speech Synthesis*, Santa Monica: CD-rom.

GOLDSMITH, H. (1993). 'Temperament: Variability in Developing Emotion Systems', in M. Lewis and J. Haviland-Jones (eds.), *Handbook of Emotions*. New York: Guilford Press, 353–64.

GRAY, J. (1994). 'Three Fundamental Emotions Systems', in P. Ekman and R. Davidson (eds.), *The Nature of Emotion: Fundamental Questions*. Oxford: Oxford University Press, 243–7.

GREENBERG, L. (1993). 'Emotion and Change Processes in Psychotherapy', in M. Lewis and J. Haviland-Jones (eds.), *Handbook of Emotions*. New York: Guilford Press, 499–508.

GUSSENHOVEN, C. (1986). 'English Plosive Allophones and Ambisyllabicity', *Gramma* 10: 119–41.

HANSON, H., AND STEVENS, K. (2002). 'A Quasi-articulatory Approach to Controlling Acoustic Source Parameters in a Klatt-type Formant Synthesizer Using HLsyn', *Journal of the Acoustical Society of America*: 1158–82.

HARDCASTLE, W., AND HEWLETT, N. (1999). *Coarticulation: Theory, Data and Techniques*. Cambridge: Cambridge University Press.

HARRÉ, R., AND PARROTT, W. (1996). *The Emotions: Social, Cultural, and Physical Dimensions of the Emotions*. London: Sage.

HAYES, B. (1995). *Metrical Stress Theory: Principles and Case Studies*. Chicago: University of Chicago Press.

HEBB, D. (1946). 'Emotion in Man and Animal: An Analysis of the Intuitive Processes of Recognition', *Psychological Review* 53: 88–106.

HEUFT, B., PORTELE, T., AND RAUTH, M. (1996). 'Emotions in Time Domain Synthesis', *Proceedings of ICLSP*, Philadelphia, 1974–7.

HOLMES, J. (1988). *Speech Synthesis and Recognition*. Wokingham: Van Nostrand Reinhold.

—— AND HOLMES, W. (2001). *Speech Synthesis and Recognition*. London: Taylor & Francis.

—— MATTINGLY, I., AND SHEARME, J. (1964). 'Speech Synthesis by Rule', *Language and Speech* 7: 127–43.

IIDA, A., CAMPBELL, N., IGA, S., HIGUCHI, F., AND YASUMURA, M. (2000). 'A Speech Synthesis System for Assisting Communication', *Proceedings of the International Speech Communication Association Workshop on Speech and Emotion*, Belfast: CD-rom. Also revised as (2003). 'A Corpus-Based Speech Synthesis System with Emotion', *Speech Communication* 40: 161–88.

—— IGA, S., HIGUCHI, F., CAMPBELL, N., AND YASUMURA, M. (1998). 'Acoustic Nature and Perceptual Testing of a Corpus of Emotional Speech', *Proceedings of ICLSP*, Sydney: 1559–92.

IZARD, C. (1977). *Human Emotions*. New York: Plenum.
—— (1992). 'Basic Emotions, Relations Among Emotions, and Emotion–Cognition Relationships', *Psychological Review* 99: 561–5.
—— (1993). 'Organization and Motivational Functions of Discrete Emotions', in M. Lewis and J. Haviland-Jones (eds.), *Handbook of Emotions*. New York: Guilford Press, 631–41.
JACKENDOFF, R. (2002). *Foundations of Language: Brain, Meaning, Grammar, Evolution*. Oxford: Oxford University Press.
JAKOBSON, R., FANT, C., AND HALLE, M. (1952). *Preliminaries to Speech Analysis*. Technical Report 13, Acoustics Laboratory, Massachusetts Institute of Technology. Repr. Cambridge, Mass.: MIT Press, 1963.
JAMES, W. (1884). 'What is an Emotion?', *Mind* 9: 188–205.
JASSEM, W., HILL, D., AND WITTEN, I. (1984). 'Isochrony in English Speech: Its Statistical Validity and Linguistic Relevance', in D. Gibbon and H. Richter (eds.), *Intonation, Accent and Rhythm*. Berlin: de Gruyter, 203–25.
JENKINS, J., OATLEY, K., AND STEIN, N. (1998). 'History and Culture', in J. Jenkins, K. Oatley, and N. Stein (eds.), *Human Emotions: A Reader*. Oxford: Blackwell, 7–12.
JIANG, J., ALWAN, A., BERNSTEIN, L., AUER, E., AND KEATING, P. (2002). 'Predicting Face Movements from Speech Acoustics Using Spectral Dynamics', *ICMA Proceedings*, Lausanne, 181–4.
JOHNSON, W., NARAYANAN, S., WITNEY, R., DAS, R., BULUT, M., AND LABORE, C. (2002). 'Limited Domain Synthesis of Expressive Military Speech for Animated Characters', *Proceedings of the IEEE Workshop on Speech Synthesis*, Santa Monica: CD-rom.
JOHNSON-LAIRD, P., AND OATLEY, K. (1992). 'Basic Emotions, Rationality, and Folk Theory', *Cognition and Emotion* 6: 201–23.
JOHNSTONE, T., BANSE, R., AND SCHERER, K. (1995). 'Acoustic Profiles in Prototypical Vocal Expressions of Emotion', *Proceedings of the International Conference of the Phonetic Sciences*, Stockholm: 2–5.
—— AND SCHERER, K. (2000). 'Vocal Communication of Emotion', in M. Lewis and J. Haviland-Jones (eds.), *Handbook of Emotions*. New York: Guilford Press, 220–35.
—— VAN REEKUM, C., AND SCHERER, K. (2001). 'Vocal Expression Correlates of Appraisal Processes', in K. Scherer, A. Schorr, and T. Johnstone (eds.), *Appraisal Processes in Emotion*. Oxford: Oxford University Press, 271–84.

KAHN, D. (1976). 'Syllable-Based Generalizations in English Phonology'. Ph.D. dissertation, Massachusetts Institute of Technology. Published New York: Garland, 1980.

KEATING, P., AND SHATTUCK-HUFNAGEL, S. (2002). 'A Prosodic View of Word Form Encoding for Speech Production', *Working Papers in Phonetics* 101. Los Angeles: University of California, 112–56.

KLATT, D. (1979). 'Synthesis by Rule of Segmental Durations in English Sentences', in B. Lindblom and S. Ohman (eds.), *Frontiers of Speech Communication*. New York: Academic Press, 287–99.

——(1980). 'Software for a Cascade/Parallel Formant Synthesizer', *Journal of the Acoustical Society of America* 67: 971–95.

——AND KLATT, L. (1990). 'Analysis, Synthesis, and Perception of Voice Quality Variations among Female and Male Talkers', *Journal of the Acoustical Society of America* 87: 820–57.

LADD, D. (1984). 'Declination: A Review and Some Hypotheses', *Phonology Yearbook* 1: 53–74.

——SILVERMAN, K., TOLKMITT, F., BERGMAN, G., AND SCHERER, K. (1985). 'Evidence for the Independent Function of Intonation Contour Type, Voice Quality, and f0 Range in Signalling Speaker Affect', *Journal of the Acoustical Society of America* 78: 435–44.

LADEFOGED, P. (1971). *Preliminaries to Linguistic Phonetics*. Chicago: University of Chicago Press.

——(1996). *Elements of Acoustic Phonetics*. Chicago: University of Chicago Press.

——AND MADDIESON, I. (1996). *The Sounds of the World's Languages*. Oxford: Blackwell.

LANE, R., NADEL, L., ALLEN, J., AND KASZNIAK, A. (2000). 'The Study of Emotion from the Perspective of Cognitive Neuroscience', in R. Lane and L. Nadel (eds.), *The Cognitive Neuroscience of Emotion*. Oxford: Oxford University Press, 3–23.

LAVER, J. (1980). *The Phonetic Description of Voice Quality*. Cambridge: Cambridge University Press.

——(1994). *Principles of Phonetics*. Cambridge: Cambridge University Press.

——AND HANSON, R. (1981). 'Describing the Normal Voice', in J. Darby (ed.), *Speech Evaluation in Psychiatry*. New York: Grune & Stratton, 51–78.

LAWRENCE, W. (1953). 'The Synthesis of Speech from Signals Which Have a Low Information Rate', in W. Jackson (ed.), *Communication Theory*. New York: Butterworth.

LAZARUS, R. (1991). *Emotion and Adaptation*. Oxford: Oxford University Press.
—— (1992). 'Thoughts on the Relation between Emotion and Cognition', *American Psychologist*, 37: 1019–24.
—— (1999). 'The Cognition–Emotion Debate: A Bit of History', in T. Dalgleish and M. Power (eds.), *Handbook of Cognition and Emotion*. Chichester: Wiley 3–19.
—— (2001). 'Relational Meaning and Discrete Emotions', in K. Scherer, A. Schorr, and T. Johnstone (eds.), *Appraisal Processes in Emotion*. Oxford: Oxford University Press, 37–69.
LEDOUX, J. (1996). *The Emotional Brain*. New York: Simon & Schuster.
—— (2000). 'Cognitive–Emotional Interactions: Listen to the Brain', in R. Lane and L. Nadel (eds.), *Cognitive Neuroscience of Emotion*. Oxford: Oxford University Press.
—— AND PHELPS, E. (2000). 'Emotional Networks in the Brain', in M. Lewis and J. Haviland-Jones (eds.), *Handbook of Emotions*. New York: Guilford Press, 157–72.
LEHISTE, I. (1977). 'Isochrony Reconsidered', *Journal of Phonetics* 5: 253–63.
LEVENSON, R. (1992). 'Autonomic Nervous System Differences among Emotions', *Psychological Science* 3: 23–7.
LEVENTHAL, H. (1984). 'A Perceptual Motor Theory of Emotion', in K. Scherer and P. Ekman (eds.), *Approaches to Emotion*. Hillsdale, NJ: Erlbaum, 271–92.
—— AND PATRICK-MILLER, L. (1993). 'Emotion and Illness: The Mind is in the Body', in M. Lewis and J. Haviland-Jones (eds.), *Handbook of Emotions*. New York: Guilford Press, 365–80.
—— AND SCHERER, K. (1987). 'The Relationship of Emotion to Cognition: a Relational Approach to a Semantic Controversy', *Cognition and Emotion* 1: 3–28.
LEWIS, M. (1993). 'The Emergence of Human Emotions', in M. Lewis and J. Haviland-Jones (eds.), *Handbook of Emotions*. New York: Guilford Press, 223–5.
—— SULLIVAN, M., STANGER, C., AND WEISS, M. (1998). 'Self Development and Self-Conscious Emotions', in J. Jenkins, K. Oatley, and N. Stein (eds.), *Human Emotions: A Reader*. Oxford: Blackwell, 159–67. Originally pub. in *Child Development* 60 (1989): 146–8, 150–2, 153–5.
LEWIS, E., AND TATHAM, M. (1991). 'SPRUCE: a New Text-to-Speech Synthesis System', *Proceedings of Eurospeech*, Genoa: 976–81.

LIEBERMAN, P., AND BLUMSTEIN, S. (1988). *Speech Physiology, Speech Perception and Acoustic Phonetics*. Cambridge: Cambridge University Press.

MCCLELLAND, J., AND RUMELHART, D. (eds.) (1986). *Parallel Distributed Processing: Exploration in the Microstructure of Cognition*. Cambridge, Mass.: MIT Press.

MACLEAN, P. (1990). *The Triune Brain*. New York: Plenum Press.

MACNEILAGE, P., AND DECLERK, J. (1969). 'On the Motor Control of Coarticulation in CVC Monosyllables', *Journal of the Acoustical Society of America* 45: 1217–33.

MANDLER, G. (1999). 'Emotion', in B. Bly and D. Rumelhart (eds.), *Cognitive Science*. London: Academic Press, 367–84.

MARR, D. (1982). *Vision: A Computational Investigation into the Human Representation and Processing of Visual Information*. San Francisco: Freeman.

MARUMOTO, T., AND CAMPBELL, N. (2000). 'Control of Speaking Types for Emotion in a Speech Re-sequencing System' [in Japanese], *Proceedings of the Acoustic Society of Japan*: 213–14.

MASAKI, M., KASHIOKA, H., AND CAMPBELL, N. (2002). 'Modeling the Timing Characteristics of Different Speaking Styles', *Proceedings of the IEEE Workshop on Speech Synthesis*, Santa Monica: CD-rom.

MASSARO, D., AND EGAN, P. (1996). 'Perceiving Affect from the Voice and the Face', *Psychonomic Bulletin and Review* 3: 215–21.

MATTINGLY, I. (1968). *Synthesis by Rule of General American English: Supplement to Status Report on Speech Research*. New York: Haskins Laboratories.

MONTERO, J., GUTIERREZ-ARRIOLA, J., PALAZUELOS, S., ENRIQUEZ, E., AGUILERA, S., AND PARDO, J. M. (1998). 'Emotional Speech Synthesis: From Speech Database to TTs', *Proceedings of the International Conference on Spoken Language Processing*, Sydney: 923–6.

MORTON, K. (1986). 'Cognitive Phonetics: Some of the Evidence', in R. Channon and L. Shockey (eds.), *In Honor of Ilse Lehiste*. Dordrecht: Foris, 191–4.

——(1996). 'Spoken Language and Speech Synthesis in CSCW', in J. H. Connolly and L. Pemberton (eds.), *Linguistics Concepts and Methods in CSCW*. London: Springer, 23–33.

——AND TATHAM, M. (1980). 'Production Instructions'. *Occasional Papers* 23, University of Essex: 104–16.

————(1995). 'Pragmatic Effects in Speech Synthesis'. *Proceedings of EuroSpeech*, Madrid: 1819–22.

—— —— AND LEWIS, E. (1999). 'A New Intonation Model for Text-to-Speech Synthesis', *Proceedings of the International Congress of Phonetic Sciences*, San Francisco: 85–8.

MOULINES, E., AND CHARPENTIER, F. (1990). 'Pitch Synchronous Waveform Processing Techniques for Text-to-Speech Synthesis Using Diphones', *Speech Communication* 9: 453–67.

MOZZICONACCI, S. (1995). 'Pitch Variation and Emotions in Speech', *Proceedings of the International Conference of the Phonetic Sciences*, Stockholm: 178–81.

—— AND HERMES, D. (1999). 'Role of Intonation Patterns in Conveying Emotion in Speech', *Proceedings of the International Conference of the Phonetic Sciences*, San Francisco: 2001–4.

MURRAY, I., AND ARNOTT, J. (1993). 'Toward the Simulation of Emotion in Synthetic Speech: A Review of the Literature on Human Vocal Emotion', *Journal of the Acoustical Society of America* 93: 1097–108.

—— —— (1995). 'Implementation and Testing of a System for Producing Emotion-by-Rule in Synthetic Speech', *Speech Communication* 16: 369–90.

NIEDENTHAL, P., HALBERSTADT, J., AND INNES-KER, A. (1999). 'Emotional Response Categorization', *Psychological Review* 106 (2): 337–61.

OATLEY, K., AND JOHNSON-LAIRD, P. (1987). 'Toward a Cognitive Theory of Emotion', *Cognition and Emotion* 1: 29–50.

—— —— (1998). 'The Communicative Theory of Emotions', in J. Jenkins, K. Oatley, and N. Stein (eds.), *Human Emotions: A Reader*. Oxford: Blackwell, 84–97. Originally pub. in L. Martin and A. Tesser (eds.), *Striving and Feeling: Interactions Among Goals, Affect, and Self-Regulation*, Hillsdale, NJ: Erlbaum, 1996, 363–6, 372–80.

OCHSNER, K., AND BARRETT, L. (2001). 'A Multiprocess Perspective on the Neuroscience of Emotion', in T. Mayne and G. Bonanno (eds.), *Emotions and Current Issues*. London: Guildford Press, 38–81.

—— AND KOSSLYN, S. (1999). 'The Cognitive Neuroscience Approach', in B. Bly and D. Rumelhart (eds.), *Cognitive Science*. London: Academic Press, 319–65.

OGDEN, R., HAWKINS, S., HOUSE, J., HUCKVALE, M., LOCAL, J., CARTER, P., DANKOVIOVÁ J., AND HEID, S. (2000). 'ProSynth: An Integrated Prosodic Approach to Device-Independent, Natural-Sounding Speech Synthesis', *Computer Speech and Language* 14: 177–210.

OHALA, J. J. (1984). 'An Ethological Perspective on Common Cross-Language Utilization of f0 of Voice', *Phonetica* 41: 1–16.

OHMAN, A., FLYKT, A., AND ESTEVES, F. (2001). 'Emotion Drives Attention: Detecting the Snake in the Grass'. *Journal of Experimental Psychology: General* 130: 466–78.

ÖHMAN, S. (1966). 'Coarticulation in VCV Utterances: Spectrographic Measurements', *Journal of the Acoustical Society of America* 39: 151–68.

O'KEEFE, J., AND NADEL, L. (1978). *The Hippocampus as a Cognitive Map*. Oxford: Clarendon Press.

ORTONY, A., CLORE, G., AND COLLINS, A. (1988). *The Cognitive Structure of Emotions*. Cambridge: Cambridge University Press.

—— AND TURNER, T. (1990). 'What's Basic About Basic Emotions?', *Psychological Review* 97: 315–31.

O'SHAUGHNESSY, D. (1987). *Speech Communication: Human and Machine*. Reading, Mass.: Addison-Wesley.

PAESCHKE, A., KIENAST, M., AND SENDLMEIER, W. (1999). 'f0-contours in Emotional Speech', *Proceedings of the International Conference of the Phonetic Sciences*, San Francisco: 929–32.

—— AND SENDLMEIER, W. (2000). 'Prosodic Characteristics of Emotional Speech: Measurements of Fundamental Frequency Movements', *Proceedings of the International Speech Communication Association Workshop on Speech and Emotion*, Belfast: CD-rom.

PANKSEPP, J. (1991). 'Affective Neuroscience: A Conceptual Framework for the Neurobiological Study of Emotions', in K. Strongman (ed.), *International Review of Studies on Emotion* 1: 59–99.

—— (1994). 'The Basics of Basic Emotion', in P. Ekman and R. Davidson (eds.), *The Nature of Emotion: Fundamental Questions*. Oxford: Oxford University Press, 20–4.

—— (1998). *Affective Neuroscience: The Foundations of Human and Animal Emotions*. Oxford: Oxford University Press.

—— (2000). 'Emotions as Natural Kinds within the Mammalian Brain', in M. Lewis and J. Haviland-Jones (eds.), *Handbook of Emotions*. New York: Guilford Press, 137–56.

—— AND MILLER A. (1996). 'Emotions and the Aging Brain', in C. Magai and S. McFadden (eds.), *Handbook of Emotion, Adult Development, and Aging*. London: Academic Press, 3–26.

PECCHINENDA, A. (2001). 'The Psychophysiology of Appraisals', in K. Scherer, A. Schorr, and T. Johnstone (eds.), *Appraisal Processes in Emotion*. Oxford: Oxford University Press, 301–14.

PETERSON, G., AND BARNEY, H. (1952). 'Control Methods Used in a Study of the Vowels', *Journal of the Acoustical Society of America* 24: 175–84.

PICARD, R. (1997). *Affective Computing*. Cambridge, Mass.: MIT Press.
PIERREHUMBERT, J. (1980). 'The Phonetics and Phonology of English Intonation'. Ph.D. thesis, Massachusetts Institute of Technology. Repr. Bloomington: Indiana University Linguistics Club, 1987.
—— (1981). 'Synthesizing Intonation', *Journal of the Acoustical Society of America* 70: 985–95.
PISONI, D., AND LAZARUS, J. (1974). 'Categorical and Noncategorical Modes of Speech Perception along the Voicing Continuum', *Journal of the Acoustical Society of America* 55: 328–33.
PLUTCHIK, R. (1984). 'Emotions; A General Psychoevolutionary Theory', in K. Scherer and P. Ekman (eds.), *Approaches to Emotion*. Hillsdale, NJ: Erlbaum, 197–219.
—— (1993). 'Emotions and their Vicissitudes: Emotion and Psychopathology', in M. Lewis and J. Haviland-Jones (eds.), *Handbook of Emotions*. New York: Guilford Press, 53–66.
—— (1994). *The Psychology and Biology of Emotion*. New York: HarperCollins.
POLZIN, T., AND WAIBEL, A. (2000). 'Emotion-Sensitive Human–Computer Interfaces', *Proceedings of the International Speech Communication Association Workshop on Speech and Emotion*, Belfast: CD-rom.
PRIBHAM, K. (1980). 'The Biology of Emotions and Other Feelings', in R. Plutchik and H. Kellerman (eds.), *Emotion Theory, Research, and Experience* 1: *Theories of Emotion*. New York: Academic Press, 245–69.
PRUDON, R., D'ALESSANDRO, C., AND BOULA DE MAREÜIL, P. (2002). 'Prosody Synthesis by Unit Selection and Transplantation on Diphones', *Proceedings of the IEEE Workshop on Speech Synthesis*, Santa Monica: CD-rom.
RANK, E., AND PIRKER, H. (1998). 'Generating Emotional Speech with a Concatenative Synthesizer', *Proceedings of ICLSP*, Sydney: 671–4.
REEVES, B., AND NASS, C. (1996). *The Media Equation*. Stanford: CSLI.
ROLLS, E. (1999). *The Brain and Emotion*. Oxford: Oxford University Press.
—— —— AND TREVES, A. (1998). *Neural Networks and Brain Function*. New York: Oxford University Press.
ROSEMAN, I., AND SMITH, C. (2001). 'Appraisal Theory: Overview, Assumptions, Varieties, Controversies', in K. Scherer, A. Schorr, and T. Johnstone (eds.), *Appraisal Processes in Emotion*. Oxford: Oxford University Press, 3–19.

RUSSELL, J. (1997). 'How Shall an Emotion be Called?', in R. Plutchik and H. Conte (eds.), *Circumplex Models of Personality and Emotions*. Washington: APA, 205–20.

SAMENGO, I. AND TREVES, A. (2001). 'Representational Capacity of a Set of Independent Neurons', *Physical Review E* 63: 11,910–24.

SCARPA, A., AND RAINE, A. (2000). 'Violence Associated with Anger and Impulsivity', in J. Borod (ed.), *The Neuropsychology of Emotion*. Oxford: Oxford University Press, 320–39.

SCHERER, K. (1974). 'Acoustic Concomitants of Emotional Dimensions: Judging Affect from Synthesised Tone Sequence', in E. Weitz (ed.), *Non Verbal Communication: Readings with Commentary*. New York: Oxford University Press, 105–11.

—— (1981). 'Speech and Emotional States', in J. Darby (ed.), *Speech Evaluation in Psychiatry*. New York: Grune & Stratton, 189–220.

—— (1985). 'Vocal Affect Signalling: A Comparative Approach', in J. Rosenblatt, C. Beer, M. Busnel, and P. Slater (eds.), *Advances in the Study of Behavior*. New York: Academic Press, 198–244.

—— (1986). 'Vocal Affect Expression: A Review and a Model for Future Research', *Psychological Bulletin* 99: 143–65.

—— (1993). 'Neuroscience Projections to Current Debates in Emotion Psychology', *Cognition and Emotion* 7: 1–41.

—— (1995). 'How Emotion is Expressed in Speech and Singing', *Proceedings of the International Congress of Phonetic Sciences*, Stockholm: 90–6.

—— (1996). 'Adding the Affective Dimension: A New Look in Speech Analysis and Synthesis', *Proceedings of the International Conference on Spoken Language Processing*, Philadelphia, 1014–17.

—— (1999). 'Appraisal Theory', in T. Dalgleish and M. Power (eds.), *Handbook of Cognition and Emotion*. Chichester: Wiley, 637–58.

—— (2000). 'Emotions as Episodes of Subsystem Synchronization Driven by Nonlinear Appraisal Processes', in M. Lewis, and I. Granic (eds.), *Emotion, Development, and Self-Organization: Dynamic Systems Approaches to Emotional Development*. Cambridge: Cambridge University Press, 70–99.

—— (2001). 'The Nature and Study of Appraisal: A Review of the Issues', in K. Scherer, A. Schorr, and T. Johnstone (eds.), *Appraisal Processes in Emotion*. Oxford: Oxford University Press, 369–91.

SCHLOSBERG, H. (1954). 'Three Dimensions of Emotion', *Psychological Review* 61: 81–8.

SCHORR, A. (2001). 'Subjective Measurement in Appraisal Research', in K. Scherer, A. Schorr, and T. Johnstone (eds.), *Appraisal Processes in Emotion*. Oxford: Oxford University Press, 331–49.

SCHRÖDER, M. (1999). 'Can Emotions be Synthesized without Controlling Voice Quality?', *Phonus: Research Report of the Institute of Phonetics*, University of the Saarland 4: 37–55.

—— (2000). 'Emotional Speech Synthesis: A Review', *Proceedings of the International Speech Communication Association Workshop on Speech and Emotion*, Belfast: CD-rom.

—— COWIE, R., DOUGLAS-COWIE, E., WESTERDIJK, M., AND GIELEN, S. (2000). 'Acoustic Correlates of Emotion Dimensions in View of Speech Synthesis', *Proceedings of the International Speech Communication Association Workshop on Speech and Emotion*, Belfast: CD-rom.

SCHRÖDINGER, E. (1944) repr. (2001). *What is Life?* Cambridge: Cambridge University Press.

SCHUMANN, J. (1999). 'A Neurobiological Basis for Decision Making in Language Pragmatics', *Pragmatics and Cognition* 7(2): 283–311.

SEDIKIDES, C. (2001). 'Glimpses of the Interplay Between Affect and Cognition', *Cognition and Emotion* 15 (1): 109–12

SILVERMAN, K., BECKMANN, M., PITRELLI, J., OSTENDORF, M., WIGHTMAN, C., PRICE, P., PIERREHUMBERT, J., AND HIRSCHBERG, J. (1992). 'ToBI: A Standard for Labeling English Prosody', *Proceedings of the International Conference on Spoken Language*, Banff: 867–70.

SOLOMON, R. (1993). 'The Philosophy of Emotion', in M. Lewis and J. Haviland-Jones (eds.), *Handbook of Emotions*. New York: Guilford Press, 3–15.

STAMPE, D. (1979). *A Dissertation on Natural Phonology*. New York: Garland.

STEVENS, K. (2002). 'Toward Formant Synthesis with Articulatory Controls', in *Proceedings of the IEEE Workshop on Speech Synthesis*, Santa Monica: CD-rom.

STEVENS, K., AND BICKLEY, C. (1991). 'Constraints among Parameters Simplify Control of Klatt Formant Synthesizer', *Journal of Phonetics* 19: 161–74.

—— AND HALLE, M. (1967). 'Remarks on Analysis by Synthesis and Distinctive Features', in W. Wathen-Dunn (ed.), *Models for the Perception of Speech and Visual Form*. Cambridge, Mass.: MIT Press, 88–102.

STIBBARD, R. (2001). 'Vocal Expression of Emotions in Non-Laboratory Speech'. Ph.D. thesis, University of Reading.

STRANGE, W., AND JENKINS, J. (1978). 'The Role of Linguistic Experience in the Perception of Speech', in R. Walk and H. Pick (eds.), *Perception and Experience*. New York: Plenum Press, 125–69.

STRONGMAN, K. (1996). 'Emotion and Memory', in C. Magai and S. McFadden (eds.), *Handbook of Emotion, Adult Development, and Aging*. London: Academic Press, 133–59.

'T HART, J., COLLIER, R., AND COHEN, A. (1990). *A Perceptual Study of Intonation: An Experimental Phonetic Approach to Speech Melody*. Cambridge: Cambridge University Press.

TAMS, A., AND TATHAM, M. (1995). 'Describing Speech Styles Using Prosody', *Proceedings of EuroSpeech*, Madrid: 2081–4.

TARTTER, V. (1980). 'Happy Talk: Perceptual and Acoustic Effects of Smiling on Speech', *Perception and Psychophysics* 27: 24–7.

—— AND BRAUN, D. (1994). 'Hearing Smiles and Frowns in Normal and Whisper Registers', *Journal of the Acoustical Society of America* 96: 2101–7.

TATHAM, M. (1970a). 'Articulatory Speech Synthesis by Rule: Implementation of a Theory of Speech Production', *Report CN-534.1*. Washington: National Science Foundation. Also in *Working Papers*, Computer and Information Science Research Center, Ohio State University, 1970.

—— (1970b). 'Speech Synthesis: A Critical Review of the State of the Art', *International Journal of Man–Machine Studies* 2: 303–8.

—— (1971). 'Classifying Allophones'. *Language and Speech* 14: 140–5.

—— (1986a). 'Towards a Cognitive Phonetics', *Journal of Phonetics* 12: 37–47.

—— (1986b). 'Cognitive Phonetics: Some of the Theory', in R. Channon, and L. Shockey (eds.), *In Honor of Ilse Lehiste*. Dordrecht: Foris, 271–6.

—— (1990). 'Cognitive Phonetics', in W. A. Ainsworth (ed.), *Advances in Speech, Hearing and Language Processing* 1. London: JAI Press, 193–218.

—— (1994). 'The Supervision of Speech Production: An Issue in Speech Theory', *Proceedings of the Institute of Acoustics* 16: 171–82.

—— (1995). 'The Supervision of Speech Production', in C. Sorin, J. Mariani, H. Meloni, and J. Schoentgen (eds.), *Levels in Speech Communication: Relations and Interactions*. Amsterdam: Elsevier, 115–25.

—— AND LEWIS, E. (1992). 'Prosodic Assignment in SPRUCE Text-to-Speech Synthesis', *Proceedings of the UK Institute of Acoustics* 14: 447–54

—— —— (1999). 'Syllable Reconstruction in Concatenated Waveform Speech Synthesis'. *Proceedings of the International Congress of Phonetic Sciences*, San Francisco: 2303–6.

—— AND MORTON, K. (1972). 'Electromyographic and Intraoral Air Pressure Studies of Bilabial Stops', *Occasional Papers* 12. University of Essex.

—— —— (1995). 'Speech Synthesis in Dialogue Systems'. *ESCA Workshop on Spoken Dialogue Systems*, Visgø: 221–5.

—— —— (2002). 'Computational Modelling of Speech Production: English Rhythm', in A. Braun and H. R. Masthoff (eds.), *Phonetics and Its Applications. Festschrift for Jens-Peter Köster on the Occasion of his 60th Birthday*. Stuttgart: Steiner, 383–405.

—— —— (2003). 'Data Structures in Speech Production', *Journal of the International Phonetics Association* 33.

—— —— AND LEWIS, E. (2000). 'SPRUCE: Speech Synthesis for Dialogue Systems', in M. M. Taylor, F. Néel, and D. G. Bouwhuis (eds.), *The Structure of Multimodal Dialogue II*. Amsterdam: Benjamins, 271–92.

TAYLOR, P., BLACK, A., AND CALEY, R. (1998). 'The Architecture of the Festival Speech Synthesis System', *European Speech Communication Association Workshop on Speech Synthesis*, Jenolan Caves: 147–51.

TOATES, F. (2001). 'Emotion', in *Biological Psychology: An Integrative Approach*. Harlow: Pearson, 318–43.

TOMKINS, S. (1962). *Affect, Imagery, Consciousness* 1: *The Positive Affects*. New York: Springer.

TREVES, A., AND SAMENGO, I. (2002). 'Standing on the Gateway to Memory: Shouldn't We Step in?', *Cognitive Neuropsychology* 19(6): 557–75.

TUCKER, D., DERRYBERRY, D., AND LUU, P. (2000). 'Anatomy and Physiology of Human Emotion: Vertical Integration of Brain Stem, Limbic, and Cortical Systems', in J. Borod (ed.), *The Neuropsychology of Emotion*. Oxford: Oxford University Press, 56–79.

VAN SANTEN, J., AND NIU, X. (2002). 'Prediction and Synthesis of Prosodic Effects on Spectral Balance', *Proceedings of the IEEE Workshop on Speech Synthesis*, Santa Monica: CD-rom.

VANNER, G., LACHERET-DUJOUR, A., AND VERGNE, J. (1999). 'Pause Location and Duration Calculated with Syntactic Dependencies and

Textual Consideration for a TTS System', *Proceedings of the International Congress on Spoken Language Processing*, San Francisco: 1569–72.

WEHRLE, T., AND SCHERER, K. (2001). 'Toward Computational Modeling of Appraisal Theories', in K. Scherer, A. Schorr, and T. Johnstone (eds.), *Appraisal Processes in Emotion*. Oxford: Oxford University Press, 350–68.

WELLS, J. C. (1982). *Accents of English*. Cambridge: Cambridge University Press.

WERNER, E., AND HAGGARD, M. (1969). 'Articulatory Synthesis by Rule', *Speech Synthesis and Perception: Progress Report* 1. Psychological Laboratory, University of Cambridge.

WHYBROW, P. (1998). *A Mood Apart*. New York: HarperPerennial.

WIERZBICKA, A. (1992). 'Talking About Emotions: Semantics, Culture, and Cognition', *Cognition and Emotion* 6(3/4): 285–319.

WILSHAW, D., AND BUCKINGHAM, J. (1990). 'An Assessment of Marr's Theory of the Hippocampus as a Temporary Memory Store', *Philosophical Transactions of the Royal Society of London B* 329: 205–15.

WOLPERT, L. (1999). *Malignant Sadness*. London: Faber & Faber.

World Wide Web Consortium: *www.w3c.org*.

WOUTERS, J., AND MACON, M. (2002a). 'Effects of Prosodic Factors on Spectral Dynamics, I: Analysis', *Journal of the Acoustical Society of America* 111: 417–27.

———— (2002b). 'Effects of Prosodic Factors on Spectral Dynamics, II: Synthesis', *Journal of the Acoustical Society of America* 111: 428–38.

WUNDT, W. (1902) (repr. 1998). *Principles of Physiological Psychology*. Bristol: Thoemmeso.

YOUNG, S., AND FALLSIDE, F. (1979). 'Speech Synthesis from Concept: A Method for Speech Output from Information Systems', *Journal of the Acoustical Society of America* 66: 685–95.

ZAJONC, R. (1980). 'Feeling and Thinking: Preferences Need no Inferences', *American Psychologist* 35: 151–75.

—— (1989). 'Feeling and Facial Efference; Implications of the Vascular Theory of Emotion', *Psychological Review* 96: 395–416.

Bibliography

During the last ten to fifteen years, a number of collections have been published. A few are listed here which might prove useful for speech researchers.

BLY, B., AND RUMELHART, D. (eds.) (1999). *Cognitive Science*. London: Academic Press
BORDEN, G., HARRIS, K., AND RAPHAEL, L. (1994). *Speech Science Primer: Physiology, Acoustics, and Perception of Speech*, 3rd edn. Baltimore: Williams & Wilkins.
BOROD, J. (ed.) (2000). *The Neuropsychology of Emotion*. Oxford: Oxford University Press.
DALGLEISH, T., AND POWER, M. (1999). *Handbook of Cognition and Emotion*. Chichester: Wiley.
DAMASIO, A. (1994). *Descartes' Error*. New York: Putnam's.
EKMAN, P., AND DAVIDSON, R. (eds.) (1994). *The Nature of Emotion: Fundamental Questions*. Oxford: Oxford University Press.
EYSENCK, M., AND KEANE, M. (1999). *Cognitive Psychology: A Student's Handbook*, 3rd edn. Hove: Taylor & Francis.
FORGAS, J. (ed.) (2000). *Feeling and Thinking: The Role of Affect in Social Cognition*. Cambridge: Cambridge University Press.
FRIJDA, N., MANSTEAD, S., AND BENN, S. (eds.), *Emotions and Beliefs*. Paris: Cambridge University Press.
GAZZANIGA, M. (ed.) (1999). *The New Cognitive Neurosciences*, 2nd edn. Cambridge, Mass: MIT Press.
—— IVRY, R., AND MANGUN, G. (1998). *Cognitive Neuroscience: the Biology of the Mind*. New York: Norton.
GRUNDY, P. (2000). *Doing Pragmatics*. London: Arnold.
HARRÉ, R., AND PARROTT, W. (eds.) (1996). *The Emotions: Social, Cultural and Biological Dimensions*. London: Sage.
JENKINS, J., OATLEY, K., AND STEIN, N. (eds.) (1998). *Human Emotions: A Reader*. Oxford: Blackwell.
LAKOFF, G., AND JOHNSON, M. (1999). *Philosophy in the Flesh: The Embodied Mind and its Challenge to Western Thought*. New York: Basic Books.
LANE, R., AND NADEL, L. (eds.) (2000). *The Cognitive Neuroscience of Emotion*. Oxford: Oxford University Press.

LeDoux, J. (1996). *The Emotional Brain*. New York: Simon & Schuster.
Lewis, M., and Haviland-Jones, J. (eds.) (1993). *Handbook of Emotions 1*. New York: Guilford Press.
—— —— (eds.) (2000). *Handbook of Emotions 2*. New York: Guilford Press.
Magai, C., and McFadden, S. (eds.) (1996). *Handbook of Emotion, Adult Development, and Aging*. London: Academic Press.
Mayne, T. and Bonanno, G. (eds.) (2001). *Emotions: Current Issues and Future Directions*. New York: Guilford Press.
Ortony, A., Clore, G., and Collins, A. (1988). *The Cognitive Structure of Emotions*. Cambridge: Cambridge University Press.
Plutchik, R., and Kellerman, H. (eds.) (1980). *Emotion Theory, Research, and Experience 1: Theories of Emotion*. New York: Academic Press.
Rakic, P., and Singer, W. (eds.) (1988). *Neurobiology of Neocortex*. New York: Wiley.
Scherer, K., and Ekman, P. (eds.) (1984). *Approaches to Emotion*. Hillsdale, NJ: Erlbaum.
—— Schorr, A., and Johnstone, T. (eds.) (2001). *Appraisal Processes in Emotion*. Oxford: Oxford University Press.
Searle, J. (1992). *Minds, Brains, Science*. Cambridge, Mass.: Harvard University Press.
Strongman, K. (ed.) (1991). *International Review of Studies on Emotion 1*. Chichester: Wiley.
Toates, F. (2001). *Biological Psychology: An Integrative Approach*. Harlow: Pearson.

Author Index

Abercrombie, D. 119, 247
Adolphs, R. 169, 176
Aitchison, J. 172
Allen, J. 30
Altova GmbH 304
Amir, N. 220
Arnott, J. 97, 105, 115, 252
Atal, B. 30
Aubergé, V. 222
Averill, J. 169, 170, 195, 202

Balkenius, C. 266
Barney, H. 226
Barrett, L. 169, 170
Bechtel, W. 169, 186
Benn, S. 411
Bickley, C. 240
Black, A. 32, 79
Blumstein, S. 101
Bly, B. 411
Bonanno, G. 411
Borden, G. 171, 411
Borod, J. 169, 175, 195, 411
Braun, D. 221
Bregman, A. 76
Browman, C. 21, 22, 209
Bruckert, E. 240
Buckingham, J. 185

Cacioppo, J. 175
Campbell, N. 32, 79, 128, 242
Carlson, R. 252
Cauldwell, R. 203, 231
Cawley, G. 120
Charpentier, J. 30, 31, 79, 82
Childers, D. 73
Chomsky, N. 172, 189, 321, 335
Clore, G. 169, 176, 177, 178, 191, 193, 411
Collins, A. 411
Cooke, M. 75
Cottingham, J. 410
Cowie, R. 154
Cruttenden, A. 189, 209

Dalgleish, T. 169, 170, 411
Damasio, A. 169, 176, 183, 222
Daniloff, R. 35
Darwin, C. 170
Davidson, R. 169, 173, 175, 178, 185, 192, 411
Davitz, J. 205
DeClerk, J. 119, 215
Deigh, J. 169
Descartes, R. 183

Egan, P. 271
Edgington, M. 127, 148
Ekman, P. 42, 169, 173, 178, 179, 192, 266, 411
Ellis, D. 75
Epstein, M. 244, 245
Eskenazi, M. 154, 226
Eysenck, M. 411

Fallside, F. 331
Fant, G. 214, 240, 246
Firth, J. 21
Flanagan, J. 35, 56
Forgas, J. 411
Fowler, C. 15, 22, 119
Friesen, W. 192
Frijda, N. 169, 170, 175, 178, 188, 189, 193, 411
Fry, D. 110

Gainotti, G. 169, 176
Gazzaniga, M. 411
George, M. 175
Gimson, A. 119, 209
Gobl, C. 246
Goldsmith, H. 170
Goldstein, L. 21, 209
Gray, J. 184
Green, A. 120
Greenberg, L. 188
Grundy, P. 411
Gussenhoven, C. 383

Haggard, M. 241
Halle, M. 189, 263, 335
Hanauer, S. 30
Hanson, H. 106, 240
Hardcastle, W. 79, 205
Harré, R. 169, 194, 202, 411
Harris, K. 411
Haviland-Jones, J. 411
Hayes, B. 21
Hebb, D. 170
Henriques, J. 175
Hermes, D. 131
Heuft, B. 148
Hewlett, N. 79, 205
Holmes, J. 28, 79, 119, 261
Holmes, W. 250, 261

Iida, A. 128
Ivry, R. 411
Izard, C. 103, 169, 188, 192

Jackendoff, R. 172
Jakobson, R. 189
James, W. 170
Jassem, W. 247
Jenkins, J. 194, 344
Jiang, J. 266
Johnson, M. 411
Johnson, W. 242
Johnson-Laird, P. 42, 104, 169, 170, 182, 190, 192
Johnstone, T. 169, 175, 181, 232, 411

Kahn, D. 383
Keane, M. 411
Keating, P. 355
Kellerman, H. 411
Klatt, D. 30, 239, 247, 252
Klatt, L. 252
Kosslyn, S. 185

Ladd, D. 216, 384, 385
Ladefoged, P. 171, 321, 334
Lakoff, G. 411
Lane, R. 169, 411
Laver, J. 98, 106, 222
Lawrence, W. 35
Lazarus, R. 42, 169, 170, 178, 180, 183, 189, 193, 298, 411
LeDoux, J. 169, 173, 184, 185, 186, 192, 196, 198
Lehiste, I. 247, 337
Lemaître, L. 22
Levenson, R. 173, 192
Leventhal, H. 169, 170, 177, 189
Lewis, E. 32, 79, 80, 244, 342, 367
Lewis, M. 179, 190, 313, 315, 411
Lieberman, P. 101

McClelland, J. 187
McFadden, S. 411
MacLean, P. 170, 280
MacNeilage, P. 119, 215
Macon, M. 244
Maddieson, I. 321
Magai, C. 411
Mandler, G. 169
Mangun, G. 411
Manstead, S. 411
Marr, D. 306
Marumoto, T. 128
Masaki, M. 248
Massaro, D. 271
Mattingly, I. 119
Mayne, T. 411
Miller, A. 280
Montero, J. 148
Moren, J. 266
Morton, K. 156, 160, 161, 181, 210, 247, 337, 360, 364, 367
Moulines, E. 30, 31, 79, 82
Mozziconacci, S. 131, 245
Mundale, J. 169, 186
Murray, I. 97, 105, 115, 252

Nadel, L. 184, 411
Nass, C. 266
Niedenthal, P. 177, 188
Niu, X. 245
Nord, L. 252

Oatley, K. 42, 104, 169, 170, 182, 190, 192, 411
Ochsner, K. 169, 170, 185
Ogden, R. 118
Ohala, J. 104
Ohman, A. 188, 266
Öhman, S. 119
O'Keefe, J. 184
Ortony, A. 104, 169, 176, 177, 180, 411
O'Shaughnessy, D. 214

Author Index

Paeschke, A. 225, 228
Panksepp, J. 169, 173–4, 185, 196, 280, 315
Parrott, W. 169, 202, 411
Patrick-Miller, L. 169, 170, 196, 280
Pecchinenda, A. 184
Peterson, G. 226
Phelps, E. 169
Picard, R. 261, 266
Pierrehumbert, J. 118, 244, 339
Pirker, H. 127, 148
Pisoni, D. 298
Plutchik, R. 42, 169, 190, 192, 206, 313, 411
Polzin, T. 266
Power, M. 169, 170, 411
Pribham, K. 169
Prudon, R. 249

Raine, A. 198, 220
Rakic, P. 411
Rank, E. 127, 148
Raphael, L. 411
Reeves, B. 266
Rolls, E. 169, 175, 186
Ron, S. 220
Roseman, I. 188
Rumelhart, D. 187, 411
Russell, J. 406

Samengo, I. 176, 186
Scarpa, A. 198, 220
Scherer, K. 102, 113, 148, 169, 175, 181, 183, 207, 232, 233, 245, 411
Schlosberg, H. 140
Schorr, A. 180, 411
Schröder, M. 126, 129, 146
Schrödinger, E. 187
Schumann, J. 176
Searle, J. 411
Sedikides, C. 176
Sendlmeier, W. 225
Shattuck-Hufnagel, S. 355
Shearme, J. 119

Silverman, K. 118, 129, 339
Singer, W. 411
Smith, C. 188
Solomon, R. 169, 170, 196
Stampe, D. 332, 362
Stein, N. 411
Stevens, K. 240, 263
Stibbard, R. 54, 202
Strange, W. 191, 344
Strongman, K. 169, 170, 411

't Hart, J. 56
Tams, A. 37
Tartter, V. 221
Tatham, M. 15, 26, 32, 79, 101, 118, 121, 156, 162, 209, 210, 255, 334, 337, 342, 360, 383
Taylor, P. 247, 342
Toates, F. 175, 411
Tomkins, S. 104, 169, 191
Treves, A. 175, 176, 186
Tucker, D. 185
Turner, T. 104

van Santen, J. 245
Vanner, G. 248

Waibel, A. 266
Wehrle, T. 182
Wells, J. 363
Werner, E. 241
Whybrow, P. 193
Wierzbicka, A. 193
Wilshaw, D. 185
Wolpert, L. 191
Wouters, J. 244
Wundt, W. 170

Young, S. 331

Zajonc, R. 169, 178, 181

Subject Index

accent group (AG) 369, 370, 384
acoustic correlates 110–11, 114, 144–8, 224, 229–31, 311
   expression 47, 53, 56, 87–9, 138, 140, 150, 200, 232, 264, 291, 318, 345, 360, 382
   waveform 21, 87, 91–4, 112, 214, 249, 294, 313, 383
Action Theory 15, 22, 119
ambisyllabicity 383
articulatory correlates 240–2
Articulatory Phonology 21, 209
attributes 291, 308, 314, 370, 372
auditory analysis 76
automatic speech recognition (ASR) 24, 80, 259–62

cognitive 121
cognitive phonetics 208–10, 221, 255, 334, 357, 362
   CPA 357–9, 363, 374, 380, 382
   processes 120, 362
context-sensitive 267
contour 255, 306, 308

databases 128, 210–13
   collection 57–61, 212, 320
   dialogue systems 266–7
derivation 366, 374
disambiguation 93, 227

elements 307, 314, 371, 373, 378
emotion
   acoustic parameters 97, 99, 140
   biological aspects 19, 20, 105, 169–70, 276–9, 280–3, 315, 375
      neural processing 186
      linking with cognition 183–6, 197, 264; reaction/response 276
      physiological descriptors 173, 185, 279, 280
   cognitive aspects 105, 169–70, 176–81, 169–70, 176–81, 279, 283–4
      appraisal 176, 181–3, 195
      definition 181

cognition and emotion 178, 180
   defined 169, 171, 172
   cognitive processing 178
   development 190
   expression of 103
   function 39, 102–3, 187–8
   parameterization 140, 189
   representation, cognitive 100
   types 113
      basic 19, 42, 89, 104, 136, 189, 191–3
      blends 190
      secondary 42, 189, 192, 219
expression
   defining 19, 39, 290
   degrees 38, 41, 91, 109, 124, 155, 233
   direct encoding 233
   dynamically varying 44, 213, 295, 297–8, 375, 378, 382
   envelope 224, 307–10
   expressive content 21, 172, 224, 295, 380, 386
   induction 164; *see also* speaker–listener system
   modes 65, 382
      neutral 40, 202–5, 253, 300, 302
      defining 310–13
   space 153–4, 226–7, 297, 345
   synthesis of 124–5, 277; assessment of 132, 150, 254; evaluation 22, 67, 132–6, 347, 380
   uniqueness hypothesis 234
   wrapper 24, 111; *see also* wrapper
expressive speech 38, 87, 309, 322
   defining for acoustics 290, 305–6, 341–3
   deriving 300–2, 306, 386
   detail in model 374
   variable 296

hearing 56
hierarchy 137, 379–81

inheritance 130–1, 308, 376
instantiation 374

intonational phrase (IP) 370
IPA 17

language
  code 194, 195
  natural expression 198–200
  linguistics 11, 19, 62–4, 144, 194
    underlying representations 201, 204,
        254–5, 310–11, 317, 332
    universals 321–5
    words as classifiers 190–6, 218, 343
  listener reaction 86, 198, 230
  sampling 303, 306

models
  classification 195, 290, 311, 345
  computational 182, 278, 355
    expressive speech 198–201, 278, 290,
        346, 355–88
    instantiation 366; see also instantiation
  conditions on 36, 69–71, 136, 168, 217
  current 21, 118–21, 158–60, 168, 252, 349
    inadequacies 18, 73, 136–7, 144, 151,
        267–9, 311, 349
    integrated 269–71
    unsolved problems 122, 217, 219, 252,
        256–8
  data structure 27, 209, 305, 356
  dynamic/static 44, 157, 182, 282, 292, 355,
      358, 360, 364–7, 382, 386–7
  emotive content of speech 277–8
  evaluation 71–3, 133–5, 148
  focus, change of 271–3
  goals 18, 217, 285
  ideal 265, 277, 289, 326, 347
  proposed model 130–1, 278–84, 289,
      346, 387
    architecture 364–7
    data structures 304–5, 356, 380–81
    speech production 223, 387
      expressive 278–84, 290, 355–72, 374
      text mark-up 304–5, 329–31, 339, 356,
          359, 368–70, 376–8; see also XML
    speech production and perception 15, 17,
        89, 227
    testing 23, 65, 88, 112–13, 122, 227,
        250–2, 281, 320
    theoretical basis 119, 278–9
      biological evidence 282
      cognitive evidence 283
      supporting evidence 280–4, 367–8
      variability 48–52

moods 193
motor control 14, 101, 102, 199

natural speech see, speech, natural
neutral utterance see, expression, neutral

parameters
  acoustic correlates 105, 140, 240
  criteria 145–9
  interacting 319
  representations 54, 167, 226, 313, 314,
      316, 318–20, 323, 348
  vs. categories 141–3
perception
  expression 61–4, 151–3, 226, 235
  goal 16, 86
  limits 88, 151, 228, 317, 323, 325, 335
  models 21, 87–8, 335
    computational model 292–3, 317
phonetics
  allophone, intrinsic 333, 334
  classical (CP) 25, 120, 204, 209, 313,
      324, 333
  coarticulation 14, 205, 215, 237, 311,
      375, 381, 383–4
  phonation see, voice quality
  precision 319, 361
  processes 361–2
  rendering 38, 292, 310, 357, 359, 381
  segmental 332, 335, 341
  voice quality 98, 106, 148, 245–7
phonology 159, 331, 334
  allophone, extrinsic 333, 364
  assimilation 332, 362, 381
  planning 38, 48, 52, 93–4, 157, 216, 310,
      349, 384, 357, 363, 371–5, 384, 386
  processes 361–2
  script 290–4
pitch see, prosody
plan, planning see, phonology, planning
processes
  cognitive phonetic 362
  phonetic 361–2
  phonological 362
prosodic detail 374
prosody 110, 118, 129, 224, 334, 376, 385
  basic to model 355
  carrier 309, 367, 376
  integration 355
  intonation 99, 110, 118, 131, 138, 216,
      225, 243, 308, 338, 385
  profile 143

Subject Index 419

spectrum 244
stress 335
suprasegmental 203, 335
wrapper 130, 302, 308, 384, 389
  tags 243–4, 305

rendering 38, 78, 93, 357, 362, 368, 375, 383–4, 386–7
  precision 16, 109, 360, 381; *see also* phonetics, rendering
research
  data collection 58–60
  paradigm 47, 67, 86, 123, 150, 159, 180, 197, 217–20, 256–8, 261, 294
  questions, naturalness 22, 67, 83, 85, 197
  strategies, naturalness 22, 84, 151
rhythm *see*, syllables

sample derivation 366, 368–71, 373, 374
script 290–4, 304–5
segmental 332
suprasegmental, *see* prosody
speech:
  expression-based 300–5
  expression in, *see* expression
    acoustics of, *see* acoustic correlates
    degrees of 41, 109, 265
    dynamic nature 44–6
    neutral 37, 40, 122, 202, 366
  natural 11–25, 78, 108, 154, 254
  naturalness 82, 121, 134,
    perception 12, 86, 94, 226; of waveform 24, 51
  objective of 87, 376
  production 12, 101, 171, 214–15, 355, 357–62, 364, 376
  production-for-perception 15, 125, 155, 156, 164, 347–8; integrating 13, 342, 348
  perception 201, 294, 343, 349
  speaker-listener system 64, 154–8, 242, 293, 303, 348, 361, 375, 378
  supervision 157–8, 265, 310, 346, 349, 358

syllables:
  isochrony 247, 337, 338
  rhythm 126, 225, 247, 318, 336, 360
  stress 225, 335
  synthesis 236, 372
synthesis
  analysis by synthesis 262–3
  current units 32–33, 116, 118
  evaluation 68, 132, 349
  expression 65, 121–3, 265
    models 82, 238, 347
    modes 65
    speakers, integrity 76
    testing, trialling 25, 35, 250, 251, 327, 347, 349, 353
  levels: high and low 23, 28, 78, 115, 119–21, 331, 338–9, 350–4
    naturalness 82; feasibility studies 65, 236
  rules 31, 120
  simulation 120, 168, 327
  syllables
  synthesizer types 125–9, 236, 239, 243, 248–9, 342, 351
  traditional units 29–32, 116

theory 119–21
  emotion
    basic questions 200–2
    disciplines 198–200
  speech production 139, 217

variables 111, 127
variability 48–51, 90, 98, 107–10, 159, 161, 239, 254, 279, 344–5, 348
attitude 378–9
vector 43, 91, 163, 297–8, 307, 316, 324

wrapper 111, 223, 297, 302, 307, 360, 367, 368, 376, 384

XML coding 120, 161, 224, 242, 304–5, 307, 330, 356–7, 359, 369, 370, 372–3, 376–9